TEXAS COAST AND THE RIO GRANDE VALLEY

TEXAS COAST AND THE RIO GRANDE VALLEY

COMPLETELY NEW 2ND EDITION

BY ROBERT R. RAFFERTY

Gulf Publishing Company
Houston, Texas

To my wife, Lyn, and our children and step-children:
Ron, Mike, Donald, Dorothy, Tim, and Robin

Printed in the United States of America.

10 9 8 7 6 5 4 3 2 1

Gulf Publishing Company
P.O. Box 2608
Houston, Texas 77252-2608

Library of Congress Cataloging-in-Publication Data

Rafferty, Robert.
Texas coast and the Rio Grande Valley / by Robert R. Rafferty. — Completely new 2nd ed.
p. cm. — (Texas monthly guidebooks)
Rev. ed. of: Texas coast, c1986.
Includes index.
ISBN 0-87719-184-0
1. Gulf Region (Tex.)—Description and travel—Guide-books. 2. Rio Grande Valley—Description and travel—Guide-books.
I. Rafferty, Robert. Texas coast. II. Title. III. Series.
F392.G9R34 1991
917.6404'63—dc20 90-22529

Cover design by Hixo, Inc.

CONTENTS

ACKNOWLEDGMENTS

Details, details, details! A guidebook is only as good as the accuracy of its details. So, I'm deeply indebted to a number of people for their help in gathering and verifying the thousands of details in this book.

In general, I'd like to thank the various chambers of commerce and visitors bureaus along the coast and in the Valley for their invaluable assistance and enthusiastic help.

In particular, I'd like to offer an extra-special thank you to the individuals listed below, most of whom went far beyond the call of duty to ensure that my research visits were fruitful.

Aransas Pass . . . Kay Wolf
Beaumont . . . Judy Stone
Brackettville . . . Lashawn Wardlaw
Brazosport . . . Jan Scott
Brownsville/Matamoros . . . Teri Gomez
Clear Lake . . . Cecilia Coleman
Corpus Christi. . . . .Judy Everett Ramos
Del Rio/Ciudad Acuna . . . Debbie Studer Green and Gloria Cruz
Eagle Pass/Piedras Negras . . . Sandra Martinez and Carmen Yolanda Arredondo
Edinburg . . . Aida Hernandez
Galveston . . . Carol Ann Anderson, Carole Ketterhagen, and Olivia Meyer

Harlingen . . . Linda Rath
Kingsville . . . Tem Miller
Laredo/Nuevo Laredo . . . Irma Garcia-Torres
McAllen/Reynosa . . . Chuck Snyder and Kitty Dailey
Mission . . . Ed White
Orange . . . Christina Bilenski
Pharr . . . Lilliana Ruiz and Toni McKee
Port Aransas . . . Lanette Nolte
Port Arthur. . . Faye Liss and Edith Huber
Port Lavaca . . . Lana Morgenroth
Port Mansfield . . . Margaret Torregrossa
Port O'Connor . . . Jimmy Crouch
Raymondville . . . Raymond Sansom
Rio Grande City/Roma . . . Crisanto (Chris) Salinas
Rockport-Fulton . . . Robert W. Lynch, Jr.
Seadrift . . . Rae Jean Jordan
South Padre Island . . . Geri Jean Wilson
Weslaco . . . Charles E. LaGrone

Not to forget the ones who helped with the "big picture": Dianne Pehl of the Texas Department of Commerce's Tourism Division, and Marge Johnson of the Rio Grande Valley Chamber of Commerce.

Finally, I would like to thank the staff at Gulf Publishing who shepherded my manuscript through the production process to produce the book you now hold.

INTRODUCTION

PLEASE READ THIS FIRST!

Why the shouting title for what's really the **Introduction**? Because studies show that guidebook users, anxious to find out about their destination, often skip anything labeled *Introduction* and any other sections in the front of the book, and thereby miss some of the guidelines that are essential to fully understanding the listings.

Please take the time to at least skim this section so you'll at least know what's covered here. Then you'll know where to look and can flip back to get the details whenever you need them.

ORGANIZATION OF THIS GUIDE

The organization is simple. The first part of the book covers the Texas coast from Port Arthur on the Louisiana border to South Padre Island that is just a few miles from the Mexican border. The second part covers the Rio Grande Valley from Brownsville to Del Rio. Cities and towns are listed alphabetically in each part. The major Mexican border cities and towns are included with the nearest city on the U.S. side of the Rio Grande.

THINGS CHANGE

It took a long time to research, write, edit, print, and distribute this book. In the meantime, things have been changing. Restaurants, for example, are notorious for changing their names, their management, menu, hours, or — even worse — closing down. Museums change hours. Attractions burn down and new ones open up. Prices go up or down (rarely down). In other words, all I can tell you is that the information in this book was as current as the publisher's staff and I could make it at the time it went to press. But the words you're reading were set when the book came out of the press and can't be changed until the next edition.

So if you use a listing for a restaurant and find the place is no longer there, or your motel doesn't have all the amenities cited, or the museum is closed on Monday when I said it was open, please try to be understanding. To help you avoid any inconvenience caused by changes, I've included telephone numbers in the listings whenever possible. A call before you go might save you a little irritation, especially if you have to travel any distance. Remember, however, phone numbers change, too. If you have trouble reaching a listing, check the phone book or call Information.

WHAT'S IN THIS GUIDE — AND WHAT'S NOT

It would take a book as thick as a Dallas phone book to list all the places of interest to visitors, restaurants, hotels/motels, etc., in the cities in this guide. Therefore, my goal is not to tell ALL, but to give you a solid sampling of the best of what's there to get you started on your visit. Once started, you can get more information from the listed local Chamber of Commerce or Convention and Visitors Bureau, the local newspaper, your hotel/motel staff, or a dozen other local sources. They can help you discover the places and/or events of particular interest to you that space forced me to omit.

If you think I really goofed by omitting your favorite place or event, or you find any errors in this guide, I'd like to hear from you so I can give consideration to your comments when preparing the next edition. Write me: Robert Rafferty, Guide to the Texas Coast and Rio Grande Valley, % Gulf Publishing Company, P.O. Box 2608, Houston, TX 77252-2608.

HOW TO READ THE LISTINGS

Each city's listings begin with the name of the county in which the city is located, the best estimate of the city's current population, and (in parenthesis) the telephone area code. For most short distances, reported mileages were actually checked. Where this was not possible, mileages were generally provided by knowledgeable local sources or taken from the Texas Department of Highways and Public Transportation's Official Highway Map. These may differ slightly from your actual driving mileage.

To make it easier for you to find the listings that interest you, each city's listings are grouped down under the headings that follow.

TOURIST SERVICES

Chambers of Commerce, Visitors Bureaus, and other organizations where you can get free information about the area are listed along with their addresses and phone numbers so you can contact them for trip planning or when you're in their town. Unless otherwise listed, chambers are usually open regular business hours Monday through Friday. Also under this heading are places and organizations that offer tours. Most of these charge fees, like tour buses and tour boats, but some are free.

GUIDEBOOKS

Only those guidebooks and other publications targeted at a particular city are listed under that city.

A GET-ACQUAINTED DRIVING TOUR

Sometimes trying to find your way around in a strange city seems to be such an overwhelming task that you just give up, eat at the nearest restaurant and then stay wherever you've settled in, passing up an opportunity to explore and enjoy what that city has to offer the visitor. It doesn't matter whether you're in town for pleasure or business, driving tours presented in this book will make it easier for you to get out and make the most of your visit.

These aren't sight-seeing tours. The idea is that by taking the tour you'll get acquainted with the main streets, traffic, distances, and the general location of the major sights and attractions before you venture out to find a specific place. The get-acquainted tours work best when taken early in your visit. Whenever possible, the major streets listed in each tour are included in the simplified map of that city. Try marking out the tour, as well as you can, on the city map before you start. Even better, get a detailed map from the Chamber of Commerce and mark your route on that. Another way to do it, to avoid confusion and map shuffling, is to read the directions into a portable tape recorder and let that be your guide as you play it back in your car.

BIRD'S-EYE VIEW

These are the best sites to get a panoramic view of the area. There aren't many of these listings because there aren't many high places, natural or man-made, along the coast or in the Valley.

MUSEUMS

One of the attractive things about the museums listed in this book is that they are all small enough to see everything there is to see — and many have a lot worth seeing — in an hour or two, or at most, a leisurely afternoon. These can be pleasant diversions — especially for children — rather than tiring undertakings that too often characterize visits to larger museums. Some of the listed museums are little gems. Others are merely haphazard collections resulting from the cleaning out of local attics and barns. But even the most poorly organized collection often contains treasures if you look closely.

The hours of operation of some of these museums often depend on volunteers, so don't be surprised if one isn't open when I say it should be.

HISTORIC PLACES

Whether you are a history buff or just curious about our heritage, there are a number of places that give you a glimpse of what life was like in Texas in our past. Many listings are for historic homes that are still private residences. If this is the case, just walk or drive by and do not bother the residents. Not included in the listings are the thousands of state historical markers and plaques attached to walls of historic buildings and set up on roadsides near historic sites. Each of these tells a fragment of Texas history, and most are worth the time it takes to stop to read and think about the events recorded there.

OTHER POINTS OF INTEREST

This is sort of a catch-all category for places of interest that aren't museums or historic places and don't fit exactly into any of the other categories listed below.

SPORTS AND ACTIVITIES

A selection of participant and spectator sports and activities available to visitors is listed. These activities range from baseball and bullfights to birdwatching and jogging. College sports open to visitors are listed under each individual school. If your favorite sport or activity isn't listed or you need more details, contact the local chamber of commerce or visitors bureau or the parks and recreation department.

Two of the most popular sports along the Texas coast are hunting and fishing. For free brochures and other information about them, as well as information about the facilities available in state parks, contact the Texas Parks and Wildlife Department, 4200 Smith School Rd. Austin, 78744. Both of these sports are closely regulated and require licenses that may be purchased at many locations around the state including county courthouses, Texas Parks and Wildlife Department offices, many tackle shops, sporting goods stores, and even convenience stores near the hunting and fishing areas. The license fees depend on what you want to do and whether you are a state resident.

COLLEGES AND UNIVERSITIES

In addition to briefly describing educational programs, these listings include information on the facilities and events at the schools that are open to the public. These may include art galleries, museums, historic buildings, concerts, plays, film and lecture series, festivals, and sporting events ranging from basketball to intercollegiate rodeos. Parking is a problem at many schools, so when available, listings include information on visitor parking.

PERFORMING ARTS

Theater, dance, and music are alive and well in Texas. Even many small towns have their own community theater group or band. Many also have some type of cultural arts group that brings in touring shows and celebrity concerts. These listings, which barely scratch the surface of what's going on, include specific performing arts organizations and the places such as theaters and civic centers that host various performing arts and other events.

SHOPPING

The major shopping malls are listed so you know where to go to find the essentials. Other listings are mostly of specialty shops that are unique, or at least different from the run-of-the-mill stores found in every city. Hours are not given unless they vary from the normal shopping hours in that area. Many malls now have Sunday hours and most of the shops in the Mexican cities along the border are open seven days a week.

KIDS' STUFF

Special places for kids of all ages.

SIDE TRIPS

The suggested side trips are rarely more than an hour's drive from the designated city or town, and usually well worth your time and effort.

ANNUAL EVENTS

Almost every community celebrates one or more annual events that makes that town unique and helps bring people together in the spirit of fun and civic pride. Many of these are just one-day affairs that really don't justify the long trip to get there. For this reason, I've used two rules to make my selections (breaking my own rules on a few occasions when I felt the festival was worth it): the event must last at least two days and it must draw visitors from out of the immediate area. Listings rarely include specific dates because, in most cases, these change from year to year. For the exact dates and details call the number in the listing.

OFFBEAT

If you're looking for something really different, listings under this heading may fill the bill.

RESTAURANTS

The key to listing a restaurant was simple: cleanliness was a given and ambiance was a factor, but most important was that the food was well-prepared and enjoyable and that the kitchen lived up to the promises on the menu. It didn't matter if it was a gourmet restaurant, a small-town cafe, or barbecue place. If it delivered in full on its promises and the meal was a pleasure, then it made the listing. If it promised and didn't deliver, it didn't make it.

But even then, too often there were more restaurants that passed the test than I had space to list. So, this is just a sampling. A little digging and questioning on your part will undoubtedly turn up more restaurants worth your business.

In general, major chain restaurants are not listed because most travelers are aware of them and can look them up in the phone book. Separate listings for hotel/motel restaurants are also only covered lightly because too often they are overpriced "nothing" places whose one big feature is that they are convenient for captive guests. An interesting and welcome trend here, however, is that the management of more and more of these places is turning its attention to making its in-house restaurant appeal to non-guests. Some places have earned a reputation as "the place to dine" and bring in local people as steady customers. Seek and you shall find.

Finally, although not listed, cafeterias are a major part of the eating-out scene in many cities. Many cafeteria chains do a superior job of providing convenient, well-prepared meals at reasonable prices. They offer a needed alternative to fast food, especially for families, and are worth a try.

In the larger cities, restaurants are listed according to type; otherwise, they're listed alphabetically. Since exact prices are hard to keep up with, the following symbols are used to indicate the approximate cost of a *typical dinner* (or lunch, if dinner is not served) for one person, exclusive of drinks, tax, and tip. If two symbols are given in the listing, it indicates the price spread on the menu.

$ = Under $7
$$ = $7 to $17
$$$ = $17 to $25
$$$$ = Over $25

The following symbols indicate what credit cards are accepted by restaurants (and clubs and bars):

AE	American Express
DC	Diners Club
DIS	Discover
MC	Master Card
V	Visa
Cr.	All major credit cards
No Cr.	No credit cards

The words "bar" or "lounge" indicate that you can buy liquor by the drink. "Private club" means you must buy a temporary membership to get an alcoholic beverage (although some places sell beer or wine without a membership). Also noted are those places that sell only beer or wine. If none of these are listed, it means no alcoholic beverages are sold (See Liquor Laws, following).

CLUBS AND BARS

This category doesn't have many listings because clubs and bars change frequently to keep up with the latest fad, and I can't change listings fast enough to keep up with them. To rate a listing, a club has to be popular, open to the public without membership, and have at least the air of permanence about it. Even then, you'll probably find more changes in this category than any other. If you're really interested in the local nightlife, check the local newspapers, your hotel/motel staff, or the chamber of commerce or visitors bureau. Symbols for credit cards accepted in the clubs are listed under Restaurants, above.

ACCOMMODATIONS

Generally, the Accommodations section lists hotels and motels, but, depending on the area, you'll also find listings for condominiums, bed and breakfast homes and inns, resorts, and beach houses.

I've tried to include information on just about everything you might want to know to find accommodations that fit your price range, your lifestyle, and your expectations. The information is compressed in these listings, so a more complete explanation is given here.

Local *Room Tax* is listed at the beginning of each city's Accommodations section. Depending on the area, room tax may be made up of a combination of state, county, and city sales taxes plus an additional occupancy tax. (In many cases, at least part of the room tax goes to supporting tourism and the arts.) It may add up to a single digit percentage or go as high as 15 percent. The thing to note is that the room tax is rarely included in quoted rates but will be added on at check-out time. To reduce the shock when you get your bill, ask for the exact tax on your room when you make your reservation or at check-in.

In **boldface type** at the start of each listing you'll find:

• The street address, and the mailing address, if they're different.

• Directions and/or highway exits where appropriate, to help you find your destination.

• Local telephone number (area code is given at beginning of the city's listing) and toll-free 800 number if there is one — usually these are for the chain's central reservations office; occasionally, they are direct lines to the property.

• A symbol for the price. Unless otherwise specified, the rate symbols used are for a double room (two people in a room without regard to the bed arrangement). If two symbols are used in a listing, they indicate the spread between the lowest- and highest-priced double rooms. For ease of comparison, the rate symbols are based on what the trade calls "rack rates" — the standard-room rate without discounts. (For discounts, see following.) For places with seasonal rates, such as resort areas along the coast, the rate symbol indicates a double in high season. Off-season rates are usually lower, sometimes substantially lower.

$ = Under $45
$$ = $46-$60
$$$ = $61-$80
$$$$ = $81-$100
$$$$$ = Over $100

I did not break out any rates over $100, so $$$$$ could mean $101 on up — and sometimes very, very up. Ask for the exact price before registering.

• A symbol for wheelchair accessibility (See following). Hotels and motels have joined the effort to make traveling easier for the handicapped with special rooms. The number of these rooms is noted in the boldface type after the symbol **W+** in each accommodation's listing If there is no wheelchair symbol, the place does not have any rooms specifically equipped for the handicapped, but it still may have rooms with a lower level of wheelchair accessibility.

• No-smoking rooms. Designated no-smoking rooms are noted. The actual number is listed in the text.

The text also provides information on the following:

• Number of stories.

• Number of units including suites and no-smoking rooms.

• Stay-free package plans for children in rooms with parents.

• Reduced-rate package plans such as a golf, fishing, or special events package. The type of plans are not listed; however, if you are interested, ask.

• Discounts. Our rate symbol is for "rack rate" without discounts. But **there are discounts!** All types of discounts — from special rates for AAA or other organization members to promotional rates. In slow season, you may even get a discount if you look like the desk clerk. Because discounts vary so widely, the only two included are the discounts for seniors and lower weekend rates. In many cases the senior discount — usually at least 10 percent — applies only to members of AARP, but even if you aren't a member, you can ask for it. Rates are based on supply and demand, so in resort areas, you'll probably find that rates are higher on weekends, because that's when hotels fill up. In every case, it's worth asking for a discount.

- Room amenities. Here you'll find out what type TV set-up is in the rooms, whether there is a coffeemaker, and whether you will be charged for local calls.
- Fire safety. By law, all hotel/motel rooms must have smoke alarms; therefore, these are not noted. However, what is noted is extra safety devices such as fire sprinklers and intercom or loudspeaker systems that let hotel personnel notify you in your room of a fire or other emergency.
- Pet privileges. If you can have your pet in your room this is noted by Pets OK. Any limits, pet charges, or deposits are also cited.
- Number of restaurants. If there is no further comment, then at least one restaurant is open for all meals. If room service is available, it is noted, but if you plan to use it, it's best to check its operating hours.
- Bar or lounge. Hours of operation and any entertainment will be noted. Clubs that operate in dry areas must be private (See Liquor Laws, following). Guests are normally automatically made members of these private clubs and temporary memberships are available for non-guests for a small fee.
- Other facilities and amenities available:

— Swimming pool, exercise room, whirlpool, sauna, or other health or recreational facilities

— Availability of temporary memberships in local health, golf, or other clubs through the hotel/motel for free or fee

— Availability of free airport transportation or other local transportation

— Other freebies such as coffee in the morning, newspaper, cocktails, breakfast

— Availability of a self-service laundry on the premises and same-day dry cleaning service

— Other noted items include such things as covered or valet parking (free or fee), microwaves or refrigerators in rooms, information about the history of the building or its location on the beach, or anything special that sets this place apart.

One final note — unless you enjoy bouncing around looking for a place to bed down for the night, I strongly recommend you make reservations whenever possible.

WHEELCHAIR ACCESSIBILITY SYMBOLS

Most public buildings and many business buildings are now accessible to the handicapped. An increasing number of tourist attractions also offer handicapped facilities and reserved parking. The following sym-

bols are used in all appropriate listings to indicate wheelchair accessibility.
W This place is accessible to persons in wheelchairs. At least one entrance is wide enough, and the entrance has no more than two steps. However, not all facilities (rest rooms, etc.) are accessible.
W Variable This place is accessible in some areas but not in others.
W+ This place and all its major facilities, including rest rooms, are accessible.
W+ But not all areas This place has handicapped facilities, but some areas are not accessible. Parks are an example.
No symbol This place is accessible only with great difficulty or not at all.

INFORMATION FOR VISITORS FROM OUT-OF-STATE

WEATHER

In general, the Texas coast and the Rio Grande Valley have mild winters — with the exception of an occasional "Norther," a north wind that brings in a short-lived Arctic blast. Corpus Christi, for example, averages only seven days a year when the temperature falls below freezing; Galveston only four, and Brownsville only two. Spring and fall are warm and pleasant all along the coast, and summers are hot. Balmy Gulf breezes can temper the weather, even when the humidity is high. But, almost everything indoors (including rental cars) is air conditioned.

DRIVING IN TEXAS

You'll need a car to get around almost everywhere. Even in the few cities with good public transportation systems, you may not always get where you want to go when you want to go. But Texas is made for drivers. A lot of money goes into maintaining what is one of the finest highway systems in the country. Of course, that maintenance means you should expect to run into road repairs as you travel. The following are a few rules of the road you should know to keep out of trouble and a few tidbits to make your life on the road easier.

The speed limit on U.S. and state highways is 55 mph unless posted at a lower speed. Watch for posted limits, especially school zone signs, that require reduced speeds. The speed limit on interstate highways is 65 mph, except through cities where it is usually reduced to 55 or less.

Texas law requires that you have proof of liability insurance for the car in the car.

It is illegal to pass a stopped school bus from either direction or a school bus that is about to stop and has its warning lights flashing.

A right turn is permitted on a red light after a full stop, unless specifically prohibited by a traffic sign.

All occupants must be buckled up in seat belts, and children under the age of four must be secured either with a belt or in a federally approved child safety seat. Infants under the age of two must be secured in a federally approved child safety seat.

Littering the highways is prohibited. The "Don't Mess With Texas" signs you'll see everywhere are a warning that if you get caught littering you'll pay a hefty fine.

Secondary roads are frequently designated FM (Farm to Market), RM (Ranch to Market) or RR (Ranch Road).

Highway mileage signs giving distances to cities or towns usually refer to the distance to a specific central location in the downtown area — the courthouse or town square, for example — and not to the city limits.

LIQUOR LAWS

The minimum drinking age is 21.

State local option laws give citizens within a county or local precinct the option to sell alcoholic beverages. Most of the cities and towns along the coast and in the Valley are "wet," which means you can buy liquor by the drink. However, where this is the exception, wet and dry precincts exist side-by-side within a municipality. The result is you can sometimes buy an alcoholic drink on one side of a street and not on the other. Where possible, information on dry areas is provided in this book under restaurant and accommodations listings (usually by the words "private club"). If you are unclear about the local option liquor law, and this is important to you, I recommend you ask the hotel clerk about it before you check in.

CROSSING INTO MEXICO

First, you should understand that most Mexican cities along the border are not typical Mexican cities. You will see a different culture, but it is a hybrid developed by the proximity to Texas cities — not a purely Mexican culture. This does not mean that most border cities are not worth the trip. They definitely are for food, fun, and a shopping bonanza. And you can enjoy a visit without worry or hassle if you understand the rules, don't be an ugly American, and exercise a little caution.

If you are a U.S citizen you can visit any border city for up to 72 hours with no special documents. All you need is some proof of who you are — like a driver's license — and this only in the rare case that you are challenged to prove your nationality when you reenter Texas. In most cases, the Mexican border customs and immigration officers will not stop your going over, and on your return the U.S. immigration officers will simply ask a question or two, such as "Where were you born?" and "What are you bringing back from Mexico?"

Resident aliens must carry their alien registration, and naturalized citizens should carry proof of naturalization.

Trips of more than 72 hours or more than 15 miles into Mexico require a tourist card and a car entry permit. These can easily be obtained in advance at Mexican consulates, Mexican tourism office in the States, and, perhaps with a little more difficulty, at the Mexican immigration offices located on the Mexican side of most of the international bridges. Definitive proof of citizenship (birth certificate, passport, voter's registration card) is required as well as a valid title for the car.

In some border towns, like Laredo/Nuevo Laredo, the twin cities are so close you can park your car on the U.S. side near the international bridge and walk across the Rio Grande to the main tourist area. In other towns, it's easier to take a bus or a taxi across the bridge. Or, you can drive across. Thousands of cars cross every day; however, if you've never done it before, you should be aware of a few things.

First, your U.S. automobile insurance is not valid in Mexico. It will not be recognized by the Mexican authorities. You must have insurance issued by a Mexican company, which you can get from insurance agents, travel agents, or the American Automobile Association's office in most Texas border cities. A short-term policy for the duration of your trip will cost between $5 and $10 a day. (It might be cheaper to take a taxi.) If you don't have Mexican insurance and you have an accident, your car can be impounded, and you can wind up in jail because under Mexican law, which is based on the Napoleonic Code, you are guilty until proven innocent.

Next, there's a lot of horn-blowing and wild-driving in most border cities. Of course, if you've driven in Houston or Los Angeles, this may seem tame. In the larger Mexican cities, when you park, even on a street — provided you should be so lucky as to find a space — you'll probably find someone dressed in a quasi-uniform who will direct you into the parking space and then watch your car or feed pesos into the parking meter for a small tip. Pay him.

For your own safety, don't go into any section of a border town, or any bar or some such place, that you wouldn't go into if it was in your hometown. This note is not intended to scare you off from your visit. There is probably more crime in the States than in Mexico, but it is still wise to be careful. This is especially true if traveling by car into the interior of Mexico. The desperate economic conditions in parts of the country have lead to an increase in crimes against tourists on the road. If you decide to drive, it's best to stick to the main highways, travel by day, and, if possible, travel in groups.

There have always been bargains for shoppers in the Mexican border towns, and the devaluation of the peso has created even more of a bonanza. Most shops on the border will gladly take U.S. dollars. But if you want to use pesos, you can exchange your dollars for pesos at many places on both sides of the border. The exchange rates are fairly steady now, but they do fluctuate wildly at times, so find out the rate before you make an exchange. A pocket calculator is helpful for making the conversions.

Time in all Mexican border cities is always Central Standard Time. These cities do not follow Daylight Savings Time, so during the months when that time is in effect in Texas, it's one hour earlier in Mexico.

Each U.S. citizen may bring back Mexican purchases up to $400 retail value per person in gifts or items for personal use every 31 days without paying duty. You can bring in more than $400 retail, but you'll have to pay customs duty on everything over that amount. Customs agents are pretty sharp at determining retail value, but if you don't want any trouble, keep your receipts. They are also experts at finding items you did not declare — which can lead to heavy fines or worse — so declare everything you bring back. Some fruits, vegetables, birds, trademarked items, all archaeological artifacts, and a host of other items may not be brought back into the United States. On the other hand, certain items such as genuine handicrafts, may qualify for exemption from the $400 duty free limit. As an out-of-state visitor you may bring back more alcoholic beverages than Texans, but there are limits and these are subject to a Texas tax and possibly a customs duty.

The best way to avoid any problems is to stop at the U.S. Customs Office before you cross the border and pick up the free pamphlets that spell out the details.

THE TASTE OF TEXAS

You can find just about any type cuisine in Texas, but for the real taste of Texas you should try barbecue, chicken-fried steak, and Tex-Mex food. All are hearty, tasty, and inexpensive.

Barbecue

They say Texans will barbecue anything, including the old tires off their Cadillac, but to most Texans barbecue means beef. Beef brisket, shoulder clod, or some other cut is cooked slowly for hours and hours in a pit over mesquite, hickory, or another wood carefully selected by the cook. Of course, barbecue pit operators realize that some people have strange and uncultivated tastes, so to keep these people from going into a frenzy, the pitman may smoke up some pork ribs, or sausages (usually called "hot links") or some other such thing. Some heretics say that barbecue is a way of cooking and it doesn't matter what meat you use. But the real Texas barbecuer knows this is just not so. His heart and soul remains with his beef.

Purists serve their barbecue beef well done, but not dry, sliced by the pound and served on butcher paper with a minimum of extras; perhaps a couple of pieces of white bread, some sauce, and maybe sliced onions, pickles, and/or a jalapeno pepper. Your choices are usually limited to how much you want and whether you want it lean or with the fat on. About the fanciest you can expect in a true Texas barbecue place — which is always casual and smelling of the wonderful pit smoke — is to be served on paper plates with plastic knife and fork and side dishes of potato salad or beans or coleslaw, or all of those mentioned.

Chicken-fried Steak

This is just what the name says. An inexpensive steak — round steak is probably top-of-the-line here — beaten until it's tender, then coated with a batter, fried like chicken, and served with a cream gravy made from the drippings. A good chicken-fried steak should be tender and the crust light and crispy. It's so well-known in Texas that many restaurant menus merely list it as CFS.

Unfortunately, it's becoming harder and harder to find a good CFS because more and more restaurants are succumbing to the convenience of the frozen packaged version — which too often tastes like the box it came in. But there are still chefs out there who care enough about their customers to do it the old-fashioned way. They may be hard to find, but they're worth the looking.

Tex-Mex

Texas abounds with restaurants serving all types of ethnic food from Czech to Greek to Vietnamese. One of the most popular, of course, is Mexican. But Mexican restaurants serving authentic Mexican dishes from interior Mexico are rare — even in the Mexican border towns. What you are more likely to find is a derivative made to please Texan taste and known affectionately as Tex-Mex. It's different, it's delicious, but you should know it bears only a distant relationship to real Mexican cuisine.

The names of Tex-Mex dishes are invariably in Mexican or Spanish, so here's a rather loosely translated short list of some of the names you should learn to recognize to get you started ordering Tex-Mex (or real Mexican, if you should be so lucky).

al carbon: charcoal grilled
arroz: rice
cabrito: kid (young goat), usually cooked on a spit over a fire
carne: meat
cerveza: beer, the preferred beverage with Tex-Mex
chile: spelled with an "e" refers to peppers — a wide variety from mild to sinus-cleaning — used in Tex-Mex cooking
chili: spelled with an "i" (also called a "bowl of Texas Red") is a stewlike dish of meat, onions, herbs, and spices, and, of course, *chiles* that may be mild or hot enough to require an asbestos mouth. There's a major on-going war among *chili*-lovers as to whether it should be made with beans or not. Try them both and make your own choice. I'm not enlisting in that war.

chorizo: spicy pork sausage

enchilada: a rolled soft *tortilla* filled with cheese, chicken, or other fillings and a *chile* sauce

fajitas: marinated and broiled or grilled strips of beef skirt (a term now corrupted, like barbecue, to include marinated grilled chicken strips and even grilled shrimp strips)

guacamole: a mashed avocado salad usually made with onions and *chiles*

huevos: eggs

jalapeno: a hot, green *chile* that is used in many dishes

migas: eggs scrambled with pieces of corn *tortilla* and sometimes with *chorizo*

picante: spicy hot

pico de gallo: a spicy sauce or side dish usually made with hot *chiles*, onions, and cilantro

pollo: chicken

queso: cheese

taco: usually a corn *tortilla* deep-fried in a U-shape and filled with a variety of fillings limited only by the cook's imagination

tamale: corn dough spread in a corn husk, topped with a meat filling, rolled, and steamed (don't eat the husk!)

tortilla: corn or flour dough flattened like a pancake, cooked on a griddle or steamed and used like bread

WELCOME TO THE TEXAS COAST

Many rhapsodize about the beaches along our east and west coasts, but they don't know about the relatively undiscovered captivating charms of the Third Coast — the sandy stretches of Texas along the Gulf of Mexico. This sun-blessed coast is the subject of the first section of this guidebook.

What's it like?

There's no one answer to that question. Portions of the Texas coast are remote and primitive with more alligators per square mile than people, others are serene, others cosmopolitan, and still others glitzy. Descriptions range from one travel writer's "funky" to the glamorous tag of "The Texas Riviera."

You'll find that all these descriptions are correct. So, just about whatever you want to do — that's legal — you can find a place to do it somewhere along the more than 360 miles of coastline of the Third Coast.

There are beaches, but the beaches are just one of the attractions of the coast. Other attractions lie in the cities and towns behind the beaches and the Gulf waters themselves.

What do you want to do?

Before you do anything, of course, you'll need a place to stay. The choices here run the gamut from world-class luxury hotels in the major cities to no-frills beach houses or fishermen's cabins scattered all along

THE TEXAS COAST

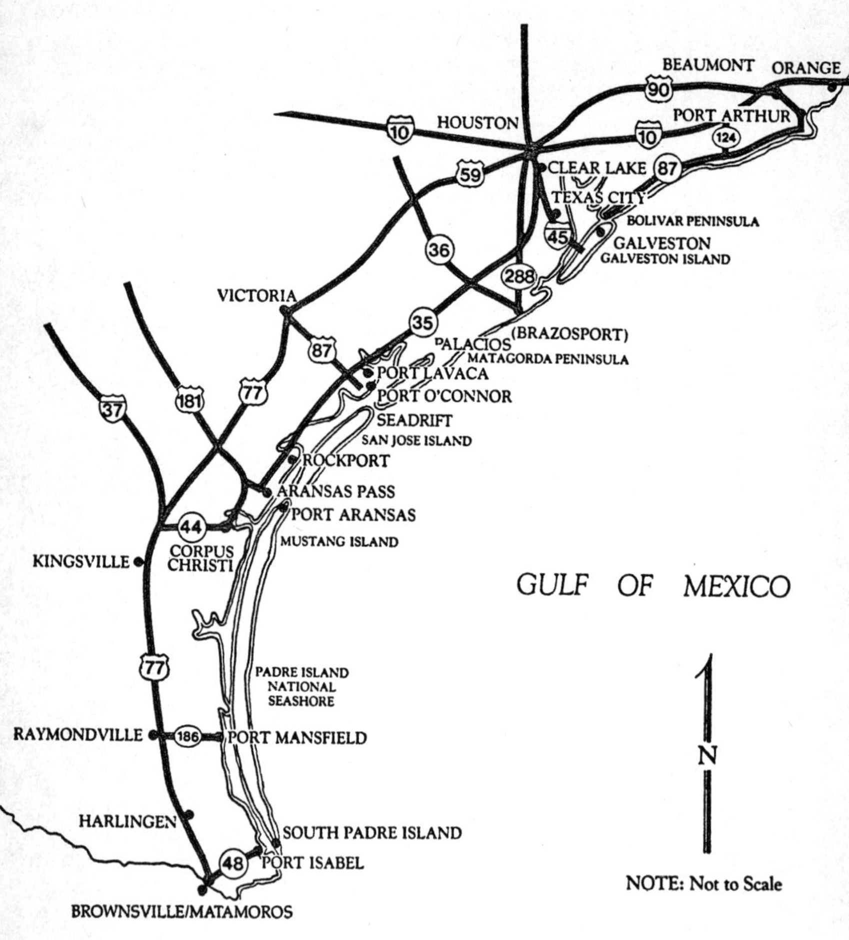

the coast. You can watch the sunrise over the Gulf from a high rise condominium apartment in places like Port Aransas or South Padre or enjoy all the comforts of home in a bed and breakfast. And, of course, motels with a wide range of prices and amenities — from major chains to Mom and Pop operations — are everywhere.

Then there's the eating. On top of the list, naturally, is seafood. The good thing is that more and more restaurants now serve up fresh instead of frozen and have learned there are more ways to cook a fish than by frying. But seafood isn't everything. Barbecue, Italian, Tex-Mex, Vietnamese, Czech, German — they're all here, even places that serve a good ol' American steak. And when it comes to atmosphere and the other ingredients that add to your dining pleasure, here too, the range is wide. You can put on the Ritz at Reflections on top of the Wyndham Hotel in Corpus Christi or Galveston's Merchant Prince or use your hands to dig into Cajun shrimp and sausage served on butcher paper at the Crazy Cajun's in Port Aransas.

What you do when you'll not eating or sleeping depends on your interest. In addition to sun and sand you can have action or solitude. Jump into the middle of elbow-to-elbow college students partying during Spring Break at Port Aransas or South Padre or beachcomb the long, quiet stretches of Padre Island National Seashore or Matagorda Island off Port O'Connor. You can observe the birds and wildlife at several national wildlife refuges and parks or play blackjack or roulette on one of the cruise ships operating out of Galveston or Port Isabel. If you want you can be surrounded by history on Galveston's Strand or in Port Arthur's Pompeiian Villa, experience the wonders of our space program at Space Center Houston in Clear Lake or life underwater at Corpus Christi's Texas State Aquarium, ride a bike on Galveston's seawall — the world's longest sidewalk — attend a symphony or let the good times roll at a Cajun dancehall. For the sports enthusiast there's sailing, windsurfing, golf, tennis, or dozens of other choices. Not to forget going after a big one. You can fish in the Gulf, the bays, or Laguna Madre from a party boat or a charter, off several public fishing piers, or from the innumerable places you can get a line in the water from Sabine Lake on the north to the jetties on South Padre.

Well, you get the idea. There's a place for you to do what you want to do somewhere along the Third Coast. And this guidebook can help you find *yours* somewhere.

This is not to say that all is perfect in paradise. As a visitor you should be aware that there are some imperfections that could blemish your holiday. For example, if you're expecting wide, white sandy beaches all along the coast, you may be in for a disappointment, at least in the northern half. The sand on most of the beaches from Sabine Pass down to Corpus Christi is dull-looking and generally coarse-textured, and, with few exceptions, the beaches are narrow. It's not until you hit Mustang Island and Padre Island, around Corpus Christi, that the beaches start to get pristine and expansive and look like they came from travel posters.

There are also some problems

Some problems are man-made, some natural. The first is that industry, especially the huge petrochemical industry, is much in evidence along the coast. Let's face it, on much of the Texas coast, industry ranks ahead of tourism as the prime provider of jobs. Ports, refineries, and industrial plants that depend on cheap ocean transport play a major role here. There are exceptions — Galveston Island, smaller towns like Port Aransas, Port O'Connor and Port Mansfield, and the developed areas on both ends of Padre Island — have little or no heavy industry. And sometimes the plants are located well away from the tourist areas, as in Corpus Christi. But, in any case, industry is there, the plants are there, and you should expect to see them. In fact, in some cases, they are part of sights to see and are mentioned in the listings.

Another problem is that occasionally man and nature can make the Gulf water inhospitable to swimmers and others who enjoy water sports, and sometimes even to fishermen. At times, especially in the summer, the shallow waters off some beaches can be invaded by a huge flotilla of jellyfish. It doesn't happen often, but it does happen. (By the way, a suggested antidote to neutralize a jellyfish sting is meat tenderizer.) Man also does his inimitable job of messing up our beaches and fishing grounds with oil spills and other polluting discharges. (If you get oil tar on you or your possessions, try using WD-40, Pine Sol, or tar or bug remover that's sold in car-parts stores.)

Finally, our beaches are fragile. The combination of natural erosion and thoughtless overdevelopment and overuse is eroding the state's beautiful shoreline at an alarming rate. Some beaches are already starting to disappear. Individual cities and counties have taken whatever steps they can afford to save this natural treasure, but, unfortunately at this time, Texas lacks a comprehensive state program dedicated to saving our coastal beaches.

Experts agree that one of the best methods of protecting the beaches is by assisting nature in strengthening the front line of sand dunes. This means giving the beach space to live and rebuild instead of building right on top of it. It also means that you and I, the ones who use the beaches, should realize what recreational delights they are and treat them with tender, loving care.

ARANSAS PASS

ARANSAS AND SAN PATRICIO COUNTIES ★ 8,500 ★ (512)

The city is located on the mainland but named after the entrance pass to Corpus Christi Bay that separates Mustang and San José islands, six miles south. Shrimping and commercial and sports fishing are the main industries here. The city boasts that it has the world's largest and most modern shrimping facilities at Conn Brown Harbor. There are shrimp fleets at many ports up and down the Texas coast, but Aransas Pass' central location on the coastal bend makes it the home port for about 500 shrimp trawlers, one of the largest fleets in Texas.

The name "Aransas" has been traced to Spanish explorers who named the city after a shrine in Spain called *Nuestra Senora de Aranzazu* (Our Lady of Aranzazu).

The city had an unusual beginning. In 1909, T. B. Wheeler and his partner, Russell Harrison, son of former President Benjamin Harrison, decided to hold a lottery to sell their 12,000 acres on Red Fish Bay that included the townsite of Aransas Pass. Interest was high because the U.S. government was about to finance the dredging of a port in this area, and because Aransas Pass was the closest outlet to the Gulf, everyone assumed it would be chosen over Corpus Christi or Rockport. Lottery tickets were sold for $100 each, and special trains brought buyers

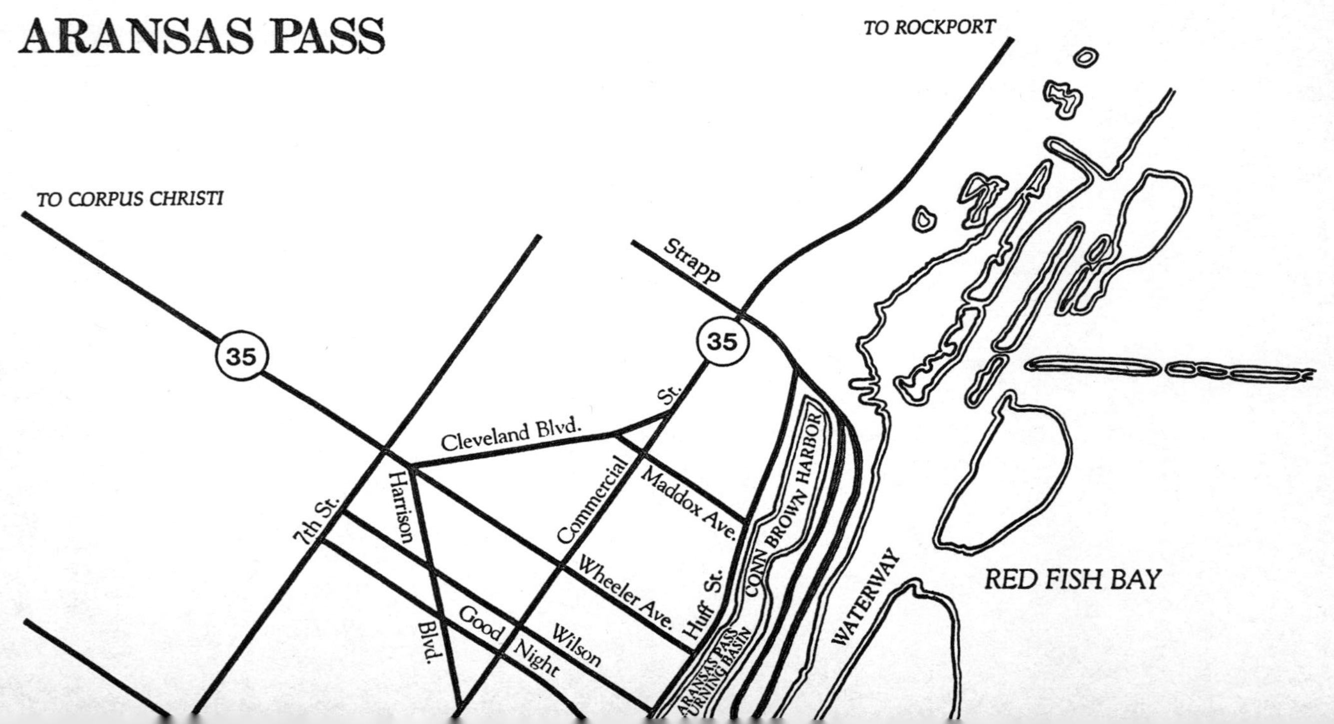
ARANSAS PASS
TO ROCKPORT
TO CORPUS CHRISTI
Strapp
35
35
St.
Cleveland Blvd.
Commercial
Maddox Ave.
7th St.
Harrison
Wheeler Ave.
Huff St.
CONN BROWN HARBOR
ARANSAS PASS
URNING BASIN
WATERWAY
RED FISH BAY
Good
Night
Wilson
Blvd.

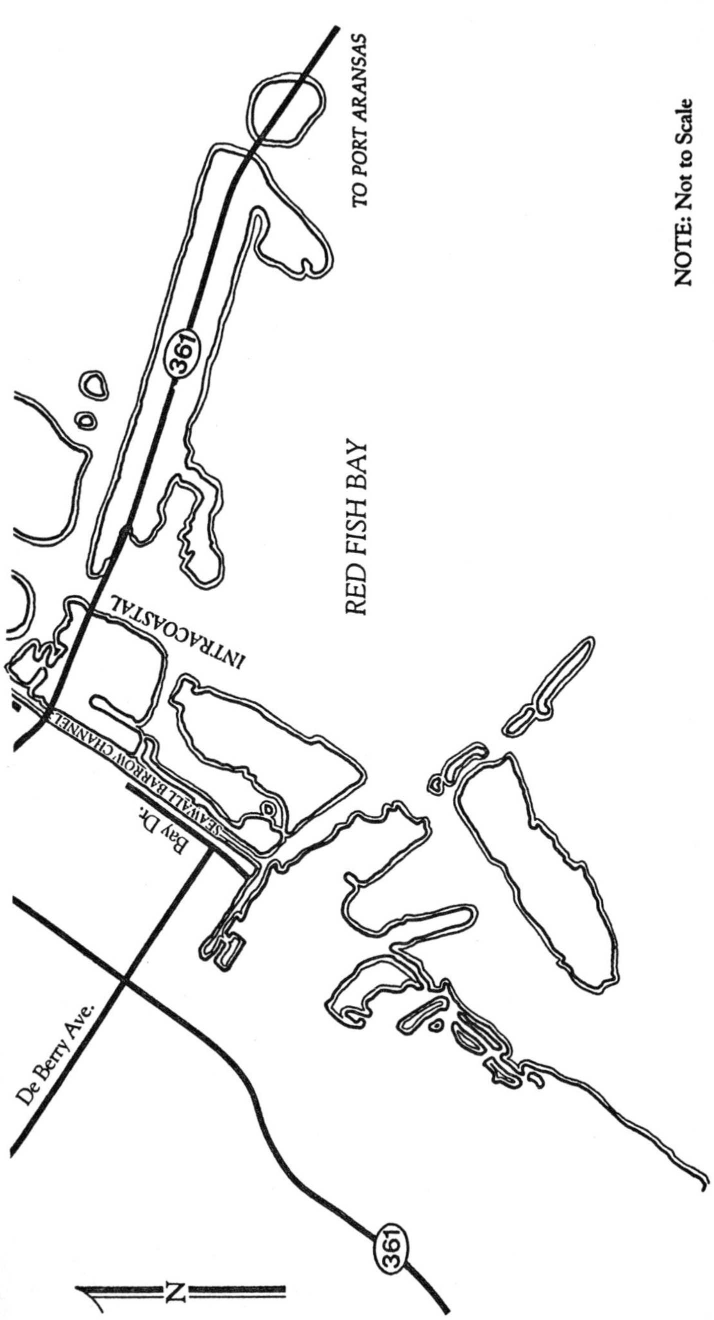
TO PORT ARANSAS
NOTE: Not to Scale
361
RED FISH BAY
INTRACOASTAL
SEAWALL BARROW CHANNEL
Bay Dr.
De Berry Ave.
361
N

from as far away as Kansas and Nebraska to try their luck in the drawings. The best thing about this lottery was that no one could lose. Only 6,000 tickets were sold for the 6,000 lots. The only gamble concerned the location of the lot each ticket holder would win. According to local historians, this was the largest and last land lottery held in the United States. The winners must have been disappointed, however, when a short time later, Washington decided to make Corpus Christi the major port instead of Aransas Pass.

TOURIST SERVICES

ARANSAS PASS CHAMBER OF COMMERCE
452 Cleveland (Texas 35) near Whitney (78336)
758-2750 or 800-633-3028
Monday–Friday 9–12, 1–5
Free
W

Information is available here on where the fish are biting, accommodations, directions, and other details about the area that you might want to know. Among the free brochures is a map of the city that includes much of the surrounding area out to Port Aransas.

POINTS OF INTEREST

CONN BROWN HARBOR
From Commercial St. (Texas 35 N) take Staff Blvd. east to the peninsula sheltering the harbor

This is the center of the local fishing industry with docks and mooring for the fleet that annually brings in millions of pounds of shrimp to the processing plants along the shore. Overlooking the port, at the south end of the peninsula, is the Seamen's Memorial Tower dedicated to the fishermen from this port who lost their lives at sea. Behind this is Harbor Park, which includes free public fishing piers.

SPORTS AND ACTIVITIES

Birdwatching

Birdwatching for shorebirds is usually good to excellent along the Texas 361 causeway to Port Aransas, especially in winter. Another nearby location popular with birders is the Welder Wildlife Refuge in nearby Sinton (See Side Trips).

Fishing

You can get a line in the water from dozens of places along the shore, the jetties, or the public piers at Harbor Park on the end of the Conn Brown Harbor peninsula. The catch here may include flounder, redfish, speckled and sand trout, and drum. Or, if you prefer Gulf fishing, it's just six miles away through the pass. Out there wait red snapper, warsaw, mackerel, ling, and many other species. The Chamber of Commerce (See Tourist Services) has information on charter boats and guides for bay and deep-sea fishing, and also duck hunting.

SHOPPING

DANIEL'S DEN ANTIQUES
315 E. Wilson, under the watertower
758-5189

Chick and JoAnna Daniel don't believe in specializing. Their shop is crammed with a wide variety of antiques, mostly small, easy-to-carry items such as silver, linens, china, art glass, and toys. A lot of their stock comes from estate sales and from "Winter Texans" who bring it down from their northern homes.

SIDE TRIPS

SINTON
Take Texas 35 west to US 181 then continue west to Sinton.

Sinton Chamber Of Commerce
218 W. Sinton (P.O. Box 217, 78387)
364-2307
W

Rob And Bessie Welder Park
About three miles north off US Hwy 181
364-2569
Open seven days dawn to dusk
Free
W Variable

The park's 300 acres includes a playground, 18-hole golf course, swimming pool, tennis courts, picnic areas, and RV campsites.

Welder Wildlife Refuge
US 77 about 7.4 miles northeast, entrance on east side of railroad tracks
364-2643
Regular tours Thursday only at 2:55. Closed holidays
Free
W Variable

This refuge is unique in that it is a working ranch containing what is said to be the largest privately endowed wildlife refuge in the world. About 55 species of mammals, 55 species of reptiles and amphibians, and more than 380 species of birds have been seen on the 7,800-acre sanctuary and research center that was established by a provision in the will of rancher Robert H. Welder. Tours normally take about two and a half hours and include a visit to portions of the preserve and the museum in the Administration Building. When they say be there at 2:55 on Thursday, that's exactly what they mean. The gates are opened at that time, everyone waiting drives in (tours are guided but you travel from place to place in your own car), and then at 3:00 the gates are closed and not opened until the tour ends. No pets are allowed on the grounds. Groups of 15 up to 72 can arrange tours at other times (except Sundays) by contacting the tour director at P.O. Drawer 1400, Sinton 78387. A good time to take the tour is during the winter after the northern birds have migrated to the preserve. The wildlife is also generally more active at that time.

ANNUAL EVENTS

September

SHRIMPOREE
Roosevelt Stadium on Texas 35 near 7th, and downtown
758-2750 (Chamber of Commerce)
Friday–Sunday late in September
Admission
W Variable

The city's ties to the shrimping industry are celebrated in this festival that opens on Friday evening with an arts and crafts fair, games, and live entertainment. But the real fun starts Saturday morning. That's when the schedule includes the Shrimporee Parade and the Great Outhouse Race. The rest of the day usually features a shrimp eating contest, a variety of entertainment, and a street dance. Sunday morning is given over to gospel singing, then in the afternoon there's more entertainment and the Men's Sexy Legs Contest. A children's area is open Saturday and Sunday. And, as would be expected, there are food booths serving fresh seafood.

OFFBEAT

BIG FISHERMAN RESTAURANT
Take Texas 35 north to FM 1069 then left (west) on FM 1069 about half a mile

See Rockport, Offbeat

RESTAURANTS

($ = under $7, $$ = $7 to $17, $$$ = $17 to $25, $$$$ = over $25 for one person excluding drinks, tax, and tip.)

BAKERY CAFE
434 S. Commercial, downtown
758-3511
Breakfast, lunch, and dinner Monday–Saturday, Closed Sunday
$-$$
MC, V
W

It started out as a bakery in 1926 and slowly expanded into a small restaurant that's widely known in the area for simple, good food at reasonable prices. Seafood, steaks, chicken, and the like are all on the menu, plus, of course, fresh bakery goodies. Because fishermen often head out before dawn, it opens at 5 a.m.

CRAB-N
Texas 35 approximately four miles north
758-2371
Open seven days for dinner only
$$
Cr.
Children's plates

The restaurant overlooks one of the canals in the City by the Sea, a housing development on the Rockport Road that's built on canals, so you can drive here or come by boat. House specialties include some Cajun entrées such as Cajun shrimp and catfish. The menu is almost equally divided between seafood and beef dishes such as steaks and blackened prime rib. If you're a shrimp lover, the Shrimp Feast features stuffed shrimp, Cajun shrimp, shrimp scampi, fried shrimp, and boiled shrimp. Lounge.

LA COCINA Y CANTINA
Texas 35 about four miles north
729-4934
Lunch and dinner Tuesday–Sunday, Closed Monday
$-$$
Cr.
W

Most of the dishes are Tex-Mex with specialties such as shrimp *enchiladas, chiles relenos,* and *fajitas.* But American-style steaks, seafood, and chicken are also on the menu. Lounge.

UNCLE SLICK'S EATERY
Texas 35 approximately half a mile north
758-9941
Lunch and dinner Monday–Saturday, closed Sunday
$$
AE, MC, V
W ramp

The dining room in this Cape Cod house is decorated with everything from old children's toys to quilts, and the lower walls are covered with corrugated tin. Somehow that combination works to make a bright and pleasant room. The menu emphasizes seafood with a touch of chicken and steaks and some Cajun-style and Tex-Mex entrées. A popular choice is the Chesapeake Casserole: a spicy concoction of shrimp, scallops, and crabmeat in a butter/sherry sauce. Bar.

ACCOMMODATIONS

($ = Under $45, $$ = $46-$60, $$$ = $61-$80, $$$$ = $81-$100, $$$$$ = Over $100)
Room Tax 10 percent

HOMEPORT INN
1515 W. Wheeler (Texas 35)
758-3213 or 800-456-9071
$
W+ one room
No-smoking rooms

The 63 units in this two-story motel include four 2-bedroom apartments ($$) and two no-smoking rooms. Children under 13 stay free in room with parents. Senior discount in winter only. Satellite TV with The Movie channel. Room phones (local calls free). Pets OK ($5 pet charge). Outdoor pool and indoor whirlpool. Free coffee in lobby, free newspaper, and free Continental breakfast. Almost every room has a piece of furniture from the famous old Warwick Hotel in Houston.

BRAZOSPORT

BRAZORIA COUNTY ★ 70,000 ★ (409)

Brazosport is not a city itself but a loose confederation of nine cities and towns clustered on the coast near the mouth of the Brazos River. Interlocking like pieces of a jigsaw puzzle are: Brazoria, Clute, Freeport, Jones Creek, Lake Jackson, Oyster Creek, Richwood, and the beach communities of Quintana and Surfside.

The cities have separate governments, but are joined in one independent school district and one Chamber of Commerce. A peculiarity of the patchwork make-up of this composite city is that each town has its own version of the local option liquor law. As a result, some of the cities are wet and some dry and in some cases wet and dry coexist on each side of a boundary street.

Geographically, Brazosport is unique in that it occupies the only "frontal mainland coastline" in Texas. That's coastline that does not have a barrier island, bays, estuaries, or tidal marsh. There is only about 20 miles of it in Texas, and it's all here.

As a recreational area, Brazosport is relatively undeveloped, but still has a lot to offer in activities in the multi-cities as well as on the beaches. In addition to the two major beach communities, there are miles of quiet beaches you can drive on to find your own private spot. It is also

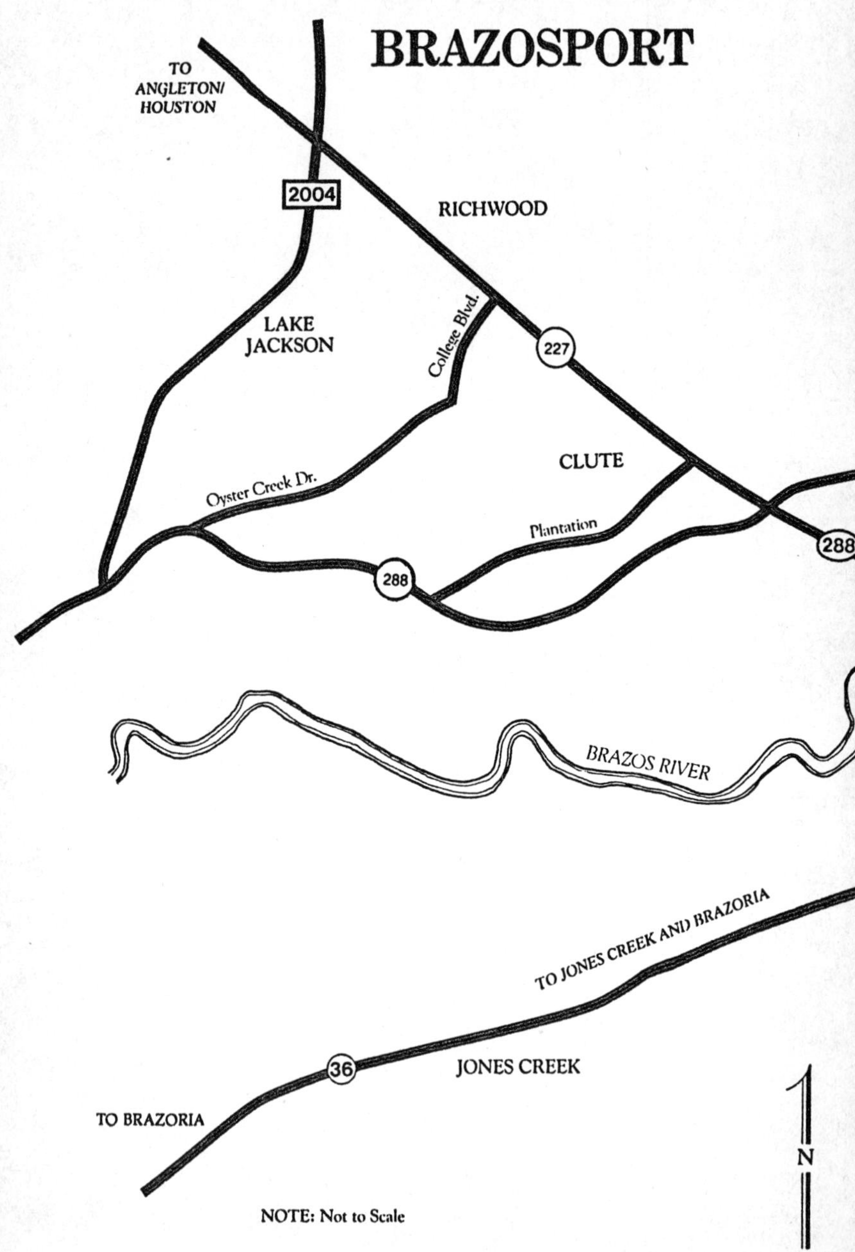
BRAZOSPORT
TO
ANGLETON/
HOUSTON
2004
RICHWOOD
LAKE
JACKSON
College Blvd.
227
CLUTE
Oyster Creek Dr.
Plantation
288
288
BRAZOS RIVER
TO JONES CREEK AND BRAZORIA
36
JONES CREEK
TO BRAZORIA
N
NOTE: Not to Scale

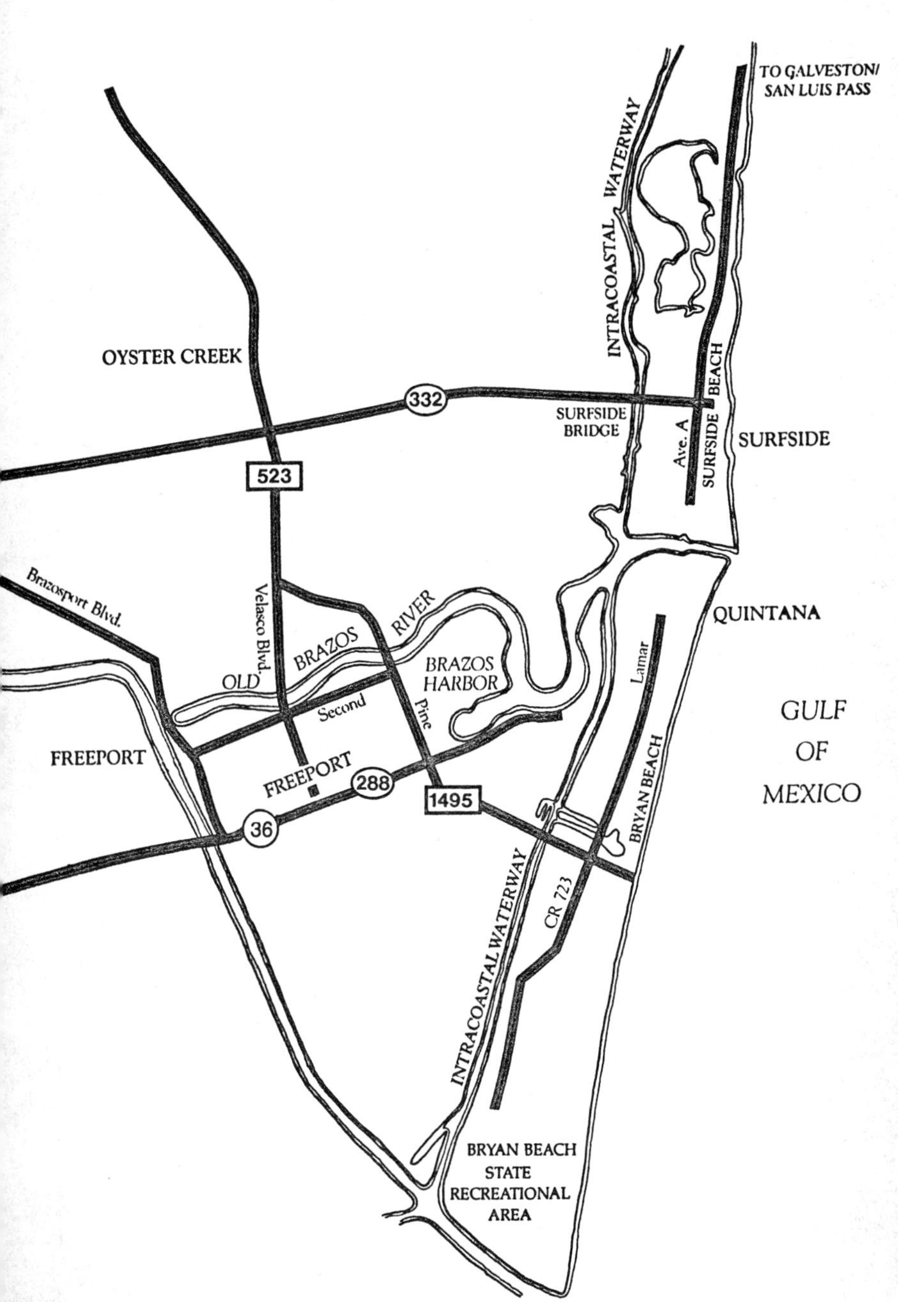
TO GALVESTON/
SAN LUIS PASS
INTRACOASTAL WATERWAY
OYSTER CREEK
332
SURFSIDE
BRIDGE
Ave. A
SURFSIDE BEACH
SURFSIDE
523
Brazosport Blvd.
Velasco Blvd.
OLD BRAZOS RIVER
BRAZOS
HARBOR
QUINTANA
Lamar
Second
Pine
GULF
OF
MEXICO
FREEPORT
FREEPORT
288
1495
36
BRYAN BEACH
CR 723
INTRACOASTAL WATERWAY
BRYAN BEACH
STATE
RECREATIONAL
AREA

a birdwatchers' paradise because it is flanked on one side by the Brazoria National Wildlife Refuge and on the other by the San Bernard National Wildlife Refuge.

In addition to the miles of beaches and other attractions, Brazosport's biggest draw is for fishermen. Deep-sea, surf, jetty, and small-boat inshore fishing are all available. On the commercial fishing side, the area is the seasonal home of a large shrimp fleet that brings in as much as 15 million pounds of shrimp annually.

As a low-key, generally low-cost recreation area, Brazosport appears to have one big handicap. It is the home of Texas' fastest growing petrochemical/industrial complex that averages about a mile and a half in width and stretches for about nine miles starting right behind the beach communities. As a result, this complex is the backdrop for everything you see or do in the area. The good news is that most visitors become accustomed to it quickly and don't even notice it after a day or two.

The area figures prominently in Texas history. It was here at the mouth of the Brazos River that Stephen F. Austin's first colonists landed in 1821 in the ship *The Lively*. True, they were lost — they were looking for the mouth of the Colorado River — but that doesn't alter the fact that this was their first landing. It was also here that the Texans first fought the Mexicans — at the Battle of Velasco in 1832, four years before the Alamo — and where Santa Anna was brought after his defeat at San Jacinto to sign the treaty that gave Texas its independence. It was also here that the new government of the Republic of Texas sat for the first time.

That first battle with the Mexicans occurred when the Mexican government built a one-cannon fort at Velasco commanding the mouth of the Brazos River. (The site is no longer visible, but it was just behind the Coast Guard Station in what is now Surfside.) The commanders of Fort Velasco, and another fort at Anahuac, to the east of Galveston Bay, irritated the Texan colonists when they started charging customs and clearance duties that the Texans considered close to outright piracy. The situation came to a head when the commander at Fort Anahuac imprisoned several of the Texans, including William B. Travis. The men of the illegally formed Texan militia at Brazoria decided to level the fort at Anahuac. They planned to load two cannon and about 120 men aboard the tiny schooner *Brazoria* and sail down the Brazos and across the Gulf to Anahuac. But when the commander at Fort Velasco refused to let the ship pass, the Texans decided to level his fort instead.

Late on the night of June 25, 1832, about a hundred Texans stole ashore from the ship and surrounded the fort, intending a surprise attack at dawn. The surprise was spoiled when one of them tripped and accidentally fired his rifle. For the rest of the night both sides fired at each other in the dark, doing little damage. With daylight, however, the Texan sharpshooters took command of the battle. The Mexicans' only cannon was on an exposed mound in the center of the fort so it could shoot over the walls in all directions. This arrangement was fine for controlling the river, but, unfortunately for the Mexican's, it also meant the walls got in the way of close-in shots. The Texans simply stayed below the cannon's angle of fire and picked off any soldier who exposed himself on the walls or the mound. After a few hours of fire from the sharpshooters, the fort surrendered.

Naturally, the Texans expected retribution from Mexico for this act of rebellion, and it wasn't long in coming in the form of five Mexican gunboats. But the whims of politics saved the day for the Texans. For a long time, the Texans had considered Mexican President Bustamante a tyrant. They therefore pledged their support to a Mexican general who was trying to overthrow the president. As it turned out, the commander of the gunboats was also a follower of that general. Instead of a bloodbath, a fiesta was held that ended with the Texans handing back Fort Velasco.

The general they favored did become the leader of Mexico. His name? General Antonio Lopez de Santa Anna.

And in another twist of fate, the colonel who surrendered Fort Velasco to the Texans also became a follower of Santa Anna and later led the Mexican troops in what is known in Texas history as the "Goliad Massacre."

TOURIST SERVICES

BRAZOSPORT VISITORS AND CONVENTION COUNCIL
Clute, in Chamber of Commerce Building, 420 Texas 332, approximately half mile from Texas 227 interchange (P.O. Box 1361, 77541)
265-2508
Monday–Friday 9–5

The large Chamber of Commerce sign makes the chamber easy to find, but it's a little hard to get to. The trick is to turn north at Main, then immediately right on the access road.

GET-ACQUAINTED DRIVING TOUR

Pick up a map at the **Visitors and Convention Council**'s office (See preceding listing) and start this tour from there. *Get back on Texas 332 and go west*, away from the Gulf. The Dow Chemical plant will be on your left and the city of Clute on your right.

During this drive you'll be going in and out of seven of the nine cities that make up Brazosport. Now you're in Clute, but, at just about the point where the Dow plant ends, you'll pass into Lake Jackson, the most populous city in the multi-city complex that was started in the 1940s as a company town for Dow. If you ever felt you didn't know whether to go this way or that way, then the place for you may be Lake Jackson where streets are named This Way, That Way, and Anyway. And, there's a church on one of these Ways with its driveway named His Way.

Stay on Texas 332 W and you'll come to **Brazos Mall** (See Shopping). Just past this, *turn right on Lake Rd.* then *right again on FM 2004*. For the next few miles you'll be driving through woodlands that includes the

T. J. Dunbar Park. Continue east on FM 2004 across the railroad tracks out of Lake Jackson and into Richwood. The next main road is *Texas 227*. A left turn would take you to Angleton (See Side Trips), but *turn right* (south), back toward the Gulf. Two miles down you'll come to the light at College Blvd. *Turn right on College* and then right again at the entrance sign to **Brazosport College** (See Colleges and Universities) and the **Brazosport Center for the Arts and Sciences** (See Museums and Performing Arts). Drive around the small campus and/or visit the Center, and then *retrace your route* going left on College and right to put you *back on Texas 227 going south.*

Shortly, you'll be back in Clute. It's about two miles to the cloverleaf intersection with Texas 332. This is almost back where you started, having gone through and circled Clute, Lake Jackson, and Richwood. (Have you ever traveled through so many cities in such a short time?) But there's more to see. After you pass the cloverleaf, Texas 227 becomes Texas 288 South and you'll find yourself crossing right through the industrial area. Some of the plants offer tours (Dow Chemical, for example, has a tour each Wednesday at 3 p.m. For details contact the Visitors and Convention Council).

About three miles south of the cloverleaf you'll see the **Mystery Monument** (See other Points of Interest) on your left. You're now in Freeport where this restored shrimp boat is set up in a city park at the head of the Old Brazos River. The gaily painted root beer stand near the boat is **Antonelli's River Inn**. Keg root beer and ice cream are the main items here, just as they were years ago when this stand was a popular spot in downtown Freeport. Donated to the Freeport League, it was moved here to once again lure root beer fans from miles around. If you care to stop for a taste, it's open weekends in spring and fall and daily in summer.

Stay on Texas 288, skirting Freeport, when *it joins Texas 36* going east toward Quintana. *At the end of 36/288, turn right (south) on FM 1495.* This road takes you across the drawbridge over the Intracoastal Waterway, and leads to **Bryan Beach** and **Quintana Beach** (See Other Points of Interest). You can't see it, but off to your right before the drawbridge is a **Department of Energy Strategic Petroleum Reserve** facility where petroleum is stored in huge underground caverns at Bryan Mound, an old sulphur mining spot. Freeport was founded in 1912 as a sulphur company town.

After the drawbridge, *turn left on County Rd. 723* to go to Quintana. If you want to go to **Bryan Beach State Recreation Area** (See Other Points of Interest), instead of turning, you continue the short distance down FM 1495 to the beach and then take a right and drive along the beach. But you better have 4-wheel drive to try this.

Follow County Rd. 723 about two miles to **Quintana Beach Park** (See other Points of Interest). This park is open dawn to dusk. From the boardwalk here, or from the nearby jetty, you can look across the Freeport Harbor Channel to **Surfside Beach** (See Other Points of Interest).

After you finish exploring the tiny town of Quintana and its park, return to FM 1495 and *head back across the drawbridge to Freeport*. Soon, on your right, you'll see the **Port of Freeport**. This port is growing as the result of a five-year program to widen and deepen the existing channel to enable the largest cargo ships to dock here. In addition to handling cargo for the petrochemical and other industries in the area, it also handles such diverse cargos as 250,000 tons of containerized bananas and 350,000 tons of rice products annually. (Half-hour tours of the port can be arranged. For information contact Freeport City Hall, 233-3526.)

When you get to *E. 4th St. take a left*, then at the next block *a right on Park Ave.*, then two blocks to *another left on E. 2nd St.*, the main street of Freeport. On your right, just before the railroad overpass, you'll see **Girouard's General Store**, a combination grocery, hardware store, and ship chandler's shop that advertises "If we don't have it, you don't need it." Girouard's is reportedly the only grocery store in the country certified as a government agent for marine charts. Further on, also on your right, you'll pass the **On the River Restaurant** (See Restaurants) and **Captain Elliott's Party Boats** (See Sports and Activities-Fishing). At the corner by Captain Elliott's, *turn right on Velasco Blvd.* As you cross the bridge, look to your right for a view of whatever part of the **shrimp fleet** that's in port. If you look further down in the same direction, you'll see a large metal rectangle sticking up above the river. This is the **Velasco Memorial Tide Gate**. When a storm tide warning is received, small boat owners steer their crafts up the Old Brazos River then the tide gate is lowered, and the boats ride out the storm safe and secure in the sealed-off waterway.

Continue on Velasco Blvd. for about two miles, through the plants again, back *to Texas 322*. If you continue straight you'll hit the town of Oyster Creek (See Restaurants — Windswept), but we'll *turn right* and head for Surfside which sits at the end of this road. The limits of this village include the site of the first town of Velasco. At the entrance to the beach you'll see the **Surfside Beach Tourist Center** (See Other Points of Interest) where you can find out all you want to know about this beachfront community. County Rd. 257, called the Bluewater Highway, runs north behind the beach up to San Luis Pass and Galveston.

Your tour to get you acquainted with Brazosport ends here. If you want to return to your starting point at the Brazosport Chamber of Commerce, just take Texas 332 back past the cloverleaf to Clute.

MUSEUMS

BRAZOSPORT CENTER FOR ARTS AND SCIENCES
Lake Jackson, 400 College Dr. on campus of Brazosport College
265-7661
W + But not all areas

This center, a cultural complex owned and operated by the Brazosport Fine Arts Council, is the home of the Museum of Natural Sciences, the Nature Center and Planetarium, the Brazosport Art League, and the Brazosport Music Theater and Little Theatre (See Performing Arts).

MUSEUM OF NATURAL SCIENCES, NATURE CENTER AND PLANETARIUM
(Museum) 265-7831 (Nature Center/Planetarium) 265-3376
Tuesday–Saturday 10–5, Sunday 2–5, Closed Monday
Free
W + But not all areas

The cornerstone of this museum is its seashell collection that is reputed to be one of the most comprehensive on the Gulf coast. There are also sections devoted to area archaeology, fossils, rocks, and minerals, and Touch Tables for children of all ages. The Nature Center has displays on plants and wildlife, and there is a three quarters of a mile nature trail on the grounds. The planetarium periodically has shows open to the general public.

BRAZOSPORT ART LEAGUE GALLERY
265-7971
Tuesday–Sunday 2–5, Closed Monday
Free

The work of local professional and amateur artists, in a variety of media, as well as traveling exhibits are featured in this gallery. Exhibits change every 4 to 6 weeks.

LAKE JACKSON HISTORICAL MUSEUM
122 S. Parking Pl.
297-6727 or 297-0617
Thursday 1–5, except if Thursday is a holiday. Tours by appointment
Free
W

Exhibits recount the history of Lake Jackson from its founding as a Dow Chemical company town in 1942 to the present. Layouts of the city's winding streets and spacious park areas that were designed by Alden Dow, architect and son of the company's founder, are also on display.

OTHER POINTS OF INTEREST

BRYAN BEACH STATE RECREATION AREA
From Freeport, take FM 1495 to end at Bryan Beach, then right and down beach approximately two miles (4-wheel drive recommended)
737-1222 (Galveston Island State Park)
Open daylight hours
Free

This 878-acre undeveloped peninsula park is bordered by the Gulf, the Brazos River Diversion Channel, and the Intracoastal Waterway. It offers a quiet beach for fishing, birdwatching, beachcombing, and primitive camping. There are no facilities and no roads in the area. High tides can dictate whether cars can get in or out over the beach driving route, so the surest way to get there is by small boat.

MYSTERY MONUMENT

Freeport, Texas 227 (400 block of Brazosport Blvd.) at head of Old Brazos River
Open at all times
Free
W

Forty tons of wood, iron, and rigging, proud bow still held high, this shrimp trawler looks eager to return to the Gulf waters that were her home for almost three decades. The 60-foot craft was once the undisputed wood-hull queen of the Gulf shrimp fleet from Mississippi to the Mexican border. There are no records to prove it, but experts estimate *The Mystery* had a career catch of close to 3.5 million pounds of shrimp. Now a monument to the pioneers of the Texas shrimping industry, she got her name when her first owners thought it a mystery how they'd pay for her.

Possibly as interesting as her life at sea is the story of the chamber of commerce's project to transform the boat into a monument. It started with the trawler abandoned and sunk at her berth. Moving her proved to be about as simple as moving the first space shuttle from the hanger to the launch pad. She was refloated, towed to another dock, hauled out of the water, cleaned up, and returned to her original mooring — where she promptly sunk again. This, plus the fact that she would almost have to be turned into a submarine to pass under a railroad bridge on the water route to her new site, encouraged the committee to decide on an overland move.

Raised again, but threatening to go under at any moment, she was carefully towed across the water to a 100-ton crane that lifted her onto a trailer. The trailer's center beam immediately sagged to about an inch off the ground. On the move, the low-slung trailer hung up on a levee and, when finally worked loose, chased two winch trucks down the other side, tied up traffic, got stuck again on a railroad track, and in two hours had moved a grand total of half a mile. Finally, *The Mystery* was hoisted onto her permanent site. It was then that the movers discovered they had moved her with a couple of tons of water in the hull.

So, in addition to being a tribute to the men who sailed her, she is also a tribute to the perseverance of the members of the chamber of commerce who moved her.

QUINTANA BEACH COUNTY PARK

Take FM 1495 from Freeport across the Intracoastal Waterway, then left on County Rd. 723 and follow signs to beach
859-5711 Ext 1541 (Brazoria County Park Commission at County Courthouse in Angleton)
Free
Open seven days dawn to dark
W +

This 50-acre park has a large deck with picnic tables, a snack bar, bathhouse, a boardwalk down to the beach, fishing pier, amphitheater, hiking trails, and camping area. Two historical homes have been moved here. The "Coveney House," was originally built in 1897 and then, after it was wrecked by the 1900 hurricane, rebuilt with walls reinforced by four layers of solid wood so it wouldn't blow away again. The "Seaburn House" dates from before the Civil War. These houses contain historical exhibits, and the Coveney House has a hands-on beach ecology display and an observation room.

SURFSIDE BEACH
Follow Texas 332 to its eastern end
233-7596 or 800-232-2414 (Surfside Beach Tourist Center)
Free
W Variable

Located on the site where Santa Anna signed the treaty that gave Texas its independence, this is the major beach community in Brazosport. Facilities for swimming, sailing, surfing, sunning, fishing, and all other beach activities are available here. There are many places to eat, bars, small motels, and other beach-type businesses. Driving is permitted on much of the beach, but you need a permit to park. Permits cost $2 a day ($10 a year) and are available at the tourist center and most beach stores. A mile of pedestrians-only beach is located between First and Thirteenth Streets. During the summer months there are free, supervised daily activities for children and families. The tourist center, located off Texas 332 at the main entrance to the beach, is usually open seven days, 9-5. There are a number of cottages and beach houses for rent in the community (See Accommodations).

SPORTS AND ACTIVITIES

Birdwatching

The Freeport Christmas Bird Count, sponsored by the national Audubon Society, frequently ranks first or second in the nation. The record count is 226 different species and it usually averages more than 200 species. Although access is difficult, two of the best places for birding are the nearby national wildlife refuges (See Side Trips).

Fishing

Brazosport is an excellent jumping-off place for deep sea fishing. From the Freeport jetties to the 100-foot depth where the big ones bite is only about three hours by boat. Surf, jetty, and small-boat inshore fishing are also popular as is crabbing in the more than 100 miles of waterways in the area. During the summer the local marinas and organizations offer a continual string of fishing tournaments. A number of charter boat outfits are listed in the phone book, but the only party boats are operated by Captain Elliott's at 1010 W. 2nd St. in Freeport (233-1811). A 12-hour (6 a.m. to 6 p.m.) deep-sea party boat trip costs about $50 (children 12 and under $30) plus $7 for tackle rental. Long range, two-day weekend deep-sea trips are also available for about $175. There is also a fishing pier at San Luis Pass (233-6902) off County Rd. 257 north of Surfside. A list of fishing locations and boat ramps is available from the Visitors and Convention Council (See Tourist Services).

Golf

FREEPORT MUNICIPAL GOLF COURSE
830 Slaughter Rd., off Texas 36
233-8311

Eighteen-hole course. Visitors' green fees: weekdays $7, weekends $9.

Tennis

Lighted courts open to the public are available at Garland Park, Jasmine Park, and Lake Jackson Intermediate School in Lake Jackson, and Freeport Community House. Other courts are located at Brazoswood High School in Clute, Brazosport High School in Freeport, and Brazosport College in Lake Jackson.

COLLEGES AND UNIVERSITIES

BRAZOSPORT COLLEGE
Lake Jackson, 500 College off Texas 227
265-6131
W

This community college offers academic and vocational/technical programs for about 4,000 students. One field of study appropriate to the school's coastal location is oceanographic technologies. Visitors are welcome to dramatic and musical programs. The Brazosport Center for Arts and Sciences is on campus.

PERFORMING ARTS

BRAZOSPORT LITTLE THEATRE and MUSIC THEATRE
Brazosport Center for Arts and Science, Lake Jackson, 400 College Dr. on campus of Brazosport College
265-7661
Admission varies with production
W +

The Little Theatre group usually presents three major productions and a children's program each year in its 199-seat arena theater, while the Music Theatre usually puts on the same number of musicals each year in its 399-seat theater. Traveling shows and musical movie classics are also on the program.

SHOPPING

BRAZOS MALL
Lake Jackson
Texas 332 W at FM 2004
297-8001
W

The only indoor shopping mall in the area, includes Dillard's, Penney's, and Sears as anchor stores, and more than 90 other stores, fast food places, a cafeteria, and a 3-screen cinema.

SIDE TRIPS

ANGLETON
Take Texas 227 north to the city

Angleton was founded in 1890 and became the Brazoria County Seat in 1897.

(The following listings are only a sampling of what's of interest to visitors in Angleton. For a fuller account, including history, annual events, and accommodations, see the *Texas Monthly Guidebook: Texas*.)

Angleton Chamber Of Commerce
445 E. Mulberry at Morgan (P.O. Box 1356, 77515)
849-6443
W ramp in rear

Brazoria County Historical Museum
Velasco Rd. (Texas 227) at Cedar
849-5711
Tuesday–Saturday 11–5
Free
W

The building that houses the museum was hastily constructed as the county courthouse in 1897 when the county seat was moved from Brazoria to Angleton. Although the building's exterior has undergone many changes, the interior remains much the same as when it was built with thick walls, wrought iron balustrades, and several steel-door vaults. Permanent exhibits tell the story of the county in three phases: pre-statehood, the plantation years, and after 1900.

BRAZORIA NATIONAL WILDLIFE REFUGE
Approximately four miles east of Surfside
849-6062 (Access difficult, call for directions)

More than 425 wildlife species, including 270 bird species, use the refuge during all or part of their life cycles. Public access is limited by the lack of facilities. Presently the refuge is open on a limited basis for birdwatching, wildlife photography, nature observation, and fishing and hunting. For information write Refuge Manager, P.O. Drawer 1088 (1212 N. Velasco Rd.), Angleton 77515.

SAN BERNARD NATIONAL WILDLIFE REFUGE
Approximately ten miles southwest of Freeport on County Rd. 306 off FM 2918
849-6062
Open seven days dawn to dusk

Easier to get to than Brazoria Wildlife Refuge, this 24,454-acre refuge is one of the winter homes of the blue and snow geese. Permissible activities include birding, wildlife studies and photography, hiking, and limited hunting and fishing. For information write Refuge Manager, Brazoria National Wildlife Refuge Complex, P.O. Drawer 1088 (1212 N. Velasco Rd.), Angleton 77515.

WEST COLUMBIA
Take Texas 36 northwest to the city.

After the Texans won their independence from Mexico they had a difficult time picking a place to set up the capital of the new nation. Columbia was chosen because it had a hotel and several rooming houses offering more accommodations for government officials than almost every other town in the area. It also had one of the few newspapers.

The first Congress met here on October 3, 1836. In its short session it accomplished much. It ratified the constitution; elected Sam Houston the first president and Mirabeau B. Lamar as vice-president; selected Stephen F. Austin as secretary of state; appointed committees; provided for the army and navy; created a judiciary, a postal department, a land office; established a financial system; and, in general, took the first steps to get the new government rolling. It also decided to move the capital and hold the next session in the growing town of Houston.

During this same period, the captured Mexican General Santa Anna was held prisoner here from shortly after his capture until his release in late 1836. And on December 27, 1836, Stephen F. Austin died here of pneumonia.

(The following listings are only a sampling of what's of interest to visitors to this city. For a fuller account, including history, annual events, and accommodations, see the *Texas Monthly Guidebook: Texas.*)

West Columbia Chamber Of Commerce
14th St. and Hamilton, one block north of Brazos (Texas 35)(P.O. Box 837, 77486)
345-3921
Monday–Friday 9–12

At the time this guidebook went to press, the chamber was housed in the Replica of the First Capitol (See following), but plans are underway to move to another location.

Varner-Hogg Plantation State Historical Park
Take FM 2852 (13th St.) about two miles north off Texas 35 (Brazos Ave.)
345-4656
Open for tours Wednesday–Saturday 10–11:30 and 1–4:30, Sunday 1–4:30. Closed Monday and Tuesday

Adults $2, children $1

The park is named after the first and last owners of the plantation — Martin Varner, one of the Old Three Hundred of Austin's Colony, who built the original cabin in the late 1820s (he also built a rum distillery which Austin said produced the first "ardent spirits" made in the colony), and former Texas governor James S. Hogg who bought the plantation in 1901. The main house was built in the 1830s by the Patton family. The architectural style is a local variant of the then-fashionable Greek Revival. The Patton family owned the property until about the time of the Civil War. There were numerous owners between the Pattons and Hogg. Soon after Hogg purchased the house, he became convinced that there was oil under the property and drilled several wells trying to find it. He died in 1906 without hitting oil, but 14 years later he was proven right when the West Columbia field was brought in. A photo on display in the house shows the mansion surrounded by a forest of derricks. Oil soon became the cornerstone of the Hogg family wealth. The house was donated to the State in 1958 by Miss Ima Hogg who furnished it with her collection of historic furnishings including Empire and Rococo Revival furniture and Currier & Ives prints. Picnic sites are available in the park. The park is administered by the Texas Parks and Wildlife Department and is listed in the National Register of Historic Places.

Replica Of First Capitol
14th St. and Hamilton, one block north of Brazos (Texas 35)
345-3921 (Chamber of Commerce)
Monday–Friday 9–12 or by appointment
Free

About 1833, Leman Kelsey built a story-and-a-half clapboard store near this location. When Columbia became the Capital of the Republic of Texas in 1836, his building was one of the two that housed the first Congress. The shed room in the rear served as Stephen F. Austin's office during his brief tenure as secretary of state before his death in December, 1836. In 1837 the government moved to Houston. The 1900 hurricane destroyed the Kelsey store. This replica was built in 1977.

ANNUAL EVENTS

APRIL

RIVERFEST
Freeport, Old River Harbor
233-3526 (Freeport City Hall)
Weekend usually late in April
Free
W Variable

This weekend of festivities includes a parade and blessing of the shrimp boats and onshore activities ranging from a seafood cooking contest to a street dance.

JULY

FISHING FIESTA
Headquarters at Freeport Municipal Park, Brazosport Blvd.
233-3526 (Freeport City Hall)
Most events free
W Variable

The Fishing Fiesta is usually tied in with the fourth of July. In addition to fishing tournaments, there are boat races, a shrimp festival, and other activities. The biggest fireworks display in the area is usually at Lake Jackson's Old Fashioned Fourth in Dunbar Park on FM 2004.

GREAT TEXAS MOSQUITO FESTIVAL
Clute Community Park, Brazoswood Dr. between Dixie Dr. and Old Angleton Rd.
265-8392 (Clute Parks and Recreation)
Thursday–Saturday late in July
Free
W Variable

Mosquitos are dear to the heart of Texans because, as the story goes, wildcatters often use them to drill for oil. This festival celebrates these playful little beasts with a parade, entertainment, an arts and crafts show, cook-offs, a carnival and all the other things you'd expect. What you might not expect, and what makes it unique are events like the Mosquito Calling Contest, the Mosquito Juice Chug-a-Lug, and a Mosquito Song Writing Competition, all under the watchful stinger of a 25-foot tall mosquito called Willy Manchew.

RESTAURANTS

($ = under $7, $$ = $7 to $17, $$$ = $17 to $25, $$$$ = over $25 for one person excluding drinks, tax, and tip.)

ON THE RIVER
Freeport. 920 W. 2nd St.
233-0503
Lunch Wednesday–Friday, Dinner seven days
$-$$
MC, V
W
Children's plates

With the exception of a few items listed under appetizers, like fried dill pickles and fried cheese, the menu here is basically seafood. Most entrées are fried, but you can also get blackened or broiled catfish. The Po' Boy sandwiches are a meal in themselves and are filled with either shrimp, oyster, catfish, or chicken. This upstairs restaurant offers a good view of the shrimp boats docked nearby.

WINDSWEPT SEAFOOD RESTAURANT
Oyster Creek, 105 Burch Circle. Take Texas 523 toward Oyster Creek and follow signs
233-1951
Lunch and dinner Sunday–Friday, Dinner only on Sunday
$$
Cr.
W
Children's plates

There's a wide variety of seafood choices on the menu, but the best deal in the house may be the all-you-can-eat fried or broiled shrimp for about $12. Also worth catching is the moderately priced seafood buffet lunch Wednesday, Thursday, and Friday that usually includes dishes like baked trout, fried catfish, and fried shrimp. Private Club membership is $5.

ACCOMMODATIONS

($ = Under $45, $$ = $46-$60, $$$ = $61-$80, $$$$ = $81-$100, $$$$$ = Over $100)
Room Tax 10 percent

BRAZOSPORT HILTON INN
Lake Jackson, 925 Texas 332W
297-1161 or in Texas 800-442-7260
$$$
W + two rooms
No-smoking rooms

The two-story Hilton has 146 rooms that include 33 no-smoking rooms. Children under 17 stay free in room with parents. Package plans available, and senior discount. Cable TV with HBO and pay channel. Room phones (charge for local calls). Small pets OK. Restaurant, room service, and private club open seven nights with occasional entertainment (guests automatically members, temporary membership for non-guests $5). Indoor heated pool. Guest memberships available in local racquet club. Free coffee in lobby and free newspaper. Same-day dry cleaning.

FLAGSHIP INN
Lake Jackson, 915 Texas 332W
297-3031 or 800-722-5094
$
W + one room
No-smoking rooms

The two-story Flagship has 100 rooms that include ten no-smoking. Children under 15 stay free in room with parents. Senior discounts.

Cable TV with HBO. Room phones (local calls free). Small pets OK (pet deposit $25). Restaurant, room service, private club open Monday-Saturday (guests automatically members, temporary membership for non-guests $3). Outdoor pool. Free full breakfast. Self-service laundry and same-day dry cleaning.

HOMEPLACE INN
Freeport, 1015 W. 2nd St.
239-1602
$$
W + two rooms
No-smoking rooms

This two-story inn has 40 units that include one suite ($$$$$) and four no-smoking rooms. Children under 17 stay free in room with parents. Senior discount. Cable TV with HBO. Room phones (local calls free). Small pets OK. Outdoor pool. Free coffee in lobby, free two-hour manager's reception every evening, and free Continental breakfast. Self-service laundry and same-day dry cleaning.

LA QUINTA INN
Clute, 1126 Texas 332W
265-7461 or 800-531-5900
$-$$
W + two rooms
No-smoking rooms

This two-story La Quinta has 136 units that include one suite ($$) and 36 no-smoking rooms. Children under 18 stay free in room with parents. Senior discount. Cable and satellite TV with Showtime and pay channel. Room phones (local calls free). Small pets OK. 24-hour restaurant adjoining. Outdoor pool. Free coffee in lobby. Same-day dry cleaning.

SOUTHERN EXECUTIVE INN
Clute, 805 Hwy 332W
265-3301
$
No-smoking rooms

The 103 rooms in this two-story inn include eight no-smoking. Children under 12 stay free in room with parents. Senior discount. TV with in-room movies. Room phones (local calls free). Small pets OK. Lounge open Monday-Saturday with entertainment nightly. Outdoor pool. Free coffee in lobby.

OTHER ACCOMMODATIONS

BEACH HOUSE RENTALS

There are nearly 200 beach houses for rent in the Surfside Beach area. Most houses rent in the $450 to $700 a week range with the rental price depending on size, amenities, and location. On the low end of the scale you can rent a no-frills two-bedroom house in high season for less than $300, and on the up side you can get a three-bedroom luxury house for around $1,000 a week. The Visitors and Convention Council (See Tourist Services) can supply information on realty companies handling rentals.

CORPUS CHRISTI

NUECES COUNTY SEAT ★ 292,138 ★ (512)

Residents of Corpus Christi obviously love their bay. Why else would they put a large picture window in their art museum so visitors could pause from looking at man-made art and look out at the natural beauty of the bay? Why else build a marina close enough to the downtown office buildings so boat owners can walk down and relax with a sail at the end of the day? Why else would the city go to the expense of buying up all the undeveloped shoreline property it could to ensure that no more condos, homes, or other obstructions could be built that would limit both access to and views of the bay?

The city owes its religious name to that bay. In 1519, Spanish explorer Alonso Álvarez de Piñeda discovered what he reported as "a beautiful bay." Since the discovery occurred on the religious feast day of Corpus Christi (The Body of Christ), he gave that name to the bay. Eventually the name carried over to the city. Today, most Texans shorten that name to Corpus, but the abbreviated version is frowned on by most residents of the city.

It was 1839, more than three centuries after Piñeda's discovery, that a frontier trading post was set up near what is now the 400 block of Broadway, and a colony slowly grew up around it. The Mexican War

CORPUS CHRISTI

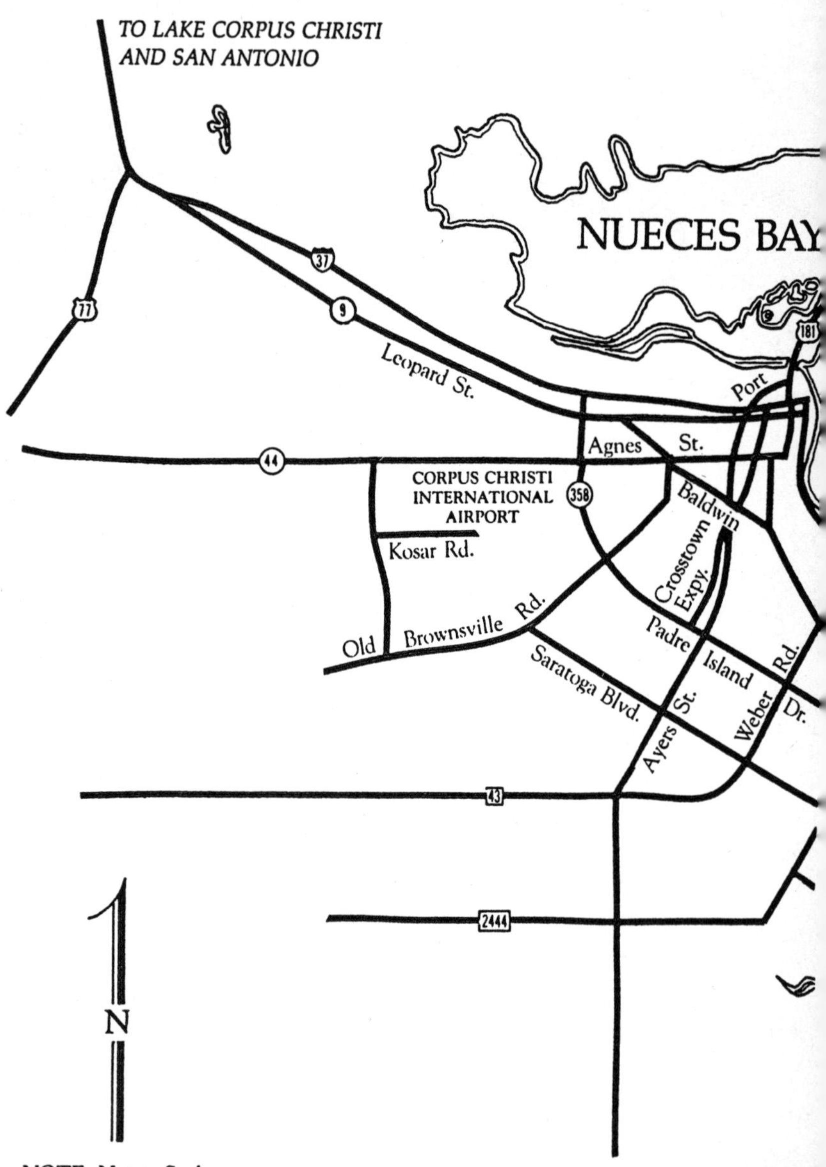

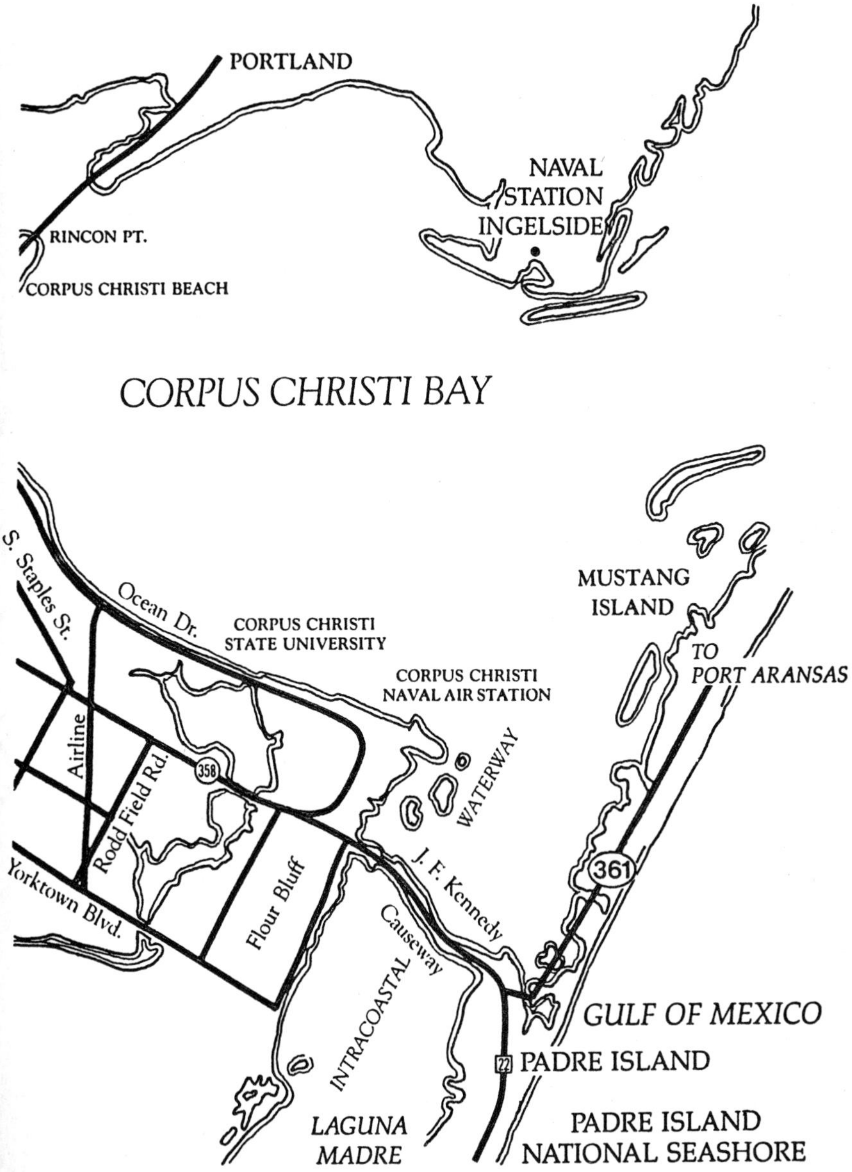

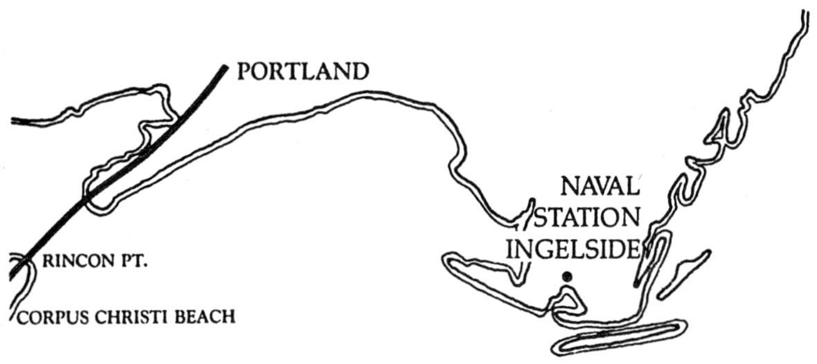

PORTLAND
NAVAL
STATION
INGELSIDE
RINCON PT.
CORPUS CHRISTI BEACH
CORPUS CHRISTI BAY
S. Staples St.
Ocean Dr.
CORPUS CHRISTI
STATE UNIVERSITY
CORPUS CHRISTI
NAVAL AIR STATION
MUSTANG
ISLAND
TO
PORT ARANSAS
Airline
Rodd Field Rd.
358
WATERWAY
361
Yorktown Blvd.
Flour Bluff
J. F. Kennedy
Causeway
INTRACOASTAL
GULF OF MEXICO
22
PADRE ISLAND
LAGUNA
MADRE
PADRE ISLAND
NATIONAL SEASHORE

gave the colony its first spurt of growth. While waiting for the diplomats to try their hand at settling the Texas border dispute with Mexico, General Zachary Taylor and a small army was sent to Corpus Christi to be ready to move south if diplomacy failed. The army set up a tent city in what in now Artesian Park near downtown. Diplomacy did fail, and Taylor and his men moved off to war. By then, Corpus Christi was established as a supply point for the Mexican War, and when that war ended, it continued as a supply point supporting operations in the West.

As the years went by, the port became a shipping point for Texas cattle and crops and the town grew up around it. But a U.S. Government decision in the 1920s to turn Corpus Christi into a deep-water port really put the city on the map. The dredges came and turned Corpus into what is still the deepest port on the Texas coast. This soon attracted the petrochemical and other industries. Fortunately, the city was already established before the refineries and other industrial complexes moved in, so the plants were built on the ship channel instead of the bay. The result is that the major plants are relatively hidden from downtown and other tourist areas. And, in spite of its industrial base, the city has repeatedly won recognition for being pollution-free.

Often called "The Texas Riviera" or "The Sparkling City by the Sea," the city itself sits like a quarter moon hugging the bay. From the air it looks long and thin, as if everyone were trying to get as close to the water as possible. On the north is Corpus Christi Beach, also called North Beach, a small resort area. Immediately behind and south of this beach, on both sides of the Harbor Bridge, is the bustling port. South of the bridge, along the bay is downtown with a concentration of major hotels as well as the business district and the cultural center at Bayfront Plaza. To the west of downtown is the industrial area. The major residential, shopping, and small business section of the city is southeast of both downtown and the industrial area. And furthest south are Padre Island and the Gulf.

Ah! Padre Island! There are beaches all along the Texas coast, but it isn't until you reach the wide, sandy beaches of Padre that everything starts to look as it would in a travel poster. Only the north end of Padre Island (near Corpus Christi) and the southern tip (South Padre Island) of the 113-mile barrier island are commercially developed. Between them sits the more than 80 miles of the Padre Island National Seashore, which many consider the most beautiful stretch of natural beach in the country.

Corpus Christi welcomes tourists. There are many fine restaurants, inviting clubs, first-class hotels, and facilities for both the arts and outdoor activities that are far and away better than what one would expect in a city this size. And these attractions are growing. For example, the Texas State Aquarium (See Museums) is now open in a seven-acre park across the ship channel from Bayfront Plaza. There's also a new greyhound race track just getting started, and plans are underway for a day-cruise gambling ship to operate out of the port. In nearby Ingleside, across Corpus Christi Bay, is the designated Navy home port for the battleship *USS Wisconsin*, the aircraft carrier *USS Lexington*, and several other ships. (See Other Points of Interest.) At press time, cutbacks in the Department of Defense budget have put the fate of this port up in the air, but if it isn't cut out of the Navy's budget, the port is scheduled to be completed in the early 1990s. A regular program of weekend and specially arranged group tours of the ships in port that will be open to the public is being planned.

TOURIST SERVICES

CORPUS CHRISTI AREA CONVENTION AND VISITORS BUREAU
1201 N. Shoreline, one block north of where the extension of I-37 ends at Shoreline (P.O. Box 2664, 78403)
882-5603 or 800-678-6232
Monday–Friday 8:30–5
Free
W

If this office is closed, there are several other places where you can pick up brochures and other tourist information. One Tourist Information Center is located on I-37 coming into the city at Exit 16 in Nueces River Park (241-1464). It is open every day 9-5. Another one is in the Padre Island National Seashore Headquarters at 9405 Padre Island Drive (937-6711). It is usually open seven days 8:30-4:30 from June through August and the same hours, Monday-Friday, December through March. And, in the Bayfront Plaza area, brochures and tourist information are also available at the Corpus Christi Museum (See Museums).

***FLAGSHIP* AND *GULF CLIPPER* SIGHTSEEING CRUISES**
People's St. T-Head and Shoreline Blvd.
643-7128 or 884-1693
Morning, afternoon, evening, and moonlight cruises
Times and prices vary by cruise and season. Closed Tuesday, October–March
W

The *Flagship* is a scaled-down version of an old Mississippi showboat that carries up to 400 passengers on an hour to an hour-and-half narrated tour of the bay and the harbor and gives a wonderful, often spectacular, view of the bayfront skyline and a close-up of operations of the port. (Day trips in high season: adults $5.25, children 11 and under $3.25.) The weekend early evening cruises and the Saturday moonlight cruise feature a live band. The *Gulf Clipper* is a smaller sightseeing vessel that occasionally alternates with the *Flagship*.

GRAY LINE TOURS
289-7113
Make tour reservations at most hotels, motels, and travel agencies
Tours $10-$28

In season, the two-and-a-half hour city tour ($10) usually starts at 9 a.m. daily except Sunday. The Loop Tour ($18), which usually lasts about four hours, goes around the bay through Padre Island, Port

Aransas, and Aransas Pass,and is given by appointment with a minimum of six passengers.

REGIONAL TRANSPORTATION AUTHORITY'S SPECIAL BUSES Printed schedules are usually available at hotels/motels and various locations in the Bayfront area. Schedules are subject to change. For latest call 289-2600

B Trolley Scenic Trail A motorized trolley with polished brass and wooden seats which operates primarily on a bayfront route with stops at the major sights.
Adults 25¢ (10¢ on Saturdays), children under 6 free.

B Bus Shopping Trail This route goes from the Bayfront area along the Seawall, past several shopping centers, and winds up at the two major malls, Sunrise Mall and Padre Staples Mall approximately every hour, afternoons and evenings, Monday through Saturday. No service is available Sundays or major holidays. Adults 50¢, (10¢ on Saturdays), children under 6 free.

Beach Bus There are several routes from various parts of the city to the beach. The buses, which only run on Saturdays, Sundays, and holidays in season, are equipped with luggage compartments to hold beach goers' paraphernalia such as coolers, lawnchairs, and surfboards. Schedule and fares vary.

GET-ACQUAINTED DRIVING TOUR

First you need to recognize that Corpus Christi is basically a long, narrow city built along the bay, so driving distances can get stretched out. Next, you need to be familiar with the numbers of the major highways in the city because many of the direction signs at critical turn-offs give those numbers rather than the street names. For example, South Padre Island Drive (also often cited as S.P.I.D.) is frequently listed on the signs as Texas 358.

The starting point for this drive-yourself tour is the **Convention and Visitors Bureau** at 1201 N. Shoreline at Power (See Tourist Services). If you haven't already stocked up, before setting out, go inside and gather up all the information, brochures, and maps you think you might need for your visit.

When you're ready to go, drive *west on Power to N. Chaparral and turn right.* A short way down, on your left, is **Heritage Park**, a restoration project that includes the **Sidbury House** (See Historic Places) and several other Victorian homes. A little farther on, on your right, is **Bayfront Arts and Sciences Park** that contains the **Harbor Playhouse, Bayfront Plaza Convention Center** (home of the Corpus Christi Symphony), the **Corpus Christi Museum**, the **Art Museum of South Texas**, and the **Watergarden**. Across the ship channel is the **Texas State Aquarium.**

Drive through the plaza back to Shoreline, then *turn right* and go back up Shoreline, past the Convention and Visitors Bureau, and make a *right and follow the signs to US 181* to Sinton and Rockport. This will take you over the **Harbor Bridge** to **Corpus Christi Beach**, also called North

Beach (See Other Points of Interest). Take the *first exit off the bridge* and follow the signs to the **Texas State Aquarium** (See Museums). From here, drive around this small resort area that includes motels, condos, restaurants, and a couple of small parks. When you've seen enough, get *back on US 181* heading towards the Harbor Bridge. Get off at the *Shoreline exit*, just over the bridge, and follow the signs *back to Shoreline Dr.*, then *turn right*.

On your right are the bayfront skyscraper hotels as well as some smaller motels and restaurants. The building with the futuristic 20- and 28-story towers between the Wyndham and the Marriott hotels is **One Shoreline Plaza**, the tallest building in Corpus Christi. The tubular section just over the entrance, between the towers, houses a private club.

On your left for the next couple of miles is the **Seawall** along the bay (See Other Points of Interest). At Shoreline and Schatzel, in the center island, is a statue of two sailfish hurling into the air. Called **"Wind in the Sails,"** it is by noted sculptor Ken Ullberg. Just past this is the **Yacht Basin** with its three man-made peninsulas, the T-Heads and L-Head, jutting out into the bay. Corpus Christi is one of the few cities where you can walk out of your downtown office building at the end of a day and be in your sailboat on the bay in minutes. In addition to being the marina for local boating enthusiasts, the Yacht Basin is also the home port for sightseeing boats, fishing party and charter boats, a floating restaurant, and the local shrimp fleet.

As you leave the skyscrapers behind, Shoreline Drive separates and the lanes going south briefly bend away from the water. At **McGee Beach**, the division of Shoreline ends and becomes a two-way street called Ocean Dr. that is the city's most affluent residential street. A grand avenue in the old tradition, it continues along the bay all the way to the **Naval Air Station**. After you pass Spohn Hospital on your right, **Cole Park** will be on your left. The amphitheater in the park is the scene of concerts under the stars on summer Sunday evenings.

For the next few miles, Ocean Dr. becomes a residential area of mostly expensive homes with well-manicured lawns. The **First Baptist Church** with its 51-bell carillon is at 3115 Ocean Dr. Hymns are played at noon and in the evening, and special carillon concerts are frequently given. Westminster chimes ring out every quarter hour.

Stay on Ocean Dr. across the little causeway to **Corpus Christi State University** (See Colleges and Universities). Go past the campus to *East University Dr.*, then *turn in* and drive through the grounds *circling back to Ocean. Turn left* to go back the way you came on Ocean. (If you go right you'll be turned around at the security gate at the **Naval Air Station.**) *At the first fork,* take *Ennis Joslin Rd.* that leads you along the little bay known as Cayo Del Oso and the **Hans Suter Wildlife Park** to Texas 358, South Padre Island Drive (S.P.I.D.).

If you want to go to **Padre Island** and **Malaquite Beach**, all you have to do is turn left and follow the signs (Texas 358 to Park Rd. 22). But that's not part of this tour to get you acquainted with the city, so turn right back towards downtown.

Soon after you get on it, S.P.I.D. becomes a controlled access highway. After you pass **Sunrise Mall**, on your right, *exit on Staples and turn right*. Once you've turned, **Padre Staples Mall** will be on your left (See Shopping). Stay on this street all the way back downtown. There's not much of sightseeing interest along this route, but it will give you a view of another residential and shopping section of the city. Stay on Staples when it meets Alameda, another major east-west street, at Six Points. *At Agnes (Texas 44) turn right* and follow it as it winds down towards downtown. Another *right on Laguna* will bring you back to the Seawall. A *left* takes you back to the bayfront hotel area and your starting point.

BIRD'S-EYE VIEW

You can get an excellent sky-high view of the shoreline and bay from the restaurants and lounges atop the Wyndham and Radison Marina hotels (See Accommodations).

MUSEUMS

ART MUSEUM OF SOUTH TEXAS
1902 N. Shoreline in Bayfront Arts and Sciences Park
884-3844
Tuesday–Friday 10–5, Saturday–Sunday 12–5, Closed Monday
Adults $2, children 6–12 50¢ (combination ticket for Art Museum and Corpus Christi Museum: adults $3)
W +

Starkly austere in design, this building is worth seeing just for itself. It stands out, white and crisp, against the background of green park lawn and sparkling bay waters. Bronze-tinted glass is used on all exterior windows and doors so there will be no distortion of color of the works of art on display inside. The museum has only a small, but growing, permanent collection, but features exhibits on loan from other institutions that cover a wide variety of periods and media. Over the years, exhibits have ranged from Andy Worhol to Frederic Remington to local artists. At Christmas time, as part of the Harbor Lights Festival, the museum is transformed by a forest of decorated Christmas trees. Gift Shop.

CORPUS CHRISTI MUSEUM OF SCIENCE AND HISTORY
1900 N. Chaparral in Bayfront Arts and Sciences Park
883-2862
Tuesday–Saturday 10–5, Sunday 1–5, Closed Monday and holidays
Adults $2, children 6–12 50¢ (combination ticket for Corpus Christi Museum and Art Museum: adults $3)
W +

History and the natural history of the coastal region are the focal points here, but exhibits stretch these limits in fascinating ways. For instance, the replica of a Spanish ship wrecked in 1554 is the center of one exhibit. You can climb aboard the main deck and forecastle to get a first-hand view of how small the ships were that Columbus and other early explorers sailed to challenge the oceans of the world. Another major exhibit relates the history of U.S. Naval aviation training, which is still conducted at the nearby Naval Air Station. There are also dioramas of wildlife native to the coast, Indian artifacts, a re-creation of a typical Corpus Christi street scene in 1930, a small aquarium, an antique gallery, and an art gallery featuring the work of local artists. For children (and the curious adult), there are several hands-on exhibits such as "touch tables" and a sit-in airplane cockpit trainer with a video showing what it's like to land on an aircraft carrier. And the staff has a sense of humor, well illustrated in its exhibit of such rarities as the head of the Headless Horseman and a snow footprint of the Abominable Snowman that melted and is now preserved as water. And best of all, this museum is diverse enough to have something for everyone, but compact enough (even at 78,000-square feet) to let you look at everything in a few hours without getting tired. Gift shop.

MUSEUM OF ORIENTAL CULTURES
418 People's, Suite 200
883-1303
Tuesday–Saturday 10–4, Sunday by appointment, Closed Monday
Adults $1, students 50¢
W +
Free parking in garage at Mesquite and People's with museum entrance on second level.

Japanese daily life, history, religion, and art are the focal points of this museum. Its collection of *Hakata* dolls is reportedly the largest private collection in the United States. There is also a collection of *Noh* and *Kabuki* masks and a bigger-than-life bronze statue of Buddha that is more than 200 years old. Although the emphasis is on Japanese culture, there are also exhibits on other Asian countries. Gift shop.

TEXAS STATE AQUARIUM
Corpus Christi Beach by the Harbor Bridge (P.O. Box 331307, 78463)
881-1200 or 800-477-GULF
Monday–Saturday 10–6, Sunday 12–6, closed Thanksgiving and Christmas
Adults $6.50, seniors, active duty military, and college students with valid ID cards $4.50, children 4 to 15 $3.50
W +

This is the first major aquarium in the country to focus on ecosystems of the Gulf of Mexico and the Caribbean Sea. Designed to be a world-class aquarium, it features interactive exhibits that let the visitor experience plant and animal life in intricately reproduced settings of their natural environments. The aquarium is being built in phases on 7.3 acres. The first phase, costing more than $31 million of the projected $60 million-plus project, is the Gulf of Mexico Exhibit Building. Here visitors are engulfed (no pun intended) in an underwater journey that stretches from the coastal marshlands, across the barrier islands, and past the oil rigs to the colorful Flower Gardens Coral Reef located about 115 miles off the Texas coast. You can watch divers feed exotic fish, play the role of a city mayor as a simulated hurricane threatens the coast, get eye-to-eye with a shark, and get your hands wet as you feel a variety of sea creatures from crabs to starfish in the Sea Star Discovery Pool, the equivilant of a petting zoo. Phase II, an education and research center, will include a state-of-the-art theater where spectacular underwater films will be featured. Phase III is the Caribbean Exhibit Building with marine plant and animal life indigenous to this tropical sea. Future phases will incorporate marine mammals and expanded predator (read that "shark") exhibits. Despite its title, this is not a state-owned facility. Designated the "official Aquarium of Texas" by the sixty-ninth Legislature, it is operated by the private, non-profit Texas State Aquarium Association. Gift shop.

HISTORIC PLACES

CENTENNIAL HOUSE
411 N. Upper Broadway
992-6003
Wednesday 2–5 and by appointment for groups
Adults $2, students $1
W

Forbes Britton was in Zachary Taylor's army when it came through Corpus Christi during the Mexican War. Shortly after Britton retired from the army in 1849, he built this house which still stands as the oldest structure in the city. During the Civil War it served as a hospital for both the Confederate and Union forces. It received its name because it was 100 years old when the Texas Historical Commission presented its medallion in 1949. The house is listed in the National Register of Historic Places. Note the address — Broadway is on two levels, and the house is on the upper level.

HERITAGE PARK
1600 Block of N. Chaparral between Hughes and Fitzgerald
883-0639 (Multicultural Center in the Galvan House at 1581 N. Chaparral)
Free

Several organizations, including LULAC (League of United Latin American Citizens that was founded in Corpus Christi in 1929) and the NAACP, have pitched in to restore nine Victorian homes moved from various locations in the city to this historic district known as Old Irishtown. Most of these historic homes now serve as offices for the organizations. They are open to visitors, but generally are of interest only to those interested in the organizations themselves. Two of the buildings, however, are set up for the public: the Sidbury House and the Galvan House. A walking tour brochure is available at the Galvan House.

The Sidbury House, 1609 N. Chaparral (883-9351), built in 1893, is the only example of High Victorian architecture in Corpus Christi and is listed in the National Register of Historic Places. It was restored by The Junior League in painstaking authentic detail. Even the wallpaper in the living room was hand-printed in Europe from original blocks used during the Victorian era. The first floor is furnished with period furniture and open to the public Tuesday-Thursday 10-1. The league office is upstairs.

The Galvan House, 1581 N. Chaparral (883-0639), was built in 1908 in the Colonial Revival style. It is now used as a Multicultural Center and has changing art exhibits. It is open Monday-Friday 10-4, Saturday 10-2.

In addition to the Sidbury House, two other houses in the park are listed in the National Register of Historic Places: the **Lichtenstein House**, 1617 N. Chaparral (888-5692), built in 1905, now used as the Creative Arts Center; and the **Gugenheim House**, 1601 N. Chaparral (887-1601), built in 1905, now the home of Camp Fire, Incorporated. The oldest house in the park, and the second oldest structure in the city, is **Merriman-Bobys House**, 1521 N. Chaparral (883-2787), built in 1851.

OTHER POINTS OF INTEREST

ART CENTER OF CORPUS CHRISTI
100 N. Shoreline
884-6406
Tuesday–Friday 10–4, Saturday and Sunday 1–5, closed Monday
Free
W

You can frequently watch artists in all media at work here and see exhibits of local and area artists. Exhibits usually change monthly. Gift shop and small restaurant.

BAYFRONT ARTS AND SCIENCES PARK AND BAYFRONT PLAZA
North end of Shoreline Blvd.
Open at all times
W Variable

Art, drama, science, history, and music are all concentrated on these few acres near the Harbor Bridge. The Art Museum of South Texas stands at the water's edge with the Watergarden leading to the entrance. Across the lawn is the Corpus Christi Museum. In the adjoining plaza are the Convention Center, home of the Corpus Christi Symphony, and the Harbor Playhouse. Nearby is an observation point where you can see the traffic on the ship channel and the Texas State Aquarium across the water. Even though all these attractions can make this a busy place on a summer weekend, there is still enough park space to relax and enjoy the sunshine.

COLE PARK
2000 block of Ocean Dr.

All the park basics are here — playground, picnic tables, restrooms — plus an amphitheater for summer Sunday evening concerts, a lighted fishing pier, and a small beach. This is a popular spot for windsurfers, and the U.S. Open Sailboard Regatta is held here on Memorial Day weekend.

CORPUS CHRISTI BEACH
North of downtown off US 181 across Harbor Bridge

Old timers still call it North Beach and speak of its 1930s heyday when it was the home of gambling casinos and amusement parks. But when the beach lost the gambling and its glamour, it turned into an eyesore. The city and the Army Corps of Engineers restored it in the late 1970s at a cost of $3.7 million. Now hotels, motels, and condos line much of the one-and-a-half mile beachfront, and the Texas State Aquarium in located here.

CORPUS CHRISTI BOTANICAL GARDENS
8500 S. Staples at Yorktown
993-7551
Tuesday–Sunday 9–5, Closed Thanksgiving, Christmas, and New Years
Admission
W

The gardens stretch along the bank of Oso Creek in the city's southwest quadrant. Surpassing 100 acres, the gardens are being opened in stages and include a nature trail, gardens of subtropicals, beds of seasonal color, a vegetable demonstration area, picnic areas, an information center, and a gift shop. Lectures on Saturday. A good place for birdwatching. Guided tours available (993-9885).

GCCA/CPL MARINE DEVELOPMENT CENTER
4300 Waldron Rd., at end of road in CPL power station compound, Flour Bluff
939-7784
Tours: Tuesday and Thursday 1 and 3, Saturday 10 and 2. Call to register for tours
Free
W

This hatching and research lab raises marine sport fish, mostly redfish and spotted seatrout, for restocking the bays. The capacity of the center is 20 million fingerlings and 100 million fry per year. A specially designed lighting system on the spawning tanks makes the fish believe that 150 days is a full year, and they therefore spawn twice in one year. The GCCA in the name is the Gulf Coast Conservation Association and the CPL is Central Power and Light, but the facility is actually run by a third party: Texas Parks and Wildlife. The tour, which lasts about 40 minutes, includes an orientation in the visitors center and then viewing of dozens of tanks holding various sized fish, including the trophy-sized "daddies."

HARBOR BRIDGE
US 181 between downtown and Corpus Christi Beach

This bridge over the ship channel at the port has a cantilever span of 620 feet, which is the longest such span on any bridge in Texas. It is 243 feet high and clears the water by 140 feet, which surprisingly, is not enough clearance for some large ships that must lower their radar equipment before passing under it. When you top the bridge going north, you have a view that includes Corpus Christi Beach and across the bay to Portland and beyond. Going south, there's an excellent view of the downtown skyline and the bay shore. If you are adventurous, there are narrow pedestrian walkways that you can take to the center of the bridge for a bird's-eye view or taking pictures. Lights outline the bridge at night.

THE INTERNATIONAL KITE MUSEUM
Best Western Sandy Shores Resort, 3200 Surfside on Corpus Christi Beach
883-7456
Seven days 10–5
Free
W

Tucked in a corner of this resort hotel, this small museum is a celebration of the fascinating history of kites from their origin in the Orient to today. Included are a vintage navy kite used for target practice, photos of early kites, a model of the Wright Brothers' 1900 glider launch, a 20-minute video on the technical aspects of the Wright Brothers' first flight, and kites of all sizes, shapes, and colors. If you want, you can buy a kite in the Kite Shoppe and take it right out on the beach to fly.

KING HIGH SCHOOL PLANETARIUM
5225 Gollihar
992-0130
Adults $2, students $1, Senior Citizens free
W

A variety of astronomy programs are open to the public on Tuesday evenings during the school year. Doors open at 7 p.m. No one allowed in after program starts at 7:30.

MARINA AND YACHT BASIN
Shoreline Dr. along the Seawall between Starr and Kinney
W Variable

This downtown marina is built around three small, man-made peninsulas that take their names from their alphabetical shapes and the streets that lead to them: the People's Street T-Head, the Lawrence Street T-Head, and the Cooper's Alley L-Head. In addition to the pleasure craft berthed here, there are also a floating restaurant, sightseeing boats, charter and party fishing boats, and the commercial shrimp fleet where you can usually buy fresh shrimp and fish right off the boats. In season, you'll also find rentals of aqua bikes, sailboards, sailboats, jet skis, paddle boats, and other water sports equipment in the marina area. Even if you never intend to go out on the bay, it's fun to walk around here, watching the real and sometime sailors at work or play and listening to the breeze humming and slapping out a tune as it wafts through the riggings and masts of the sailboats

McGEE BEACH
Shoreline Dr. across from the Memorial Coliseum

The sand on this 250-yard long, man-made beach has burned a lot of feet since the beach was built in 1940, and it is still a popular place. Lifeguards are on duty Memorial Day to Labor Day. There's a pier, concession stand, and freshwater showers. For fishing, or a different view of the bayfront skyline, walk out on the quarter-mile long lighted breakwater that protects the yacht basin.

NAVAL AIR STATION AND ARMY DEPOT
Gates at east end of Ocean Dr. and at end of Texas 358 after it turns off South Padre Island Dr.
Bus tour available, usually Wednesday at 1 p.m. Call Public Affairs Office, 939-2674, for information
Free
W

Once the largest Naval Air Station in the world, it remains the training station for naval pilots of multi-engine propeller aircraft. From here they may go on to jet training stations, including those at nearby Kingsville and Beeville. The other major tenant on the station is the army's helicopter repair depot, the largest in the nation. Also at the station are the training facilities for naval air navigators and a coast guard search and rescue unit. The station is closed to the public except for official tours which start at the North Gate on Ocean Drive.

NAVAL STATION INGLESIDE
From Ingleside, take FM 1069 south to the base
882-5603 or 800-678-6232 (Convention and Visitors Bureau)
Weekend tours
Free
W Variable

If all goes according to plan, and the budget isn't cut, the battleship *USS Wisconsin*, the aircraft carrier *USS Lexington*, a guided missile cruiser, a destroyer and six other active duty and reserve ships will be calling this their homeport sometime in 1991. It will be the largest homeport on the gulf coast. Though the base will be closed, one ship will be made available each weekend for public tours.

NUECES COUNTY PARKS
Park Rd. 22, Padre Island
949-8121

Open at all times
Free
W Variable

Nueces County Park Number 2 is a small park with a pavilion and restrooms located on Packery Channel just off the JFK Causeway. Park Number 1, Padre Balli Park, is about two miles farther along Park Rd. 22, just north of the Nueces-Kleberg County line. This park has a long stretch of beach on the Gulf. The Bob Hall Fishing Pier (fee) is located here and extends out into the Gulf for more than 1200 feet. There are also campsites with hookups (fee), a bathhouse, and picnic area. The so-called "Beachcomber's Museum" in the park office just north of Bob Hall Pier (888-0268) is a showplace for the odd items found on the beach. Because it is the closest Gulf beach to the city, it is extremely popular and often crowded. If it's too crowded for you, you can always drive on further to Malaquite Beach on the National Seashore.

PADRE ISLAND NATIONAL SEASHORE AND MALAQUITE BEACH
Approximately 25 miles south of JFK Causeway on Park Rd. 22
937-2621
Open at all times
Admission
W Variable

Padre Island, stretching 113 miles from Corpus Christi on the north almost to the Mexican border on the south, is the longest in the string of barrier islands protecting the Texas coast. The island ranges in width from a few hundred yards to about three miles and is separated from the mainland by Laguna Madre, a generally shallow body of water with a maximum width of ten miles.

A little more than 80 miles, starting near the north end of the island, has been designated a National Seashore, administered by the U. S. Department of the Interior. Commercial development is restricted to the two ends of the island.

Malaquite Beach is the only developed area within the National Seashore itself. There is a pavilion with visitors center and facilities for swimming, picnicking, and camping (fee). There are also nature trails, and park rangers and naturalists conduct a number of programs for visitors during the summer. These include beach discovery walks, instructions on net fishing and crabbing, and evening slide shows.

The paved road continues for a few miles past Malaquite, but from then on you need a 4-wheel drive vehicle (with water and other safety supplies). With one of these, you can venture south for more than 50 miles to the Mansfield Cut. Hiking and primitive camping is also permitted, but requires a great deal of planning because there is no water and no shade. For your own safety, you are required to check in at the ranger station before going into the area past Malaquite Beach.

For general information, contact the National Park Service's Padre Island Headquarters on the mainland at 9405 S. Padre Island Dr., Corpus

Christi 78412 (937-2621), open normal business hours Monday-Friday. The phone number at Malaquite Beach is 949-8068. For beach, weather, and driving conditions only, call 949-8175.

PORT OF CORPUS CHRISTI
Office at 222 Power St
882-5633

A protected bay leading to a 400-foot wide and 45-foot deep ship channel has helped make this the sixth largest saltwater port in the nation in terms of cargo handled. One way to view port operations is through the telescope in the observation pavilion in Channelview Park on the north shore of the channel. To do this cross the Harbor Bridge to Corpus Christi Beach, then double back under the bridge to the pavilion near the Texas State Aquarium. For a better view, take the harbor tour on one of the sightseeing boats (See Tourist Services). Finally, for the fearless and hearty only, the pedestrian walkways on the Harbor Bridge offer a clear view of most of the port.

There are plans to convert a warehouse in the port into a pavilion that will include the Windsurf Hall of Fame (See Sports and Activities-Windsurfing).

THE SEAWALL

More than 2.5 miles long, this 14-foot high seawall was designed by sculptor Gutzon Borglum and was built just before World War II (1939-1941) while he was still putting the finishing touches to his most famous project, Mount Rushmore. What is unique about this seawall is that it steps down into the water. The steps are wide enough to sit — or doze — on, and many people working in the nearby buildings find it an ideal place for a brown-bag lunch while watching the seagulls and other shorebirds. The sidewalk atop the seawall is 20 feet wide, making it a favorite track for joggers, roller skaters, and bicyclists, as well as strollers. You can also rent pedal-powered two-person surreys with the fringe on top.

WATERGARDEN
Bayfront Science Park, in front of the Art Museum of South Texas
Open at all times, but fountain operates Tuesday–Sunday, 10 a.m. to midnight
Free
W

The Watergarden begins at a terrace near the entrance to the Art Museum. From here a 10-foot wide, 231-foot long rill acts like a babbling brook that culminates in a waterfall. From both sides of the waterfall, a large circular pool with 150 fountain jets and eleven concentric waterfall steps form an 84-foot ring. You can go inside the water ring and relax on a large "grass rug" or the seating wall. You can also watch from a promenade with a vine-covered pergola outside the circular pool. The fountains are illuminated at night.

SPORTS AND ACTIVITIES

Bicycling

Regular bicycles can be rented ($4-5 an hour or about $12 a day) at several locations including: **Adventure Bicycle Rentals** at the Radisson Marina, 300 N. Shoreline; and **Park Avenue Bicycles,** 218 Park Ave. Or two adults and a couple of small children can ride along the Seawall in a pedal-powered surrey with the fringe on top for about $10 an hour. These can be rented from **Jomark Surreys,** Shoreline Dr. near the Art Center (887-8717). Deposit required.

Birdwatching

HANS SUTER WILDLIFE PARK
Ennis Joslin Rd. along Oso Bay
882-1971 (Parks Dept.)
Seven days sunrise to 10 p.m.
Free
W

There's an 800-foot long boardwalk spanning the marshy flats of Oso Bay in this 22-acre park that's ideal for birdwatching. You can expect to see pelicans, roseate spoonbills, great blue herons, and various other shorebirds and waterfowl.

Other good birdwatching areas include Corpus Christi Botanical Gardens and Padre Island National Seashore (See Other Points of Interest), Mustang Island State Park (See Port Aransas) and Aransas National Wildlife Refuge (See Rockport-Fulton).

Fishing

Fishing the inshore waters around Corpus Christi is made easy by the many fishing piers and jetties. Surf fishing is good from the beaches on Padre and Mustang Islands. For wade fishing the Laguna Madre and Cayo del Oso (near the Naval Air Station) are both reportedly excellent. Party boats for bay fishing operate from the People's Street T-Head. These usually run four-hour trips morning, afternoon, and evening. The usual fare is about $12 per adult and $6 for children under 11. Bait is furnished and tackle is available for rent. Charter boats are also available at the T-Head for private fishing parties. Most deep-sea charters operate out of Port Aransas, which is really Corpus Christi's outlet to the Gulf (See Port Aransas). A list of party and charter boats and fishing guides operating from Corpus Christi, Port Aransas, Aransas Pass, and Rockport-Fulton and a list of fishing piers and jetties are available from the Corpus Christi Convention and Visitors Bureau (See Tourist Services). Lake Corpus Christi, about 40 miles northwest, near Mathis, offers excellent freshwater fishing (See Side Trips).

Golf

GABE LOZANO SR. GOLF CENTER
4401 Old Brownsville Rd. between Navigation and Airport
883-3696

Eighteen-hole public course. Green fees: weekdays $6, weekends $7.25. Also Executive 9, green fees: $3 for 9 holes, $4 for 18 holes.

OSO BEACH GOLF COURSE
5601 S. Alameda at Glenmore
991-5351

Eighteen-hole municipal course. Green fees: weekdays $6, weekends $7.25

Greyhound Racing

CORPUS CHRISTI GREYHOUND PARK
I-37 between Navigation and McBride
888-4385, or 882-5603 or 800-678-6232 (Convention and Visitors Bureau)
Grandstand: Adults $1, children (over 12) 50¢, children (under 12) free; Clubhouse: Adults and children $2
W Varied

An $18 million complex offering year-round pari-mutuel greyhound racing with 450 race programs — 300 evening and 150 days of both matinee and evening programs with 13 races per program — scheduled during the year. Restaurant.

Jogging

Several places are ideal for joggers. In the north is Corpus Christi Beach where you can get a runner's guide from Best Western Sandy Shores Resort (See Accommodations) that marks out four routes ranging from one to 12 miles. Or you can just jog the beach. Joggers use the Seawall and the marked jogging (and bicycle) lane on Ocean Dr. that continues south all the way to the Naval Air Station. All the way south, of course, are the miles and miles of beach on Mustang and Padre Islands.

Sailing

Almost any Wednesday afternoon, the downtown marina and yacht basin looks like mad confusion with crews hustling to make their boats ready and dozens of sailboats dodging each other as they jockey to get into the bay. But there's actually a method to the madness, for what they're all doing is making ready to take off in the weekly sailboat races. You can watch them from the yacht basin or the Seawall. Corpus Christi Bay is just about a perfect place for sailing because it has protected waters and good breezes.

If you want to sail yourself, small sailboats and catamarans are available for rent, in season, at the yacht basin as are captained and bare boat (no crew) charters. For a list of rental and charter companies throughout the area, contact the Convention and Visitors Bureau.

You can also learn to sail at the International School of Sailing located on the L-Head (881-8503). A Saturday and Sunday basic course costs about $125, a three-day live-aboard course about $400, and a seven-day live-aboard course about $900.

If you just want a catamaran ride, try **The Boat House,** #1 Surfside Park on Corpus Christi Beach (888-8333). A ride for up to four people costs about $30 an hour.

Stock Car Racing

CORPUS CHRISTI SPEEDWAY
241 Flato Rd., near Agnes
289-8847
Closed November–February (851-2383 off season)
Adults $7, children under 12 free with adult
W

Opened in 1945, this is the oldest racing complex in Corpus Christi. Races are held every Saturday from March through September on the quarter-mile, high-banked, oval, asphalt stock car track. (Call for times.)

Surfing

J. P. LUBY YOUTH PARK
Zahn Rd. off Park Rd. 53
888-0268

Normally the waters in this area are not too great for surfing. But this park has 600-feet of pilings in the Gulf to create waves. It's not the Banzai Pipeline, but it should please beginners.

Swimming

Bay and Gulf swimming is available at Corpus Christi Beach, Cole Park, McGee Beach, Nueces County Parks, and Padre Island National Seashore's Malaquite Beach (See Other Points of Interest). A little further away, you can swim at Mustang Island State Park (See Port Aransas).

Tennis

AL KRUZE TENNIS CENTER
502 King
883-6942

Ten courts. Days: $1.50 for 1½ hours; nights: $2 for 1½ hours.

H.E.B. TENNIS CENTER
1520 Shely near Ayers in H. E. Butt Park
888-5681

Twenty-four courts. Days: $1.50 for 1½ hours; nights: $2 for 1½ hours.

Windsurfing

OLEANDER POINT
Cole Park, 2000 block of Ocean Dr.

It goes by several names: windsurfing, sailboarding, or boardsailing; but it's all the same sport of riding an enlarged surfboard equipped with a sail. With consistent winds of 15 to 25 miles per hour blowing across the waters of the bay — which are generally warm enough not to require a wetsuit — and a mild climate that offers the possibility of sailing 12 months a year, Corpus Christi is vying to become the nation's windsurfing capital. To draw the boardsailors, the city built a breakwater at Oleander Point and created what is claimed to be "the only city-sanctioned surfboard park in the world." It has also promoted windsurfing competitions at various locations on the bay, including the annual *Caller-Times* U. S. Open Sailboard Regatta and the Mistral World Competitions. And a Windsurf Hall of Fame is in the works to be set up in a warehouse at the port.

If you want to get into the sport, instruction leading to certification is available from Texas Excursions, 2705A Laguna Shores Rd., 78418 (937-2375), and there are a number of sailboard rental shops in town.

COLLEGES AND UNIVERSITIES

CORPUS CHRISTI STATE UNIVERSITY
6300 Ocean Dr.
991-6810 Ext 335 (Public Affairs Office)
W Variable

More than 3,700 students are enrolled in this upper level university and graduate school on a 250-acre island campus between the end of the Ocean Drive residential area and the Naval Air Station. Visitors can take advanatage of traveling and local art exhibits in the Weil Gallery in the Center for the Arts (Ext 314), open weekdays; productions in the University Theatre and in the Center for the Arts; concerts by music majors and the school's jazz band; plus film, visiting artist, and lecture series. Now that the university is part of the Texas A&M System, there are plans to make it a four-year school by the mid-1990s. In addition to being the home of the Center for Coastal Studies, the campus also is the home of the National Spill Control School where students learn techniques for controlling and handling spills of all types of hazardous materials.

DEL MAR COLLEGE
Baldwin and Ayers
881-6200
W Variable

A two-year community college, Del Mar has approximately 10,000 students enrolled in its vocational/technical and academic programs.

Visitors are welcome at the Fine Arts Center that includes the Joseph A. Cain Memorial Art Gallery (881-6216), open weekdays, and at drama department productions in the Neil Tribble Bartlett Theatre. Frequent concerts by the school's jazz band are open to the public as well as recitals by students and faculty of the music department and visiting artists.

PERFORMING ARTS

(Also see Colleges and Universities)

CORPUS CHRISTI SYMPHONY
Bayfront Plaza Auditorium
1901 N. Shoreline
882-2717
Admission Varies
W +

Usually seven or eight concerts are held during the October through April season. The Symphony also performs at some of the free Sunday summer evening concerts in Cole Park. The Corpus Christi Ballet also occasionally performs in this auditorium.

HARBOR PLAYHOUSE
1 Bayfront Park
882-3356
Admission varies
W +

The local theater group puts on about a half dozen productions here ranging from drama to musicals during its August through May season plus a melodrama series during the summer. The Youth Theatre usually has two productions for children in the fall and two in the spring. The Playhouse is also used for musical events.

ENCORE THEATRE
Naval Air Station
289-1088
Admission Varies
W +

The productions here are usually put on by the local community theater and include everything from historic plays, such as *The Battle of Corpus Christi,* to Gilbert and Sullivan.

SHOPPING

ANTIQUES

A listing and map of antique shops in Corpus Christi and surrounding area is available from the Convention and Visitors Bureau (See Tourist Services).

CORPUS CHRISTI GALLERY
3209 S. Alameda in Alameda Shopping Center
854-1057
W

Features contemporary realism by area and national artists. Emphasis is on original paintings and sculpture by more than 70 professional artists including about half the artists in the National Academy of Western Art.

CORPUS CHRISTI TRADE CENTER
2833 S. Padre Island Dr. (exit at Ayers)
854-4943
Friday–Sunday 9–6
W

About 100 merchants have booths in this 50,000-square-foot center that bills itself as "the largest indoor market in South Texas." Merchandise ranges from western hats and boots and Mexican dresses to furniture, jewelry, and antiques.

THE PADRE ISLANDER
14514 S. Padre Island Dr., intersection of Park Rds. 53 and 22
949-8800
Open seven days
W

Just about everything you'd want for the beach is available at this one-stop, warehouse-sized shop.

PADRE STAPLES MALL
South Padre Island Dr. at S. Staples
991-5718
W

There are more than 100 stores and places to eat and a six-screen cinema in this mall that is anchored by Beall's, Dillard's, Foley's, Palais Royal, and Penney's. An old-fashioned carousel is located in the Center Court (See Kids' Stuff).

PILAR
3814 S. Alameda at Doddridge, in Lamar Park Center
883-7171
W

A distinctive women's shop brimming with selections from all over the world including embroidered dresses, wearable art, nubby woolens and cottons, jewelry, folk art, rugs, and tapestries.

SUNRISE MALL
South Padre Island Dr. at Airline
993-2900
W

This two-level shopping center has more than 100 stores and places to eat, a cinema, a supermarket, a playpark for children, and is anchored by Mervyn's, Sears, and Wards.

WATER STREET MARKET
309 N. Water St.
W

A grouping of several specialty shops in the bayfront area convenient to the major hotels. One of the shops is Totally Texas (883-9768) where you'll find a wide selection of Texas-related gifts and novelty items including armadillo purses, chili pepper jewelry, and bluebonnet pottery.

KIDS' STUFF

CAROUSEL CARNAVAL
Padre Staples Mall, S. Padre Island Dr. and S. Staples
Open seven days during mall hours
$1

An elaborately colorful, two-deck Italian-built carousel that is a near-copy of a 1898 German original. It stands 25 feet high, is 36 feet in diameter, and seats 70 riders.

YOUTH THEATRE
Harbor Playhouse, 1 Bayfront Park
882-3356
Admission varies
W +

Children's theater productions performed by and for children. Usually four productions a year are held with two in the spring and two in the fall.

SIDE TRIPS

CORPUS CHRISTI BAY LOOP DRIVE

You can make the 75 miles or so of this complete circle around Corpus Christi Bay in about two hours of easy driving. Or you can plan some stop-overs and make it a full-day excursion. Since it is a loop, you can go either direction. To go the northern way, take US 181 across the Harbor Bridge, past Portland to Texas 361. Then follow 361 to Aransas Pass (See Aransas Pass) and continue on the causeway across Redfish Bay to the ferry at Port Aransas (See Port Aransas). Then pick up Park Rd. 53 and go south the full length of Mustang Island until Park Rd. 53 runs into Park Rd. 22 on Padre Island. Turn right (west), cross the JFK Causeway and get on Texas 358 (South Padre Island Dr.). Turn right again at Ennis Joslin Rd. which ends at Ocean Dr. A left here will put you on Ocean, which becomes Shoreline and winds up back downtown.

KING RANCH
Kingsville
Take Texas 44 to US 77 to Kingsville, then Texas 141 to ranch gate west of city. Approximately 40 miles
Visitors Center 592-8055

Possibly the most famous ranch in the world, at one time it owned and operated almost 10 million acres in seven countries. It encompasses more than 825,000 acres in four divisions and is a designated National Historic Landmark. Guided tours are available at the Visitors Center located just inside the main gate. There are about 20 designated stops at educational signs on the tour, the main one at the Plomo cattle pens where you can watch cowboys at work. Also visit the Henrietta Memorial, an ice house transformed into a museum displaying the family's memorabilia including saddles and custom-made cars (See Kingsville).

LAKE CORPUS CHRISTI STATE RECREATION AREA
Mathis
Take I-37 to Texas 359 at Mathis, then southwest six miles to Park Rd. 25 to the recreation area. Approximately 35 miles
1-547-2635
Open seven days 8–10 for day use, at all times for camping
$2 per vehicle per day
W + But not all areas

Want a change from saltwater? Try this 350-acre park on the southern end of the 24-mile long freshwater lake that has facilities for boating (rental boats available), fishing (two lighted fishing piers), swimming, waterskiing, picnicking, and camping (fee). The park overlooks a former part of the Nueces River that was the disputed boundary between Texas and Mexico until the Rio Grande became the boundary as a result of the Mexican War. For information write: Park Superintendent, Box 1167, Mathis 78368. There are also numerous commercial campsites, parks, and other recreational facilities along the rest of the 200-mile shoreline of the lake. For information on these, contact the Lake Corpus Christi Area Chamber of Commerce (1-547-6112).

MUSTANG ISLAND STATE PARK
Take S. Padre Island Dr. across the JFK Causeway to Mustang Island, then left on Texas 361 (formerly Park Rd. 53) to the park
(See Port Aransas)

ANNUAL EVENTS

April

BUCCANEER DAYS
Various locations in the city
882-3242
About 11 days near end of the month

Free (Admission to some events)
W Variable

For more than 50 years, the city has been celebrating the 1519 discovery of Corpus Christi Bay with this festival. The festivities are kicked off with the capture of the city by pirate girls (actually the contestants in the Buc Days beauty contest) who make the Mayor "walk the plank." Activities include the junior parade, the illuminated night parade, fireworks, a carnival, music festivals, street dance, sports events on both land and sea, arts and crafts show, a sailboat regatta, and a carnival.

June

FIESTA DE CORPUS CHRISTI
Watergarden in Bayfront Park
882-5603 or 800-678-6232 (Convention and Visitors Bureau)
Three-day weekend late in June
Free
W

A celebration of the city's Hispanic heritage that dates back to its naming after the Feast day of Corpus Christi. Festivities include mariachis and other musical groups, folkloric dances, and historical exhibits.

July

TEXAS JAZZ FESTIVAL
Various locations in the city
992-4540
Three-day weekend
Most activities are free
W Variable

Jazz musicians, many of them famous, donate their time to come here from all over the country to put on this festival. Activities include free clinics, concerts, and jam sessions; a scenic jazz festival cruise (pay) on Friday evening, and a Jazz Mass on Sunday.

September

BAYFEST
Shoreline Blvd. and Bayfront Arts and Sciences Park
887-0868
Usually last weekend in September or first in October
Free
***W Variable**

It began as a bicentennial celebration and since then this three-day family fall festival has mushroomed into a major event drawing more than 350,000 visitors. Activities include an arts and crafts show, fireworks, a boat parade and a street parade, a sailboat regatta, and the "Anything-That-Can-Float-But-A-Boat Race." For children there are puppet and magic shows and contests.

December

HARBOR LIGHTS FESTIVAL
Bayfront and various locations in the city
882-5603 or 800-678-6232 (Convention and Visitors Bureau)
First weekend in December (with some activities scattered throughout the month)
Most activities free
W Variable

Santa comes early to Corpus Christi to get this festival rolling, and he travels by boat. The weekend events include the official lighting ceremony that not only lights up the official tree but also the marina, office buildings, and the Harbor Bridge. The Art Museum opens its annual Christmas Tree Forest and the Wyndham Hotel becomes the mecca for chocoholics with its annual Chocolate Festival. There are two parades down Shoreline Blvd., live entertainment, street dancing, an arts and crafts show, and special events for children. Throughout the month there are plays, dances, musical events, art shows, and other Christmasy activities.

RESTAURANTS

($ = under $7, $$ = $7 to $17, $$$ = $17 to $25, $$$$ = over $25 for one person excluding drinks, tax, and tip.)

Putting on the Ritz

REFLECTIONS
Wyndham Hotel, 900 N. Shoreline Dr.
886-3515
Dinner only Tuesday–Saturday, Closed Sunday and Monday
Reservations suggested on weekends
$$$-$$$$
Cr.
W Call ahead
Validated parking in hotel garage

Three walls of glass encase this plush, tri-level restaurant on the 20th floor, giving an unobstructed view of much of the shoreline. Entrées are divided simply into "sea" and "land." The sea choices include *Cajun Shrimp Dianne, Lobster Fettucine,* and *Shrimp Lavaca* — sauteed shrimp and spinach, topped with a peppery cheese and served in a flour tortilla egg roll. The land entrées include smoked duckling, mesquite broiled lamb chops, steaks and Veal Amarillo — medallions sauteed with mushroom, red peppers, brandy, and lemon. And you can light up your evening with a choice of *flambe* desserts made at your table. Piano music, dim lighting, and a dance floor round out the romantic setting. Bar.

American

ELMO'S CITY DINER AND OYSTER BAR
622 N. Water at Starr
883-1643
Lunch and dinner seven days
$$
Cr.
W
Children's plates

Except for the shape, all the traditional standards of a diner are here, such as the checkerboard black and white tile, stainless steel and neon decor. The fare includes burgers and poorboys and "blue plate specials," but it also goes upscale with entrées like flounder filet stuffed with crab and shrimp stuffing, fried River Catfish, Chicken Florentine, and Mesquite Roasted Prime Rib of Beef. Bar. Look for hometown girl Farrah Fawcett as a teenager in old yearbook photos on the wall.

Barbecue

COUNTY LINE
6102 Ocean Dr., just north of Corpus Christi State University
991-RIBS (991-7427)
Lunch and dinner Wednesday–Sunday, closed Monday and Tuesday
$$
AE, MC, V
W
Children's plates

The menu here is more extensive than you'll find in most barbecue places. There are the staples, of course — barbecued ribs, beef, sausage, and chicken — but they also offer smoked duck, smoked turkey, prime rib, and grilled steaks, chicken, and more and more seafood dishes are being added to the menu. If you're with a group of hungry barbecue lovers, try the Country Style (about $12 for adults, half for kids), a big platter of ribs, brisket, and sausage, big bowls of potato salad, cold slaw, and beans, and homemade bread — with seconds on everything. And, if you want to really bust your diet you can top dinner off with homemade ice cream. All this plus a view of the bay. Bar.

Continental

LA PARISIENNE
42 Lamar Park, in Lamar Park Center, Alameda at Doddridge
857-2736
Lunch Monday–Saturday, dinner Friday and Saturday, closed Sunday
Reservations suggested for dinner
$$$
Cr.
W

Chef Bruno and his wife Frederika started out as caterers who soon won the hearts and appetites of the gourmets of the city. They expanded the business by opening this French bakery and small restaurant. The lunch menu ($6-$8) offers such taste treats as *quiche lorraine* and smoked salmon sandwiches as well as the chef's version of the more traditional club sandwich and BLT. What the chef prepares for dinner depends on what is the best that is available. It may be rack of lamb, black pepper steak, or a veal, poultry, or seafood entree. Bakery is open from 7 a.m. to 6:30 p.m. Beer and wine.

Italian

FRANK'S SPAGHETTI HOUSE
2724 Leopard at Palm
882-0075
Lunch and dinner Monday–Friday, dinner only Saturday, closed Sunday
$$
AE, MC, V
W
Children's plates

The typical wine bottles, checkered tablecloths, and tables crowded into the rooms of an old house give this restaurant the feeling of a neighborhood *trattoria* in Italy. The menu lists a good sampling of the most popular Italian dishes plus seafood prepared in a variety of styles from grilled to parmesan. Bar.

LUCIANO'S
1618 S. Staples, one block north of Six Points
884-1832
Lunch and dinner Tuesday–Friday, dinner only Saturday and Sunday, closed Monday
$$
AE, MC, V
W
Children's plate

A local favorite for years and years, the restaurant remains popular even though the Luciano family, who introduced *pizza* to Corpus Christi in 1949, no longer guides the kitchen here. The house speciality is an entrée called "Around the World" that gives you a hearty taste of *lasagna, parmigiana, cannelloni,* eggplant *parmigiana,* and *spaghetti* with meat sauce, plus soup and a dinner salad. The menu also includes choices like *Salsiccia Castiglioni* — homemade Italian sausage in a casserole — and veal and seafood entrees. Bar.

PAESANO'S RISTORANTE
3812 S. Alameda at Doddridge in Lamar Park Center
852-7971
Lunch and dinner seven days
$$
AE, MC, V

W
Children's plates

Many Italian restaurants in Texas specialize in cuisine of Sicily and Southern Italy so most Texans think Italian food is always flavored with tomato sauces. There are several southern dishes like that on Paesano's menu, but it also ranges the whole Italian peninsula offering a variety of that country's creative cuisines that use lighter doses of tomatos and depend more on butter and a variety of spices to enhance the flavor. For example, the veal entrées include authentic dishes from Milan, Bologna, and Genoa, and you can order Beef Steak *Florentine* (Florence style) or a Filet of Red Snapper *Livornese* (Livorno style). Bar.

Seafood

BAJA COAST
5253 S. Staples, near South Padre Island Dr.
992-FISH (992-3474)
Lunch and dinner Monday–Friday and Sunday, dinner only Saturday
$$
Cr.
W

The dining area in this highly popular seafood house is tiered so you can watch the cooks at work behind the long counter, grilling the seafood over coals made from mesquite wood and stir-frying the vegetables. In addition to the local catch from the Gulf, seafood is also frequently flown in from the other two coasts. If you're not into seafood, they also use the grill to make *fajitas*. There's an oyster bar and, if you want to take some fish home with you, a fish market is just inside the entrance. Bar.

BLACK DIAMOND OYSTER BAR
7202 S. Padre Island Dr. at Rodd Field Rd.
992-2432
Lunch and dinner seven days
$$
AE, MC, V
W +

When the only Black Diamond was the original on Gollihar, your choices for how they prepared your seafood were fried, fried, or fried. At this fancier location, however, you can get it mesquite grilled or several other ways. But no matter how they cook it, it's still good and lives up to the reputation established at the original that made this restaurant an institution in the city. If you want to try the hole-in-the-wall original, it's at 5712 Gollihar at Airline (992-2382). The hours are different, so call.

CATFISH CHARLIE'S
5830 McArdle at Airline, in Crossroads Shopping Center
993-0363

Lunch and dinner seven days
$-$$
AE, MC, V
Children's plates

A mild version of a Cajun fish-fry is what you walk into when you enter this barn-like restaurant. As you could guess, the menu mainstay is all-you-can-eat fried catfish fillets. They also offer Cajun-style frog legs, Creole shrimp on rice, fried oysters, seafood gumbo, and Louisiana-style red beans and rice with ham. A good sampler is the Bayou Country Feast that has catfish, shrimp, oysters, and seafood gumbo. Beer and wine.

C. C. DOCKSIDE
600 N. Shoreline at People's St. T-Head
882-6666
Lunch and dinner seven days
$$
AE, MC, V
W
Children's plates

This restored quarters barge transformed into a floating restaurant offers such entrées as baked flounder fillet in lemon-pepper sauce, and a combination plate of broiled fish, shrimp, oysters, and scallops. Other seafood entrées come fried, grilled, blackened, or baked. There's an early bird special nightly from 5 to 7 and all day Sunday that includes a choice of one of two special entrées and all the trimmings including dessert (and tax and tip) for about $10. Good view of the bayfront skyline or the bay. If you want to enjoy the view outdoors, the Deck at Dockside offers a more casual menu of fried seafood and burgers. ($-$$). Bar.

FRENCHY'S CRABHOUSE
13309 S. Padre Island Dr., actually off S. Padre Island Dr. *under* the east end of the JFK Causeway
949-8710
$-$$
Lunch and dinner seven days in season. Call for off-season hours
AE, MC, V
W

Casual dress here doesn't mean just no ties. At Frenchy's, laid-back is a way of life so just about any clothing that won't cause a riot or a police raid is welcome. Seafood comes grilled over mesquite, broiled, blackened or fried and the house specialty of a Seafood Feast For Two should fill both of you without emptying your wallet. Watch the sun set over the Intracoastal Waterway or visit Frenchy's Museum displaying his collection from 50 years of beachcombing. Occasional live entertainment. Bar.

THE LIGHTHOUSE
444 N. Shoreline at the Lawrence St. T-Head
883-3982
Lunch and dinner seven days
$$
Cr.
W Elevator

Casual dining with a menu that ranges from u-peel-em shrimp to oysters *en brochette* and steak sandwiches to the catch of the day. But the real catch of the day — or night — here is the wide-angle view of the bay. This makes it a favorite spot for watching the sailboat races held early every Wednesday evening in season. Bar.

SNOOPY'S PIER
13313 S. Padre Island Dr., actually off S. Padre Island Dr. *under* the east end of the JFK Causeway
949-8815
Lunch and dinner seven days
$-$$
No Cr.
W

The decor is strictly "old fishermen's hangout," which it was; the dress is whatever you're wearing, and the menu is simple: mostly shrimp, the local catch of the day, and burgers. Sit outside on the deck and enjoy the evening breeze and watch the sun set over the water. Bar.

WATER STREET OYSTER BAR
309 N. Water at Williams, in Water St. Market
881-9448
Lunch and dinner seven days
$$
AE, MC, V
W +

This popular spot was once a transmission shop, but now serves mostly fresh Gulf catches grilled over mesquite, fried, or blackened. Be sure to look at the house specials on the huge blackboard over the open kitchen. Blackened redfish is usually on the menu. This searing technique is also used to prepare shark. Stand-up oyster bar and large patio. Bar.

WATER STREET SEAFOOD COMPANY
309 N. Water, in rear of courtyard at Water St. Market
882-8684
Lunch and dinner seven days
Reservations taken for large parties only
$$
Cr.
W
Children's plates

For starters there are appetizers like *ceviche*, or a quarter-pound of Blue Crab Cocktail (in season), or oysters on the half shell. And the entrée menu is just as varied with choices like *Red Snapper Nueces* — sauteed snapper filet topped with shrimp and blue crabmeat in a browned butter sauce — or, if you prefer your seafood deep fried, the combination dinner includes shrimp, oysters, crab cake, soft shell crab, and frogs legs. Daily specials on the blackboard. Bar.

THE YARDARM
4310 Ocean Dr., just south of Robert Dr.
855-8157
Dinner only Wednesday–Sunday, usually closed November through February
$$
Cr.

The only bad thing the locals say about this restaurant is it's closed too often. But when it is open, this weathered Cape Cod house on the bay continues to draw the crowds for its culinary skills with entrées like herb-poached salmon, red snapper *en papillote*, frogs legs *Provencal*, and *Coquilles St. Jacques*. All dinners include homemade soup or chowder, a salad served family-style in a large bowl, and a potato. Bar.

ACCOMMODATIONS

($ = Under $45, $$ = $46-$60, $$$ = $61-$80, $$$$ = $81-$100, $$$$$ = Over $100)

Note: Most accommodations in Corpus Christi have seasonal rates. Rate symbols used are for high season summer months. Ask about lower rates in low season.

Hotels and Motels

Room Tax 13 percent

BEST WESTERN SANDY SHORES RESORT
3200 Surfside, on Corpus Christi Beach north of Harbor Bridge
883-7456 or 800-528-1234
$$-$$$$$
W + five rooms
No-smoking rooms

This resort has a two-story section around the pool and seven-story section on the beach. The 253 units include six suites ($$$$$) and 14 no-smoking rooms. Children under 12 are free in room with parents. Senior discount. Limited covered parking. Cable TV with HBO and pay channel. Room phones (local calls free). Pets OK ($8 charge). Four restaurants and snack shops, room service, and lounge open seven nights with entertainment Tuesday-Saturday. Outdoor pool, indoor saunas, and whirlpool. Sports courts. Guest memberships available for country club. Free wine tasting every evening. Self-service laundry and same-day dry cleaning. Gift shop. Maps for joggers available. The International Kite Museum is located here (See Other Points of Interest). On the beach.

CORPUS CHRISTI MARRIOTT
Bayfront
707 N. Shoreline
882-1700 or 800-228-9290
$$$$$
W + four rooms
No-smoking rooms

The 20-story Marriott has 346 units that include 16 suites ($$$$$) and 21 no-smoking rooms. Children under 18 free in room with parents. Senior discount, weekend rates, and package plans available. Free garage parking for guests. Cable TV with HBO and pay channel. Room phones (charge for local calls). Fire sprinklers in rooms and fire intercom system. Pets OK. Restaurant, room service, and lounge open seven nights with DJ. Outdoor heated pool, indoor whirlpool, sauna, exercise room, and sundeck. Guest memberships available in country club. Free airport transportation. Same-day dry cleaning. On the bayfront.

DRURY INN CORPUS CHRISTI
2021 N. Padre Island Dr., take Texas 358 (Leopard St.) exit off I-37
289-8200 or 800-325-8300
$-$$
W + five rooms
No-smoking rooms

This four-story inn has 105 rooms that include 30 no-smoking. Children under 18 free in room with parents. Senior discount and package plans available. Satellite TV with Showtime and pay channel. Room phones (local calls free). Fire sprinklers in rooms. Pets OK. Outdoor pool. Free airport transportation, free cocktails Monday-Saturday, and free continental breakfast. Same-day dry cleaning.

EMBASSY SUITES HOTEL
4337 S. Padre Island Dr., near Weber exit
853-7899 or 800-EMBASSY (800-362-2779) or 800-678-7533
$$$$-$$$$$
W + two suites
No-smoking suites

In this three-story hotel all 150 units are suites of which 68 are no-smoking. Children under 12 free in room with parents. Senior discount, weekend rates, and package plans available. Cable TV with HBO and pay channel. VCR rentals. Room phones (charge for local calls). Coffeemakers in rooms. Pets OK ($10 charge). Lounge open Monday-Saturday with occasional entertainment. Indoor heated pool, indoor whirlpool, sauna. Memberships available for guests in YWCA and country club. Two hours of free cocktails in evening, free full breakfast, free newspaper, and free airport and local area transportation. Same-day dry cleaning. Guests can charge meals to their hotel bills at several area restaurants.

HOLIDAY INN-CORPUS CHRISTI AIRPORT
5549 Leopard St. (Texas 9) at Texas 358 and 44
289-5100 or 800-465-4329
$$
W + two rooms
No-smoking rooms

The six-story Airport Inn offers 247 units including six suites with whirlpools ($$$$$) and 25 no-smoking rooms. Children under 18 free in room with parents. Senior discount, package plans available. Cable TV with Showtime and pay channel. VCR rentals. Room phones (local calls free). Coffeemakers in rooms. Pets OK. Restaurant, room service, and lounge open seven nights with DJ. Indoor heated pool, indoor whirlpool, saunas, sundeck. Guest memberships available in health club and country club. Gift shop. Atrium lobby with waterfall.

HOLIDAY INN-EMERALD BEACH
1102 S. Shoreline
883-5731 or 800-465-4329
$$$-$$$$
W + one room
No-smoking rooms

This Holiday Inn is a five- and seven-story inn that has 368 units including four suites ($$$$$) and 39 no-smoking rooms. Children under 18 free in room with parents. Senior discounts and package plans available. Cable TV with Showtime and pay channel. VCR rentals. Room phones (charge for local calls). Pets OK. Two restaurants (one seasonal), lobby bar, and lounge open seven nights with DJ. Indoor heated pool, children's pool, exercise room, whirlpool, sauna. Guest memberships available in country club. Free airport transportation. Children's playground. Same-day dry cleaning. Gift shop. This is the only bayfront hotel/motel located right on the bay.

HOLIDAY INN-NORTH PADRE ISLAND
15202 Windward Dr.
949-8041 or 800-465-4329
$$$$-$$$$$
W + two rooms
No-smoking rooms

This six-story inn offers 148 units including two suites ($$$$$) and 30 no-smoking rooms. Children under 19 free in parent's room. Senior discount and package plans available. Cable TV with Showtime and pay channel. Room phones (local calls free). Pets OK. Restaurant, room service, and lounge open seven days with live entertainment Wednesday-Sunday in high season. Outdoor pool with bar. Guest memberships available in country club. Self-service laundry, and same-day dry cleaning. Located on the beach.

RADISSON MARINA
300 N.Shoreline
883-5111 or 800-333-3333
$$$-$$$$
No-smoking rooms

The 11-story Sheraton offers 175 units including five suites ($$$$$) and 49 no-smoking rooms. Children under 17 free in room with parents. Senior discount, package plans, and weekend rates in off-season. Some covered parking. Cable TV with pay channel. Room phones (charge for local calls). Pets OK. Restaurant, room service, lounge open seven nights with entertainment Wednesday-Saturday, and music and dancing in restaurant/lounge after dinner. Outdoor pool with bar, sauna, tennis courts. Memberships available for guests in YMCA and country club. Free airport and local transportation, free coffee in lobby, and free newspaper. Self-service laundry, and same-day dry cleaning. Rafts, bicycles and tennis racquets for rent. Bird's-eye view of shoreline from 11th floor restaurant/lounge. On the bayfront.

ROYAL NUECES-DAYS
800-325-2525
888-4461 or 800-531-5900
$$$
W + 2 rooms
No-smoking rooms

This ten-story hotel offers 200 units that include seven suites ($$$-$$$$$) and 48 no-smoking rooms. Children under 18 stay free in room with parents. Package plans available, senior discount, and weekend rates. Cable TV with HBO. Room phones (local calls free). No pets. Restaurant and club open Monday-Saturday with entertainment on weekends. Outdoor pool. Guest memberships available in YMCA. Free airport transportation. Same-day dry cleaning. One block from the bay.

WYNDHAM CORPUS CHRISTI HOTEL
900 N. Shoreline
887-1600 or 800-822-4200
$$$$-$$$$$
W + eight rooms
No-smoking rooms

The 20-story Wyndham Hotel has 474 units including 27 suites ($$$$$) and 25 no-smoking rooms. Children under 18 free in parent's room. Senior discount, package plans, and weekend rates in off-season. Free valet/garage parking. Cable TV with HBO and pay channel. Room phones (charge for local calls). Fire sprinklers in rooms and fire intercom system. No pets. Two restaurants, room service, and three lounges open seven days. Outdoor pool with bar in season, exercise room, whirlpool, sauna, racquetball court. Memberships available for guests in several golf clubs. Free coffee in lobby in morning. Same day dry cleaning. Comedy Club Tuesday-Saturday, $3 for guests, $5 for others. On the bayfront.

OTHER ACCOMMODATIONS

Condominiums

GULFSTREAM
North Padre Island
14810 Windward Rd.
949-8061 or 800-542-RENT (800-542-7368)
$$$$$

The six-story Gulfstream has 94 two-bedroom/two-bath units in rental pool. Senior discount in off-season. Minimum stay two nights with reservation. Satellite TV with HBO. Room phones (charge for local calls). No pets. Outdoor heated pool, outdoor whirlpool. Memberships available for guests in country club. Free coffee in lobby. On the beach.

ISLAND HOUSE CONDOMINIUMS
North Padre Island
15340 Leeward Dr.
949-8166 or 800-333-8806
$$$$$

The three-story Island House has about 58 units in the rental pool that include one, two, and three bedrooms. Minimum stay two nights with reservation. Satellite TV with HBO/Cinemax. Room phones (charge for local calls). Pets OK in winter season only (pet deposit $50). Outdoor heated pool, children's pool. Memberships available for guests in country club. Free coffee in lobby. Self-service laundry. On the beach.

VILLA DEL SOL CONDOMINIUM HOTEL
Corpus Christi Beach
3938 Surfside
883-9748 or 800-242-3291
$$$-$$$$$
No-smoking units

This four-story condominium hotel has 280 one-bedroom/one bath units in the rental pool of which 32 are no-smoking. Up to four adults and two children may stay in a unit. Senior discount and package plans are available. Two night minimum stay on holiday weekends is required. Some covered parking. Satellite TV with pay channel. Room phones (local calls free). No pets. Two outdoor heated pools, three outdoor whirlpools, sailboat and jet ski rentals. Self-service laundry and same-day dry cleaning. Gift shop in summer. On the beach.

CONDOMINIUM AND BEACH HOUSE RENTAL AGENCIES

Several agencies in the Corpus Christi area handle condominium and beach house rentals. In most cases a minimum stay of two days is required with rates ranging from about $60 to $250 a day. Weekly and monthly rates are available. Two of these agencies are: Century 21, 14517 South Padre Island Dr., 949-8110. Padre Island Rentals, 14200 Padre Island Dr., 949-7036 or 800-234-0117.

GALVESTON

GALVESTON COUNTY SEAT ★ 72,000 ★ (409)

Over the past 25 years or so, Galveston has undergone a renaissance. Part of this is due to the unceasing labors of the Galveston Historical Foundation that saved whole areas of the city from the bulldozer. Part is due to the bounty of the Moody Foundation, that substantially contributed money to worthwhile projects. And part is due to the far-sighted city fathers, business people and investors, like George Mitchell, who have pulled the area out of its decline and are slowly putting it back on the throne as Queen of the Texas Coast.

From the luxury of its splendid hotels to the playland atmosphere of Stewart Beach Park, Galveston is now a place with a bit of everything you'd expect in a resort city. There is something to do here rain or shine. You can swim in the Gulf or waterski the bayous, wear your bathing suit as you shell and eat shrimp at a restaurant on the seawall or dress up for more formal dining in one of the several first class restaurants, shop on the Strand, admire the intricate craftsmanship of the woodwork in the Bishop's Palace, stroll a tree-shaded street in a historic district, or do any one of a thousand other things to make your stay enjoyable.

Despite the long list of lures thrown out to tourists — in a city that recognizes that tourism is a major factor in its economy — the two

GALVESTON

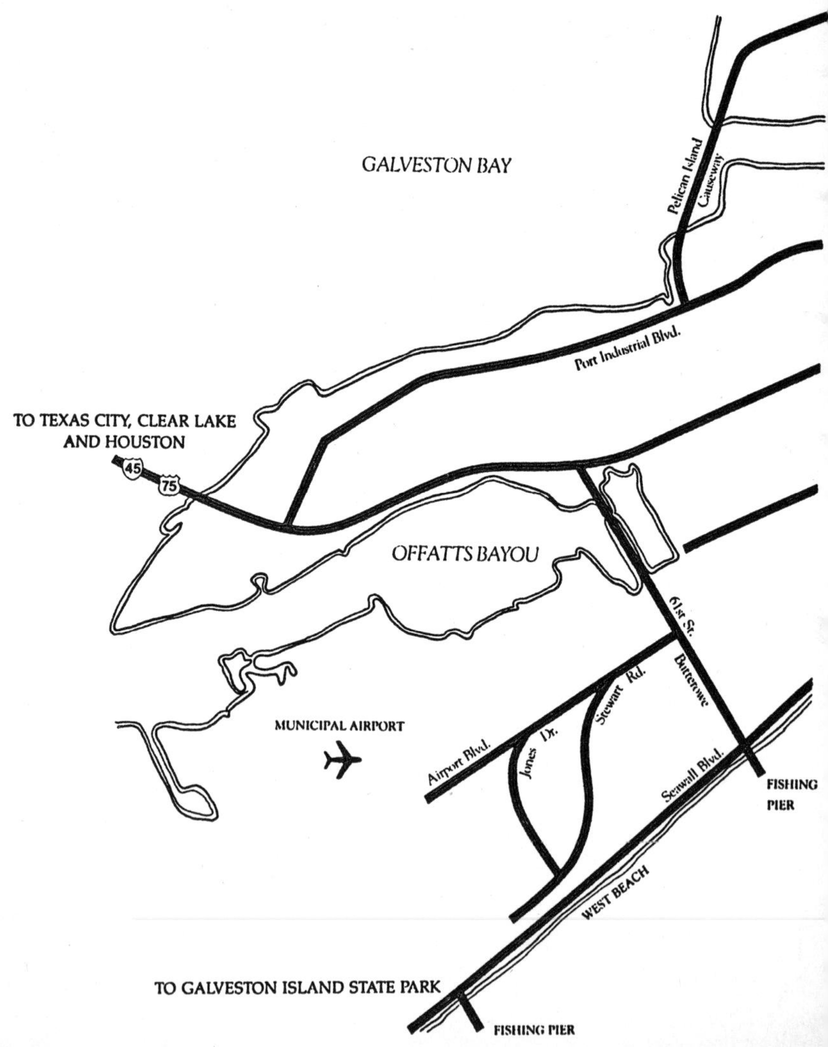

GALVESTON BAY
Pelican Island Causeway
Port Industrial Blvd.
TO TEXAS CITY, CLEAR LAKE AND HOUSTON
45
75
OFFATTS BAYOU
61st St.
Butterowe
Stewart Rd.
Jones Dr.
Airport Blvd.
MUNICIPAL AIRPORT
Seawall Blvd.
FISHING PIER
WEST BEACH
TO GALVESTON ISLAND STATE PARK
FISHING PIER

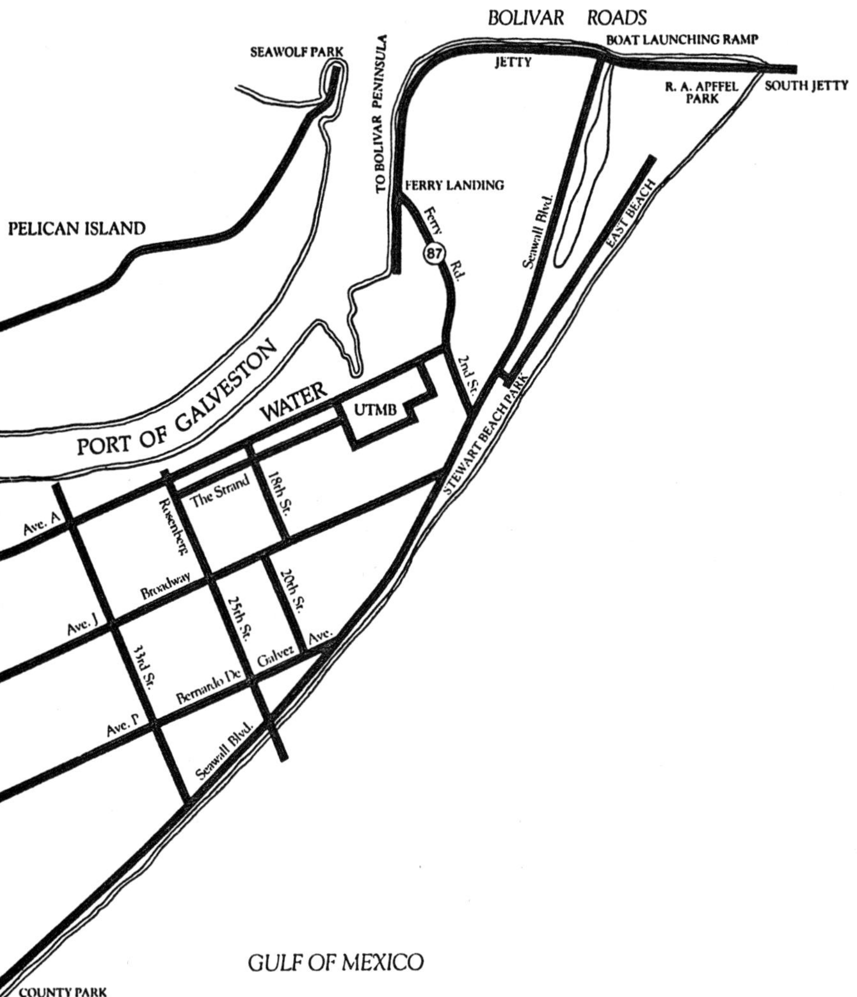
BOLIVAR ROADS
BOAT LAUNCHING RAMP
SEAWOLF PARK
TO BOLIVAR PENINSULA
JETTY
R. A. APFFEL PARK
SOUTH JETTY
FERRY LANDING
PELICAN ISLAND
Ferry Rd.
87
Seawall Blvd.
EAST BEACH
PORT OF GALVESTON
WATER
UTMB
2nd St.
STEWART BEACH PARK
The Strand
18th St.
Ave. A
Rosenberg
Broadway
20th St.
25th St.
Ave. J
Galvez Ave.
33rd St.
Bernardo De
Ave. P
Seawall Blvd.
GULF OF MEXICO
COUNTY PARK
N
NOTE: Not to Scale

biggest draws for visitors are still sun and sea. The city is located on one end of Galveston Island, a barrier island about two miles off the coast, so there are miles and miles of beaches — 32, in fact. These may not be as sparkling nor as wide as those further south on Padre Island, but they are clean and convenient. As for fishing, why brave the discomforts of an isolated fishing camp when the fish are waiting all around the island and all the comforts of a resort city are available?

Galveston's colorful history goes back to 1528 when it was discovered by Cabeza de Vaca, a Spanish explorer. The discovery, however, was made when he was shipwrecked and kept prisoner for six years by the Karankawa Indians, a fact that may belie that vanished tribe's reputation for cannibalism. A company of Spanish soldiers, stationed on the island in the mid-1700s, named it after Count Bernardo de Galvez, viceroy of Mexico. The flags changed — Spanish, French, Mexican — but the island stayed the same until Jean Lafitte, the buccaneer, set up his base there in 1817. Lafitte, who had become an American hero when he came to the aid of General Andrew Jackson at the Battle of New Orleans in the War of 1812, founded the town of Campeche, which was literally a pirates' den. From here he and his men ravaged the Spanish ships in the Gulf. He stayed until 1821 when the U.S. Government forced him to leave after his men made the undiplomatic mistake of privateering against an American ship. When Lafitte left, the settlers came.

During the Texas War for Independence, Galveston was one of the temporary capitals of the provisional government, and a Galvestonian, Samuel May Williams, was a major financial backer of that revolution. It was also the home port of four ships of the Texas Navy that prevented a Mexican blockade of the Texas coast. After the Texans won, Michael B. Menard bought most of the eastern end of the island from the new republic for $50,000 and laid out the townsite with the streets much as they exist today. The first Custom House was established here in 1836, with Gail Borden, who later invented condensed milk, as collector of the port. It is said that Borden also was locally famous for occasionally riding down the Strand on a pet bull.

During the Civil War, Galveston fell to Federal troops, but a Confederate force, lead by General J. B. Magruder, launched a surprise attack — with a force that included two river steamboats turned into "Cottonclads" by piling bales of cotton on the decks to protect the riflemen — and recaptured it. It was also during this battle that the Confederates loaded a heavy piece of artillery on a railroad car and pushed it along the tracks on the waterfront, stopping to fire at the Union ships in the harbor. Reportedly, this was the first use of railroad artillery in American military history. After that victory, Galveston remained in the Confederate ranks until the war ended.

By the late 1800s, Galveston's natural deep water port had become the third largest port in the nation, and The Strand, modeled and named after a street in London, became known as the "Wall Street of the Southwest." Fortunes were made, elegant homes were built, and the city became a cultural center.

Unfortunately, the Galvestonians forgot that their city was built on a barrier island. In 1900 disaster struck in the form of an unexpected hurricane that lashed the low-lying island with devastating winds and tidal waves. At least 6,000 perished in what is still listed as the greatest natural disaster in American history. The flourishing port and many of the buildings on the island were destroyed.

Undaunted, the survivors started to rebuild. But first they had to work out a way to protect their island from future hurricanes. The plan they decided on would take heroic efforts, high purpose, perseverance, and years to complete. They started by building the seawall (originally less than four miles long, now more than ten). Then, behind this protective barrier, they worked for eight years dredging sand from the waterways and using it to raise, by 3 to 17 feet, the elevation of the entire city of more than 2,000 buildings and all the streets. This prodigious project was severely tested by a storm in 1915 that was reportedly worse than the one in 1900. There were some casualties and some buildings were lost, but overall, the seawall held and the raised city survived.

It almost didn't survive the economic disaster that followed. The business leaders of Houston, a city sitting more than 40 miles inland, had a ship channel dug to the Gulf. And when the Houston Ship Channel opened, the railroads decided Houston was easier to serve than Galveston. They located their major terminals there turning it into a major inland port and killing the economy of Galveston.

The decline was halted during the '30s and '40s when the island city became known as the gambling playground of the Southwest. In a play on words, people going to Galveston spoke of going south of the Maceo-Dickinson Line, referring to the Maceo family who ran some gambling nightclubs and the town of Dickinson, about 30 miles north of the island. The glamor lasted up into the 1950s when a crackdown on vice sent the city into another nosedive.

The latest upswing started with a rebirth of the port. City officials began to realize that visitors would be interested in the city's historical treasures as well as its beaches. In some ways the economic stagnation in the 1950s proved a blessing in disguise because no urban renewal programs or major corporations had torn down old houses to build office skyscrapers. The homes built on nineteenth-century wealth were in disrepair, but they were still there — about 1,500 of them — making Galveston one of the finest collections of Victorian architecture in the United States. It was at this time that the forerunner of the present Galveston Historical Foundation was started with the express purpose of preserving, restoring, and adapting these structures for present day use — a purpose that literally saved the city.

Today the city has four major sources of economic activity: the port; the large medical complex (built around the University of Texas Medical Branch), which is the largest single employer in the city; financial institutions, including a number of banks and two large insurance companies; and tourism that brings in more than five million visitors a year.

Galveston lays claim to a number of firsts for Texas. Among these are: The oldest newspaper now surviving in Texas was established here in 1842, the first gaslights appeared here in 1856 and the first electric lights in 1888, the first YMCA was established here in 1856, the first medical college in Texas was started here in 1891, and the first brewery in the state opened here about 1894. Despite what some may say, no historical connection has been found between the opening of the college and the opening of the brewery nor the subsequent opening here of the first golf course and country club in Texas in 1898.

Galveston is often called "Oleander City" because it boasts the most extensive collection of that flower found anywhere in the world. More than sixty varieties are found here, and in the spring, the city is saturated in colors ranging from white, reds, pinks to creams, and yellows.

TOURIST SERVICES

Galveston Island is geared for tourists. Detailed information is available at the Convention and Visitors Bureau and The Strand Visitors Center, but you'll find brochures popping up almost everywhere that give information on sights to see and places to go and the wide variety of tours to take.

GALVESTON ISLAND CONVENTION AND VISITORS BUREAU
2106 Seawall at 21st St., on ground floor of Moody Civic Center
763-4311 or in Texas 800-351-4236. Outside Texas 800-351-4237
Open seven days 9–5
Free
W + Back entrance.

In addition to the tons of information they can provide you here, they usually have discount coupons for everything from accommodations to shopping. This is also the place to buy tickets and board the Treasure Island Tour Train and the Trolley (see following).

ALL ABOUT TOWN TOURS
744-6371
Call for schedule
Adults $5, children $4

The Galveston Flyer, an air conditioned bus designed to look like a 1920s trolley, makes several tours of the major sights daily except Wednesday with pick-ups from hotels on the beachfront and historic district.

CARRIAGE TOURS

You can usually pick up one of these horse-drawn carriages near The Strand Visitors Center. They offer narrated tours through The Strand, the historic districts, or just about anywhere else you want to go as long as it isn't hazardous to the horse and you're willing to pay for it. **Classic Carriage Tours**, 1604 Ave. M (762-1260), operates every day in summer, but usually only on weekends or during special events, like

Dickens on the Strand, in winter. Prices depend on the route and the number of passengers.

***THE COLONEL* PADDLEWHEELER**
Pier 22, 22nd St (Office at 111 Tremont)
763-4666
April through Labor Day: two day cruises daily, dinner/jazz cruise Tuesday–Saturday, moonlight cruise Saturday only. Cruises on weekends only from September through March. Call for times
Day cruises: Adults $8, children (4–12) $4. Dinner/Jazz Cruises: Adults: $24, children (under 12) $15. Moonlight cruise: Adults only $8
W
Free parking Strand at 25th St.

Actually a floating period museum built in Mississippi for the non-profit Moody Foundation at a cost of three million dollars, this authentic reproduction of an 1860s stern wheeler is named in honor of Colonel W. L. Moody, a Virginian who came to Texas in 1854 to practice law. *The Colonel* is 152 feet long and holds up to 800 passengers on its three public decks. The daily sightseeing cruises last about two hours and include a narration on Galveston's historic past and views of present port activities. The dinner/jazz cruise and the moonlight cruise also last about two hours. *The Colonel* is berthed at Pier 22, next to the *Elissa*. Boarding begins a half hour prior to all cruises.

GALVESTON HISTORICAL FOUNDATION TOUR SERVICE
2016 Strand
765-7834
Fees vary by tour
W

Now that the members of the foundation have helped save much of historic Galveston, they welcome the opportunity to show visitors around. Among the several step-on guide tours offered is a tour of the Foundation's properties: Ashton Villa, The 1839 Williams Home, the *Elissa*, and the Galveston County Historical Museum. Also available are narrated driving tours. In most cases, guides are paid $20 an hour with a two hour minimum.

GALVESTON ISLAND TROLLEY
Loops from the Moody Civic Center at Seawall and 21st St. to the Strand area and back
For schedule information call 763-4311 (Convention and Visitors Bureau)
Adults $1 each way, children and seniors 50¢

These are replicas of the fixed-rail commuter trolleys used here in the early 1900s. The round trip up Rosenberg Ave. from the Seawall to The Strand and back takes about one hour, and you can get on or off at any stop. The cars run every 30 minutes in the summer and every hour in the winter. Rubber-wheeled trolley vehicles run an east and west feeder route connecting major hotels, Moody Gardens, and other attractions with the trolley station at the Moody Civic Center.

THE STRAND VISITORS CENTER
2016 Strand
765-7834
Open Monday–Friday and Sunday 9:30–6, Saturday 9:30–9. Closed Christmas and Thanksgiving
Free
W ramp to see movie

This should be your first stop when you hit The Strand. Located in the street's oldest restored structure, the 1859 Hendley Building, it's another project of the Galveston Historical Foundation whose office is upstairs. The staff offers expert information and there's a seemingly endless stock of brochures on The Strand and other historic districts and buildings and a 12-minute orientation film called *Galveston: Island of Discovery*. You can pick up a map for a self-guided tour or rent a cassette ($2) that will guide you through a walking tour of the area. Tickets to the trolley, the various foundation properties, and important events are for sale. The Ticketron office also has tickets for events in Houston.

TREASURE ISLAND TOUR TRAIN
Departs from Moody Civic Center, Seawall and 21st St.
765-9564
Seven days. Number of tours per day vary from two a day in low season to nine a day in summer. Call for tour times
Adults about $4, children about $2.50
W

This pink-awninged, open-air train carries up to 64 passengers on a leisurely, 17-mile, narrated trip that takes about an hour and a half and covers the highlights of old and new Galveston.

GUIDEBOOKS

BOB'S GALVESTON ISLAND READER
by Bob Nesbitt
Published by the author
$5.95

An old-time Galvestonian's tongue-in-cheek view of the island's history and sights. Available at The Strand Visitors Center.

HISTORIC GALVESTON
by Payne, Leavenworth, and Herring
Herring Press, Houston
$49.95

A book of richly detailed photographs reaching back in time by focusing on architecture and beauty that even many Galvestonians are not aware of. Available in bookstores.

RAY MILLER'S GALVESTON
by Ray Miller
Cordovan Press (Gulf Publishing Co.), Houston
$19.95

A little bit of history, a little bit of gossip, and lots of old photos bring the past to life. Available in bookstores.

A GET-ACQUAINTED DRIVING TOUR

The place to start, of course, is the **Convention and Visitors Bureau** in the **Moody Civic Center** at Seawall and 21st St. Here you can pick up a map and a number of brochures that will make your tour more interesting and meaningful. You might especially want to pick up the maps and brochures on the several historic districts.

But, before you start driving, there are three things to note about the way the city is laid out. First, many streets and avenues have two names: 21 St. (next to the Civic Center), for example, is also appropriately named Moody Street, and Ave. B is The Strand. Sometimes both names appear on the street sign or on a map, sometimes only one. Next, the numbered streets run north and south starting at the east end of the island near Ferry Rd. (Texas 87) and the street numbers get higher as you go west. The lettered avenues start at the port on the bay side of the island and go through the alphabet as they work south to the seawall. And, perhaps just to make it more interesting, the city fathers have occasionally stuck in a half avenue: like Ave. M ½ or Avenue P ½. Finally, most east-west avenues are cut up and go in spurts, a piece here, a piece there, with breaks between them. Broadway (Ave. J) is the best two-way east-west in the north section of the city, Ave. O is the major uninterrupted one-way going west and Ave. P the major one-way going east in the center, and Seawall Blvd., the main east-west road in the south. There are a number of uninterrupted north-south streets, but the best are Rosenberg (25th St.) and 61st St. (Butterowe).

Confused? You won't be once you've looked at this on a map and after you've finished this tour.

From the Visitors Center, head *west on Seawall Blvd.*, putting the seawall and the Gulf on your left. The first tall building you encounter is the **Moody House**, a retirement home. Then as you continue along Seawall, you'll pass a number of motels, hotels, restaurants, and beach shops. As you approach 61st St. (Butterowe) get in the right turn lane. If you continued straight you'd be heading out the island to **Galveston Island State Park** and the **Mary Moody Northern Amphitheater** (See Performing Arts) and on to San Luis Pass, but *turn right (north) on 61st St.*

At Stewart Rd. (Ave. S) turn left (west), as if heading to the airport. Go to *Jones Dr.*, then *right on Hope Blvd.* which will take you to **Moody Gardens** (See Other Points of Interest). Here are Hope Arena, The Garden of Life, and Palm Beach, the first stages of a 20-year, $120 million recreational project of the Moody Foundation. Drive around and take a look, then reverse and work your way *back to 61st St. and turn left (north).*

A little further on, 61st St. crosses **Offatt's Bayou** where, on any good day, you'll see dozens of small sailboats and wind surfers taking advantage of the protected waters and steady breezes. Beyond this is the intersection with US 75. Go left on US 75 and it will take you to **Texas City, Clear Lake,** and **Houston** (See Side Trips). And if you go left on the US 75 access road, you'll be at **Galvez Mall**, the city's largest (See Shopping) which is at the northwest corner of US 75 and 61st Street. But we'll *turn right (east) on Broadway* and continue heading east to Rosenberg (25th St.). With the exception of Moody Gardens, there hasn't been much to see of tourist interest along this route since you left the seawall, but you've done one thing. The rectangle you've driven has pretty well boxed in the area containing most of the places of tourist interest, so you should have an easier time finding each one when you want to. And from here on there's plenty to see, starting with the **Texas Heroes Monument** at Rosenberg and Broadway. This 72-foot memorial is dedicated to the heroes of the Texas Revolution. Today the figure on top seems to point the way to The Strand and the waterfront attractions, but legend has it that the pointing figure originally showed sailors the way to the town's old red-light district. We'll fight off the temptation to follow that pointing hand and *turn right (south) on Rosenberg.*

In two blocks, turn left (east) on Ave. L. You've now entered the **Silk Stocking Historic District** (See Historic Places) which covers the area between Rosenberg (25th St.) and 23rd St. from Ave. L to Ave. N. A number of historically interesting homes in this area are being restored. One is the blue and white-trimmed **Sweeney-Royston House** at Ave. L and 24th St. This Victorian cottage, built in 1885, is listed in the National Register of Historic Places.

Continue on Ave. L to 21st St. (Moody) and turn right (south). The large building on your right is a retirement home. In the next block, on the right, is the former **Island City Protestant Orphans Home** founded in 1878. After the original home was destroyed in the 1900 hurricane, William Randolph Hearst hosted a charity affair in New York to raise money for the present building.

Turn right (west) on Ave. O and go back to cross Rosenberg. The **Las Palmas House** on the northwest corner of Rosenberg and Ave. O has been a setting in several films. At Ave. O and 27th is **Garten Verein** (See Historic Places). About six blocks further on, at 3427 Ave. O is the **Powhatan House** (See Historic Places). Built in 1847, it is now the home of the Galveston Garden Club and is open for visitors Saturday and Sunday 1-5 p.m. (For information: 763-0077.)

Turn left (south) off Ave. O onto 37th St. The next turn is Ave. P, but that's not one block, it's two because they stuck in Ave. O ½. *Turn left (east) on Ave. P (Bernardo de Galvez).* On your right, at 3601 is the **1839 Samuel May Williams Home** (See Historic Places), built by one of Texas' earliest entrepreneurs. Continue on Ave. P *back to Rosenberg (25th St.) and turn left (north).* At the Heroes Monument, *turn right (east) on Broadway (Ave. J).*

Immediately on your left, on the northeast corner of Rosenberg and Broadway is the **Sealy Mansion**, called "Open Gates." This castle-like 1889 home is now owned by the University of Texas Medical Center. On the next block, also on your left, is the **Ashton Villa** (See Historic Places). Starting at 19th St., you enter the **East End Historic District**, a residential area of about 40 square blocks listed as an entity in the National Register of Historic Places. From where you are, the district continues east to 11th and north about six blocks to Market (Ave. D). The house on your right at 1515 Broadway is a good example of historic homes in this area. Built in 1871, it is notable for the porches with slender columns, arches, and imaginative gingerbread trim. The major attraction in this area is at 14th St. where, on your left, you'll see what may be the most well-known building in Galveston, the **Bishop's Palace** (See Historic Places). Next to it is Sacred Heart Catholic Church, built in 1903. The statue on the dome, added in 1950, is a copy of the famous Christ of the Andes.

Turn left (north) on 12th St., go one block to Sealy and turn left (west) again. On your right at the next corner, at 1228, is the **Burr House**, built in 1876 in a blend of Classical and Gothic Victorian styles. The Queen-Anne-style **Skinner House** at 1318 dates from 1895. The original iron fence still encloses the yard. The **Smith-Chubb House** at 1417, on your left behind the Bishop's Palace, built in 1859, is called the "Flat Roof House." What has been described as "the strangest house in a city of strange house" is the **Trube House** on your left at the corner of Sealy and 17th St. Built in 1890, it is a cross between Gothic and Moorish design. Note that the sculptured burning torch decoration on the octagonal tower is repeated on the iron fence posts. On your right at the corner of Sealy and 19th is the **Sonnentheil House** which was built by one of the best-known carpenters in the area in 1886 and is notable for its woodworking details.

Turn right (north) on 19th St. the **First Presbyterian Church** is on the corner of Church (Ave. F) and 19th. This was the first church congregation in Galveston, organized in 1840. The present church building was started in 1872 and completed 17 years later. *Turn left on Church.* Behind the First Presbyterian, standing back-to-back with it at 21st St., is the oldest surviving church building in the city and the oldest cathedral in Texas, **St. Mary's Cathedral**. It was built in 1847 with half million bricks brought in from Belgium. In an act of thanksgiving after the church survived a disastrous flood in 1875, the tower was crowned with a statue of Mary, Star of the Sea. Its survival of the 1900 hurricane and every storm since has inspired the growth of a legend that as long as the statue stands, Galveston will stand.

Turn right (north) on Moody (21st St.) and right (east) again at the next corner onto Post Office (Ave. E). On your left is the **1894 Grand Opera House** (See Performing Arts). *Go two blocks to 19th and turn left (north).* Ahead at Market (Ave. D) is the **American National Insurance Company** tower; at 20 stories high, it is Galveston's tallest building. Go a block past this *to Mechanic (Ave. C) and turn left (west).* On the corner of Moody (21st St.) is the **old cotton exchange**. Between 23rd St. and 24th St. is the Tremont Hotel (See Accommodations) and across the street **The Strand Street Theater** (See Performing Arts).

At Rosenberg (25th St. — are you getting this dual name system yet?) *turn right (north).* On your left is the **Railroad Museum** (See Museums). *At the next block, turn right (east) onto* **The Strand** (See Historic Places), the street of nineteenth-century commercial buildings that have been restored to their former glory and now house a number of fine shops and restaurants. A *left (north) on 20th St.* will take you to the waterfront where you make a *right (east) on Water St. (Ave. A or Port Industrial Blvd.).* Along here are the docks of the tour paddlewheeler, *The Colonel,* the 1877 tall ship *Elissa* at the **Texas Seaport Museum**, the Mosquito Fleet (Galveston's shrimpers) and a variety of other ships in the port. If you want a better view of all this, stop at **Hill's Pier 19 Restaurant** (See Restaurants) and climb the outside stairs to the observation deck.

Continue down Water St. until it runs into the eastern end of The Strand at the **University of Texas Medical Branch** that will be on your right. The large, old red-brick building you'll see near one of the entrances to the medical complex is **Old Red**, the Ashbel Smith Building (See Colleges and Universities). Before the turn of the century this was the first medical school in Texas, and this building housed the entire school.

A little way further down The Strand, on your left, you'll be able to see the huge cranes at the container ship terminal. At the water tower (on your right), *turn left (north) onto Holiday Dr.* At the end of this road is the **Galveston Yacht Club** where many large pleasure craft are berthed. From here you can get another view of the container ship cranes. Turn left into the parking lot, make a loop, *get back on Holiday Dr. and go back south* to the water tower. *Turn left (east), which will put you back on The Strand.* From here, it's one block to Ferry Rd. If you wanted to take the free ferry to the Bolivar Peninsula (See Side Trips), you'd turn left (north), but instead *turn right and go south on Ferry* to Seawall Blvd. When you reach there you'll be at the **Stewart Beach Park** and back at the Gulf. If you want to expand this tour to loop out to the east end of the island with its south jetty and **R. A. Apffel Beach Park**, take a left (east). Otherwise, follow Seawall Blvd, (staying on Seawall by making the left turn at the intersection with Broadway) and return back to your starting place at the Convention and Visitors Bureau.

BIRD'S-EYE VIEW

GALV-AERO FLIGHT CENTER
Scholes Field Executive Terminal, Hope Blvd.
740-1223 (Call for directions)

See the island from the air. Light planes can give you a bird's-eye view of the city and a wide area around it on a one-hour flight that costs about $60 for up to three passengers.

MUSEUMS

GALVESTON ART CENTER ON THE STRAND

2127 Strand
763-2403
Monday–Saturday 10–5, Sunday 12–5; Extended hours in summer
Free
W call ahead

Although the works of major artists are frequently shown here, the thrust of this storefront art gallery is to feature the works of emerging artists in all media from all over the country. The center offers about 11 shows a year plus art lectures. The gift shop, called Artworks, features the works of regional artists in all media.

GALVESTON COUNTY HISTORICAL MUSEUM

2219 Market (Ave. D)
766-2340
Memorial Day to Labor Day: Monday–Saturday 10–5, Sunday noon–5; rest of year closes one hour earlier
Donation $1
W call ahead

This compact museum is housed in a narrow old bank building, built in 1919, and operated for the county by the Galveston Historical Foundation. The exhibits tell the story of Galveston County, a story that features Jean Lafitte, the Civil War Battle of Galveston, and the devastating 1900 hurricane. Permanent exhibits include a re-creation of a late 1800s railroad depot, where the varied farming and ranching products from the county were brought together as they made their way to market, and an early 1900s general store. There is also an exhibit on Nicholas Clayton, the architect who changed the face of the city in the late 1800s by designing such landmarks as the Bishop's Palace, Old Red, and about fifty other buildings that survived the 1900 hurricane. The museum is downtown, so parking space can be difficult to find. Try parking on the less-trafficked streets to the east or between the museum and The Strand.

LONE STAR FLIGHT MUSEUM

2002 Terminal Dr., Scholes Field
740-7722
Open seven days 10–5, except Thanksgiving and Christmas
Adults 50¢, children under 13 and seniors $2.50
W +

While there are several vintage aircraft museums throughout the country, the goal of this museum is to be the home of the "Best of Type." The current collection of 24 vintage aircraft on display is mostly from the World War II era and include a restored B-17, B-25, P-38 and a P-47. In addition to aircraft, there is also a display of restored autos including a 1941 Ford staff car and a 1943 jeep. Gift Shop.

MOODY MANSION AND MUSEUM
2628 Broadway
762-7668
Open seven days 10–4
Admission
W Ground floor only

The terreted, 42-room, 28,000 square-foot mansion was built around 1892 as the home of W. L. Moody, Jr, who was then the head of one of the wealthiest and most powerful families in Texas. It was one of the first houses in Texas to be constructed on a steel frame and to be equipped to take advantage of the first electrical power plant in the state. Severely damaged in the 1983 hurricane, the mansion has been restored and turned into a museum by the Mary Moody Northern Foundation at a cost of $10 million. The Victorian interior has been restored to reflect a period regarded as one of the highlights of the Moody's lives — Mary Moody's debut in 1911. One-hour guided tours leave approximately every half hour and include a short orientation film about the Moody family and the mansion. Restaurant and gift shop.

THE RAILROAD MUSEUM
123 Rosenberg (25th St.) at the west end of The Strand
765-5700
Open seven days 10–5, except Thanksgiving and Christmas
Adults $4, children $2, seniors $3
W +
Free parking at entrance on Santa Fe Place, one block west of Rosenberg

Located in the old Santa Fe railroad station, two of the museum's prize exhibits are the waiting room, set up with more than 30 life-sized sculptures of travelers frozen in a moment in time in the 1930s, and the dozens of old railroad locomotives and cars displayed on the station's tracks. The entrance to this five-acre world of railroading is through a replica of an 1875 depot complete with recordings of sounds you'd have heard at a station in that era. Inside, you'll progress through five rooms of imaginative sound and light shows that cover the island's history from its discovery to the present. There is also a working scale model of the Port of Galveston (that kids can pop their heads up in plastic bubbles in the middle of and watch the model trains run around them). Then on to the "waiting room." With its art deco splendor carefully restored, it is the setting for the "people's gallery" of life-sized travellers frozen in a moment in time in 1932. The authentically dressed models are made of ghostlike white plaster from original castings taken directly from live models in casual poses. Headphones located near each grouping let you eavesdrop on conversations that might have taken place back then. This modeling technique is carried over to the outside display of railway cars. As you wander through the cars you might see a child climbing into a berth, a gentleman shaving, or other "people" doing the ordinary things train travelers do. Among the collection of rail cars is the "Anacapa," a luxurious private car from the 1920s. Both Harry Truman and Dwight Eisenhower made trips on this car. The restaurant

"Dinner on the Diner" is located in several of the restored dining cars (See Restaurants), and this is the depot for the Texas Limited (See Side Trips) on its runs to Houston.

TEXAS SEAPORT MUSEUM AND *ELISSA*
Pier 21 off Water (Port Industrial Blvd.)
763-1877 or 763-0027
Open seven days 10–5, extended hours in summer
Admission
Museum W +, *Elissa* W deck only
Parking nearby

The story of the search for the *Elissa,* an iron-hulled sailing vessel, is almost as fascinating as a visit to the ship itself. The Galveston Historical Foundation wanted a ship to represent that city's role as an important nineteenth-century port. The long search ended in Piraeus, Greece, where they found the *Elissa,* a 150-foot square-rigged barque that had called at Galveston several times in the 1880s. She was a tramp merchant ship carrying a variety of cargoes to more than a hundred different ports from the day she was launched from a Scottish shipyard in 1877 until 1970 when she made her last voyage carrying a load of smuggled cigarettes. Towed back to Galveston, she was restored at a cost of more than $4.5 million. *Elissa* is the third oldest ship afloat, giving way only to England's *Cutty Sark* and the *Star of India* berthed in San Diego. Although well over a century old, she still is sailed at least once a year, which may make her the only operational nineteenth-century sailing ship in the world. A multi-media show in the 70-person theater in the new museum gives you a simulated experience of sailing this tall ship. The museum also features 3,500 square-feet of exhibits depicting the maritime history of Galveston. There is also a viewing platform where you can watch the activities in the working port. Gift shop.

HISTORIC PLACES

The Galveston Historical Foundation is responsible for Ashton Villa, the Texas Seaport Museum and *Elissa,* the Galveston County Historical Museum, the St. Joseph's Church Museum, and the 1839 Williams Home. Combination tickets are available at The Strand Visitors Center or any of the Foundation properties that offer a discount off the total of separate admissions for several of these historic places.

ASHTON VILLA
2328 Broadway
762-3933
Open seven days, except Thanksgiving and Christmas
Tours seven days June 1 through Labor Day: 10–5; rest of year: Monday–Friday 10–4, Saturday–Sunday 10–5
Adults $3, children $2
W first floor and multi-media show

Parking in rear

This gracious Italianate mansion was built in 1859 during Galveston's reign as the leading seaport of the Southwest. The three-story structure is furnished with possessions of the James M. Brown family, the original owners, and other authentic antiques of the mid-1800s. The hour long tour covers the dramatic history of Victorian Galveston and the role the Brown family and this home played in that era when it was a focal point for local society. It includes an audio-visual presentation on the 1900 hurricane and the gigantic projects of building the seawall and raising the elevation of the city. Also on view are artifacts illustrating the backstairs servants' life in the Villa that were uncovered in archaeological digs to the level of the house before the post-hurricane fill. The Villa is listed in the National Register of Historic Places. Gift shop.

THE BISHOP'S PALACE
1402 Broadway
762-2475
May 31 to Labor Day: tours Monday–Saturday 10–5, Sunday noon–5; rest of year: tours Wednesday–Monday 12–4, closed Tuesday
Adults $3.50, children over 13 $1.50, under 13 50¢
Parking on street

Beautiful examples of the attention to detail that was the hallmark of the old-time craftsmen abound in Galveston, but nowhere is there a greater concentration of them in one place than in the Bishop's Palace. This grandiose home is often considered the crowning achievement of the well-known Galveston architect Nicholas Clayton, whose work left a lasting stamp on the city. He designed the home for Colonel Walter Gresham, a local attorney who served as a representative to Congress. Completed in 1886, it cost an estimated quarter of a million dollars and took seven years to build. The American Institute of Architecture included this home on its list of the hundred most architecturally significant buildings in the United States, the only residence in Texas to receive this honor. It is also on the selected list of 14 structures included in the Archives of the Library of Congress as representative of early American architecture. Originally called the Gresham House, its name was changed in 1923 when the Catholic Diocese of Galveston-Houston purchased it for the bishop's residence, a role it still serves when the bishop is in Galveston. The tour lasts approximately one hour.

EAST END HISTORIC DISTRICT
11th St. to 19th St. between Mechanic (Ave. C) and Broadway (Ave. J)

The well-to-do of the city lived in this area from the late 1800s through the early 1900s. A few homes here date back as far as the 1850s, but most were built between 1875 and the turn of the century. The entire district is listed in the National Register of Historic Places and designated a National Historic Landmark. The best way to enjoy the architectural beauty of this 40-block district near The Strand is to stop first at the Convention and Visitors Bureau or The Strand Visitors Center and pick up a riding and walking tour map that designates the historically significant buildings and gives details on each. An audio-tape tour is also available for rent — $5 for cassette and portable tape player, $3 for cassette only to play in car recorder. Deposit or credit card required.

GARTEN VEREIN
Ave. O and Ursuline at 27th St.
766-2138
Free

German residents formed a social club and built this octagonal dancing pavilion in 1876. It was designed by the noted architect Nicholas Clayton. The site was donated to the city by Stanley Kempner in 1923 and is now a park named after him.

HISTORIC CHURCHES

There are a number of historic churches in Galveston, but the three oldest that are still actively used for religious services are St. Mary's Cathedral, Trinity Episcopal, and First Presbyterian. The oldest church in the city and the oldest Catholic cathedral in Texas is **St. Mary's**, at 2011 Church, which was built in 1848. It is listed in the National Register of Historic Places. **Trinity Episcopal**, Winnie and 22nd St., dating from 1855, is the oldest Episcopal church building in continuous use in Texas. **First Presbyterian Church** was started in 1872 and completed in 1889 replacing a small frame building that had served the congregation from the early 1840s.

POWHATAN HOUSE
35th St. and Ave. O
763-0077
Saturday–Sunday 1–5 (or by appointment for groups) except closed Christmas Week and major holidays
Adults $2, students/seniors $1

The core of this Greek Revival style house was built in 1847. It was moved from its original site to this location and remodeled in 1893. Once a family residence-hotel, it served as an academy in the 1850s, a military school during the Civil War, an orphanage in the 1880s, and later the residence of several prominent families until it was taken over and made the headquarters of the Galveston Garden Club in 1965. There are no formal tours, except for groups, but "picture books" in each room explain that room's architectural details, the furniture, and the appointments.

1839 SAMUEL MAY WILLIAMS HOME
3601 Ave. P (Bernardo de Galvez)
765-1839
Open seven days except Thanksgiving and Christmas. Monday–Saturday 10–5, Sunday noon–5, closes at 4 in off-season
Adults $2.50, children $1.50
W

One of the oldest houses on the island, it is an example of an early 1800s prefabricated house. It was built in Maine then carefully taken apart and shipped to Galveston where it was reassembled. It was the home of a relatively unknown man who worked behind the scenes in the War for Texas Independence. Samuel May Williams was the business mind behind Austin's colony, and when the Texans declared their independence, he used his financial savvy and some of his own money to buy the first ships for the Texas Navy, recruit volunteers for the army, and purchase supplies and munitions for both. A venture capitalist, he is often called the "Father of Texas Banking." The home comes to life through a multi-image show and audio presentations about Williams and his place in Texas history. There is an audio system that is activated as you enter each room so you can hear conversations that might have taken place in that room when the Williamses lived here.

SILK STOCKING HISTORIC DISTRICT
Along 24th St. and 25th St. between Ave. L and Ave. O

Formerly a political precinct of the city, its name supposedly came from the time when only the well-to-do ladies could afford silk stockings, and most of the ladies in the district were well-to-do. Excellent examples of nineteenth-century architecture in this district include the **Sweeny-Royston House** at 24th St. and Ave. L. Designed by popular architect, Nicholas Clayton, it was built in 1885 as a wedding gift from J. M. Brown, who built the Ashton Villa, to one of his daughters. It is listed in the National Register of Historic Places.

ST. JOSEPH'S CHURCH
2202 Avenue K
765-7834 Galveston Historical Foundation

This simple frame structure with rich Victorian Gothic interior was built by German immigrants in 1859 and served as a church until 1968. The massive doors, hand-carved altars and coffered ceilings reflect the skilled hands of its early parishioners. Now leased to the Galveston Historical Foundation, it is open for special events and by appointment for group tours.

STRAND HISTORIC DISTRICT
20th St. to 25th St. between Water (Ave. A) and Mechanic (Ave. C)

Many cities have lost the battle to save their downtown areas from urban rot. Galveston is one city that won that battle. Instead of tearing down the old buildings, the civic-minded have turned the very age of the buildings into a tourist attraction. The restoration of most of the iron-front buildings in just a six-block section of this avenue has led to a rebirth of the whole area. When King Cotton reigned supreme and Galveston was *the* port on the Texas coast, the Strand was rightly called the "Wall Street of the Southwest." No longer lined with banks, cotton tracers, and commercial houses, it is now a sightseers' and shoppers' delight with shops, restaurants for every taste and pocketbook, and interesting galleries. If you want to get the most from your visit, stop first at The Strand Visitors Center at 2016 Strand (See Tourist Services) and pick up a walking tour brochure.

OTHER POINTS OF INTEREST

DAVID TAYLOR'S CLASSICS
1918 Mechanic St.
765-6590
Open Tuesday–Sunday, noon–6
Admission
W
Parking on street

The "classics" here are more than a dozen vintage cars that include a 1931 Cadillac V8 roadster, a 1934 Ford roadster, and a 1955 Thunderbird convertible. Also on display are automotive memorabilia including old car manuals and parts and dealer signs.

GALVESTON ISLAND STATE PARK
West Beach, FM 3005 (Seawall Blvd.) near 13 Mile Rd.
737-1222
$2 per vehicle per day
W But not all areas

The 2,000 acres of this park cut across the narrow center of the island taking in a 1.6 mile beach on the Gulf on one side and the marshes on Galveston Bay on the other. Facilities are provided for surf-fishing on the beach and wade-fishing in the marshes, swimming, picnicking, camping (fee), birdwatching and nature walks. The Mary Moody Northern Amphitheater, which features outdoor musicals in summer, adjoins the park on the bay side. For information write: Route 1, Box 156A, Galveston 77551.

MOODY GARDENS
From 61st St., take Stewart Rd. (Ave. S)/Jones Dr. to Hope Blvd. then right. Next to airport
744-HOPE
Hours of various facilities differ, call
Admission to some facilities
W +

The Moody Foundation is putting some $120 million into a project to turn 142 acres of property on Offatts Bayou near the airport into a garden fantasyland. The project is scheduled to be completed in eight phases spread over a 20 year period, but several major phases are already finished and open to the public. These include **Hope Arena**, a 60,000-square-foot building used for special events (See Performing Arts); **Palm Beach**, built on Offatts Bayou with barge loads of white sand brought in from Florida (See Sports and Activities — Swimming); the **Garden of Life**, which is the first of the botanical complex's formal gardens; and **Seaside Safari**, where visitors can touch both domestic and exotic animals (See Kids' Stuff). Ongoing plans to be completed in the near future include construction of a one-acre greenhouse housing growing replicas of the major tropical forests of the world, a 3-D IMAX theatre, desert and Alpine conservatories, and the Historic Gardens of Man that will trace the evolution of man's use of landscaping and gardens from ancient Egypt to nineteenth-century England. Longer range plans include construction of a Wetlands Interpretive Center to expand the botanical complex, and a resort hotel. (A model of the completed project is on display both at the Gardens and in the Railroad Museum.) A continuing mission at the Gardens and the primary reason for building Hope Arena is to provide therapeutic programs for patients with head injuries. One such program involves therapeutic horseback riding.

NATIONAL MARINE FISHERIES CENTER
4700 Ave. U
766-3523
By appointment only

The full name is the National Marine Fisheries Service's Southeast Fisheries Center and one of its major missions is to help save the critically endangered Kemp's ridley sea turtle from extinction. (See Also South Padre Island — The Turtle Lady.) One way this is done is by raising many hundreds of these turtles from hatchlings each year and, when they reach the size of a small dinner plate, releasing them in the Gulf each May or June. At this lab you will see racks containing hundreds of individual plastic buckets that are perforated to permit seawater to flow through. In each bucket is a turtle. These turtles are kept separated because the Kemp's ridley is very aggressive. The best time to visit is Spring, before the yearly release. This working research lab is not staffed for tours, so call well in advance so they can work you in.

PELICAN ISLAND
Take 51st St. north over Pelican Island Causeway onto Seawolf Parkway

Largely a man-made island across from the Port of Galveston, it is the home of Seawolf Park (See Seawolf Park, following), Texas A&M University at Galveston (See Colleges and Universities), as well as shipyards and other industrial sites.

PORT OF GALVESTON
Along Water St. on north side of the island from 9th St. to 41st St.

Banana boats, shrimpers, grain carriers, and container ships, and now cruise ships — all use this port that claims to have the fastest access to the open seas of any major American port. It is also unique in being the only port in the nation where all facilities — from railroad switching to crating — are coordinated under one management. This results in a highly efficient system and has gained the port the title of "Port of Quickest Dispatch." For a better understanding of port operations, see the working scale model in the Railroad Museum (See Museums).

ROSENBERG LIBRARY
2310 Ave. I (Sealy), immediately behind Ashton Villa
763-8854
Monday–Thursday 9—9, Friday–Saturday 9–6
Free
W ramp in alley
Parking at Ave. H (Ball) and 24th St.

The Rosenberg is the oldest Texas public library in continuous operation and one of the oldest in the Southwest. In addition to being a city library, it also houses several art and history galleries, a rare book room, and the Galveston and Texas History Center. The extensive archives of the history center include Galveston newspapers starting in 1844 and a letter from Andrew Jackson to Sam Houston. Among the architectural drawings on file are those of Nicholas Clayton who designed approximately 120 buildings in the city between 1872 and the early 1900s, including the Bishop's Palace. Some of the special facilities have different open hours from the main library. Call for schedule. The library also offers adult and children's programs, lectures, and a free film series.

THE SEAWALL
Starting near the east end of the Island and stretching about ten miles west

In addition to its protective role, the seawall is also a monument to the spirit of the Galvestonians who say this city is worth saving at any cost. After the devastating hurricane of 1900, in which more than 6,000 died, residents decided to build the seawall and, using sand dredged from the bayous and waterways, raise the elevation of the entire city. This project took eight years, but it worked and is still working. The first seawall was less than four miles long, but it has been gradually lengthened over the years and now protects about one third of the island from the Gulf's surf. One of the engineers who worked on the original design was Brigadier General Henry M. Roberts, who is more famous for his Robert's Rules of Order. The solid concrete wall was constructed to the height of 17 feet above mean low tide. Seawall Blvd., behind it, is one of the island's best known streets and is lined with hotels, motels, restaurants, and shops. The seawall also claims the title of the world's longest continuous sidewalk, which makes it great for strolling, jogging, bicycling, skateboarding, and roller skating.

SEAWOLF PARK
Take 51st St. causeway to Pelican Island, continue on approximately two miles
744-5738
Open seven days dawn to dusk
Parking $2; fishing: adults $2, children $1; tour of ships: adults $2,

children $1
W + except for ship tour

Fishing from the rocks or the 380-foot fishing pier, an imaginative children's playground, picnic areas, a snack bar, an observation deck, and two World War II combat ships to explore — all are available in this park. One of the ships you can climb all over is the *USS Cavalla,* a submarine that includes a Japanese aircraft carrier among its kills. The other is the destroyer escort the *USS Stewart,* which had the unusual distinction of sailing under both the U.S. and Japanese flags in World War II. Originally a U.S. ship, the navy had attempted to scuttle her to prevent capture by the Japanese. However, the Japanese refloated and re-outfitted her and sent her out as one of their own. Reports of an enemy ship that "looks like one of ours" were explained when the *Stewart* was found in Japan at the end of the war. There's a great view from the upper level of the three-level pavilion. From there you can see the Port of Galveston, the University of Texas Medical Branch, the many ships plying the Houston Ship Channel, the Bolivar Ferry on its route from Point Bolivar to its landing on Galveston Island, and the Texas City Dike. You can also see the hulk of the *Selma,* a World War I experimental concrete ship that sank in shallow water.

UNIVERSITY OF TEXAS MEDICAL BRANCH COMPLEX
Between Strand and Market from about 4th St. (Holiday) to 14th St.

Legend has it that the pirate Jean Lafitte had his headquarters where this medical complex stands today. And if there's any consistency in the stories and legends about pirates it is that they always buried their loot. That's why treasure hunters today would jump at the chance to dig under here. But even if Lafitte did bury a fortune, the real treasure is in these buildings. It's found in the dedicated labors of the 9,000 health professionals who work in the complex of hospitals and graduate institutions built around the University of Texas Medical Branch (See Colleges and Universities). Here they provide health care not only to Galvestonians, but, at times, to patients from all over the world. The medical complex includes John Sealy Hospital, Shriners Burn Institute, Jennie Sealy Hospital, Mary Moody Northern Pavilion, R. Waverly Smith Pavilion, St. Mary's Hospital, Ambulatory Care Center, Child Health Center, and the Texas Department of Corrections Hospital. The University of Texas Medical Branch operates a Visitor Information Center at 6th St. and Market.

SPORTS AND ACTIVITIES

Bicycling

Bicycling along the seawall and through the quiet streets of the historic districts are popular activities. Rental bicycles are available at several shops along the seawall. You can also rent four-wheel surreys, but these are banned on the seawall because too many visitors drove them over the edge.

Birdwatching

Galveston is noted for the wide variety of species observed including black shouldered kits, American oystercatchers, roseate spoonbills, herons, whitewing doves, and white and brown pelicans. Nearby Bolivar Flats is famous for waders and shorebirds including flocks of avocets. Galveston Island State Park has observation points for birdwatchers (See Other Points of Interest).

Boating

You can boat in Galveston Bay, the bayous, or the Gulf. Boat rental and charter firms, marinas, and public and commercial boat ramps are listed in the phone book, or contact the Convention and Visitors Bureau (See Tourist Services) for a list of boat ramps and other boating information.

Fishing

Any type of saltwater fishing you want, Galveston has it. There's the bay, the piers, the jetties, the surf, and offshore in the Gulf. Some 52 varieties of saltwater fish populate the warm waters along and offshore from the island. Red snapper, ling, dolphin, and jackfish make up the principal offshore species. Inshore anglers are most likely to catch speckled trout, redfish, pompano, whiting, flounder, and catfish. A number of charter and party boats operate daily from the docks around Pier 19 and the Yacht Basin. Charter boats charge by the boat. Party boats prices depend on whether it's a full or half-day trip, bay or deep-sea, and run from $10 to $75. Several commercial piers and numerous rock groin piers extend well into the Gulf from the beachfront. Most commercial piers charge about $2, are lighted for night fishing, and have rental tackle and bait available. For additional information contact the Convention and Visitors Bureau (See Tourist Services).

Golf

GALVESTON ISLAND MUNICIPAL GOLF COURSE
1700 Sydnor Lane, west of airport
744-2366

Eighteen-hole course. Green fees: weekdays $12, weekends $15.

Horseback Riding

There are two riding stables near each other on West Beach. You can ride on sections of the beach for about $10 an hour.

GULFSTREAM STABLES
FM 3005 at 8 Mile Rd.
744-1004

SANDY HOOF STABLES
FM 3005 at 7½ Mile Rd.
740-3481

Roller Skating

Rental skates are available at several shops along Seawall Blvd. — and the seawall is famous as one of the world's longest sidewalks.

Scuba Diving

Many good spots are near the offshore oil rigs that sit from one to fifty miles out in the Gulf. The watery wonderland of the live coral reef called the Flower Gardens is 110 miles offshore. For information contact any of the dive shops listed in the phone book.

Swimming

There are 32 miles of Gulf beaches on Galveston Island, and every mile is public. Lifeguards are provided at designated areas by The Galveston County Sheriff's Department Beach Patrol. There is an admission charge at some parks. Restrooms and other facilities are available at the following parks:
R. A. Apffel Beach Park, Seawall and Boddecker (extreme eastern end of island), 763-0166. Facilities include an 11,000 square foot recreation center.
Stewart Beach Park, Seawall near Broadway, 765-5023 (See Kids' Stuff). Pavilion and amusement park.
Galveston County Beach Pocket Parks:
Beach Park #1, FM3005 at 7½ Mile Rd.
Beach Park #2, FM 3005 at 9½Mile Rd.
Beach Park #3, FM 3005 at 11 Mile Rd.
Galveston Island State Park, Fm 3005 (Seawall Blvd.) at 13 Mile Rd. (See Other Points of Interest)

And if the Gulf doesn't satisfy you, you can go to the man-made Palm Beach at Moody Gardens on Offatts Bayou (from 61st St., take Stewart Rd.(Ave. S) and Jones Dr. to Hope Blvd., then right). White sand from Orlando, Florida was brought in by ocean barges for this beach that will accommodate about 3,000. Palm Beach has two huge freshwater lagoons complete with a 12 foot waterfall and white sand bottoms, lockers, a jogging trail, and a picnic area. Open daily in summer and weekends in spring and fall. Admission: Adults $3.50, children $2, seniors over 65 and children under 3 free. Free parking and free tram ride to the main entrance. All facilities are designed and equipped for the handicapped.

Tennis

Free, no-reservation lighted courts are available at:
Lasker Park, Ave. Q and 43rd St.
Menard Park, Seawall and 27th St.
Schreiber Park, 81st St. and Beluche

Water-skiing and Windsurfing

Water-skiers and windsurfers seem to prefer the bay and Offatts Bayou. For information on rentals, lessons, and tows see the listings in the phone book or contact the Convention and Visitors Bureau (See Tourist Services).

COLLEGES AND UNIVERSITIES

GALVESTON COLLEGE
Administration: 4015 Ave. Q; Fort Crockett Campus: 5001 Ave. U (take 53rd St. north from Seawall to Ave. U)
763-6551
W Variable

This community college offers a wide variety of academic and vocational/technical programs to its more than 2,400 students. Visitors are welcome at musical concerts and at drama productions given in the Upper Deck Theatre, a 150-seat arena theater on the third floor of the Fort Crockett building. There are usually four or five productions during the October-May season, including some dinner theater performances at the San Luis Hotel. For information and reservations call 744-9661.

TEXAS A&M UNIVERSITY AT GALVESTON
Mitchell Campus: take 51st St. causeway north to Pelican Island, campus on right; Fort Crockett campus: Ave. U and 51st St., next to Galveston College campus
740-4400
W Variable

This branch of A&M trains students in marine-oriented programs as well as officers for the U.S. Merchant Marine. Its academic programs include Marine Biology, Marine Sciences, Marine Transportation, Marine Engineering, Marine Fisheries, Maritime Systems Engineering and Maritime Administration. The biggest attraction for visitors is the training ship *Texas Clipper*. Built in World War II as a troop carrier, she was later converted to a cruise liner. Since 1965 the ship has served as a dormitory and floating classroom in winter, and the summer training ship for the maritime cadets at the school who are required to complete three cruises in preparation for Merchant Marine licensing. The ship is usually in port from early September to late April and visitors are welcome aboard on most weekend afternoons. For information, contact the Public Information Office at 740-4559.

THE UNIVERSITY OF TEXAS MEDICAL BRANCH (UTMB)
Between Strand and Market from 4th St. to 14th St. Visitor Information Center at 6th St. and Market
761-1111
W Variable

Starting with a class of 23 in 1891, UTMB now has about 2,100 students enrolled in its four schools: School of Medicine, School of Nursing, School of Biomedical Sciences, and School of Allied Health Sciences. The largest, as well as the oldest, medical school in the state, it offers a full spectrum of health care services in its seven hospitals and 85 specialty and sub-specialty outpatient clinics. The major architectural attraction on the campus is another structure designed by Nicholas Clayton, the **Ashbel Smith Building** at 916 Strand. Fondly called "Old Red," for its red sandstone exterior, it was completed in 1890. Two places of special interest in the building are the Hall of Medicine, which contains 12 statutes of outstanding individuals in the history of medicine, and the old surgical amphitheater. "Old Red" is listed in the National Register of Historic Places. A visit to this building is included in the UTMB campus tours offered weekdays between the hours of 9 and 4.

PERFORMING ARTS

GALVESTON ISLAND OUTDOOR MUSICALS
Mary Moody Northern Amphitheatre, Galveston Island State Park, FM 3005 (Seawall Blvd.) at 13 Mile Rd.
737-1744
Usually end of June to late–August, Monday–Saturday at 8 p.m.
Adults $10-$22, discounts available for groups of 20 or more
W Call ahead

This 1,800-seat outdoor theater is the setting for the revivals of big and classic Broadway musicals that are especially appropriate for the large outdoor stage like "The Sound of Music" and "The Music Man." The amphitheatre restaurant, decorated with theater memorabilia, is open before the show.

THE 1894 GRAND OPERA HOUSE
2020 Post Office (Ave. E) near 21st St.
765-1894
AE, MC, V
W +

This grand old building has been painstakingly restored so it is now as close in design as possible to the original house where Sarah Bernhardt, Paderewski, Anna Pavlova, George Burns and Gracie Allen and other greats performed. It features double curved balconies and no seat is further than 70 feet from the stage. Everything from ballet and opera to rock and pop concerts and classic films are performed here now. **The Galveston Symphony** performs most of its five concerts a year in the Opera House. Open Monday-Saturday 9-5 and Sunday noon to 5 for self-guided tours (Admission). Conducted tours can be arranged for groups. Parking is a slight problem during major production. It's first come, first park on the street, or there is a pay garage at 21st St. and Market (Ave. D).

HOPE ARENA AT MOODY GARDENS
1812 Hope Blvd. From 61st St. take Stewart Rd. (Ave. S)/Jones Dr. to Hope Blvd., then right
740-HOPE
W +

This 60,000-square-foot facility includes a 30,000-square-foot clear span arena area seating up to 3,000. It plays host to concerts, rodeos, circuses, sports events, expositions, and agricultural, trade, and horse shows. Parking is free and there are trams for getting from the parking lot to the arena and other facilities in Moody Gardens (See Other Points of Interest). The primary purpose of the facility is to house a program aiding victims of head injuries through therapeutic horseback riding.

STRAND STREET THEATRE
2317 Ship Mechanic Row (Ave. C)
763-4591
Admission varies by performance
W

Galveston's only year-round professional repertory company produces about seven shows a year in this intimate playhouse that seats 110. Most are dramas and comedies, with an occasional musical. Performances are usually Thursday through Saturday at 8 and Sunday matinee.

UPPER DECK THEATRE

See Colleges and Universities — Galveston College.

SHOPPING

BASTIEN'S
2317 Strand
765-9394

If your appreciation of the beauty of stained glass is heightened after visiting the Bishop's Palace or some other Victorian home in Galveston, this is the place to go. Usually there are only small, decorative stained glass pieces on display among the giftware of crystal, lace, and potpourri, but larger pieces can be made to order. The studio is in the rear and sometimes you can watch the artists at work through the half door.

DON ROUSE'S WILDLIFE GALLERY
2314 Strand
763-1391
W

They claim this is Texas' largest selection of wildlife art and gifts, and they may be right. The favorite subjects seem to be ducks and other waterfowl, which appear on everything from doormats to collector plates to jewelry to duck stamp prints. The gallery features signed and numbered prints by well-known wildlife artists.

GALVEZ MALL
6402 Broadway at 61st St.
744-5241
W

This is Galveston's largest mall. It offers the usual collection of specialty shops, fast food shops, a cafeteria, and a cinema all anchored by Beall's, Eiband's, the city's grand lady of department stores, and Sears.

HENDLEY MARKET
2010 Strand
762-2610
W

This next-door neighbor of The Strand Visitors Center is worth a drop-in. Housed in one of the city's oldest commercial buildings, the shop offers a delightfully eclectic collection of Victorian clothing (a place to go for authentic costumes for the annual celebration of "Dickens on the Strand"), tintypes, old photos, South American folk art, Mexican toys, antiques, and old maps, books, and magazines.

NORMA'S
6019 Stewart Rd. near 61st St.
744-5268

Surroundings of antiques, flowering plants, and gentle lighting help make shopping at this woman's fashion shop a pleasant experience. Norma's has designer clothes and famous labels in everything from sports clothes to formal wear. Branch at the Tremont House (See Accommodations).

THE OLD PEANUT BUTTER WAREHOUSE
100 20th St., just north of The Strand
762-8358
W Variable

You can still get peanut butter here, in the Peanut Pantry, but most of the items in this 22,000-square-foot assemblage of shops are antiques, collectibles, gifts, and souvenirs.

KIDS' STUFF

BOLIVAR FERRY

See Side Trips.

SEAWOLF PARK

See Other Points of Interest.

STEWART BEACH PARK
Seawall at Broadway
765-5023
W Variable

The most developed of the county's beach parks, this is a miniature Coney Island. Attractions include water slides, bumper cars and bumper boats, miniature golf, go-karts, pavilion with bathhouse, restaurant, and concessions. The amusement area is open seven days from 9 to 8:30 in summer and 9 to dusk in winter, and closed from November to mid-February. Cost of rides vary. Parking $5.

SEASIDE SAFARI
Moody Gardens, from 61st St., take Stewart Rd. (Ave. S)/Jones Dr. to Hope Blvd. then right. Next to airport
744-PETT
$1.50
W +
Free parking

Although designed to provide animal-contact therapy to patients and educational programs, this part of Moody Gardens is much like a first class petting zoo open to the public. Safari guides lead tours that include a multi-media show in the Fauna Gallery, viewing of animals in the Garden Parlour, and experiencing them in the Fantasy and Encounter Gardens. From May-August Seaside Safari opens Tuesday-Friday at 9, Saturday-Sunday at 10, and Monday at 1. The last tour every day starts at 5 p.m. September-April. It opens Tuesday-Saturday at 9 and Sunday-Monday at 1, with the last tour again at 5 p.m.

SPACE CENTER HOUSTON

See Side Trips.

WATER SLIDES

In addition to the **Sky Rapids** slide at Stewart Beach Park (See Stewart Beach), there is also the **Water Coaster** at 215 Seawall (762-6022) and **Jungle Surf** at Seawall and 92nd St.(744-4737). Prices vary.

SIDE TRIPS

BOLIVAR PENINSULA

This peninsula is a narrow strip sandwiched between the Gulf and East Galveston Bay for about 30 miles from Port Bolivar, across the Houston Ship Channel from Galveston, to High Island. To reach it, take the free Bolivar Ferry from the north end of Ferry Rd. in Galveston. The only road on the peninsula is Texas 87 that actually goes all the way along the coast from Port Bolivar to Sabine Pass, but because it is just behind an eroding beach, it's not always open past High Island. At High Island Texas 87 intersects with Texas 124 that goes north, past the Anahuac Wildlife Refuge, to Winnie at I-10. The four small towns on the peninsula, made up mainly of beach houses, are Crystal Beach,

Gilcrist, High Island, and Port Bolivar. Fishing and other beach activities are the main things going on here.

Bolivar Peninsula Chamber of Commerce
P.O. Box 1170, Crystal Beach, 77650
(409) 684-5940

Bolivar Ferry North end of Ferry Rd. (Texas 87)
763-2386
Free
W

You might call this the Texas Navy in action. The Texas Department of Highways and Public Transportation operates this fleet of ferries providing the only direct link between Galveston and the Bolivar Peninsula. The ferries leave about every 20 minutes offering 24-hour service in almost anything short of a hurricane. The trip takes about 15 minutes each way, just long enough to get out of your car and enjoy an excellent view of Galveston, the five-mile dike jutting out from Texas City, and the variety of large ships and small boats sailing the waters of the Houston Ship Channel through Bolivar Roads. You don't need a car to ride. On nice days there are always some people who walk on board and make the free round-trip just for the seabreeze and the view and to feed the seagulls and other birds that follow the boats.

Bolivar Lighthouse
Port Bolivar, Texas 87 approximately one mile east of the ferry landing

The first lighthouse, built here in 1852, was made of cast iron, so the Confederates dismantled it for the metal during the Civil War. The present tower was completed in 1872 and kept in service until 1933. In addition to the lives it may have saved by guiding ships at sea, it also served as a storm shelter and saved many from floods during several hurricanes. You can look at it from the road, but it's now on private property and no visitors are allowed.

Ft. Travis Seashore Park
Port Bolivar, Texas 87 approximately one mile east of the ferry landing
Admission
W Variable

A county park set on 66 acres of grass covering four World War I coast artillery gun emplacements it offers a beach, restrooms, showers, playground, cabanas, and tent camping.

CLEAR LAKE AREA

(This listing covers only a sampling of the highlights of this area that includes nine small cities around Clear Lake and on Galveston Bay. For a fuller account of Clear Lake including history, restaurants, accommodations, etc., see *The Texas Monthly Guidebook: Texas.)*

Clear Lake Area Convention and Visitors Bureau
1201 NASA Rd. 1 (Houston 77058-3391). Take NASA Rd. 1 exit off I-45 and go east
488-7676
Monday–Friday 8:30–5
W

If this office in the Chamber of Commerce building is closed, a free Visitors' Guide Map is available at all local hotel/motel registration desks.

Armand Bayou Nature Center
8600 Bay Area Blvd. behind the Johnson Space Center near Red Bluff Rd. (P.O. Box 58828, Houston 77258). Take Bay Area Blvd. exit off I-45 and go east to Center
474-2551
Seven days 9–5. Closed major holidays
Monday (except holidays) free, rest of week: Adults $2.50, children (5–17) $2
W Variable

Much of the 1,800 acres is wilderness on a bayou preserved in its natural state for nature study. You can explore on hiking trails or rented canoe. Facilities include an Interpretive Center with hands-on exhibits, a reproduction of a Charruco Indian Village, and the Jimmy Martyn Farm, a working farm restored to its turn-of-the-century condition. Informal demonstrations are given every Saturday and Sunday afternoons on topics such as bird and wildflower identification, quilting, butter churning, and woodworking. There are also trail hikes and farm tours on Saturday and Sunday. Call for schedule.

Bayou Wildlife Park
Take I-45 north about 20 miles to FM 517, then west (left) about six miles (P.O.Box 808, Rt 6, Alvin 77511)
337-6376
April–October: Seven days 10–6; November–March: Tuesday–Sunday 10–4, Closed Monday. Closed Christmas and New Year's Day
Adults $7, children (3-12) $5
W Variable

A two and a half-mile narrated tram ride takes you over 86 acres of a natural setting for a variety of animals and birds including camels, giraffes, ostriches, and a rhino. Some of the animals will come up to the tram for feeding. Subject to closing during bad weather, so call first.

Clear Lake Queen
NASA Rd. 1 at Clear Lake Park. Take NASA Rd. 1 exit off I-45 and go east to the lake
333-3334
Tours April–December: weekends and holidays, one-hour narrated tours starting at 1 p.m. with last tour at 4 p.m.
Adults $5, children (under 12) $3
W Lower deck only

The *Queen* is a three-deck paddlewheel boat built from an adaptation of plans from one of America's premier river boat builders of the 1800s. Unlike some other paddlewheel boat reproductions, she is actually propelled by the paddles, not propellers. A Jazz Dinner Dance Cruise is offered on Saturday nights in season. They last about three-hours, include dinner and dancing, champagne, beer and wine, and cost about $35 (plus tax) per person. Reservations required for the dinner cruises.

Space Center Houston
Inside main gate of Johnson Space Center on NASA Rd. 1. From 1-45 take NASA Rd. 1 exit and go about three miles east to main gate
W +

They may shoot the astronauts into space in Florida, but this is where you'll find the brains of the Manned Space Flight Program. It's here, at the Johnson Space Center, that our space explorers are trained, the design and fabrication of the manned spacecraft is managed, and manned space flights are controlled from after-launch to landing. This visitors center, scheduled to open in the fall of 1991, will open up more of the inner working of NASA and the Johnson Space Center than ever seen by the public before.

The goal is to make you more aware of the challenges of space flight and offer the opportunity to touch, feel, and be inspired by man's explorations of space. To do this, the Manned Space Flight Education Foundation, the not-for-profit organization funding the construction of Space Center Houston, called in Walt Disney Imagineering, the firm that designed Disney World and the Epcot Center, to design this 140,000-square-foot structure that is expected to cost well over $60 million when completed. The Visitors' Center is the jumping off place for a tour by tram to the major facilities of the Johnson Space Center, including some buildings never opened to public tours before. On the tour you'll visit Mission Control and a number of astronaut training areas. Among the many activities at the Visitors' Center itself is an up-to-the-minute briefing at the Mission Status Center on that day's activities in space, including shuttle or other flights if you are there when any of these are taking place. There are also many items designed to give you a hands-on feel of being an astronaut, from actual astronaut training devices to a simulator that lets you try your hand at landing the huge space shuttle. And in the theater, featuring a large-screen 70 mm format, you'll feel like you're right in the midst of the spectacular films of space exploration.

The Johnson Space Center attracts more than one million visitors a year; it is expected that Space Center Houston will draw at least twice that number.

Until Space Center Houston opens, you'll still be able to take the free, but limited, self-guided tour of the Johnson Space Center which is open 9-4 daily.

DAY CRUISES

The 504-foot *Pride of Mississippi*, sailing from Pier 21, is listed as the world's largest day-cruiser carrying up to 1,000 passengers. It also offers live entertainment, dancing, a buffet dinner, and once it reaches international waters off the coast, Las Vegas-style gambling. You can also swim in one of the two swimming pools, and participate in activities like aerobics and table tennis. Staterooms are available both for the day cruises and for two-day cruises that it runs periodically. For schedule, prices, and reservations call 800-284-5780. Information on these ships is also available from the Galveston Island Convention and Visitors Bureau (See Tourist Services).

HOUSTON

The largest city in the state and the fourth largest in the nation, Houston is just about an hour's drive north of Galveston on I-45. For details on what to see, where to stay, and where to eat in this sprawling city, see *The Texas Monthly Guidebook: Texas* or *The Texas Monthly Guidebook: Houston.*

TEXAS CITY and LA MARQUE

(These two cities are just north of Galveston off I-45. This listing covers only a few highlights of this area. For a fuller account of Texas City and La Marque including history, restaurants, accommodations, etc., see *The Texas Monthly Guidebook: Texas.*)

Greater Texas City-La Marque Chamber of Commerce
419 E. F. Lowry Expressway (FM 1764) just west of the College of the Mainland, (P.O. Box 3330, 77592-3330). Take FM 1764 off I-45 and go east
(409) 935-1408
W

Texas City Dike
From I-45 take E. F. Lowry Expressway/FM 1764 exit and go east to end at Bay St., then right to red light and left onto the Dike
Open at all times
W Variable

When Texas City says the dike projects five miles into Galveston Bay, that's not hype. They also claim it is the world's largest fishing pier because this is a wide dike you can drive on, not just a walk-on jetty. Along the dike are boat launching sites, bait shops, ship stores, two municipal fishing piers, and a marina. On the drive expect to see ocean-going ships on the Houston Ship Channel and Galveston Bay, and sailboats and other pleasure craft as well as shrimpers. The dike road is only two-lane so traffic can crawl on a summer weekend.

TEXAS LIMITED EXCURSION TRAIN TO HOUSTON
Departs Galveston Railroad Museum (Strand and Rosenberg)
765-5700 or in Houston (713) 522-9090
Thursday–Sunday*
Adults roundtrip $25-$40, children $18-$28
Free parking

Five refurbished passenger cars from the 1930s, '40s, and '50s make up this train that makes its run between the Railroad Museum and Houston's AMTRAK station at 902 Washington Avenue near the downtown post office. If you drove on the high-speed I-45, it would take you about an hour to make the trip while this train takes about 2 hours and 15 minutes. But speed isn't why you ride these rails — the reason is a nostalgic trip back in time to when first class trains like this were the way to travel in America. Tickets may be purchased through TICKETRON outlets.

ANNUAL EVENTS

February

MARDI GRAS FESTIVAL
Various locations around the city
Approximately two weeks in February ending the Sunday before Ash Wednesday
763-4311 (Convention and Visitors Bureau)
Free. Admission to some events
W Variable

It's not as big as the New Orleans bash *yet,* but it's growing and already draws over 200,000 spectators and participants. The two weeks of pre-Lenten festivities include 10 parades, masked balls, art exhibits, pageants, costume contests, and entertainment. The biggest night is the final Saturday before Ash Wednesday when the Grand Night Momus Parade takes place from Seawall Blvd. to the Strand, and a series of costumed and masked balls are held.

March

GALVESTON FILM FESTIVAL
Various locations including the Arts Center and Opera House
763-2403
About four days near end of March
Admission to most events
W Variable

Films and seminars, parties and celebrity receptions are a major part of this festival that honors the Texas film industry.

April

BLESSING OF THE FLEET
Pier 21
763-4311 (Convention and Visitors Bureau)
Usually third weekend in April
Free. Admission to some events
W Variable

Shrimp Boats A'Comin' — and berthing here. This festival marks both the importance of the shrimpers' Mosquito Fleet to Galveston and the good times the shrimpers have when ashore. Saturday activities include a Gumbo Cookoff, live entertainment, a "Light Up the Night Parade" and a dockside dance that night. The colorful Blessing of the Fleet takes place on Sunday with more live entertainment before and after the ceremony.

May

HISTORIC HOMES TOURS
765-7834 (Galveston Historical Foundation)
Two weekends early in month
$14 (Advance sale tickets $12)
W Variable

Seven or eight restored nineteenth-century homes are usually on each tour. These are private homes not normally open to the public. You must get from home to home on your own, but at each home you are given a guided tour. Related special events and activities are either free or discounted to ticket holders.

November

GALVESTON ISLAND JAZZ FESTIVAL
Various locations
763-1894 or 763-7080
Friday–Sunday in mid month
Most day activities free. Night performances admission varies with performer
W Variable

Jazz greats, like Dizzy Gillespie, entertain during this three day festival. Free concerts are put on in Old Galveston Square on The Strand and other outdoor locations. Other shows (admission) are held at places like the 1894 Grand Opera House and on the paddlewheeler *The Colonel*. Many of the larger hotels/motels feature jazz performances in their lounges.

December

DICKENS ON THE STRAND
Seventeen block area in Strand Historic District
765-7834 (Galveston Historical Foundation)
Usually first Saturday–Sunday in month
Adults $6, children (over 6) $3 (lower prices for advance sale tickets)
W Variable

A pre-Christmas festival in which The Strand area is turned into an authentic re-creation of The Strand in London just as it was during the nineteenth-century. There are English bobbies chasing pickpockets, street performers and street vendors, two parades a day, strolling carolers, and Scrooge and other characters from Dickens's stories wandering through the crowd. Free entertainment is provided almost continuously on seven stages scattered throughout the area. The streets are blocked off to car traffic and only horse-drawn vehicles, other "beasts of burden" and bicycles are allowed. The thousands of volunteers who work on the festival wear period costumes and you can get in free if you wear a Victorian costume — and there are prizes for the best. The Dickens Handbell Festival, held Saturday evening near The Strand Visitors Center, is reportedly the world's largest outdoor handbell event.

OFFBEAT

COLONEL BUBBIE'S STRAND SURPLUS SENTER
2202 Strand
762-7397
Monday–Saturday 10–4 "usually"

This warehouse-type building, designed by Nicholas Clayton (who else?), is stacked with surplus from the armed forces of more than 50 different countries. REAL military surplus — no fakes here — with bargains like wool sweaters from the British Navy, shorts from the German Army, and Danish Army sheepskin hats. Few countries skimp on quality in military uniforms, so all-wool and 100 percent cotton items abound. There's not much space inside, the packed aisles are narrow and twisting, but a visit to Colonel Bubbie's bonanza is an experience every bargain shopper should have.

RESTAURANTS

($ = under $7, $$ = $7 to $17, $$$ = $17 to $25, $$$$ = over $25 for one person excluding drinks, tax, and tip.)

Putting on the Ritz

THE MERCHANT PRINCE
Tremont House, 2300 Ship's Mechanic Row
763-0300
Breakfast and lunch seven days, dinner Wednesday–Sunday
$$-$$$$
Cr.

The light that falls from the glass ceiling, 65-feet above, casts a warm glow over the dining room with tables surrounding a fountain. The tasteful decor and elegance carries over to the mostly continental menu that offers gourmet choices from pasta to seafood. Valet parking. Bar.

THE WENTLETRAP
2301 Strand at Tremont
765-5545

Lunch and dinner Monday–Saturday, Sunday brunch
Reservations suggested for dinner on weekends
$$$-$$$$
Cr.
W

There is a bright and airy feeling to the restored 1871 building that is the home of this restaurant. The staff is well-trained and attentive and the continental menu is equal to the ambiance. Selections vary by season, but among the seafood choices you are likely to find *Trout Capucine* (sauteed with mushrooms, shrimp and capers). Other choices include *Veal Oscar* (topped with king crab and hollandaise) and rack of lamb. Valet parking. Jackets required for men at dinner. Bar.

Dinner for Two

DINNER ON THE DINER
Track #1, The Railroad Museum, Rosenberg (25th St.) at the The Strand
763-4759
Lunch and dinner Monday–Saturday, Sunday brunch
Reservations suggested
$$$-$$$$
Cr.
W

This is dining as it was — or we'd like to think it was — on the luxurious super trains that crossed our country in the 1940s and 1950s. Even the recipes served in these restored dining cars are adapted from recipes used on those trains and include entrées of beef, veal, seafood, fresh water fish, quail, and desserts like Rocky Railroad Cheesecake. Meals are fixed price, going from about $10 for lunch to around $25 for dinner. Free parking at museum lot at entrance on Santa Fe Place, one block west of Rosenberg, valet parking at night. To get in without paying admission when the museum is open, just tell the ticket office you're going to the diner. Beer and wine.

Continental

CAFE TORREFIE
2126 Strand
763-9088
Lunch and dinner Monday–Saturday
$$-$$$
AE, MC, V
W Call ahead

Quiche, crepes, *coq au vin*, seafood, steaks — they're all on the menu at this restaurant named after a brand of Belgian coffee. Definitely not continental cuisine, but a dish for the true coastal Texan, is Jalapeno Shrimp — jumbo shrimp stuffed with cheddar cheese and jalapeno and deep fried. The wine cellar was once the vault of a wholesale grocery business. Bar.

Italian

NASH D'AMICO'S PASTA AND CLAM BAR
2328 Strand
763-6500
Lunch and dinner seven days
$$
AE, MC, V

What the name doesn't say is that the pasta, which is the basic at this restaurant, is homemade. It comes in a variety of forms from *fettucine* to *ravioli* and combined with seafood, chicken, or veal to make up entrees that offer the taste of Italy. The setting was once a staid, old bank building but now is decorated in keeping with the space-age. Bar.

Mexican

APACHE TORTILLA FACTORY AND MEXICAN FOOD
511 20th St. near Post Office (Ave E)
765-5646
Breakfast, lunch, and dinner Tuesday–Saturday, breakfast and lunch only Sunday, closed Monday
$
No Cr.
W

A few bullfight posters and Mexican records on the jukebox are all the atmosphere you get here. But menu items like a hearty lunch special of *papas con carne* or a breakfast of eggs and *chorizo* make up for that. Beer.

EL NAPALITO
614 42nd St. between Church (Ave F) and Winnie (Ave. G). Take Broadway to 41st St., then right on 41st, left on Winnie and right on 42nd St.
763-9815
Breakfast and lunch Tuesday-Sunday, closed Monday
$
No Cr.
W

Another cafe where the attention is given to the food not the decor. Definitely not in the tourist area, and since 42nd St. is not a through street, a little hard to find, but if you are a Tex-Mex devotee, you'll welcome the Martinez family cooking of classics like *huevos rancheros* for breakfast or chicken *mole* or *chile relenno* for lunch. If you want a taste of just about everything on the menu, try a Mixed Plate. Beer and wine coolers.

Seafood

BENNO'S ON THE BEACH
200 Seawall
762-4621
Lunch and dinner seven days
$-$$
MC, V
W

It may look like a fast food place, but the emphasis here is definitely on feed not speed. One of the best buys on the beachfront is their boiled shrimp served with seasoned corn. Almost everything is done with a touch of Cajun, but if you want more than just a touch of that spicy cuisine try the Peppered Shrimp or Cajun Crabs. Other items on the short menu include oyster loaf, shrimp loaf, or fish loaf, and Gumbo. Beer.

CAPTAIN JACK'S SEAFOOD RESTAURANT
1700 Seawall
762-5950
Lunch and dinner seven days
$$
CR.
W

Located on the first floor of the old Seawall Hotel, this restaurant offers a Gulf view and a variety of seafood entrées including house specialties that feature several versions of snapper, like *Snapper Amandine,* broiled and topped with lump crabmeat Amandine; and *Snapper St. Thomas,* grilled and topped with sauteed tomatoes, mushrooms, onions, bell peppers, shrimp, and crabmeat. Chicken and steaks are also available, and the selections on the lunch menu are marked with hearts when they are low in fat, calories, and sodium. Bar.

CHRISTIE'S BEACHCOMBER
Stewart Beach, Seawall and 4th St.
762-8648
Lunch and dinner seven days
$$
MC, V
W

Two things that set this restaurant apart are its location right on the beach and its luncheon buffet which has long been a favorite of both locals and visitors making return trips to the island. Fresh Gulf seafood is a natural choice in the evening when you can sit inside or out and watch the waters from which your meal came. Bar.

CLARY'S
8509 Teichman, across from the *Galveston Daily News.* Take Teichman exit off I-45

740-0771
Lunch and dinner Monday–Friday, dinner only Saturday, closed Sunday and last two weeks in November
Reservations suggested
$$-$$$
MC, V
W call ahead

There's a Cajun touch to many of the dishes, like *Shrimp au Seasoned,* but the spices are so expertly handled that it's more of a pleasant hint than the more common overpowering spicy taste. This is one of the few restaurants on the coast — or in the State — that offers you a choice between broiled and grilled instead of fried on its seafood platter. That platter, by the way, is a house specialty, but you have to ask for it, it's not on the menu. Some tables in the rear dining room have a view of Offatts Bayou. Jackets suggested for men at dinner. Bar.

GAIDO'S
3828 Seawall
762-9625
Lunch and dinner seven days
$$-$$$$
AE, MC, V
W
Children's plates

This family restaurant has something in common with the stately Hotel Galvez — they both opened in 1911 and are still going strong. If you don't believe it, just look at the line to get in on weekends. The lure, of course, is the Gaido family is smart enough to put the emphasis on making the best possible use of fresh local seafood instead of the frozen or processed product. And on many entrées they give you a choice of broiled, grilled, or fried. The freshest catch is always listed on typed sheets in the menu. If you're over 65, they offer a moderately priced senior dinner that includes everything from appetizer to dessert. An indication of the high esteem Galvestonians hold for this restaurant's founder is on the street sign outside — 39th St. is also called Mike Gaido Blvd. Bar.

HILL'S PIER 19
Wharf at 20th St.
763-7087
Lunch and dinner seven days
$-$$
CR.
W downstairs only

The winning combination here is the close-up view of waterfront scenery — the shrimp fleet, seagulls, pelicans — and the cafeteria-style serving line offering fresh seafood, much of it right off the boats docked behind the restaurant. For a hearty lunch try a poorboy, generously filled with shrimp, oysters, or fish. Then take it up to the top deck and munch on while you watch the world flow by. Beer and wine.

SHRIMP 'N STUFF
39th St. at Ave. O
763-2805
Lunch and dinner seven days
$-$$
No Cr.
W
Children's plates

In a city saturated with good seafood restaurants, the question is where do the locals go to eat that's both good and inexpensive. This is one place — or actually two since there's another location at 6801 Stewart Rd. (740-2428). No frills here, just a simple fish house where you go up to the counter and order your fill of shrimp, oysters, or other seafood and get change for a $10 bill. Patio. Beer and wine. The Stewart Rd. location is a little fancier with waitress service, a menu that is mostly seafood but also has steaks, a bar, and higher prices.

TUFFY'S SEAFOOD HOUSE
Pirates Beach Center, FM 3005 approximately seven miles west of end of seawall
737-4336
Lunch and dinner seven days
$$-$$$
Cr.
W

Red snapper steak, broiled lobster, shrimp, and oysters are among the many entrées offered. And you can have them broiled, boiled, fried or on the half-shell. There are a couple of steak entrées on the menu, but if that's your dish of choice you can get it closer into town at Tuffy's Steakhouse at 53rd St. and Seawall (744-7179).

Sweet Stuff

LA KING'S CONFECTIONERY
2323 Strand
762-6100
Open seven days
$
W

This ice cream parlor and candy factory is a throwback to the Gay Nineties with its metal frame sweetheart chairs, wooden floors, ceiling fans, and a working soda fountain. Come at the right time and you can see them making lollipops, peppermint sticks, toffee, peanut brittle and other candy using antique candy-making equipment in the rear of the store.

ACCOMMODATIONS

($ = Under $45, $$ = $46-$60, $$$ = $61-$80, $$$$ = $81-$100, $$$$$ = Over $100)

Hotels and Motels

As a beach resort, Galveston has high and low seasons. Rates given are for a double in high season that runs from about the middle of May to the middle of September and during certain special events like Mardi Gras. Rates usually drop considerably in low season.
Room Tax 13 percent

GALVESTON RESORT INN
600 Strand (at the Yacht Basin)
765-5544 or 800-528-1234
$$-$$$$
W + four rooms
No-smoking rooms

The two- and four-story resort offers 232 units that include four suites ($$$$-$$$$$) and 50 no-smoking rooms. Children under 16 free in room with parents. Senior discount. Cable TV with The Movie Channel. Room phones (charge for local calls). Fire sprinklers in rooms. No pets. Atrium bar and lounge open seven nights with occasional live entertainment. Restaurant. Outdoor pool, children's pool, outdoor whirlpool, sauna, and game room. Same-day dry cleaning. Across street from University of Texas Medical Branch.

FLAGSHIP HOTEL
2501 Seawall
762-9000 or in Texas 800-392-6542, outside Texas 800-231-7128
$$$$-$$$$$
W + five rooms
No-smoking rooms

This seven-story hotel has 230 units that include nine suites ($$$$$) and 25 no-smoking rooms. Children under 18 stay free in room with parents. Package plans available and senior discount. Cable and satellite TV with HBO and Showtime. Room phones (charge for local calls). Pets OK ($50 deposit). Two restaurants, room service, and lounge open seven nights with entertainment Tuesday-Saturday. Outdoor pool with bar and sauna. Guest memberships available for golf. Free transportation anywhere on the island. Same-day dry cleaning. On a steel and concrete pier jutting out into the Gulf, the Flagship reportedly is the only hotel in America built entirely over water.

GAIDO'S SEASIDE INN
3800 Seawall
762-9625 or 800-525-0064
$-$$$

W + one room
No-smoking room

Built on one level, Gaido's has 107 rooms including one no-smoking. Up to five adults may stay in a room. Senior discount. Cable TV and room phones (charge for local calls). No pets. Gaido's Restaurant next door (See Restaurants). Outdoor pool. Same-day dry cleaning. Guests receive a pass that moves them to head of line at the family's popular restaurant next door. Guests are welcome to visit Mrs. Gaido's greenhouse on the property.

HOTEL GALVEZ
2024 Seawall
765-7721 or in Texas 800-392-4285
$$$$-$$$$$
W + 4 rooms
No-smoking rooms

This eight-story hotel has 228 units including three suites ($$$$$) and 34 no-smoking rooms. Children under 12 stay free in room with parents. Package plans available and senior discount. Cable TV with HBO and pay channel. Room phones (charge for local calls). No pets. Restaurant, room service, and lounge open seven nights with entertainment six nights in high season. Outdoor pool and indoor pool, indoor whirlpool, sauna, and game room. Guest memberships in country club and racquet club. Free transportation on the island. Same-day dry cleaning. Gift shop. Often called the Grand Old Lady of Galveston, this luxury hotel, built in 1911, has been restored to recapture its colorful past.

HOLIDAY INN ON THE BEACH
5002 Seawall
740-3581 or 800-HOLIDAY
$$$$-$$$$$
W + two rooms
No-smoking rooms

This eight-story Holiday Inn offers 178 units that include two suites ($$$$$) and 30 no-smoking rooms. Children under 18 stay free in parents room. Package plans available and senior discount. Cable TV with HBO. Room phones (charge for local calls). No pets. Restaurant, room service, and lounge open seven nights with entertainment Tuesday-Saturday. Outdoor pool, exercise room, and sauna. Self-service laundry and same-day dry cleaning. Gift shop. All rooms have Gulf view.

KEY LARGO RESORT HOTEL
Seawall and 54th St.
744-5000 or in Texas 800-833-0120
$$$-$$$$$
W + one room
No-smoking rooms

This six-story hotel has 150 units including three suites ($$$$$) and 20 no-smoking rooms. Children under 12 stay free in room with parents.

Package plans available and senior discount. Cable and satellite TV with HBO and pay channel. Room phones (charge for local calls). No pets. Restaurant, room service, atrium lounge and nightclub open Monday-Saturday with entertainment every night. Outdoor pool with swim-up bar, outdoor whirlpool, putting green, and lighted tennis court. Free transportation anywhere on island. Same-day dry cleaning. Gift shop.

LA QUINTA MOTOR INN
1402 Seawall
763-1224 or 800-531-5900
$$$
W + six rooms
No-smoking rooms

The three-story La Quinta offers 117 units that include two suites ($$$$$) and 38 no-smoking rooms. Children under 18 stay free in room with parents. Package plans available and senior discount. Cable TV with HBO. Room phones (local calls free). Pets OK. Restaurant adjacent. Outdoor pool. Free coffee in lobby and free news magazine in rooms. Same-day dry cleaning.

RAMADA INN
Seawall and 56th St.
740-1261 or 800-2-RAMADA
$-$$$
W + two rooms
No-smoking rooms

The three-story Ramada offers 151 units that include three suites ($$$$-$$$$$) and 20 no-smoking rooms. Children under 18 stay free in room with parents. Senior discount. Cable TV. Room phones (charge for local calls). Pets OK. Restaurant, room service, and lounge open Monday-Saturday. Outdoor heated pool, pool bar in summer. Free coffee in lobby and free newspaper. Same-day dry cleaning. Some covered parking available.

SAN LUIS HOTEL AND CONDOMINIUMS
Seawall and 53rd St.
744-1500 or in Texas 800-327-2029, outside Texas 800-445-0090
$$$$-$$$$$
W + five rooms

This 16-story hotel has 244 units that include two suites ($$$$$). Children under 12 stay free in room with parents. Package plans available and senior discount. Cable TV with pay channel. Room phones (charge for local calls). Fire sprinklers and fire intercom system in rooms. No pets. Two restaurants (fine dining restaurant open weekends only) and lounge open seven nights with entertainment on weekends. Outdoor heated pool with swim-up bar, outdoor whirlpool, two lighted tennis courts, guest memberships in country club and racquet club.

Gift shop. Limited covered self-parking area and valet parking ($5). Condo rentals available in adjoining San Luis Condominiums ($$$$$).

THE TREMONT HOUSE
2300 Ship's Mechanic Row between 23rd St. and 24th St. (Mechanic St. renamed for this one block)
763-0300 or 800-874-2300
$$$$$
W + four rooms
No-smoking rooms

The four-story Tremont has 111 units that include nine suites ($$$$$) and four no-smoking rooms. Children under 18 stay free in room with parents. Package plans available and senior discount. Cable TV. Room phones (charge for local calls). Fire sprinklers and fire intercom in rooms. No pets. Restaurant (See Restaurants), lobby bar with piano Wednesday-Sunday, and Irish Pub across street with entertainment on weekends. Guest memberships available in country club and health club. Free transportation on the island in a London cab or a limo, free shoeshines, and free newspaper. Same-day dry cleaning. Gift and other shops. The Tremont is a historical restoration of a 1870 hotel with Victorian-inspired guestrooms located one block from The Strand.

Condominiums

Rates are for one bedroom/one bath apartment in high season.

BY THE SEA CONDOMINIUMS
7310 Seawall (77551)
740-0905 or 800-666-0905
$$$-$$$$
One No-smoking unit

This 12-story condominium usually has about 35 units in the rental pool ranging from efficiencies to two-bedroom apartments. Package plans available and senior discount. Cable TV and VCR rentals. Room phones (local calls free). Coffemakers in rooms. No pets. Outdoor pool and tennis court. Self-service laundry. All apartments have balconies with view of Gulf. Minimum stay two night. On the beach.

ISLANDER EAST CONDOMINIUMS
415 East Beach Dr. (77550)
765-9301
$$$-$$$$$

About 40 units are usually in the rental pool in this nine-story condominium. Package plans available and senior discount. Cable TV. Room phones (local calls free). Coffeemakers in rooms. No pets. Outdoor pool and two lighted tennis courts. Self-service laundry. Minimum stay during high season with reservations is two nights, three nights on holiday weekends. On the beach.

THE VICTORIAN CONDO-HOTEL
6300 Seawall (77551), just west of 61st St.(Texas Spur 342)
740-3555 or in Texas 800-392-1215 or outside Texas 800-231-6363
$$$$$

The three-story Victorian offers 230 one- and two-bedroom units. Package plans available and senior discount. Cable and satellite TV with HBO and pay channel. Room phones (charge for local calls). Coffeemakers in rooms. No pets. Two outdoor pools (one heated), three outdoor whirlpools,and two lighted tennis courts. Self-service laundry. Some covered parking. Free Continental breakfast November to February only. All units have balconies with view of the Gulf.

Bed & Breakfast

The bed and breakfast phenomenon, which is spreading throughout the United States, has taken hold in Galveston's historic districts and each season the number of B&Bs increases. The following are a few that have at least three rooms for guests. Rates are for a double room in high season. Some take credit cards, some do not. Check when making your reservation. For an up-to-date list, contact the Convention and Visitors Bureau. Five of the bed and breakfast inns can also be booked through Bed and Breakfast Reservations, P.O. Box 1326, 77553 (762-1668 or 800-628-4644).

THE GILDED THISTLE
1805 Broadway (77550)
763-0194
$$$$$

One room with private bath, two with shared bath. Children over 12 are welcome. Children under 15 stay free in room with parents. Weekend rates. Cable TV. No pets. Self-service laundry. Full breakfast. Wine and cheese tray in evening. Coffee and juice tray at door in morning. Prefers no-smoking in bedrooms. Parking behind house. Home built in 1893.

HAZELWOOD HOUSE
1127 Church
762-1668 or 800-628-4644
$$$-$$$$$

Two rooms with private baths, one with shared bath. Package plans available. No children. Cable TV. No pets. Guest memberships available in Galveston Yacht Club. Expanded continental breakfast. Wine tray on arrival. Coffee/tea tray outside door in morning. Bicycle rentals. Non-smokers preferred. Home built in 1877.

INN ON THE STRAND
2021 Strand (77550)
762-4444
$$$$-$$$$$

Four bedrooms and two suites ($$$$$) all with private baths. Children under 12 stay free in room with parents. TV. No pets. Continental breakfast. One suite with jacuzzi. Upstairs in converted 1856 warehouse on The Strand across from The Strand Visitors Center. Pay parking lots in area. Two nights miniumum stay during Mardi Gras and Dickens on the Strand.

MICHAEL'S
1715 35th St. (77550) near Ave. O
763-3760
$$$$
No-smoking in bedrooms

Four rooms all with shared bath. Senior discount. Children over 12 welcome. No pets. Free newspaper. Full breakfast. Dessert at night. Bicycles available for guests. Rose garden with fishpond. Home built in 1915. Two nights miniumum stay during Mardi Gras and Dickens on the Strand.

VICTORIAN INN
511 17th St. (Mailing address: 6655 Hillcroft, Suite #206, Houston 77081)
762-3235
$$$$

Four bedrooms and one suite ($$$$$). No children. Package plans available. Senior discount. Weekend rates. No pets. Free newspaper. Continental breakfast. House built in 1899. Each room has its own balcony.

THE WHITE HORSE INN
2217 Broadway (77550)
76 B AND B (762-2632) or 800-762-2632
$$$$-$$$$$
No-smoking in bedrooms

Two rooms in the mainhouse and four rooms in the carriage house all with private baths. Package plans available. Senior discount. No pets. Full breakfast. House built in 1885. Off-street parking arranged for guests. Tours of house offered daily. Two nights miniumum stay during Mardi Gras and Dickens on the Strand.

Beach Houses

Most rental houses are located on the island west of 100th Street. Usually they come fully equipped and with maid and linen service. Some may be rented for as short a time as two nights, but most rent by the weekend or the week. Everything from one to five bedroom houses are available, some on the beach and some on the bay. They range from simple beach houses to luxury homes decorated by high-priced interior decorators. Prices depend on size, location, amenities, and season. In the summer (high season) the prices run from about $150 to $700 for a weekend and $300 to $1500 for a week. For a list of agencies that rent these homes contact the Convention and Visitors Bureau.

KINGSVILLE

KLEBERG COUNTY SEAT ★ 31,000 ★ (512)

The early history of Kingsville is really the history of Captain Richard King and his descendents and the growth of the world-famous King Ranch.

King, who had spent most of his early life at sea, came to the Rio Grande in 1847, at the age of 23, to captain one of the river steamboats that supplied General Zachary Taylor's army during the Mexican War. In the early 1850s, King quit working as a riverboat captain, bought part of a Spanish land grant called the Santa Gertrudis, and started what was to be one of the largest ranches in the world. After Captain King died, his widow, Henrietta, put up considerable acreage of the ranch to help finance the building of the St. Louis, Brownsville and Mexico Railroad. One of the provisions of her financing was that the new town of Kingsville would be the headquarters for the railroad. She selected the site for the town on a spot near the center of the original Santa Gertrudis Land Grant and personally directed the laying out of the streets of the townsite. On July 4, 1904, the railroad made its first trip to the new town of Kingsville.

The King Ranch and the railroad were two of the three ingredients that came together to put Kingsville permanently on the map. The other ingredient was the successful sinking of wells by Robert Kleberg, Sr., in 1899, that provided a permanent source of water in the arid country.

But Kingsville is no longer strictly a ranch town. One of the world's largest chemical and plastics plants is just outside the city, and it is also the home of Texas A&I University and a U.S. Naval Air Station where pilots are given advanced flight training.

TOURIST SERVICES

KINGSVILLE TOURIST INFORMATION DEPOT
1501 N. Hwy 77 Bypass at Corral
592-4121
Open seven days 9–5
W

You might want to stop at this roadside building on the Bypass to pick up maps, brochures and other information before heading into the city, especially if you arrive on a weekend when the downtown Visitors Center is closed.

KINGSVILLE VISITORS CENTER
101 N. 3rd at King (P.O. Box 1562, 78363)
592-8516 or 800-333-5032
Monday–Friday 8–5
W

You can find out just about everything you want to know about everything of interest to visitors at this center.

KING RANCH TOURS

See Other Points of Interest-King Ranch

RIO PAISANO RANCH TOURS
Riviera (P.O. Box 130, Riviera 78379) Take US 77 south to Texas 285 at Riviera, then west about nine miles
595-5753
By appointment
$30 a person, minimum of eight

Primarily a hunting resort (See Sports and Activities-Hunting), this ranch also runs tours for those who just want to see or photograph the wildlife. Tours are run both morning and afternoon, last 2½ to 3 hours, and include lunch.

MUSEUMS

JOHN E. CONNOR MUSEUM
821 Santa Gertrudis at Armstrong on campus of Texas A&I University
595-2819

Monday–Saturday 9–5, Sunday 2:30–5, Closed university holidays
Free
W +

The emphasis here is on the bicultural heritage of South Texas. Displays range from fossils and the findings at the La Paloma Mammoth site to chronological history and current economic development. Among the displays in the ranching section is a chuck wagon and a typical 1910-1920 ranch kitchen, including a handcranked washing machine. Also featured is one of the largest collections of cattle brands and branding irons in the state. The natural history exhibits include dioramas of native wildlife. There are changing exhibits monthly and Brown Bag Luncheon Lectures are given each Monday from November to April. Gift Shop.

KING RANCH MUSEUM

Henrietta Memorial Building, 405 N. 6th St.
595-1881
Monday–Saturday 10–2, Sunday 1–5
Adults $4, children (5–12) $2

What was once the town's ice factory has been transformed into a museum that features King Ranch memorabilia including items like the family's custom cars and saddles. There are also some impressive large-scale photos of ranch operations in the 1930s and 1940s. A guided tour lasts about an hour.

OTHER POINTS OF INTEREST

DICK KLEBERG PARK

South edge of city between US 77 Bus and US 77 Bypass
592-5229
Free
W Variable

The 211-acre park includes picnic areas, fishing pier on a small lake, playground, ball fields, horse stalls, and a swimming pool.

KING RANCH

Texas 141 approximately 2.5 miles west (P.O. Box 1090, 78364)
592-8055
Visitors Center open seven days 9–5, Tours on the hour 10–3
Adults $6, children (over 5–12) $4
W

In 1853, Richard King, who was a captain of a steamboat on the Rio Grande, went with friends to Corpus Christi for the Lone Star State Fair. On the way they stopped at Santa Gertrudis Creek in the wild area south of Corpus Christi known as the Wild Horse Desert. This was an oasis, the first live water they had seen in more than 100 miles. At the fair, King and a friend, Texas Ranger Captain Gideon Lewis, formed a partnership to set up a cattle ranch with headquarters at the oasis. King purchased part of the Spanish land grant, called the Santa Gertrudis, which included the creek. This area was so sparsely settled then he had to go to Mexico to buy the cattle to stock his land and find men to work the ranch. But, this was the start of the ranch that was to become one of the largest and most-famous ranches in the world and the site of the present day city of Kingsville.

During the Civil War, the King Ranch became a way station on Cotton Road, the lifeline of the southern states over which thousands of bales of cotton were hauled south to Mexico to trade for war materials. Despite Union efforts to arrest him, King helped keep the Cotton Road open and supplied beef and horses to the Confederate forces. After the war, more than 100,000 head of cattle carrying the famous "Running W" brand followed the trails to northern markets. And at every occasion, King bought more land. Prior to his death in 1885, he had increased the ranch size to about 600,000 acres.

After 1885, purchases by his widow, Henrietta, and son-in-law, Robert Kleberg, who had married the King's youngest daughter, Alice, brought the ranch to its maximum size of 1,250,000 acres. At one time the King Ranch holdings included close to 10 million acres in seven countries. At present the ranch has shrunk to a mere 825,000 acres spread over several counties from north of Kingsville south to Raymondville. Covering more than 1,300 square miles, it is larger than the entire state of Rhode Island.

Among the achievements of the ranch are the improvement of the herds by King-Kleberg descendants that eventually lead to the production of a new breed of cattle called the Santa Gertrudis, a cross between the Indian Brahman and the British Shorthorn. There are about 50,000 Santa Gertrudis cattle on the ranch today. It is also the home of a stable that in the past produced several Kentucky Derby winners — including Assault, winner of the Triple Crown in 1946 — but now concentrates on breeding and training championship quarter horses. When the American Quarter Horse Association was formed in 1940, it recognized the importance of King Ranch breeding stock by giving registration Number One to one of the ranch's stallions. Championship cutting horses are also raised here.

Bus tours leave from the Visitors Center, just inside the main gate, every hour on the hour from 10 to 3. The tours take about 1¾ hours to cover the ranch headquarters area. There is a stop at the cattle pens where a cowboy explains how the pens work, and you might see cowboys actually working the cattle, if that's on the day's work schedule. Another stop is made at Santa Gertrudis Creek, near the location where Captain Richard King had stopped and decided to go into the cattle business. The bus also drives by the main house and the auction arena. There is also a 20-minute video shown at the Visitors Center either before or after the bus tour.

Private tours are also available for groups of two to eight. These go almost anyplace you want to on the ranch and into places, like the main house, that aren't open for the bus tours. Called VIP tours, they cost $40 per person and reservations must be made because arrangements must be made for a vehicle and guide.

SPORTS AND ACTIVITIES

Golf

GOLF L. E. RAMEY GOLF COURSE
Take US 77 Bypass south to Trant Rd., then east (left) to course
592-1101

Eighteen-hole course. Green fees: weekdays $6.75, weekends and holidays $8.25. Also six lighted tennis courts.

Hunting

Two large hunting resorts in the area offer hunts for both native and exotic wildlife and migratory birds. Both offer package deals that provide luxurious quarters, meals, guides, and the promise of a successful hunt. The 10,000-acre **Rio Paisano Ranch**, south of Kingsville and about nine miles west of Riviera on Texas 285, is strictly a hunting ranch that is surrounded by a game fence. For information contact Horlock Land & Cattle, P.O. Box 130, Riviera 78379 (294-5281). A little further south, **Sarita Safaris** operates a hunting resort on the 435,000-acre Kenedy Ranch. In addition to hunts, they also offer fishing trips both on the Kenedy Ranch shoreline on Laguna Madre and deepsea in the Gulf. For information contact Sarita Safaris, P.O. Box 27, Sarita 78385 (294-5290).

COLLEGES AND UNIVERSITIES

TEXAS A&I UNIVERSITY
University Blvd.
595-2111
W + But not all areas
Visitor parking available all over campus

About 5,500 students take classes in the five colleges: Agriculture and Home Economics, Engineering, Arts and Sciences, Business Administration, and Teacher Education. The 240-acre campus includes a 1,000 seat theater, the Caesar Kleberg Wildlife Research Institute, the Ben Bailey Art Gallery, an observatory with a sixteen-inch reflecting telescope, and an indoor arena for English and Western horseback riding. Visitors are welcome to sports events, recitals and other musical performances, and theatrical productions. The John E. Connor Museum (see Museums) is also on campus.

SHOPPING

KING RANCH SADDLE SHOP
6th St. and Kleberg
595-5761 or 1-800-282-KING
W

An outgrowth of the saddle shop established by Captain King to outfit his ranchhands, this shop is located in the restored Ragsland Building. Built in 1904, it was the first mercantile building in town and is listed in the National Register of Historic Places. The shop carries a custom line of luggage, purses, and other leather goods, all branded with the ranch's Running W. It also carries western ware, as they call it, for horses and people.

SELLERS MARKET
205 E. Kleberg
595-4992
Thursday and Friday 10–5:30, Saturday 10–4, or by appointment
W

Area artists and craftsmen are provided a marketplace for their work here. Located under the old Opera House, it offers paintings, crafts, and homemade baked goods. There is also a tearoom.

SIDE TRIPS

KAUFER HUBERT PARK
Take US 77 south about nine miles, then east (left) on FM 628 about nine miles
297-5738
W Variable

There are two freshwater lakes in this county park near Baffin Bay. It also has a 500 foot lighted fishing pier, picnic area, sandy beach, birdwatching area, public boat ramp, recreation facility, playground, access to Baffin Bay and Laguna Madre, tent camping (fee) and an RV resort (fee). For information write: Route 1, Box 77D, Rivera 78379.

ANNUAL EVENTS

January

KLEBERG COUNTY FAIR
J. K. Northway Exposition Center, Dick Kleberg Park, south edge of city between US 77 Bus and US 77 By-Pass
592-3316
Monday–Saturday near end of month
Admission
W

Events include a parade, livestock show, exhibition and sale, queen contest, horse show, arts and crafts, cooking and other contests, and a carnival.

June

GEORGE STRAIT TEAM ROPING AND CONCERT
J. K. Northway Exposition Center, Dick Kleberg Park, south edge of city between US 77 Bus and US 77 Bypass

592-8516 (Kingsville Visitor Center)
Admission
W

The three days of team roping by teams from all over the country, in which Country and Western singing star George Strait and his brothers compete, winds up with a Saturday night concert by Strait.

RESTAURANTS

($ = under $7, $$ = $7 to $17, $$$ = $17 to $25, $$$$ = over $25 for one person excluding drinks, tax, and tip.)

KING'S INN
Take US 77 south about 11 miles, then east (left) on FM 628 about 9 miles
297-5265
Lunch and dinner seven days
Reservations recommended on weekends
$$-$$$
Cr.
W

In this unpretentious building perched at the water's edge is yet another proof that a restaurant in the middle of nowhere will draw customers as long as it feeds them well. It's about 20 miles from Kingsville, and many more from Corpus Christi, but customers come from there, too. So many come that, if you don't have reservations, especially on weekends, be prepared to wait. The menu is by word-of-waiter and includes fried shrimp, fried fish, oysters, frogs' legs, crab legs, crab cakes, broiled catch of the day, lobster, you-peel'em shrimp, and oysters on the half-shell. Most of it is sold by the pound and served family style. If you have a group you can order a pound of this and a pound of that and share. For the single diner who has a hearty appetite and wants a taste of several items, there's a combination plate for about $16. Beer.

ACCOMMODATIONS

($ = Under $45, $$ = $46-$60, $$$ = $61-$80, $$$$ = $81-$100, $$$$$ = Over $100)
Room Tax 11 percent

BEST WESTERN KINGSVILLE INN
2402 E. King (Texas 141) at US 77 Bypass
595-5656 or 800-528-1234
$
W + one room
No-smoking rooms

The 50 rooms in this two-story Best Western include ten no-smoking. Children under 12 stay free in room with parents. Senior discount.

Cable TV with HBO. Room phones (local calls free). Pets limited. Outdoor pool. Free coffee in lobby.

HOLIDAY INN
221 S. US 77 Bypass just south of King (Texas 141)
592-5251 or 800-HOLIDAY
$-$$
W + one room
No-smoking rooms

The two-story Holiday Inn has 117 rooms that include 20 no-smoking. Senior discount. Cable TV. Room phones (charge for local calls). Pets OK. Restaurant and private club (guests automatically members) with entertainment most nights. Outdoor pool.

MATAGORDA

MATAGORDA COUNTY ★ 700 ★ (409)

The town was established in 1829 at the mouth of the Colorado River as a port for Stephen F. Austin's colony. During the Texas Revolution, men from here were among those who joined the ill-fated Fannin expedition. The town grew rapidly until the first railroad in the area bypassed it in the 1850s. That, plus several devastating hurricanes, sent it into a decline from which it never fully recovered.

When the town was founded, the Colorado River flowed into East Matagorda Bay. But in the late 1920s, when demolitions were used to break up the great log jam that had blocked the river for almost half a century, the silt that was carried down built up what amounted to an alluvial causeway for the river to cross the bay. It cut the bay in half, letting the river flow directly into the Gulf.

HISTORIC PLACES

CHRIST EPISCOPAL CHURCH
Cypress and Lewis

The original church, built here in 1841, was destroyed by the hurricane of 1854. But the church members salvaged as much of the hand-hewn cypress timbers and other parts of the building as possible and used them to build the present church in 1856. This is reportedly the oldest Episcopal Church in Texas. It has survived several other hurricanes and is still used for services.

OTHER HISTORIC BUILDINGS

The *Culver Home,* Caney and Wrightman, was built in 1890. *Dale-Rugeley-Sisk Home,* Texas 60 at the east city limits, built in the 1830s, was at one time the home of A. C. Horton, the first lieutenant governor of Texas and governor for seven months. *United Methodist Church,* Fisher St., built in 1893, contains the cypress pews and bell from the original church destroyed in the 1854 hurricane.

SIDE TRIPS

SOUTH TEXAS PROJECT
Take Texas 60 north about nine miles to Wadsworth, then west (left) on FM 521 about eight miles to the Visitors Center across from the main entrance to the nuclear power station, (P.O. Box 246, Wadsworth 77483)
972-5023 or 972-3748
Visitors Center open Monday–Saturday 9–5, closed Sunday
Free
W

The array of exhibits in the twin geodesic domes of the Visitors Center explains how electricity is produced using nuclear fuel in the huge $5.5 billion generating station across the road. When fully operational, this plant could produce over 17 billion kilowatt hours of electricity per year, which is the energy equivalent of 25 million barrels of oil. Narrated driving tours of the outside of the plant site are conducted Monday through Friday at 10 a.m. and 1:30 p.m. Reservations are suggested for this tour that takes about 45 minutes.

PALACIOS

MATAGORDA COUNTY ★ 5,000 ★ (512)

There are two stories about the origin of the name of this town — pronounced Pay-lash-yus, with the accent on the 'lash.' The romantic one says that a storm-driven Spanish ship was saved when the sailors steered toward a mirage of three palaces *(trespalacios)* and wound up in the safety of the bay, which they promptly named Tres Palacios Bay. The more realistic version is that the bay was named in honor of Jose Felix Trespalacios, governor of the area when Austin was establishing his colony. Take your pick, but in either case, the town was named after the bay, in the early 1900s, when it was carved out of the estate of the famed cattle baron, "Shanghai" Pierce by a Houston real estate agent and an investor group from Jennings, Louisiana.

A fleet of about 300 shrimp boats make this their home port, and the largest blue crab processing plant in the country is also here.

TOURIST SERVICES

PALACIOS CHAMBER OF COMMERCE
312 Main (Texas 35 Bus) (P.O. Box 774, 77465)
972-2615
Monday, Thursday and Friday 9–5

MUSEUMS

PALACIOS AREA HISTORIC ASSOCIATION MUSEUM
401 Commerce
Friday 10–5
Free

Exhibits tell the story of the development of Palacios, the "City by the Sea," including the history of nearby Camp Hulen that was used by the Texas National Guard in the 1920s and 1930s.

SPORTS AND ACTIVITIES

Fishing

Palacios offers seven miles of shoreline, two lighted and free fishing piers plus jetties, and free boat ramps.

SIDE TRIPS

BLESSING
Take Texas 36 north to FM 616, then left (west) to Blessing.

For years, around the turn of the century, the biggest name in this area was famed cattle baron Abel Head "Shanghai" Pierce who located the headquarters for his huge ranch near here. But it was after Shanghai's death that his brother Jonathan founded the town. It happened when the railroad came in 1903, and, according to the legend, Jonathan expressed his gratitude for the railroad putting an end to the long, dusty cattle drives to shipping points by naming the town Thank God. But postal authorities made him back off on that, and perhaps as a compromise, the town wound up being called Blessing. Shanghai and his brother are buried in the nearby Old Hawley Cemetery, where Shanghai's statue towers over the tombstones.

Blessing Hotel Coffee Shop
FM 616 (Ave. B) at 10th
588-6623
Breakfast and lunch seven days
$
No Cr.
W

It's called a coffee shop, but it's really the aging ballroom of the Blessing Hotel converted into a dining room with old cook stoves set up in it. It's deservedly famed for its family-style service that is the height of informality. You just go up and dish out your own servings from the pots and pans lined up on the iron stoves. The menu changes daily, but you can usually count on two meats and several vegetables, and because this is rice country, loads of rice. A Thanksgiving-style dinner featuring turkey and ham is served every Sunday. Price includes salad, beverage, and dessert. All for about $5 with children under 10 eating for about $2.

MARINE FISHERIES RESEARCH STATION

Take Texas 35 west 7.5 miles, then south (left) on Well Point Rd. about 5.5 miles
972-5483
Tours by appointment
Free
W

Scientists at this Texas Parks and Wildlife Department facility study the marine life in the Matagorda Basin with an emphasis on saltwater game fish. There are 21 ponds stocked with fish and fingerlings and two wet labs especially designed for providing a unique look at the fish in their own environment. Persons knowledgeable of marine biology are especially welcome to tour.

SOUTH TEXAS PROJECT

Take Texas 36 north to FM 521, then right (east) to the Visitors Center across from the main entrance to the nuclear power station, approximately 12 miles from Palacios (P.O. Box 246, Wadsworth 77483)
972-5023 or 972-3748
Visitors Center open Monday–Saturday 9–5, closed Sunday
Free
W

The array of exhibits in the twin geodesic domes of the Visitors Center explains how electricity is produced using nuclear fuel in the huge $5.5 billion generating station across the road. When fully operational, this plant could produce over 17 billion kilowatt hours of electricity per year, which is the energy equivalent of 25 million barrels of oil. Narrated driving tours of the outside of the plant site are conducted Monday through Friday at 10 a.m. and 1:30 p.m. Reservations are suggested for this tour that takes about 45 minutes.

ANNUAL EVENTS

October

PALACIOS BAYFEST

South Bay Park across from the Luther Hotel
972-2615 (Chamber of Commerce)
First Friday and Saturday in October
Free
W Variable

The festivities begin with a Friday night dance. Events on Saturday include a fiddler's contest, barbecue cookoff, ethnic dances, various contests, and entertainment. It all winds up with another dance that night.

RESTAURANTS

($ = under $7, $$ = $7 to $17, $$$ = $17 to $25, $$$$ = over $25 for one person excluding drinks, tax, and tip.)

PETERSEN'S RESTAURANT
416 Main
972-2413
Breakfast, lunch, and dinner seven days
$$
Cr.
W
Children's plates

The seafood dishes have been the most popular since they opened at this location in 1944. If you love crab, for example, you can get a crab meat platter that's made up of a crab finger cocktail, crab meat, fried crab pattie, and stuffed tomato with crab meat. But the menu also includes steaks, pork chops, chicken, hamburgers, and sandwiches. Even though most customers say they come for the seafood, in their hearts they know they come for the homemade pies. Beer and wine.

ACCOMMODATIONS

($ = Under $45, $$ = $46-$60, $$$ = $61-$80, $$$$ = $81-$100, $$$$$ = Over $100)
Room Tax 6 percent

LUTHER HOTEL
408 S. Bay Blvd.
972-2312
$-$$$

This hotel has about 20 rooms and 46 suites/apartments in the three-story main building and a motel section. All the motel units and some of the hotel units have air conditioning. No pets. Built on the bay in 1903, this rambling, white-frame building with a large porch and manicured lawn remains one of the few surviving grand old dames of the coast. It has been designated a Texas Historic Landmark.

PORT ARANSAS

NUECES COUNTY ★ 2,450 ★ (512)

Located on the northern tip of Mustang Island, one of the chain of barrier islands that protect the coastal mainland from Galveston to the Mexican border, Port Aransas is actually one shoulder of Aransas Pass, not the city but the outlet to the Gulf for Corpus Christi and more than 100 miles of inland bays and waterways. Fishermen, including President Franklin D. Roosevelt, discovered this rustic fishing village many years ago, but it is only within the past 20 years or so that the tourists and developers have discovered it.

The Karankawa Indians were the first real settlers here. Definitely unfriendly themselves, they survived the unfriendly visits by the Spanish, French, and pirates like Jean Lafitte, but finally succumbed to the onslaughts of the Texan colonists and the Comanches. The first recorded permanent settlers were an Englishman, R. L. Mercer, and his family who came in the mid-1850s to fish and raise cattle. Mercer also set up a small dock and warehouse for servicing visiting ships. They were soon followed by others and a tiny community took root. In 1870, a New Yorker bought St. Joseph's Island (now known as San José and still private property) and many of the settlers left there to join Mercer's settlement.

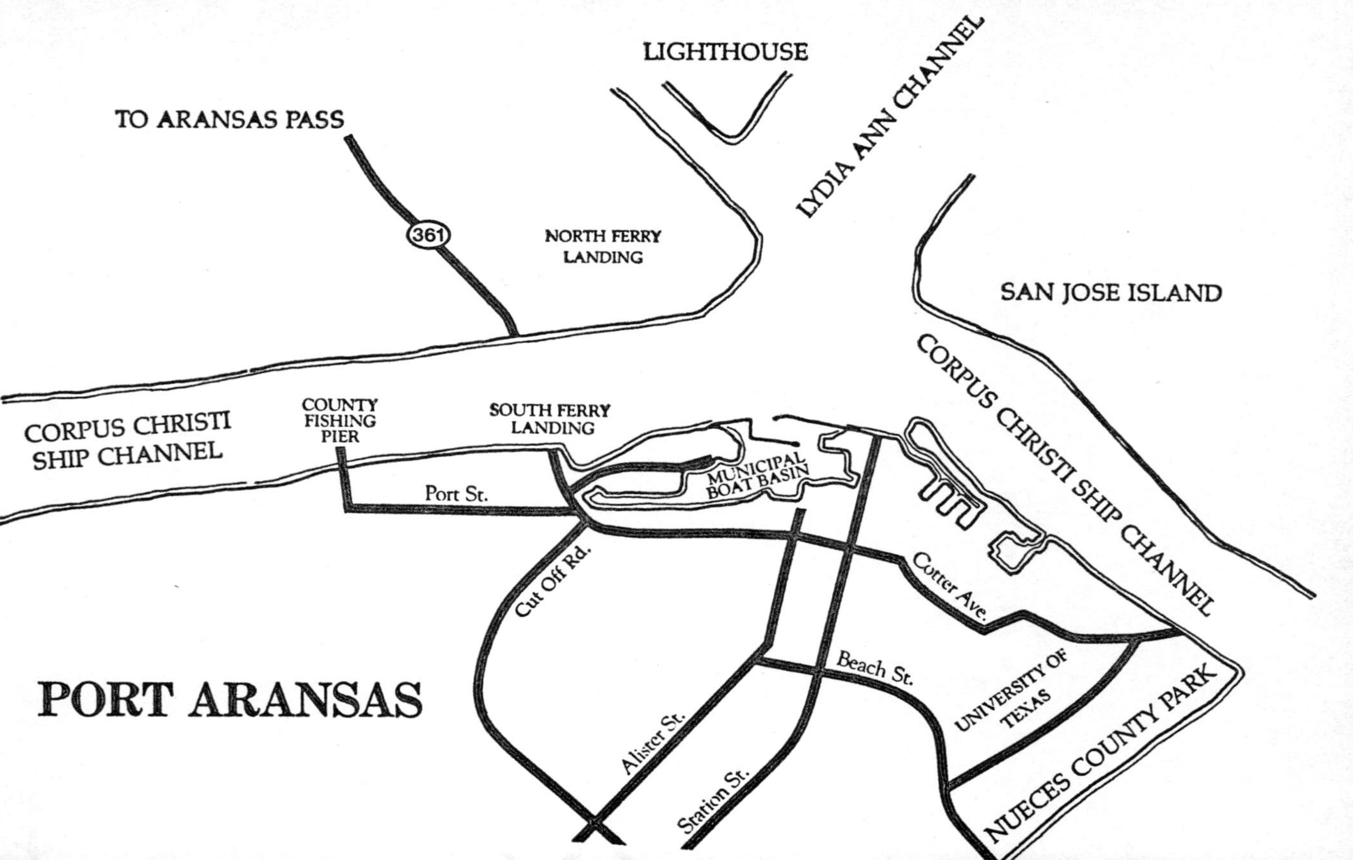
LIGHTHOUSE
TO ARANSAS PASS
LYDIA ANN CHANNEL
361
NORTH FERRY LANDING
SAN JOSE ISLAND
CORPUS CHRISTI SHIP CHANNEL
COUNTY FISHING PIER
SOUTH FERRY LANDING
CORPUS CHRISTI SHIP CHANNEL
MUNICIPAL BOAT BASIN
Port St.
Cut Off Rd.
Cotter Ave.
Beach St.
UNIVERSITY OF TEXAS
PORT ARANSAS
Alister St.
Station St.
NUECES COUNTY PARK

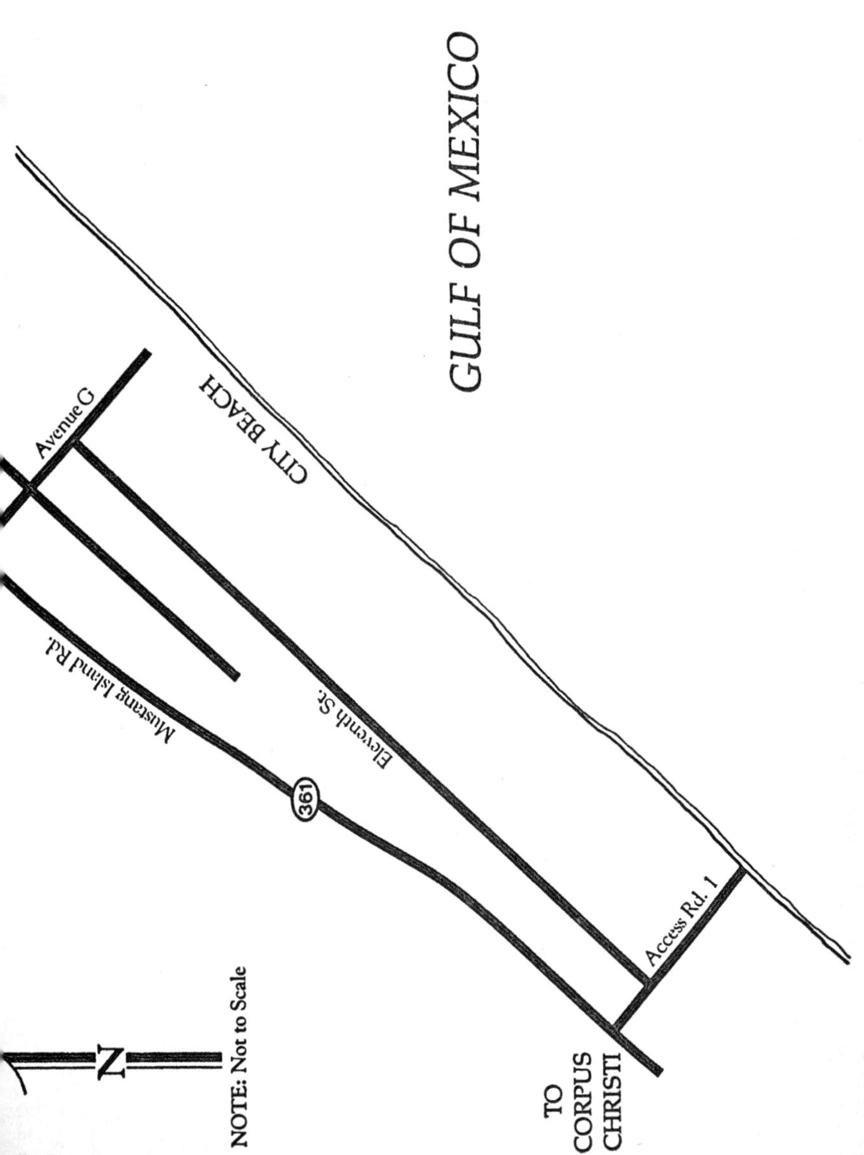
GULF OF MEXICO
CITY BEACH
Avenue G
Eleventh St.
Mustang Island Rd.
361
Access Rd. 1
N
NOTE: Not to Scale
TO
CORPUS
CHRISTI

In addition to fishing, the turn-of-the-century villagers also made money catching sea turtles. Some of these weighed 500 pounds and were shipped to market live, on their backs.

The rock jetties were built in 1909 and 1910 with the base rocks hauled in from a quarry near San Antonio and the huge granite blocks, which can be seen above the water, from Granite Mountain in Marble Falls.

During this time the village had several names, including Tarpon after the popular sport fish that was a prime catch in the area. It wasn't until 1911 that the present name became official — unofficially, most locals shorten it from Port Aransas to Port A. Shortly after that, in 1919, a hurricane all but flattened the town, but it was rebuilt.

For a long time the only way to get to Port A was by boat or train. If you wanted to drive on the island, you put your car on a railroad flatcar that was pulled by a truck mounted on train wheels. The train ran from the town of Aransas Pass to the ferry at Harbor Island. The ferry carried the cars across to the island where a ramp was lowered and the cars drove through the shallow water to the beach. Later the railroad paved over its roadbed, planked the bridges, and opened a toll road.

The island really opened up for visitors in 1954 when the Mustang Island Highway linking the town with Corpus Christi was opened. The present causeway from the city of Aransas Pass to the ferry landing was opened in 1960 providing an easy second route in, and the first condominium soon followed in 1965.

Today, Texas 361 hops from island to island on the six-mile causeway that connects the mainland city of Aransas Pass with Port Aransas. On your left as you drive toward Port A you'll see shrimpers and other boats heading for the Gulf and coming back in. But the highway stops just short of its target and you have to take a free five-minute ferry ride across the Corpus Christi Ship Channel for the last thousand yards. The free ferries, operated by the Texas Department of Highways and Public Transportation, are in service 24 hours a day. For a number of years, on weekends in season, the wait for the ferry could go on for several hours. But in 1989 several 20-car ferries replaced a couple of the nine-car boats and cut waiting time considerably. Now it is only a minor inconvenience, even at times like Spring Break (See Annual Events). For information on ferry waiting times put your AM radio on 530.

If you look to your left as your approach the ferry landing you should see the Port Aransas Lighthouse (See Historic Places), the Brown and Root facility with some of the largest offshore drilling platforms in the world, and San José Island (See Other Points of Interest).

Today, Port A is a town with a split personality — still basically an unsophisticated fisherman's haven but its cottages and bait shops are now intermingled with luxury condos and some of the better restaurants on the coast. And by the time you read this, a day cruise casino ship might be operating out of the terminal just off the ferry. So, while fishing is still a major lure, recent surveys show that close to 80 percent of the visitors come to luxuriate in the sun and surf.

(Note: Park Rd. 53, which may still appear on some maps, has been renamed Texas 361. This road runs the length of Mustang Island between Port Aransas and Corpus Christi.)

TOURIST SERVICES

PORT ARANSAS AREA CHAMBER OF COMMERCE
421 W. Cotter near Cut-Off Rd. (P.O. Box 356, 78373)
749-5919 or in Texas 800-242-3084, outside Texas 800-221-9198
Monday–Saturday 9–5
Free
W

This office is one of the first buildings on your right after you leave the ferry area. If you want to set yourself an impossible task, try coming up with a question about Port A that Lanette Nolte, long-time Chamber of Commerce manager, can't answer. The Texas Tourist Development Association has recognized her accomplishments by awarding her its annual Texas Hospitality Award.

BOAT TOURS

A five-hour narrated tour aboard the *Scat Cat*, an 80-foot catamaran, takes you on a 60-mile round trip to see the whooping cranes and other birds and animals that spend the winter at the Aransas National Wildlife Refuge. Tours leave from Fisherman's Wharf, off Cotter St. from the last Sunday in December through early April. Call 749-5760 for schedule and reservations. Adult fares are about $20 and children go for about $12. There's also a one-and-a-half-hour narrated scenic sunset cruise that leaves Fisherman's Wharf every evening from Memorial Day through August and Saturday evenings the rest of the year. Adults about $7, children about $4. Call for schedule. Other narrated sightseeing tours leave Deep Sea Headquarters daily. These tours last about one-and-a-half-hours and cost $12 for adults and $8 for children under 14. For schedule and reservations call 749-5597.

HISTORIC PLACES

Among the many brochures available at the Chamber of Commerce is one marking out the Port Aransas Historical Trail, which is sponsored by the local Boy Scout Troop. Those who complete the 14 stops on the trail — and you don't have to be a scout — can earn a patch award.

PORT ARANSAS LIGHTHOUSE
Located on Lydia Ann Flats, north of the Corpus Christi Ship Channel

Built of brick in 1855, this New England-style octagonal lighthouse was partially destroyed in the Civil War and rebuilt in 1867, making it the oldest surviving structure in the area. It was used for navigation until the early 1950s and then went dark. The original lens is now on display in the Civic Center Historical Exhibit. However, the lighthouse has been re-certified by the Coast Guard and is one of only 11 manned-lighthouses in the United States and the only non-automated one of the Texas Gulf Coast. Its present nineteenth-century lens, bought from a private collector, magnifies a 100-watt lightbulb so it can be seen for seven miles. The lighthouse is on private property and visitors are not allowed. To prevent name confusion with the Coast Guard's Port Aransas beacon, it is officially called the Lydia Ann Light, named for the channel on which it is located.

OTHER POINTS OF INTEREST

THE BEACHES

The Gulf side of Mustang Island is one long beach. The width varies, but here at Port A, the beach is generally wide enough at low tide to almost lay out a football field between the water's edge and the dune line. Permits to park on the beach are available at most stores in town for $5. The money goes to a good cause — keeping the beaches clean. The motels and condos that line the beach provide facilities for their guests, but the only public facilities are at the 167-acre Port Aransas Park at the northernmost point of the island. Operated by Nueces County Parks and Recreation Department (10901 S. Padre Island Dr., Corpus Christi, 78418, 749-6117) it has restrooms, showers, a 1240-foot long lighted fishing pier, and 75 RV campsites (fee) with electricity and water. Primitive camping is permitted on the beach.

CIVIC CENTER HISTORICAL EXHIBIT

Cut-Off Rd. at Ave. A
749-4111
Monday–Friday 8–5
Free
W +

This exhibit recaps the history of Port A. It includes a model of the town in the old days when the Tarpon Inn was in its prime, fascinating items washed up from shipwrecks, and the original lens from the lighthouse that is complete except for a chip knocked out of it when the Confederates tried to blow up the lighthouse to prevent its capture by Union troops.

ROBERTS POINT PARK

First road to the left off ferry

This city park on the Corpus Christi Ship Channel includes the city marina, public boat launching ramp, a free fishing pier, several pavilions, including one for fish cleaning, sports fields, bike and jogging trails, a playground, an amphitheater, and an observation tower. This is a good place to stop and watch the big ships slicing through the waters of the ship channel and the antics of the pelicans and other shore birds that spend their days near the ferry landing.

SAN JOSÉ ISLAND
Jetty Boat at Woody's Boat Basin off Cotter St.
749-5252
Departures at frequent intervals from 6:30 a.m. to 6 p.m.
Adults $7.50, children $4

St. Jo's, as it's called locally, is a private island; however, the area near the jetty and the beaches is open to the public. Accessible only by boat, it has NO facilities, just miles and miles of white sand beach for swimming, fishing, picnicking, surfing, beachcombing, some of the best shelling on the coast, or enjoying an unsullied and uncrowded beach. It only takes about 15 minutes to go over on the jetty boat that runs every day all year long. Your ticket is good for any return trip during the day. If you're going to be there awhile, as a minimum take food, drinks, and sunscreen

U. S. COAST GUARD STATION
800 N. Station
749-5217
Free

A Life Saving Station, authorized by Congress, opened here in 1880 and later became this USCG Station. The 82-foot Cutter *Point Baker* operates out of here covering the Gulf from Freeport to Brownsville, and four search and rescue boats also stationed here have an operational area from south of Baffin Bay to just north of Rockport and 50 nautical miles offshore. Visitors may usually visit the cutter and the boats if they are at the station during the conducted tours. Tours of the station may be given for walk-ins if personnel are available, but it's better to make reservations *at least* a day in advance. Reservations are required for groups over 15.

UNIVERSITY OF TEXAS MARINE SCIENCE INSTITUTE
At the beach end of Cotter St. across from the Port Aransas Park
749-6711
Visitors Center open Monday–Friday 8–5
Free
W +

From its start in a fisherman's shack on the beach back in 1935, this research institute has grown into an 80-acre complex. The researchers here are interested in just about everything to do with the ecosystem of the Texas coastal zone from the natural phenomena to the impact that man has on the coast. A brochure is available for a self-guided walking tour of the seven aquaria and other exhibits in the Visitors Center and the Laboratory and Main Building. Special films related to the Institute's many projects are shown in the Visitors Center at 11 a.m. and 2 p.m. Monday–Thursday. Guided group tours are usually available with at least two weeks' notice.

SPORTS AND ACTIVITIES

Birdwatching

Laughing gulls, cormorants, terns, pelicans, and herons are among the many full-time residents of Port A and Mustang Island. All seem to have a fondness for the ferry and jetty areas, but you'll also see them on the beaches, including the beaches on San José Island (See Other Points of Interest) and at Mustang Island State Park (See Side Trips). Migrating birds, including ducks, add significantly to the bird population, especially in the spring.

Fishing

The numbers of strictly sun-and-surfers may be increasing, but fishing is still the name of the biggest game at Port Aransas whose residents boast that it's the place "where they bite every day." You can fish in the surf, on the jetties or piers, in the bay, or offshore. Two city piers, one at Roberts Point Park and the other at the north end of Station St., offer free fishing in the ship channel, and it only costs fifty cents per person and a dollar a pole to fish off the Horace Caldwell Pier on the Gulf in Nueces County's Port Aransas Park. A number of boats offering bay and deep sea fishing are located on the ship channel. Party boat rates start at about $20-$25 for a four-hour bay trip and about $40 for a deep sea trip. Party boats include: the *Scat Cat* and the *Wharf Cat* at Fisherman's Wharf, 90 N. Tarpon St. (749-5760); the *Kingfisher* and *Pelican* at Deep Sea Headquarters, 416 W. Cotter (749-5597); the *Island Queen* at Woody's Sports Center on Trout St. (749-5252); and the *New Shark Hunter* and the *Dolphin* at Dolphin Express, 300 W. Cotter (749-4188 or 800-456-9156). Charter boat rates start at about $150-$175 for a half day for two people and go up depending on size of the boat, length of trip, and number of fisherman. For an up-to-date list of both charter and party boats contact the Chamber of Commerce (See Tourist Services). In June, July, and August there's a fishing tournament just about every week, including two for women only and the five-day Deep Sea Roundup (See Annual Events).

Horseback Riding

MUSTANG RIDING STABLES
Texas 361 about eight miles west of Port Aransas
749-5055 (In Corpus Christi 991-RIDE)

For about $15 an hour you can ride on the beach on horses trained to handle both first timers and experienced riders.

Hunting

The tidal flats and marshlands make Mustang Island another prime stopping place for migrating ducks and other game birds in season. For information on seasons, game limits, and a list of guides, contact the Chamber of Commerce.

SHOPPING

THE COTTAGE
104 E. Cotter
749-6087

This tiny shop, set in a cottage next to the Tarpon Inn (See Offbeat) offers a surprisingly large selection of paintings, prints, stained glass, ceramics, shell art, and ironwood carvings, including works of the owners, Kathy Sayre and Toni Hair.

SIDE TRIPS

MUSTANG ISLAND STATE PARK
Texas 361 (formerly Park Rd. 53), approximately 14 miles south of Port Aransas
1-749-5246
Open seven days 8–10 for day use, at all times for camping
$2 per day per vehicle
W + But not all areas

This 3,704-acre park is almost equidistant from Port Aransas and Corpus Christi — about 14 miles either way. It slices a cross section of Mustang Island between Corpus Christi Bay and the Gulf and includes five miles of Gulf beach frontage. Facilities are available for fishing, swimming, picnicking, nature walks, and camping (fee). Birdwatching is excellent. For information write: Box 326, Port Aransas 78373.

ANNUAL EVENTS

March

SPRING BREAK
All over Port Aransas
749-5919 (Chamber of Commerce)

At any one time from late February, through all of March, and on through Easter Weekend in April, there are probably as many college students enjoying their spring break from studies here as there are students in the total enrollment of many large colleges. This influx of 150,000 to 175,000 students can be overwhelming to the 2,400 or so residents of Port A. Each year the Chamber of Commerce issues a list of spring vacations for area high schools and some 60 colleges and universities from as far away as Colorado and Missouri. That way the local merchants can decide whether to capitalize on the invasion or board up and hide out. The major gatherings usually hit for about two weeks in the middle of March. Much of the students' partying is just doing their own thing on the beach, but there are also usually name band concerts and other activities to help keep them happy — and coming back next year. So, unless you're a student yourself or you enjoy being surrounded by hordes of exuberant students, fender-to-fender parking on the beach, long lines for ferries, restrooms, and everything else; you might want to plan your visit to Port A for other times.

July

DEEP SEA ROUNDUP
Marina and other locations
749-5919 (Chamber of Commerce)
Monday–Friday early in month
Admission to some on-shore events

One of the reasons anglers love Port A is the many fishing tournaments held here. The first one, called the Tarpon Rodeo, took place in 1932. Of the 22 contestants, about half were women, and they won most of the prizes. When the tarpon were overfished and ran out, organizers kept the tournament going but switched to calling it the Roundup, making it the oldest of all the fishing tournaments on the Texas Coast. The grand prize for a record-breaking sailfish can run up to $50,000 and champions are crowned for the biggest catch in several divisions. Entry fee is about $70. On-shore activities include an Activity Day with fun and games for all ages, dinners, and a closing day dance.

OFFBEAT

TARPON INN
200 E. Cotter
749-5555

The original was built in 1886, but fire and hurricanes knocked it and several replacements out. The present barracks-like building was built in 1925. The inn is best known for its collection of thousands of tarpon scales that decorate the lobby. Each scale is marked with the fisherman's name and hometown and the date the tarpon was caught. The prize in this collection is that of President Franklin D. Roosevelt, dated May 8, 1937. The tarpon, once a prize sport fish in these waters, is now rarely seen.

There are 26 rooms for rent (call for rates). They are air conditioned, but otherwise basic, no-frills accommodations. Their lure is living a little bit of history and enjoying the gentle Gulf breezes on the wide second-story veranda. Set in the front walk are a number of tiles with handprints, shells, and other designs that were put there by island residents as part of the inn's 100th birthday celebration in 1986. The inn is listed in the National Register of Historic Places.

RESTAURANTS

($ = under $7, $$ = $7 to $17, $$$ = $17 to $25, $$$$ = over $25 for one person excluding drinks, tax, and tip.)

CRAZY CAJUN SEAFOOD RESTAURANT
Alister St. Square
749-5069
$-$$
Dinner only Tuesday–Friday, lunch and dinner Saturday–Sunday, closed Monday
MC, V
W +
Children's plates

The special here is The Hungry Cajun that serves two with a combination of a half-pound of shrimp, a half-pound smoked sausage, new potatoes, corn on the cob, crab, and crawfish. It's all boiled in a blend of Cajun spices then dumped in the middle of your table on butcher paper. It's cooked as you order it so you can chose from no spices to volcanic hot. Half orders are available for one. They also have the ingredients as a la carte entrees, plus gumbo, red beans and rice, dirty rice, and *Jambalaya*. Beer and wine.

PELICAN'S LANDING
407 Alister
749-6405
Dinner seven days
$$-$$$
Cr.
W
Children's plates

With entrées ranging from deep fried beer batter shrimp and oysters on the half shell to steaks and beef *teri yaki* to *fettucini Alfredo*, there's probably something for everyone here. For the real seafood lover, Pelican's Feast, the highest priced item on the menu (about $20), will fill you up with a combination that usually includes beer batter shrimp, charbroiled fish, shrimp *en brochette*, stuffed blue crab, Australian lobster tail, Alaskan king crab, and baked oysters. Bar.

SEAFOOD AND SPAGHETTI WORKS
710 Alister at Ave. G
749-5666
Dinner seven days
$$
Cr.
Children's plates
W through kitchen

This geodesic-domed restaurant is an oasis for creative cookery. The menu offers pasta, pizza, steaks, chicken and veal, and a variety of imaginative seafood entrées including shrimp prepared seven ways. You can order shrimp with lemon cream sauce; with spicy crabmeat stuffing; in green sauce tossed with linguini; scampi tossed with spaghetti; broiled and topped with sauteed onions, poblano peppers, tomatoes and avocados; sauteed in picante sauce and tossed with linguini; or just plain fried. Bar.

TORTUGA FLATS
821 Trout, across from Woody's Sport Center
749-5255
Lunch and dinner seven days
$-$$
AE, MC, V
W ramp in rear

One of the favorites with patrons here is the Sampler Basket, a combo of shrimp, oysters, and fish all fried in beer batter with french fries or onion rings and cole slaw. Take it out on the porch and watch the activities in the boat basin as you munch away. Other items on the menu include charbroiled fresh fish, shrimp *flautas*, Cajun *Boudin*, "hamburguesas," *ceviche*, grilled marinated chicken, large shrimp and crab salads, and chalkboard specials. Live entertainment Friday and Saturday evenings. Bar.

YANKEE'S 'N' BETTY'S SEAFOOD GALLEY
417 Alister
749-4869
Dinner Tuesday–Friday, lunch and dinner Saturday–Sunday, closed Monday
Reservations suggested in summer
$-$$
MC, V, Discover
W
Children's plates

Shrimp, Alaskan whitefish, and oysters are the major items on the menu here. Almost all the seafood is fried, but you can get several of the fish and shrimp entrées broiled or baked to your order for just 50 cents extra. If you catch your own, you can bring the filets here and they'll cook'em up for you and serve'em with garlic bread for about $3.50 a pound. They also have a variety of pizzas. Bar.

ACCOMMODATIONS

($ = Under $45, $$ = $46-$60, $$$ = $61-$80, $$$$ = $81-$100, $$$$$ = Over $100)

There are several small motels in Port A, most cater to families and fishermen, and only one is a chain operation (Best Western). The majority of available accommodations in the town and on Mustang Island are in condominiums.

Room Tax 12 percent in city limits, 6 percent outside

Motels

Rates given are for a double in high season. Low season rates are usually considerably lower. All P.O. box numbers are in area 78373.

SEASIDE MOTEL
Sandcastle Dr. at the beach (P.O. Box 519)
749-4105
$$-$$$

This two-story motel has 46 units that include 10 one-bedroom condominium units ($$$$). Children under 12 stay free in room with parents. Package plans available and senior discount. TV and room phones (local calls free). Pets OK ($25 pet deposit). Coffee shop. Outdoor pool. On the beach.

SPORTSMANS LODGE
104 Alister (P.O. Box 367)
749-5522
$

The ten units here are one- and two-bedroom kitchenette apartments. Children under 12 stay free in apartment with parents. TV with The Movie Channel. Caters to fishermen with fish cleaning house and large freezer for keeping catch. Minimum stay two nights in summer.

TROPIC ISLAND MOTEL
315 Cut-Off Rd. (P.O. Box 748)
749-6128
$-$$

The 38 units include 16 motel rooms and 22 one- and two-bedroom apartments. Children under 12 stay free with parents. Senior discount. Cable TV with Showtime and The Movie Channel. Pets OK. Outddoor heated pool. Self-service laundry. Fish cleaning facility. Also 41 RV spaces that go for $9 a night.

Condominiums

Rates are high season (summer and Spring Break and Easter) for two persons in the smallest-sized apartment available. All P.O. box numbers are in area 78373.

ARANSAS PRINCESS
720 Beach Access Rd, 1-A (P.O. Box 309)
749-5118 or 800-347-1819
$$$$$
No-smoking units

The eight-story Aransas Princess has 32 two- and three-bedroom units in the rental pool of which ten are no-smoking. Cable TV. Room phones (local calls free). Pets limited. Two outdoor heated pools, outdoor whirlpool, two tennis courts, sauna. Guest memberships available in country club. One covered parking space for each unit. Minimum stay two nights on weekends, three nights over holidays. Deposit of $100 for all stays less than one month. On the beach.

BEACHHEAD RESORT
1319 11th St. (P.O. Box 1577)
749-6261
$$$$
No-smoking units

This is a cluster of five 2-story buildings each with eight 2-bedroom apartments of which about 35 are in the rental pool including two no-smoking units. Senior discount. Cable TV. Room phones (charge for local calls). No pets. Outdoor heated pool, 2 tennis courts, game room. Guest memberships available in country club. Self-service laundry. Minimum stay two nights on weekends in summer. On the beach.

CHANNELVIEW
631 Channel View Dr., east of the Coast Guard Station (P.O. Box 776)
749-6156
$$$$$

There are about 20 one-, two-, and three-bedroom units in the rental pool in this four-story condominium. Cable TV with Showtime and a pay channel. Room phones (local calls free). No pets. Outdoor pool. Lighted private fishing pier. Covered parking. Boat slips available at marina next door. Minimum stay two nights on weekends, three nights over major holidays. On the ship channel.

CLINE'S LANDING
1000 N. Station St. (P.O. Box 1628)
749-5274 or 800-999-7651
$$$$$
No-smoking unit

There are about 21 two- and three-bedroom units including one no-smoking in the rental pool at seven-story Cline's Landing. Cable TV. Room phones (local calls free). No pets. Outdoor heated pool, outdoor whirlpool, two tennis courts, marina, and playground. Electronic security gate. Fish cleaning stations. Minimum stay two nights with reservations in summer. On the ship channel.

MAYAN PRINCESS
Texas 361 (formerly Park Rd. 53), about nine miles south of Port Aransas (P.O. Box 281)
749-5183 or 800-662-8907
$$$$$

The four-story Mayan Princess has about 54 one-and two-bedroom units in the rental pool. Senior discounts. TV and room phones (charge for local calls). No pets. Bar open on weekends. Three outdoor pools, outdoor whirlpool, and tennis courts. Free coffee in lobby. Continental breakfast. Whirlpool-type tubs in all apartments. Minimum stay two-nights in summer. On the beach.

PORT ROYAL
Texas 361 (formerly Park Rd. 53) about seven miles south (P.O. Box 336)
749-5011 or in Texas 800-242-1034, outside Texas 800-847-5659
$$$$$
W + one unit
No-smoking units

There are three 4-story buildings at Port Royal with about 175 one-, two- and three-bedroom units in the rental pool including 15 no-smoking units. Cable TV with HBO and room phones (local calls free). No pets. Restaurant, room service, and lounge open seven nights with entertainment in high season. 500-foot lagoon-style outdoor pool with two swim-up bars, four outdoor whirlpools. Two lighted tennis courts. Guest memberships available in country club. Covered parking for most units. Whirlpool tub with steambaths in all units. Convenience store, boutique, gift shop. Two night minimum on weekends and three nights over major holidays in high season. On the beach.

SAND CASTLE
Sand Castle Dr. off 11th St. (P.O. Box 1688)
749-6201 or 800-727-6201
$$$-$$$$$

The six-story Sand Castle has about 100 efficiencies and one-and two-bedroom units in rental pool. Cable TV and room phones (local calls free). No pets. Outdoor pool, two lighted tennis courts. Some covered parking. On the beach.

SEA GULL
Texas 361 (formerly Park Rd. 53) about seven miles south (P.O. Box 1207)
749-4191
$$$$$

There are about 45 one-, two- and three-bedroom units in the rental pool in this 11-story condominium. Satellite TV with Showtime. Room phones (local calls free). No pets. Outdoor heated pool, tennis court and playground. Free coffee in lobby. Self-service laundry. Two night minimum weekends in summer. On the beach.

SAND PIPER
Texas 361 (formerly Park Rd. 53) about seven miles south (P.O. Box 1268)
749-4181
$$$$$

The 12-story Sand Piper has about 42 one-, two-, and three-bedroom units in the rental pool. Cable TV with Showtime and room phones (local calls free). No pets. Outdoor heated pool, outdoor whirlpool, and two tennis courts. Free coffee in lobby. Self-service laundry. Two night minimum stay, three nights over major holidays. On the beach.

PORT ARTHUR

JEFFERSON COUNTY ★ 64,000 ★ (409)

The lifeblood of Port Arthur is oil. It pours through a monstrous refinery complex that is listed as one of the world's largest and feeds a number of huge petrochemical plants. So it's easy to see why the city lays claim to the title "Energy City" and boasts "We Oil the World."

The city also lives up to its name as a port — a fact often brought home to the uninitiated visitor by the startling sight of tankers and other large ships that, from a block or so inland, appear to be gliding down a nearby street. What they're doing, of course, is sailing the Sabine-Neches Ship Channel that flows through the city.

Port Arthur became a city and a port in the late 1890s when Arthur Stilwell pushed his Kansas City, Pittsburgh, and Gulf Railroad down from the north, drained the swamps and dredged a canal from Lake Sabine to the Gulf. Stilwell said he chose this location as his Gulf terminus because of advice of "Brownies" from the spirit world, and in dreams he saw the city exact in every detail. Unfortunately for Stilwell and his dreams, he ran out of money and made the mistake of going for help to John "Bet-a-Million" Gates, a wheeler-dealer. Before Stilwell knew what hit him, all that remained of his interests in the area was his first name, with which he had christened the new port. "Bet-a-Million" really reaped the harvest of Arthur Stilwell's foresight when, in 1901, Spindletop blew in just ten miles north of the city and the "black gold" rush ushered in a boom.

In truth, however, even though Port Arthur itself is an industrial city that at first glance doesn't appear to offer much to the visitor, those who take the time to dig below the surface will find this easternmost corner of the state is filled with hidden treasures. It is also a delightful kaleidoscope of colorful contrasts.

The nature lover can thrill to the spillover of the Old South in the moss-laden trees that are interlaced with tropical palms. The mysterious swamps, salt marshes, and bayous give sanctuary to wildlife ranging from alligators to hundreds of species of birds. It is estimated that at peak times close to a million ducks, geese, and other birds make their temporary homes in the marshland parks, refuge areas, and rice fields surrounding the city, which is located on the "Central Fly-way" for migrating waterfowl. The majestic beauty of huge flocks of these birds on the wing is a sight worth a trip by itself. And while it is a birdwatcher's delight, this seasonal inundation of game birds also sends out a clarion call to the hunter.

This is also a fisherman's paradise — one of many on the Texas coast — but this one is slightly different because of the fresh waters of Lake Sabine so close to the Gulf. Freshwater catches are plentiful in the rivers, bayous, and upper reaches of the lake, while saltwater fish eager for the hook are found in the lower lake and Gulf.

The mix of cultures in Port Arthur adds to the local color. Prominent among these is Cajun. Although there are some other outposts of the Louisiana Cajuns farther down the Texas coast, Port Arthur is the only real Texas bastion of the descendants of the displaced Acadians whose tragic tale is told in Longfellow's *Evangeline.* Two of the many fine things the Cajuns brought with them is a distinctive style of cooking and the philosophy these hard-working people express when their work is done. *"Laissez les bons temps rouler"* is their credo. Loosely translated that means "Let the good times roll." And they make sure the good times roll and roll and roll at their favorite night spots and many local festivals.

Also in the cultural mix are the good ole boy Texans, the never-say-die Janis Joplin fans (this was that famed rock singer's home town), the urban cowboys, Southern gentlefolk, hispanics, blacks, and, most recently, the Vietnamese who have carved out their own enclaves in the city. The polygot population is also laced with descendants of the Dutch who are centered in Nederland, a city in its own right but lacking distinguishable boundaries with Port Arthur except to the quick-eyed who can see the city limits signs that flash by on the highway.

Sabine Pass, 14 miles to the south, is an annexed part of the city. This little town in the corner of Texas has the distinction of having been laid out by Sam Houston in 1836. A high point in the town's history was the Civil War battle fought here in which a handful of Confederates with a few cannon and a lot of guts whipped a Federal invasion force that some reports say was more than a hundred times its strength.

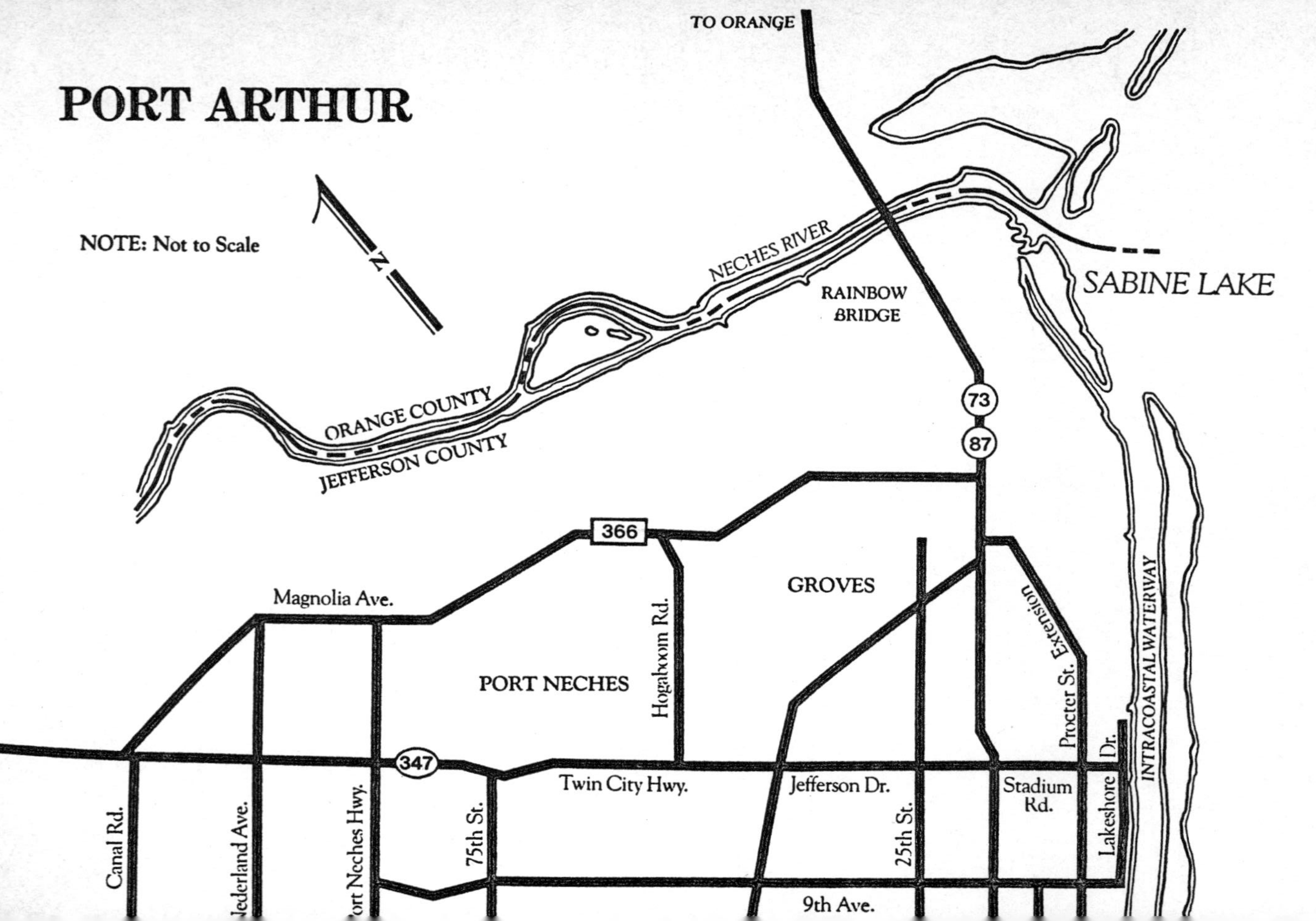
PORT ARTHUR
NOTE: Not to Scale
N
TO ORANGE
NECHES RIVER
RAINBOW BRIDGE
SABINE LAKE
73
87
ORANGE COUNTY
JEFFERSON COUNTY
366
GROVES
Magnolia Ave.
PORT NECHES
Hogaboom Rd.
Procter St. Extension
INTRACOASTAL WATERWAY
347
Twin City Hwy.
Jefferson Dr.
Stadium Rd.
Lakeshore Dr.
Canal Rd.
ederland Ave.
ort Neches Hwy.
75th St.
25th St.
9th Ave.

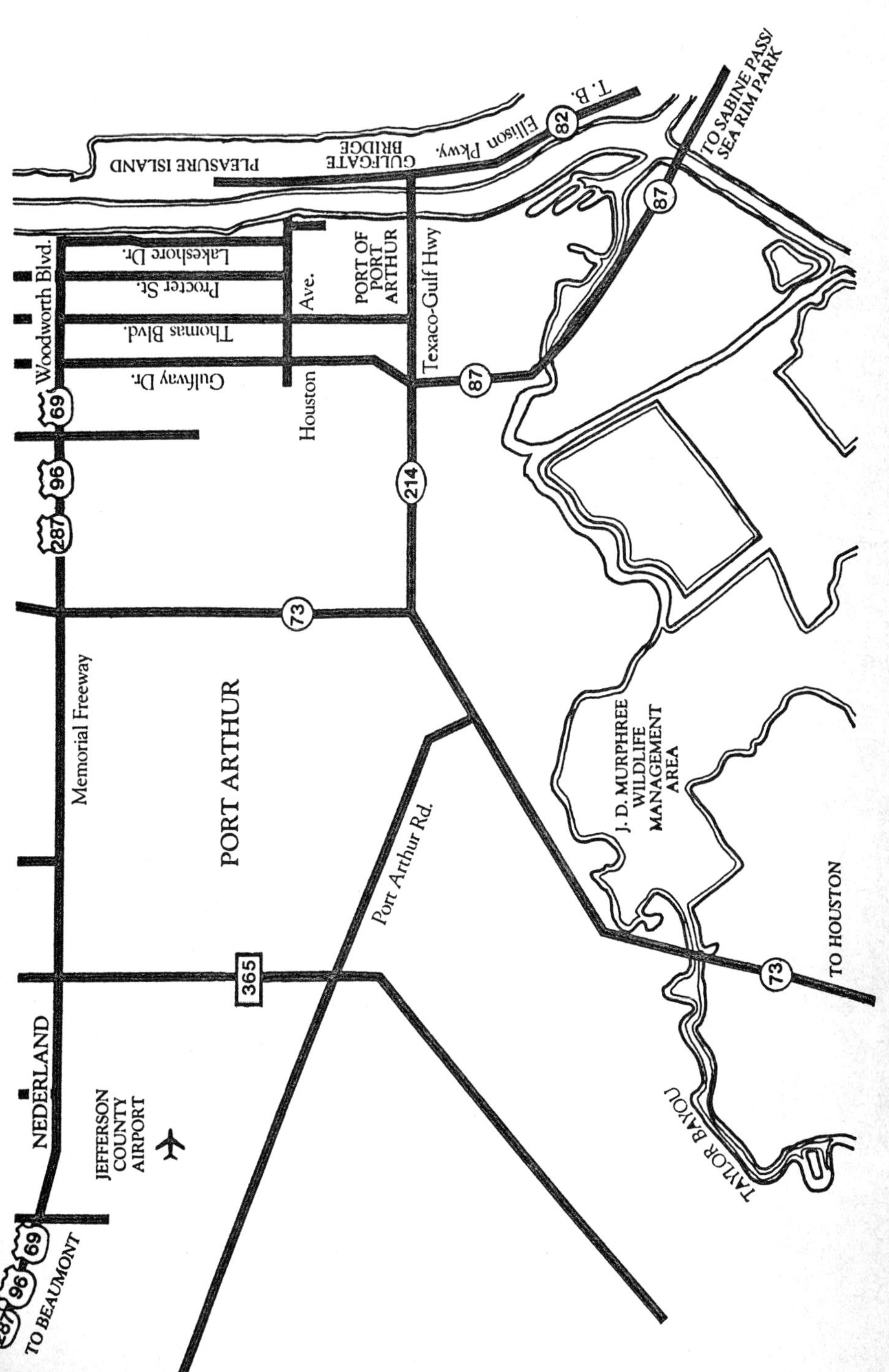

PLEASURE ISLAND
GULFGATE BRIDGE
Ellison Pkwy.
T. B.
82
TO SABINE PASS/ SEA RIM PARK
87
Woodworth Blvd.
Lakeshore Dr.
Procter St.
Thomas Blvd.
Gulfway Dr.
Houston Ave.
PORT OF PORT ARTHUR
Texaco-Gulf Hwy
69
96
287
214
73
Memorial Freeway
PORT ARTHUR
Port Arthur Rd.
J. D. MURPHREE WILDLIFE MANAGEMENT AREA
TO HOUSTON
365
NEDERLAND
JEFFERSON COUNTY AIRPORT
TAYLOR BAYOU
TO BEAUMONT

In recent years, the area has felt the sharp sting of the decline in the oil industry. From a tourist standpoint, however, this situation brings to mind the old saying that every dark cloud has a silver lining. The downturn in the economy forced the city fathers to look again at their area's natural and other attractions. The result is renewed emphasis on making the city more attractive for visitors. Plans are underway for the continuing development of Pleasure Island and the improvement of the waterfront area near the City Hall complex as a tourist attraction. In all probability Port Arthur will be — perhaps by the time you read this — a port for a cruise ship offering casino-style gambling.

Port Arthur and the nearby cities of Beaumont and Orange (See Side Trips) are known locally as the Golden Triangle.

TOURIST SERVICES

PORT ARTHUR CONVENTION AND VISITORS BUREAU
3401 Cultural Center (Texas 73 frontage road near 9th Ave., inside the Civic Center)
985-7822 Answering machine on weekends
W +

Here you can get a map, brochures, activities calendar, directions, and answers to your questions on everything from what to see to what's biting in the lake. On the wall outside the office is one of those maps that flashes a light at the spot you're seeking when you push a button. This is a good way to get oriented even if the office is closed.

GET-ACQUAINTED DRIVING TOUR

(A driving tour brochure is available from the Convention and Visitors Bureau.)

The first thing to note is that Port Arthur has both numbered streets and numbered avenues. The way to retain your sense of direction is to remember that the numbered streets run east and west while the numbered avenues run north and south.

A good starting place is the Convention and Visitors Bureau in the Civic Center on Texas 73 frontage road near 9th (See Tourist Services). Then, armed with a city map and brochures, you'll be able to get the most out of the tour.

Swing by the **Texas Artists Museum**, located near the Civic Center (See Museums) and then go east, past the library *to 9th Ave.* The library gallery features changing exhibits of art and history. At 9th Ave. *turn right under Texas 73.* A little over a mile down, on your right, is the Hughen School. What makes this school special is not just that it is the oldest institution in the state training children with severe orthopedic handicaps, but the number of celebrities involved with the school. If you look closely you'll see the name of one benefactor on the drive leading into the school — Bob Hope Drive. The high school is also named after him, and each year Hope comes here to sponsor a Celebrity

Golf Tournament and a benefit show bringing in many headline performer friends. Another old time benefactor was Jimmy Durante who donated the indoor swimming pool.

Just past the school, *turn left on 25th St.*, which leads into *Griffing Dr.* just past the railroad tracks. Here you will find Griffing Park, a section of Port Arthur with many large and carefully landscaped homes. Make your own route on the side streets, like Forest, Rosedale, or Evergreen. There are many gardens here and this area is usually part of the Spring Azalea Trail. When ready to continue the tour, work your way back to Griffing, *turn west* and go back to *9th Ave.* and *turn left* and continue *south.*

St. Mary's Hospital will be on your right just past 22nd St. About half a mile further on, you'll see several flags flying from flagpoles on your left. These mark Howard's Supermarket (950 9th Ave.). This is the largest home-owned grocery store in Texas and, like most other supermarkets, it has a bakery, florist, pharmacy, and gourmet food departments. But what makes Howard's unique is it also sells items like quince, cactus leaves, Mexican and oriental vegetables and other products not found in most supermarkets. It also contains a full-line hardware store and a cafeteria built to resemble an old grocery store. Howard's also stands out among supermarkets because it has a covered parking lot. And it recognizes who its customers are with signs in English, Spanish, and Vietnamese. This last because as you continue past this store (still on 9th) you'll be in a section heavily populated by Vietnamese. Here you'll find the **Queen of Peace Statue** (See Other Points of Interest) and a number of oriental shops.

Go past 5th St. and *turn right (west) on Proctor.* (The ill-fated rock star Janis Joplin was born at 4048 Proctor, but that's in the other direction and the building is no longer standing.) About a quarter mile down, on the left at 3300, is Eddingston Courts, the oldest large apartment complex in the city built in 1929, which is fenced in by a **wall made of shells** from the Cayman Islands (See Other Points of Interest). On your right at 2701 Proctor is the **Buu Mon Buddhist Temple** (See Other Points of Interest). Just past this is **Lamar University in Port Arthur** (See Colleges and Universities) with the **Gates Memorial Library**, which houses what was the Port Arthur Historical Museum and now expanded to include the temporary home of the **Museum of the Gulf Coast** until its new home is ready (See Museums). On your left at 700 Proctor is the site of the new Museum of the Gulf Coast that is scheduled to open around 1992. Ahead is the downtown area. Like many downtowns, it has deteriorated, but the city is moving forward with plans to revitalize it.

Turn left (south) at Fort Worth, then left again at 4th St. so you're heading east. On your right is the **City Hall** complex. You might want to stop at City Hall for an excellent view of the city and the lake from the fifth floor observation deck (See Bird's-Eye View). Continuing on, next to City Hall is the courthouse with its park and fish pond, and on your left the Port Arthur News Building and the police and fire stations.

Further along, on your right, 4th St. becomes *Lakeshore Dr.* At 1045 Lakeshore is the **Seaman's Memorial Sundial,** a tribute to the men of the ship *Texaco Oklahoma* that was lost at sea in 1971 and all others who have gone down to the sea in ships from Port Arthur. Just past this, if it's open to car traffic, angle *right* onto the **Walking Wall** (See Other Points of Interest). As you drive along the wall you'll pass Woodrow Wilson Junior High School on your left. Note the school's dome that is covered with gold leaf 1/2000 inch thick. On your right you might see an ocean-going vessel only a stone's throw away using the Sabine-Neches Waterway that is part of the Intracoastal Waterway. And beyond this is **Pleasure Island.** When you come off the Walking Wall, right ahead of you will be **Rose Hill Manor** (See Historic Places).

The tour bends back on itself at this point as you turn back onto *Lakeshore Dr. going west.* (If a U-turn is not permitted — the rules change now and then — go up Woodworth Blvd. in front of Rose Hill and go around the block to get back on Lakeshore going west.)

There are several historic homes on this street. At 2605 is the **Hogan House** built in 1915. Also from 1915 is the classic Greek Revival house **White Haven** at 2549. It is one of the three historic buildings along here that you can tour (See Historic Places). Another, which is probably the best known historic building in the city, is the **Pompeiian Villa,** the pink house at 1953 Lakeshore. Just past this, the three-story yellow brick building is the Masonic Temple, a relative newcomer, having been built in 1928, and at 1831 is the third home open to the public (by appointment), the Dutch colonial **Vuylsteke House** that was built by the Dutch Consul. Many of the other older homes along this street are in the process of being restored. Continue on Lakeshore as it turns back into 4th until it ends at Houston. To your left is the **Port of Port Arthur** that you can tour (See Other Points of Interest).

Turn right (north) on Houston. Continue past 11th St. and *turn left (west) at the light on Thomas.* This will take you into the refinery area where you'll pass some of the world's largest refineries. *At Texas 82, turn left (south)* and cross the **Martin Luther King Gulfgate Bridge** to **Pleasure Island** (See Other Points of Interest). This bridge over the Sabine-Neches Waterway is both narrow and steep, rising 138 feet above mean low tide, so the driver shouldn't be sightseeing. But even the driver can get a grand view of **Sabine Lake** and across into neighboring Louisiana as the car comes down from the high point on the bridge. *At the stop sign, turn right* and go back under the bridge to see the facilities on Pleasure Island. If you want a waterside view of the Port, this is a good place to stop.

After you explore the island, turn back and go back over the bridge to the mainland. Be sure to take the left onto the bridge access road or, if you go straight, you'll wind up in Louisiana. Coming down off the bridge, you can see all the refineries laid out in front of you.

The Get-Acquainted Tour ends here. If you want to get back to your starting point at the Civic Center, continue straight on Texas 82, across 87 onto 214 which will take you back to Texas 73. Turn right on 73 and follow it back to the start.

Want to expand the tour? Just take a left at Texas 87 and follow it out to **Sabine Pass** and **Sea Rim State Park** (See Side Trips). Don't worry, you can't get lost — Texas 87 is all there is.

BIRD'S-EYE VIEW

CITY HALL OBSERVATION BALCONY
444 4th St.
983-8100
Monday–Friday 8–5
Free
W +

From various locations on the covered fifth-floor balcony you can see the Intracoastal Waterway, Pleasure Island, Sabine Lake, Lakeshore Drive, the downtown area, and the acres and acres of refineries. If the weather isn't right for balcony viewing, you can still see a lot from inside through the windowed walls of The Heritage Room, where old photos and other memorabilia of Port Arthur's past are on display.

MUSEUMS

LA MAISONS DES ACADIENS AND DUTCH WINDMILL MUSEUM
Tex Ritter Park, 1500 Boston near 17th St., five blocks west of Twin City Hwy, Nederland
722-0279 (Nederland Chamber of Commerce)
March 1 through Labor Day: Tuesday–Sunday 1–5; after Labor Day: Thursday–Sunday 1–5
Free

It's an unusual grouping: a park dedicated to the memory of country singing star "Tex" Ritter containing two small museums commemorating two diverse groups, the Cajuns and the Dutch. The House of the Acadians is a replica of an early, rustic home of the French immigrants who settled in Louisiana after being forced out of Nova Scotia by the British in the eighteenth century. Their descendants are the Cajuns who came to Texas. Towering over the park is a 40-foot high replica of a Dutch windmill with 25-foot blades. Inside are memorabilia of "Tex" Ritter, who grew up in Nederland, and the Dutch and other nationalities who settled the area. Wooden shoes and other items imported from the Netherlands are for sale in the gift shop. If you want any other information on Nederland, that city's Chamber of Commerce office is across from the park at 1515 Boston.

MUSEUM OF THE GULF COAST
Gates Memorial Library, Stilwell at Proctor
983-4921
Monday–Friday 9–5 or by appointment
Free
W

Located in a wing of the library of Lamar University at Port Arthur, this small museum is crowded with an interesting hodgepodge of exhibits designed to tell the story of both the city and the Gulf Coast from Houston to New Orleans. Featured is the American Pop Culture exhibit that pays tribute to the contributions made in music, sports, arts, and entertainment by people who lived along this coast. These include musicians ranging from Janis Joplin and "Tex" Ritter to Ivory Joe Hunter and Clarence "Gatemouth" Brown; sports greats including "Bum" Phillips, "Babe" Didrikson Zaharias, and "Bubba" Smith; and artists such as Robert Rauchenberg. And if you take the time to browse among the other exhibits you'll find items ranging from a contract to pay a dowry executed by James Bowie in 1831 to a photo of the first Queen of Port Arthur taken in 1923. The library facility is too small to display the many other items in the museum's permanent collection that tell the story of the Gulf coast from the earliest known history to the present. These must await the new building to have their day in the sun.

TEXAS ARTISTS MUSEUM
3501 Cultural Center Dr.
983-4881
Tuesday–Wednesday 1–5, Friday 9–1, Saturday 10–2
Free
W +

This small, private museum, located just north of the Civic Center, features the works of local and regional artists in a variety of media.

HISTORIC PLACES

LA MAISON BEAUSOLEIL
701 Rue Beausoleil in Port Neches Park off Grigsby Ave., Port Neches
722-3466
By appointment for groups only

Built in 1810, this house was barged in from Vermillion Parish, Louisiana by *"Les Acadien du Texas,"* an organization with the mission of preserving the culture and language of the Acadian people who were deported to Louisiana from Nova Scotia in 1755. The name *"Beausoleil,"* which means beautiful sunshine, was originally the name of a town in Nova Scotia founded by the Acadian freedom fighter Joseph Brossard dit Beausoleil.

POMPEIIAN VILLA
1953 Lakeshore near Richmond
983-5977
Monday–Friday 9–4 or by appointment
Adults $2, children under 12 free

Sometimes called the "Billion Dollar House," this building's history is almost as fascinating as the villa itself. At the turn of the century, three tycoons bought a strip of waterfront land on Lakeshore Dr. where they planned to build adjoining "winter cottages." John W. "Bet-a-Million" Gates built a 20-room, Virginia-style colonial, while Isaac Ellwood, "the Barbed-Wire King," built a modest 10-room "cottage" that was an authentic copy of a Pompeiian home of 79 A.D. The rooms of this house were built around a traditional Roman peristyle, a three-sided courtyard with access to each room. Shortly after it was completed, Ellwood sold the house to the third member of the group, James Hopkins, president of the Diamond Match Company, who had never built on his lot. Hopkins brought his wife down from St. Louis, but when she arrived and faced the heat, mosquitos, and muddy streets of early Port Arthur, she promptly turned around and went back up north. So Hopkins traded his house to George Craig, banker and land developer, for 10 percent of the stock in the newly formed Texas Company, a forerunner of Texaco. When asked later why he gave up all this stock for the house, Craig said, "Oil companies were a dime a dozen then. How did I know the Texas Company would survive." But survive it did, and the stock traded for the house would now be worth close to three billion dollars. The Gates colonial was torn down in 1960 and in the early 1970s the Villa, one of the last houses remaining from the colorful early days of the city, was close to meeting the same fate. The Port Arthur Historical Society came to its rescue and has since restored its former opulence.

The pink stucco villa has been refurbished with antiques that might be typical of the furnishings used by the Craig family, including a Louis XVI parlor set, Savannerie rug, Baccarat crystal, Sheffield candelabras, and a George Hepplewhite chest of drawers dating from about 1790. The Villa is listed in the National Register of Historic Places.

ROSE HILL MANOR
100 Woodworth at Lakeshore
985-7292
Tuesday–Friday 8:30–5, Saturday 8:30–noon, or by appointment
Free
W ramp in rear

Another home listed in the National Register of Historic Places and one of the oldest landmarks in the city, this colonial-style mansion was built in 1906 by Rome H. Woodworth, an early banker and mayor. It remained in the Woodworth family until 1948 when it was deeded to the city and is now maintained by the Rose Hill Committee, which is working to restore the house to its original appearance. This lovely house is often rented for weddings and other social and civic events, so call to find out if it's open before making a special trip there.

SABINE PASS BATTLEGROUND STATE HISTORICAL PARK
Take Texas 87 south about 14 miles to Sabine Pass, then south about 1.5 miles on FM 3322
971-2559 (Sea Rim State Park)
Open at all times
W

The story of the Civil War battle fought here sounds like a Texas Tall Tale, but it's true. On September 8, 1863, a Union fleet numbering some

20 vessels and about 4,000 men tried to invade Texas through Sabine Pass. Facing them all alone was Company F of the Texas Heavy Artillery that consisted of some 40 Irish dockworkers lead by a lieutenant, who was a young barkeep from Houston named Dick Dowling, and six cannon set up in unfinished earthworks reinforced with railroad iron and ships' timbers. The battle started when four Union gunboats attacked the tiny Confederate force, bombarding Dowling's position. Dowling held fire until the ships were in close range, then the gunners quickly disabled two of the ships. Directing their fire at the troop carriers, the Confederates forced the fleet to turn tail and head back to New Orleans. The battle lasted less than an hour. Final score: Dowling wound up with all six of his cannon and no casualties while the Union force lost two gunboats, 65 men killed, wounded, or missing; and 315 captured. Needless to say, Dowling was a hero to Texans for the rest of his life. Time and erosion have wiped out all evidence of the exact site of gun emplacements, but this 56-acre park was built on the probable site and Dowling's victory is commemorated with a statue. Also the battle is reenacted here occasionally during "Dick Dowling Days" (See Annual Events). The park offers visitors an interpretive center with details of the battle, picnic sites, restrooms, a boat ramp, and a fish-cleaning station.

VUYLSTEKE DUTCH HOME
1831 Lakeshore
983-4921
Tours by appointment only
Free

This two-story house was built in 1906 in Dutch style by the Dutch Consul to Port Arthur. The home has been restored to its original condition with original furnishings. Among its features are three fireplaces that share one central chimney. It is owned by Lamar University at Port Arthur.

WHITE HAVEN
2545 Lakeshore
982-3068
Monday, Wednesday, and Friday 10–1, Sunday 1–4
$2 donation requested

Originally built as a New England colonial style mansion in 1915, it was changed by a subsequent owner to a Southern Greek Revival style by the addition of large verandas and columns. The Whites, the last owners of the house, filled it with a large collection of Victorian furnishings and other antiques. On display are early pieces of Wedgewood china, a French-made screen from the collection of Empress Carlotta of Mexico, and candelabras from the Shah of Persia. Stella White, who was a founder of the local chapter of the Daughters of the American Revolution (DAR), left the two-story house to that chapter on her death in 1985.

OTHER POINTS OF INTEREST

BUU MON BUDDHIST TEMPLE
2701 Proctor
982-9319
Free

Built as a Baptist church more than 40 years ago, this building was converted to a Catholic church by the Vietnamese community in 1976 and then in 1987 remodeled into a Buddhist temple which included changing the steeple to the characteristic Stupa, the three-tiered pogoda-style tower that contains a sacred relic. Visitors are welcome at the worship service for the public every Sunday afternoon at 2:30.

CONCH SHELL WALL
3300 Proctor

Captain A. Eddingston paid Cayman Islands divers to dive for the more than 5,200 pearly-pink conch shells used in the wall at the entrance to the Eddingston Court apartments, which he opened in 1929. The shells were hauled to Port Arthur in two barges and artisans were brought in from Mexico to construct the wall. Reportedly, this is the only shell wall of this size outside the Caribbean.

ELAINE EITEL DOLLHOUSE MUSEUM
2234 Nederland Ave., Port Neches
722-0103
By appointment only
Free (Donations accepted for "My Wish, Inc.")

Among the many unusual houses in Elaine Eitel's large collection of doll houses are an adobe house, a Cajun home, one with a miniature working TV, and four large dollhouses decorated to reflect the four seasons. The collection is located in a small building behind the Port Neches Clinic.

PLEASURE ISLAND
Take Texas 82 over Martin Luther King-Gulfgate Bridge
982-4675 (Pleasure Island Commission)

Slowly but surely, this 3,500-acre island located between the 400-foot wide Sabine-Neches Ship Channel and Sabine Lake is being developed to live up to its name and become an all-round resort. Facilities include a 10-acre concert park, a marina, picnic areas, lighted fishing pier, boat launches, charter fishing boats, RV parks and free camping areas, a sailboard club, condominiums, and restaurants. The island's north levee gives Texas City's Dike competition for the title of the "world's longest fishing pier." Plans? Well, they are grandiose and may not all come true, but on the drawing boards are a golf course, tennis courts, a public beach, and at least one hotel.

PORT OF PORT ARTHUR
East end of Houston St. near 4th
983-2029
Free
W

Even though it's small, this port bustles with all the normal activities found at much larger ports, but its size makes it easier to see them all. One of the highlights, especially if you see it in action, is a 75-ton gantry crane appropriately named "Big Arthur." To tour, stop at the gate and the guard will get you a guide. Conducted group tours can be arranged through the Convention and Visitors Bureau (985-7822).

QUEEN OF PEACE PARK
9th Ave. near 9th St.
983-7676 (Church)
Free
W

This pocket park was established by the parishioners of Queen of Vietnamese Martyrs Catholic Church, which is across the street, in thanksgiving for their escape from Vietnam. About 95 percent of the Vietnamese immigrants who came here in the early 1970s are Catholic and the other 5 percent are of the Buddhist faith (See Buu Mon Temple, above). The centerpiece of the park is a three-times lifesize statue of Mary, Queen of Peace. At Christmas time more than 700,000 lights are strung here depicting scenes from scripture. Many of the Vietnamese still wear their native clothing at Sunday Mass in the church to which visitors are welcome.

RAINBOW BRIDGE
Over the Neches River on Texas 87 north of city

This bridge, completed in 1938, is the tallest on the Gulf coast, rising to the height of a 20-story building and clearing the river by 177 feet. This exceptional clearance is the result of over-diligent designers who wanted to ensure that everything afloat at the time could pass under it. The determining "tallest" ship then was a U. S. Navy dirigible tender with a huge dirigible mooring mast on its aft deck. Ironically, by the time the bridge was built the ship was out of service. The height does make for a spectacular view for everyone but the driver who may compare it to driving a roller coaster. The rainbow-style arch of the bridge and its original orange-red coloring lead to its name. The new companion bridge to the east has only 133 feet navigational clearance, but its claim to fame is that it is the only cable-stayed bridge built on a Texas highway. The marshy area surrounding the bridges is the home of many wildlife species including ducks, geese, cranes, and alligators.

THE REFINERIES
West and south of downtown along Texas 82, 87, and 73

Group tours only
W

From a distance at night, this area looks like a city of lights or Christmas trees lying on their sides. Unfortunately, the magic disappears in daylight. Still, the major plants here for Chevron, Texaco, and American Petrofina, lead city boosters to call this "the world's largest oil refinery-petrochemical complex." The Chevron refinery, for example, boasts both the largest crude processing unit and largest catalytic reformer in the world, so it's worth driving by on the highways for a closer look. A guided tour for bus groups can be arranged through the Convention and Visitors Bureau with about two weeks notice.

SABINE LAKE
Bordering the city on the east

This 78-square mile lake is really not a lake at all, but a bay system leading to the Gulf. As a result, it is a mixture of fresh water from the feeding Neches and Sabine Rivers on the north end and incoming tidal salt water from the Gulf on the south. The lake is popular locally for fishing, boating, sailboarding and other water sports. It forms part of the border between Texas and Louisiana.

SABINE PASS LIGHTHOUSE

Technically, it's in Louisiana, but you can see it across the Sabine-Neches Waterway just below the battleground park. Built in 1856, this 85-foot tower sent the light from its Belgian-constructed lens as far as 18 miles into the Gulf. Decommissioned in 1952, it is now owned by the Louisiana Game and Fish Department. The lens is on display in the Museum of the Gulf Coast in Port Arthur.

WALKING WALL
Between Lakeshore Dr. and the Intracoastal Waterway from Savannah to Woodworth

This is part of the city's $89 million flood protection system, a virtual dike around the city. Cars can drive on it weekdays between 8 a.m. and 5 p.m. Auto traffic is one-way (south to north). Cars are not permitted at other times and on weekends. Then it's reserved for walkers and joggers and those who want to sit on the bank and wave at the ships passing on the Intracoastal Waterway or watch activities on Pleasure Island across the channel.

SPORTS AND ACTIVITIES

Birdwatching

Port Arthur is located on the Central Fly-way for waterfowl, so during the migratory season, birds are everywhere. Pleasure Island is one of the more accessible places to observe them. Not as accessible, but also not as disturbed by civilization are:

McFaddin Marsh National Wildlife Refuge, along the Gulf coast west of Sea Rim State Park. Office at Shell Oil Company Rd. off Texas 87. Refuge Headquarters at Anahuac (409) 267-3337.

Texas Point National Wildlife Refuge, Sabine Pass. Also contains one of the densest populations of American Alligators in Texas. Refuge Headquarters at Anahuac (409) 267-3337.

J. D. Murphree Wildlife Management Area, Texas 73 approximately five miles west of Port Arthur. 736-2551.

Sea Rim State Park (See Side Trips)

Fishing

Port Arthur is doubly blessed because freshwater catches are plentiful in the rivers and bayous and upper reaches of the lake, while saltwater fish eager for the hook are found in the lower lake and the Gulf. And, of course, there's excellent fishing in some of the wildlife areas (See Birdwatching). And don't forget the greedy crabs that always seem to be waiting for the bait in the area waterways. Strict and sometimes confusing licensing and limit requirements are set by the game wardens from two states who patrol the area. Check locally to see what you need for your particular fishing spot. Or go charter and let the Captain straighten it out. Charter boats are usually available for $600-$800 a day for up to six persons. For a complete list of guides and charter boat services contact the Convention and Visitors Bureau (985-7822).

Golf

BABE DIDRIKSON ZAHARIAS MEMORIAL GOLF COURSE
75TH St. just off US 69
722-8286

Eighteen-hole course. Green fees $4-$5.

PORT ARTHUR COUNTRY CLUB
Texas 73 and Port Arthur Country Club Rd.
796-1312

Eighteen-hole course. Open to public Mondays only. Green fees $7.

PORT GROVES GOLF CLUB
5721 Monroe Blvd., Groves
926-0406

Nine-hole course open to the public. Green fees about $2.50 for nine holes, weekends $3.50.

Hunting

Birds, birds, birds, and more birds! Plus deer, wild turkeys, and a number of other game animals can be hunted in this area in season.

And now that alligators have been protected into over-population, there's even an occasional season for them. Hunting is permitted in some of the wildlife preserves and Sea Rim State Park, and there are hunting leases and a number of hunting clubs available. For information contact the Convention and Visitors Bureau (985-7822).

Jogging

For interesting scenery as you jog, try the Walking Wall or Pleasure Island (See other Points of Interest).

Tennis

Courts — some lighted — can be found at most of the high schools and the following parks:

Adams Park, 61st St. between 9th Ave. and US 69.
Babe Didrikson Zaharias Memorial Golf Course, 75th St. and US 69.
Doornbos Park, Nederland, Ave. H between S. 24th St. and S. 27th. St.
Reynolds Park, 4100 block of 36th St.
Rose Hill Park, 2900 Proctor at Woodworth.

COLLEGES AND UNIVERSITIES

LAMAR UNIVERSITY AT PORT ARTHUR
1500 Proctor near Stilwell
983-4921
W Variable

This school's emphasis is on academic transfer and technical arts courses, and since 1975, when the Texas Legislature approved the merger of Port Arthur College with Beaumont's Lamar University to establish a branch here, its enrollment has increased more than ten-fold from about 150 to over 2,000. An interesting sidelight of the merger is that the Legislature did not authorize funds for buildings until 1983, eight years later. The people of Port Arthur solved that problem by donating buildings. The Renaissance-style Gates Memorial Library was one of those donated. It was designed by the same architects who designed New York's Grand Central Station and was originally donated to the city by the wife of John "Bet-a-Million" Gates for use as a library. The building, which is listed in the National Register of Historic Places, is now the home to the student library and the university's rare book collection as well as the temporary lodging for the Museum of the Gulf Coast (See Museums). The Ruby Ruth Fuller Building was another donation. Originally the First Methodist Church from 1916 to 1976, it was often used as an auditorium for famous visiting speakers. It continues in that role and additionally is used for touring entertainers who put on shows open to the public. For information on scheduled performances call 724-0886. Tours of both these buildings can be arranged through the school or the Port Arthur Convention and Visitors Bureau.

PERFORMING ARTS

PORT ARTHUR CIVIC CENTER
3401 Cultural Center Dr. (Texas 73 near 9th Ave.)
985-8801
Admission depends on event
W + But not all areas

Concerts and other musical events are scheduled here throughout the year. It is also the site of trade fairs, car and boat shows, and several annual festivals.

PORT ARTHUR LITTLE THEATER
4701 75th St.
722-7732
Admission
W

This community group usually stages about five productions at its theater and the Civic Center during its October through June season.

SHOPPING

CENTRAL MALL
Texas 365 and Memorial Hwy (US 69)
727-5592
W

This one-story mall has over 70 stores and restaurants anchored by Beall's, Dillard's, Penney's, and Sears.

MIDWAY TRADE FAIR
Nederland Ave. at 27th St., Nederland
721-9900
Open Friday–Sunday
W

This is a collection of small shops in a large store on the corner of a shopping strip. Costumed clerks sell a variety of items ranging from country crafts to hand-painted dresses to antiques.

SNOOPER'S PARADISE
5509 East Parkway in Cambridge Square (39th St. exit off Texas 73), Groves
962-8427
W

Here are 57 rooms (26,000 square feet) filled mostly with European furniture and other antiques from the nineteenth century. The owners make several trips a year to personally comb Europe for their stock. A catalog is available by mail.

SIDE TRIPS

ANAHUAC NATIONAL WILDLIFE REFUGE

Take Texas 73 west to Texas 124 near Winnie, then south on Texas 124 to FM 1985, then west approximately 10.5 miles to refuge sign, then left approximately three miles
267-3337
Open at all times
Free
W

Roseate spoonbills, herons, egrets, pelicans, and snow and blue geese are among the more than 40 species of birds that winter in this 24,293-acre refuge on East Bay. These are among the major temporary tenants here, but more than 250 species visit regularly and are included on the checklist provided for birdwatchers. In addition to wildlife observation and photography, other activities for visitors at the refuge include limited hunting, fishing, and camping. For information contact the refuge manager at P.O. Box 278, Anahuac, TX 77514.

BEAUMONT

Beaumont is often called the Museum Capital of Texas because it features close to a dozen museums. This listing covers only a sampling of the highlights of the city. For a fuller account of Beaumont including history, restaurants, accommodations, etc., see *The Texas Monthly Guidebook: Texas.*

Beaumont Convention And Visitors Bureau
701 Main near College, in Civic Center (P.O. Box 3827, 77704)
838-3421
W +

The bureau also operates an information center at the Babe Didrikson Zaharias Museum (See Zaharias Museum) and a 24-hour phone line (838-3634 or in Texas 800-392-4401) with a recording telling what's happening in Beaumont, Port Arthur, and Orange.

Port of Beaumont Observation Deck
Milam off Main, south of Jefferson County Courthouse
832-1546
Monday–Friday 8:30–4:30
Free

Even though it is located 42 miles inland from the Gulf of Mexico, on the deep-water Neches River ship channel, this is one of the busiest ports in Texas, handling over 30 million tons of cargo annually. Admission is free, but you must check in with the security guard at the main gate. The observation deck is located on top of the huge Harbor Island Transit Warehouse, about a quarter mile from the main gate. There is also a scale model of the early and present port with a short audio presentation. Tours are available by reservation.

Mary and John Grey Library
Lamar University, 4400 Martin Luther King Parkway
880-8118
Open during school term, hours vary
Free
W

You can get a good bird's-eye view of Lamar University, Beaumont and all the way to Port Arthur from the eighth floor. And while you're in the building, stop on the seventh floor to see the replica of Congressman Jack Brook's office in Washington. It's usually open Monday-Friday 9-4. While on the university campus you might also want to visit the Gladys City Boom Town (See Gladys City) and the Dishman Art Gallery (Lavaca and Martin Luther King, open Monday-Friday 8-4:30).

Art Museum Of Southeast Texas
500 Main
832-3432
Tuesday–Saturday 9–5 (until 8 on Thursday only), Sunday 2–5, closed Monday
Free
W

The permanent collection of paintings, sculpture, and mixed media features mostly Texas artists. There are also a number of national and international traveling exhibitions scheduled here each year, showings of classic and contemporary films, a highly regarded lecture series, and occasional performances by musical and theatrical groups. Gift shop and tea room.

Babe Didrikson Zaharias Museum and Visitors Center
I-10 at Gulf exit
833-4622
Open seven days 9–5
Free
W +

Mildred "Babe" Didrikson Zaharias grew up in Beaumont and the city has honored her as she honored it. The museum, with a design symbolizing the five Olympic circles, displays the memorabilia of the Babe's outstanding athletic career that earned her the Associated Press award as "Woman Athlete of the Year" six times. Among the exhibits is a short film showing her in action and a 15-foot, 250-pound key given to her by the City of Denver. Gift shop. Visitors Center normally open longer hours in summer.

Beaumont Police Museum
255 College
880-3814
Monday–Friday 8–5
Free
W

The exhibits in this small museum, located in the basement, depict the history of the Beaumont police force with displays of uniforms, guns, criminal case histories, and other memorabilia.

Edison Plaza Museum
350 Pine, behind the Gulf States Utilities Bldg
839-3089
Monday–Friday 8–5 (Summer 7:30–4:30) or by appointment, closed major holidays
Free
W Downstairs only
Some visitor parking usually available in Gulf States employees' lot

Thomas Alva Edison is credited with 1,093 inventions during his life, and examples or illustrations of many of these are on display here, including a replica of the original electric light. Of course, after he invented the light bulb, he had to invent generators and other commercial electrical equipment to produce and distribute the power to the people who used the electric light. Appropriately housed in the restored Travis Street Power Substation, which was built in the 1920s, the museum exhibits are displayed in three sections, Yesterday, Today, and Tomorrow. These tell the story of how the electric industry, stemming from Edison's inventive genius, has become an integral part of our lives. Gift shop sells Edison-related items including booklets with Edison's experiments that students can do, and patent drawings of the first phonograph, telegraph, and some of his other inventions.

Gladys City Boom Town
Lamar University, University Dr. and US 69/96/287 (Cardinal Dr.)
880-8896
Tuesday–Friday and Sunday 1–5, Saturday 9–5, closed Monday
Adults 50¢, children 25¢
W

This is a reconstruction of the oil boom town that appeared almost overnight after Spindletop blew in on January 10, 1901. It is operated by Lamar University as an outdoor living history museum. The 15 clapboard buildings grouped around a plank sidewalk square include a log cabin saloon, barber shop, oil company offices, livery stable, general store, pharmacy and doctor's office. All that's missing is the smell of oil, the sea of mud, and the excited crowds of boomers who jammed the streets during the town's heyday. In the same area is a National Historic Landmark, the Lucas Gusher Monument, a memorial to the Spindletop pioneers.

John Jay French Historic House Museum
2995 French Rd. off Delaware
898-0348
Tuesday–Saturday 10–4, Sunday 1–4, closed Monday
Adults $2, students 50¢

This is the oldest house in Beaumont, built in 1845. French, a tanner and merchant, brought his family from Connecticut, built this simple

Greek Revival House, opened a tannery nearby, and began trading goods. The home was the first two-story house in Beaumont, the first built with lumber instead of logs, and the first painted house. It remained in the French family for 95 years. The museum depicts the life and times of a typical East Texas settler of the mid-nineteenth century with authentic furnishings and some original pieces donated by descendants of the French family. Gift shop.

Julie Rogers Theatre For The Performing Arts
765 Pearl at Forsythe, across from the Civic Center
838-3421
Admission varies by event
W +
Pay parking for some events

This is the center for cultural events in the city. With seating for about 1,700, the refurbished theater is the home of the Beaumont Symphony Orchestra, the Civic Ballet, the Ballet Theatre, and the Civic Opera.

McFaddin-Ward House
1906 McFaddin; Visitors Center on Calder at 3rd
832-1906
Tuesday–Sunday 10–4, closed Monday
$3

This is one of the best-preserved, large-scale examples of Beaux Arts Colonial-style homes in the United States. Built in 1906, the 12,800-square-foot, 17-room mansion reflects the lifestyle of the wealthy Southeast Texas family that owned and managed ranches, rice farms, and oil fields. It is elegantly furnished with fine furniture, oriental rugs, sparkling silver, European porcelains, and American brilliant-period cutglass collected over a span of 60 years by the McFaddin family. Guided tours take approximately one hour. The house is listed in the National Register of Historic Places.

Telephone Pioneer Museum
555 Main, in Southwestern Bell Bldg.
839-6510
By appointment only
Free
W

Another small, specialized museum displaying mostly old telephone equipment and memorabilia.

Texas Energy Museum
600 Main at Forsythe
833-0247
Tuesday–Saturday 9–5, Sunday 1–5
Admission
W +

The nucleus of this new 30,000-square-foot museum is the exhibits from The Western Company Museum, formerly in Fort Worth, that the Smithsonian Institution called "the most perfectly conceptualized oil and gas museum in the United States and Europe" and those of Beaumont's Spindletop Museum. Added to these are new exhibits to round out the story of energy in the broadest perspective from macroscopic, the birth of the universe and our Earth, to the microscopic, the hydrocarbon molecular structures that provide the energy we use. Much of this is highlighted in a 120-foot history wall that shows the various forms of energy. Naturally, since this is a Texas museum, the focus is on oil and gas energy and exhibits go into detail on all phases of exploration, production, transportation, refining, and marketing.

Texas State Fire Museum
400 Walnut at Mulberry, in Beaumont Fire Department Headquarters
838-0620
Monday–Friday 8–4:30
Free (donations accepted)
W

Among the displays of fire fighting equipment here are an 1856 hand-drawn tub pumper, an 1879 American Steamer, a 1909 aerial ladder truck, and the first searchlight truck used by firemen in the United States, which was constructed in Beaumont in 1931. The oldest piece of fire fighting memorabilia in the museum is a fire rattle from Boston that was used to alert the villagers of night fires in the mid-1600s. For the kids — and those of us who always dreamed of being a fireman — there's a demonstration pole to slide down. Beaumont is an appropriate location for this museum since the city is the site of one of the two largest fire fighters' training facilities in the world. The other is at Texas A&M and thousands of fire fighters from all over the world come to these two facilities for training.

LOUISIANA'S CREOLE NATURE TRAIL

If you drive over to Pleasure Island and take the road to Louisiana, you'll wind up in Cameron Parish where you can follow the looping Creole Nature Trail. Along the trail you can visit the Sabine Wildlife Refuge, the Rockefeller Wildlife Refuge, the town of Hackberry, which proclaims itself the "Crab Capital of the World," and wind up in Lake Charles, the largest city in Southwest Louisiana. A brochure with map is usually available from the Port Arthur Convention and Visitors Bureau or write the Southwest Louisiana Convention and Visitors Bureau, 1211 N. Lakeshore Dr. (P.O. Box 1912), Lake Charles, LA 70601 (318/436-9588).

ORANGE

Orange is Texas' easternmost city, sitting on the border with Louisiana. This listing covers only a sampling of the highlights of the city. For a fuller account of Orange including history, restaurants, accommodations, etc., see *The Texas Monthly Guidebook: Texas.*

Greater Orange Chamber of Commerce
1012 Green Ave. at 10th
833-3536
W

On weekends, brochures and maps are available in the gas stations on I-10 and in local hotels.

Texas Travel Information Center
I-10 at Louisiana state line
883-9416
Open seven days 8–5
W +

One of 12 roadside information centers operated by the Texas Department of Highways and Public Transportation on key highways entering the state. Trained travel counselors can provide a wealth of free information, official highway maps, and tons of other travel literature on Orange and the rest of Texas.

Civic Plaza
Downtown Orange around Green and 7th
Best parking at Green and 7th across from art museum and Main and 5th across from library

This is the center for a number of tourist attractions and important buildings. Within walking distance are the historic City Hall, County Courthouse, Lutcher Theater, Stark Museum, Stark Mansion, Heritage House Museum, the First Presbyterian Church and Farmer's Mercantile.

Farmer's Mercantile
702 W. Division at 6th
883-2941
W

A browser's delight, this old-time wooden-floored farm and general store was opened in 1928 and is still run by the same family who still stock many items that were in vogue on opening day. If you're looking for hog rings, a horse collar, or a butter churn you'll probably find them here. And in the grocery department you can pick up an empty egg carton and fill it with your choice of eggs from a basket.

First Presbyterian Church (Lutcher Memorial Building)
902 W. Green Ave. at 8th
883-2097
Visitors welcome anytime the church is open (access through 8th St. entrance), group tours by appointment only
W

This stately memorial to the H. J. Lutcher family took four years (1908-1912) to build, but the appealing results of this investment of time and money are still beautifully evident. The stained glass windows were made in New York by hand techniques that are no longer commercially available, and the three above the front door won prizes in the Chicago World's Fair in 1893. Much of the marble was imported from Italy, the pews and woodwork are mahogany, the church has the only opalescent glass dome in the United States, and many of the decorations are overlaid in gold leaf. The church also has the distinction of being one of the first public buildings in the world to be air conditioned.

Heritage House Museum
905 Division, just west of Civic Plaza
886-5385
Tuesday–Friday 10–4, closed Saturday through Monday
Adults $1, students and senior citizens 50¢

Part of this rambling, two-story, turn-of-the-century home is furnished to reflect the lifestyle of an upper-middle-class family in the early 1900s. The rest of the house is a museum relating the history of Orange County with both permanent and changing exhibits. The house is listed in the National Register of Historic Places.

Lutcher Theater for the Performing Art
707 W. Main at Civic Plaza (P.O. Box 2310, 77630), 886- 5535
Admission varies with show
W

A modern 1,500 seat theater offering about a dozen professional productions a year ranging from cowboy comedy to touring Broadway shows and light opera.

Petrochemical Row
FM 1006 south of town

A mile-long complex of plants producing a variety of products derived from petroleum. The many companies located on the row represent an investment of nearly $3 billion.

Stark Museum of Art
712 Green at 7th, Civic Plaza
883-6661
Wednesday–Saturday 10–5, Sunday 1–5, closed Monday, Tuesday, and major holidays
Free
W

The building itself is a work of art having won an award for excellence of concept, design and construction in the use of natural stone. Inside, the exhibits reflect the Stark family's wide-ranging interests in land, wildlife, and the people of the American West. Significant among the exhibits are American Indian pottery and artifacts, original Audubon folios of birds of Texas and Louisiana, bronze sculptures by Remington and Russell, a collection of lifesize porcelain birds by Margaret Doughty and Edward Boehm that rival the Audubon prints in attention to detail. There is also a collection of Stueben glass bowls called "The United

States in Crystal," a series etched with scenes representing the history of each of the fifty states. Perhaps to offset the dignity of these impressive works, there is also a group of "Andy" Anderson's humorous "whittlings" in wood going by such aptly descriptive titles as "The Shotgun Wedding."

W. H. Stark House
Green at 6th, Civic Plaza
Entrance through Carriage House at 610 W. Main
Tuesday–Saturday 10–3, closed Sunday and Monday
Reservations required. Children 14 and over welcome if accompanied by an adult
$2

If the Heritage House reflects the life of the upper-middle-class, this house tells in many ways what it was like to be one of the richest families in the area at the turn of the century. The restored 1894 Queen Anne Victorian home is the only surviving structure of the many fine houses that once lined the tree-shaded streets of this neighborhood. The 15-room, three-story home with its many gables, galleries, and distinctive windowed turrets shows the influence of several architectural styles. Today the house stands much as it did when the H. J. Lutcher and W. H. Stark families lived here, with its original furniture, rugs, silver, ceramics, woodwork, and family portraits. It is listed in the National Register of Historic Places.

SEA RIM STATE PARK
About 14 miles west of Sabine Pass on Texas 87
971-2559
March–October open seven days 8–10 for day use; November-February open seven days 8–5 for day use; at all times for camping but gates close at day use closing hours
$2 per vehicle per day
W + but not all areas

This park is unique because it is the only marshland park in the state. It is also the best beach park on the eastern end of the Texas coast. The highway divides the 15,109-acre park into two distinct areas. South, on the Gulf, is the Beach Unit with three miles of wide, sandy beach, a 3,650-foot boardwalk nature trail, and a little over two miles of a biologically important zone where the salt tidal marshlands meet the Gulf waters. Behind the beach is the park headquarters, observation deck, camping area (fee) and Interpretive Center. Across the highway, the Marshlands Unit has a boat ramp, a channel with canoe and pirogue trails that allow access to the marsh, and several observation platforms and blinds that provide a base for nature lovers, birdwatchers, photographers, fishermen, and even campers — but don't forget the insect repellent. Airboat rides through this unit are sometimes available. For information write: Park Superintendent, P.O. Box 1066, Sabine Pass 77655.

ANNUAL EVENTS

April

PLEASURE ISLAND MUSIC FESTIVAL
Pleasure Island Music Park
985-7822 (Convention and Visitors Bureau)
Last Friday, Saturday, and Sunday in April
One day admission $10, three day pass $20, children under 12 free
W +

Musical variety is the spice of life at this festival. The Big Band sound, jazz, blues, gospel, C&W, Cajun, rock, and pop can all be heard at various times. The musical entertainment is continuous. During the day there are groups performing on stages throughout the 10-acre park. In the evenings there's a big name show on the main stage. Other activities include an arts and crafts show, special events like fiddlin' and kite flying contests, and a children's tent with a puppet theater, face painting, and games.

May

CAJUN FESTIVAL
Bishop Byrne Wellness Center, 9th Ave. and Texas 73
985-5057 or 985-7822 (Convention and Visitors Bureau)
Last Friday, Saturday, and Sunday in May
Adults $1, children 50¢
W

Cajun music, dancing, crawfish races, Cajun food, a carnival and an antique show all in the Cajun spirit of "Let the good times roll."

S.A.L.T. FISHING RODEO
Headquarters: Pleasure Island Pier
962-8371 or 722-8784
Memorial Day weekend

There are $50,000 in prizes to be caught in the in-shore, off-shore and blue water divisions of this tournament. Other Memorial Day weekend activities are tied in.

September

CAYMANFEST IN PORT ARTHUR
Civic Center
985-7822 (Convention and Visitors Bureau)
First Thursday through Monday in September
$10
W +

Close ties between the Cayman Islands in the Caribbean and Port Arthur go back to the 1920s when Cayman seafarers sailed in and decided to settle. Now more than 500 Cayman families call Southeast Texas their home. And each year they are joined by bands and other entertainers, sports figures, and beauty queens from that British Crown Colony who come to party. Events include music ranging from ragae and calypso to American country and western, limbo dancing, fire-eaters, soccer matches, contests, and both Caribbean and Texas food.

DICK DOWLING DAYS
Sabine Pass Battleground State Historical Park
Take Texas 87 south about 14 miles to Sabine Pass, then south about 1.5 miles on FM 3322
971-2147
Saturday and Sunday early in September (usually over Labor Day weekend)
Free
W

There's entertainment, music, a parade, the blessing of the shrimp fleet, an arts and crafts show, and street dances every year at this festival. But every other year, in even numbered years, the cannons blast and once again Confederate Lieutenant Dick Dowling and about 40 men with six cannons drive off the huge Union force attacking Sabine Pass. This reenactment of the Battle of Sabine Pass (See Historic Places, above) is the highlight of the festivities celebrating Dowling's spectacular Civil War victory.

October

CAV-OIL-CADE CELEBRATION
Various places in city with most events in and around the Civic Center, Texas 73 near 9th Ave.
982-8094
Week during October, time varies
Admission to some events. Most outdoor events free.
W Variable

This is the big one for the city, celebrating its ties to the oil industry. The first Cav-Oil-Cade was held in 1952 and it has grown bigger and better every year. Events include a downtown parade, dances, entertainment by local and name entertainers, golf and tennis tournaments, other competitions and contests of all kinds from fire-hose fights to races, banquets, carnival, fireworks, antique car show, regattas, and a fishing rodeo.

SHRIMPFEST
Pleasure Island Concert Park
963-1107 (Chamber of Commerce)
Last Friday, Saturday, Sunday in October
$2

W +
Pay parking

This salute to the local shrimping industry (about 400 shrimp boats make Port Arthur their home port) includes a Shrimp Foodfest, a Shrimp Calling Contest, and a Shrimp Gumbo Cookoff. There are also bands, dancers and other entertainment, a street dance, and sports contests including a windsurfing competition.

RESTAURANTS

($ = under $7, $$ = $7 to $17, $$$ = $17 to $25, $$$$ = over $25 for one person excluding drinks, tax, and tip.)

Dinner for Two

EELLEE'S
4748 Main at Monroe, Groves
962-9585
Lunch and dinner Tuesday–Friday, dinner only Saturday. Closed Sunday and Monday
$$
AE, MC, V
W
Children's plates

This converted house provides a charming setting for a quiet and cozy dinner. The seemingly meaningless name has a real meaning. New Orleans trained chef J. L. Lee is the owner, and the restaurant's name is just Lee spelled backward and forward. The menu offers a variety ranging from seafood to Italian entrees to barbecued quail. Just remember to save room for one of the sinful but exquisite desserts. No smoking area. Bar.

American

STOREY'S OLD SANTA FE
4300 FM 365
724-2615
Lunch and dinner seven days
Reservations suggested Friday and Saturday dinner
$$
AE, Discovery, MC, V
W +
Children's plates

The decor is New Mexican with Indian blankets and other artifacts, and there are a few Santa Fe entrées on the menu, but mostly it features a wide choice of steaks, chicken, and seafood. Half dinners are available for diners interested in lighter fare. Luncheon buffet every day but Saturday. Bar.

Cajun

FARM ROYAL
2701 Memorial Hwy (US 69/96/287) at 26th
982-6483
Breakfast, lunch, and dinner Monday-Saturday. Closed Sunday
$$
No Cr.
W

It may look like a typical highway restaurant, but there aren't many roadside restaurants that offer frogs legs and quail and a wine list. Featured are dishes cooked Cajun style, like *gumbo* and *etouffee*. Cajun *gumbo* is a cross between a soup and a stew and, though often loaded with seafood, is liable to have everything in it but the cook's apron. If crawfish, which Cajuns call "mudbugs," is listed as *etouffee* it will probably be cooked in a mixture of flour and oil, smothered in peppers and onions, and served over rice. Ask about the Farm Royal Cookbook. Beer and wine.

Oriental

LUCKY INN
3801 Twin City Hwy (Texas 347) in Jefferson City Shopping Center
962-6252
Lunch and dinner Monday–Saturday. Closed Sunday
$-$$
AE, MC, V
Children's plates

The emphasis here is on Chinese cuisine — and just about all the most popular dishes are available — but you can also get entrées like chicken fried steak and fried catfish. Wine and beer.

MOON PALACE
4940 Gulfway Dr. (Texas 87) at Twin City Hwy (Texas 347)
983-2888
Lunch and dinner seven days
$$
Cr.
W
Children's plates

If your party consists of two or more, you might want to try the Family Dinner in which you get a choice of soups, egg roll, B.B.Q pork, fried rice, and a choice from a number of entrées for each diner so you can have a taste of several dishes. The extensive menu includes pork, poultry, beef, and seafood entrées. No smoking area. Bar.

Seafood

THE BOONDOCKS
Take Texas 73 west toward Winnie to Jap Rd., turn right and go a little over a mile to small sign on left marking entrance. Approximately 13 miles from Port Arthur
794-2769 or 796-1482
Dinner Tuesday–Friday, lunch and dinner Saturday–Sunday. Closed Monday
$$
AE, MC, V
W

This is one restaurant where the name really tells it like it is — it is out in the boondocks of Taylor Bayou. But, it's well worth the trip and the possible wait for a table (no reservations), especially if you enjoy catfish. Bill and Mae Northern started this restaurant in the mid-seventies as a fish camp beer joint and then, when local fishermen and hunters wanted something to eat as well as drink, they turned it into a restaurant. And since catfish are plentiful in the area, they worked out a mild, medium, and spicy recipe for Cajun style whole catfish and made that the house specialty, a specialty that has turned The Boondocks into a Mecca for catfish lovers. For variety, the menu also includes shrimp, chicken-fried steak, and other routine alternatives. The decorations come from the customers — thousands of business cards stapled to everything that doesn't move. When you're finished, ask for a gator bag, or buy an extra basket of hushpuppies, and go outside to feed the bayou fish, turtles, and alligators that flock here because they also know a good thing when they taste it. Beer and Wine.

CHANNEL INN
Sabine Pass, Texas 87 at entrance to Sabine Pass
971-2400
Lunch and dinner seven days
$$
MC, V
W
Children's plates

This restaurant grew out of the owner's decision to branch out from just pulling in seafood on his commercial fishing boats. Two features here are barbecued crabs and "platter service." The crabs aren't really barbecued, they're seasoned and deep fried, but the spices used in the cooking makes them taste like no other crab dish. As to the platter service, don't mistake this for the usual seafood platter found on the menu of almost every seafood restaurant in the country. They have regular seafood platters, of course, but for this order the word "service" is the key. They serve you overflowing platters of seafood. The actual kinds depends on the season, but usually you can expect barbecued crabs, broiled and fried fish, stuffed crab, fried shrimp, frog legs, and *gumbo*. And the platters will continue to be served until you're stuffed or, more likely, overstuffed. All this for about $13 a person. (Half price for children under 10.) In season, oysters can be added to the platters for $2 extra. Beer and wine.

DOROTHY'S FRONT PORCH
1000 Holmes Rd. off Beaux Art Gardens Rd., Nederland
722-1472
Lunch and dinner Tuesday–Sunday. Closed Monday.
No reservations Friday or Saturday dinner
$-$$
AE, MC, V
W +
Children's plates

What actually started as a tiny restaurant on Dorothy and Cooper Burrough's front porch caught a mess of fish lovers so it has grown to a 5,000-square-foot building. Catfish is the big item and it comes fried (in peanut oil), mesquite smoked, broiled several ways including Cajun, and blackened. Other seafood entrées include barbecued crab, shrimp, oysters, and gumbo.

ESTHER'S SEAFOOD AND OYSTER BAR
Rainbow Lane at the foot of Rainbow Bridge. Take Texas 87 north, then left under the Rainbow Bridge to Rainbow Lane.
962-6238
Lunch and dinner Tuesday–Saturday, Closed Monday
$$
AE, MC, V
W call ahead
Children's plates

Even though only a few items on the menu are actually listed as Cajun Specialties, like crawfish *etoufee* and broiled stuffed Cajun catfish, there's a hint of Cajun spices in many of the seafood entrées here. A good way to test that, if you have a hearty appetite, is with the Seafood Platter (about $15) that also gives you a choice of *Jambalaya* as a side order. Other seafood items on the menu include charbroiled shrimp, broiled lump crab, stuffed red snapper steak, Bar-B-Que crabs, and fried froglegs. Steaks and chicken are also available. Beer and wine.

THE JETTY SEAFOOD AND OYSTER BAR
8484 Central Mall (in separate building behind east end of mall)
727-5465
Lunch and dinner seven days
$$
Cr.
W +
Children's plates

How about a "Mudbug Platter" — half fried crawfish, half Crawfish *Etouffee*? That's just one example of the Cajun style seafood that is the house specialty here. They also have Creole dishes and other seafood entrees cooked in a variety of ways from blackened to such delights as Redfish Maison, which is prepared with crabmeat, artichoke hearts and mushrooms in a brown butter lemon sauce. And, of course, fresh Gulf oysters. Also live lobster you can choose from the tank. No smoking area. Bar.

CLUBS AND BARS

BARBARY COAST
5333 Twin City Hwy (Texas 347) near Hogaboom
962-6326
Closed Sunday and Monday
AE, MC, V
W

They feature local bands here one or two nights a week, but mostly it's a DJ who plays a variety from rock to country so you can dance. Two bars and pool tables.

CHARLIE'S CLUB
8901 US 69
722-5639
Open seven days
Cover Saturday night
AE, Discover, MC, V
W

You can dance here to country and western or Cajun music from live bands every night but Monday. Attached is Charlie's Kitchen famed locally for its Cajun food including Boudin Balls. Pool tables. Beer, wine, or BYOB.

RODAIR CLUB
FM 365 about four miles west of the intersection with US 69-96-287, near the bridge
736-1721
Friday and Saturday 8:30–1, Sunday 3–8, closed rest of week
Cover
No Cr.
W

If you think Cajun food is different, wait until you try the Cajun two-step (with a hip shake) to the fiddlin' of a live band. This frame building doesn't look like much — in fact, parts of it look like they are just one rusty nail away from falling down — but it's one of the great spots in Texas for hearing the music that slipped over from Louisiana and got an alligator lock on the local scene. The theme is always "Let the good times roll." Beer and wine or BYOB.

ACCOMMODATIONS

($ = Under $45, $$ = $46-$60, $$$ = $61-$80, $$$$ = $81-$100, $$$$$ = Over $100)
Room Tax 13 percent

BEST WESTERN AIRPORT INN
200 Memorial Hwy (US 69) near Nederland Ave., Nederland
727-1631 or 800-528-1234
$
No smoking rooms

This two-story motel offers 115 rooms that include five no-smoking rooms. Children under 12 free in room with parents. Senior discount. Satellite TV with Showtime. Room phones (free local calls). No pets. Restaurant with room service and private lounge open daily except Sunday with occasional live entertainment (guests automatically members, temporary membership for non-guests $5). Outdoor pool and wading pool. Free airport transportation, free coffee in lobby in mornings, and free full breakfast. Same day dry cleaning service. Located across from Jefferson County Airport.

HOLIDAY INN PARK CENTRAL
Memorial Hwy (US 69) at 75th St.
724-5000 or 800-HOLIDAY
$$$
W + two rooms
No-smoking rooms

This four-story Holiday Inn offers 164 units including eight suites ($$$$$) and 32 no-smoking rooms. Children under 12 free in room with parents. Senior discount and weekend rates. Satellite TV with HBO. Room phones (charge for local calls). No pets. Restaurant with room service, lounge with DJ, and lobby bar. Outdoor pool, outdoor whirlpool. Guest memberships available in YMCA. Free transportation to airport and golf course and free coffee in morning. Same day dry cleaning service. Municipal golf course and jogging track across street.

RAMADA INN
3801 Texas 73 (9th Ave. exit)
962-9858 or 800-2-RAMADA
$$-$$$
W + five rooms
No-smoking rooms

The two-story Ramada has 125 units including two suites ($$$$$) and 13 no-smoking rooms, Children under 18 free in room with parents. Senior discount and weekend rates. Cable TV with Showtime. Room phones (charge for local calls). Pets OK. Restaurant open daily and lounge open Monday-Saturday with live entertainment Wednesday-Saturday. Outdoor pool, jogging track, two lighted tennis courts. Guest memberships available in YMCA. Free transportation to airport and around city. Same day dry cleaning service.

PORT LAVACA

CALHOUN COUNTY SEAT ★ 12,000 ★ (512)

In 1830, John Linn built a wharf and warehouse about three miles north of the present site of Port Lavaca. Ships brought goods from New Orleans and New York and then wagon trains carried the goods to San Antonio and points north. A small colony grew up around the wharf. Then in 1840, the budding village of Linnville was wiped out by a Comanche raid.

But Linnville probably would have died anyway because by then another port had been established south of that village which, by 1843, had seven long wharfs and was thriving by shipping large quantities of cotton, hides, and tallow. With all the cattle brought into the area for processing, the new port soon became known by the Spanish word for cow, *la vaca*.

Soon after Texas became a state, Calhoun County was formed, named after John C. Calhoun, a senator from South Carolina who had used his influence to get Texas admitted as a slave state. Port Lavaca was named the county seat.

Then another competing port grew up on the peninsula south of Port Lavaca. Located on deepwater, it was called Indianola, and by 1856 it had taken so much business away from Port Lavaca that the county seat was moved there. Port Lavaca remained a backwater until two

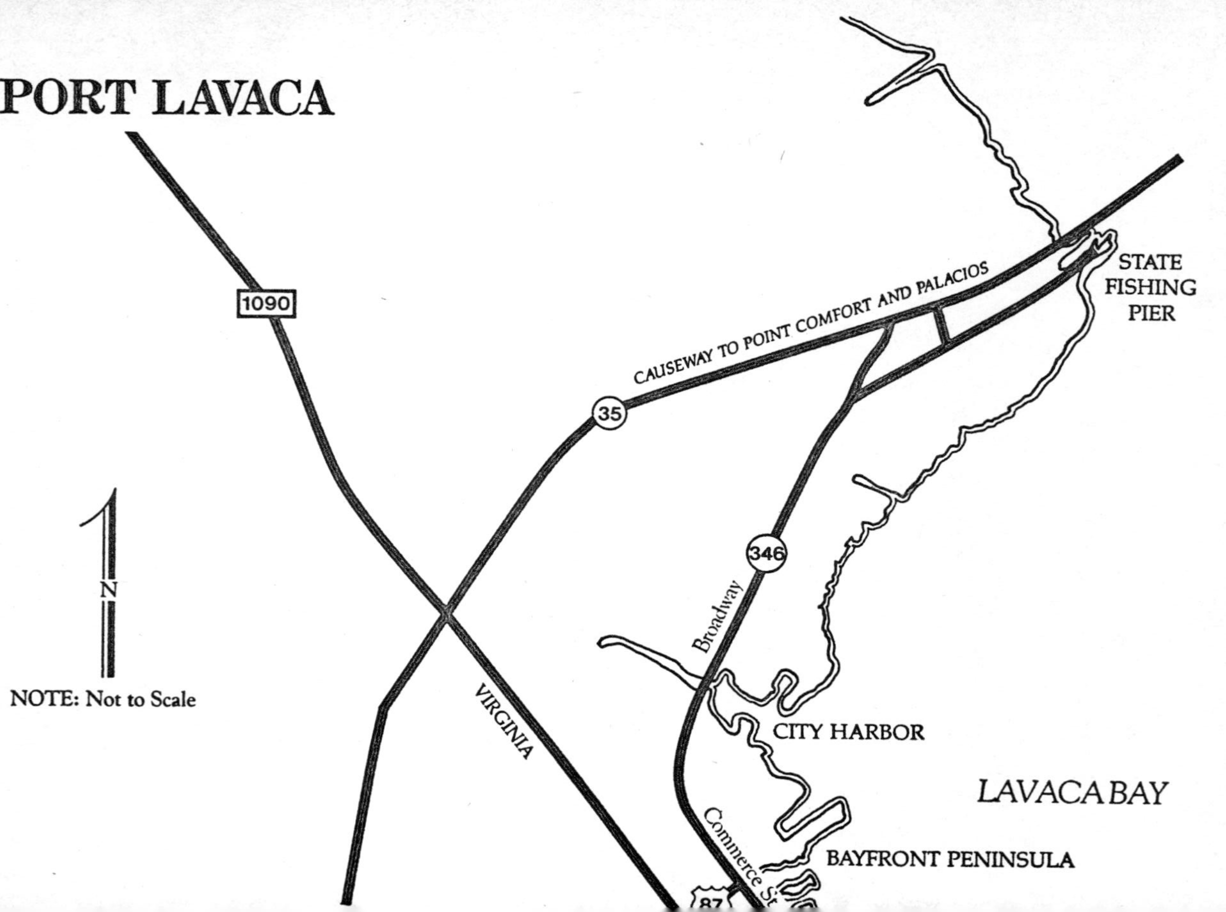
PORT LAVACA
1090
CAUSEWAY TO POINT COMFORT AND PALACIOS
STATE FISHING PIER
35
346
Broadway
N
NOTE: Not to Scale
VIRGINIA
CITY HARBOR
LAVACA BAY
Commerce St
BAYFRONT PENINSULA

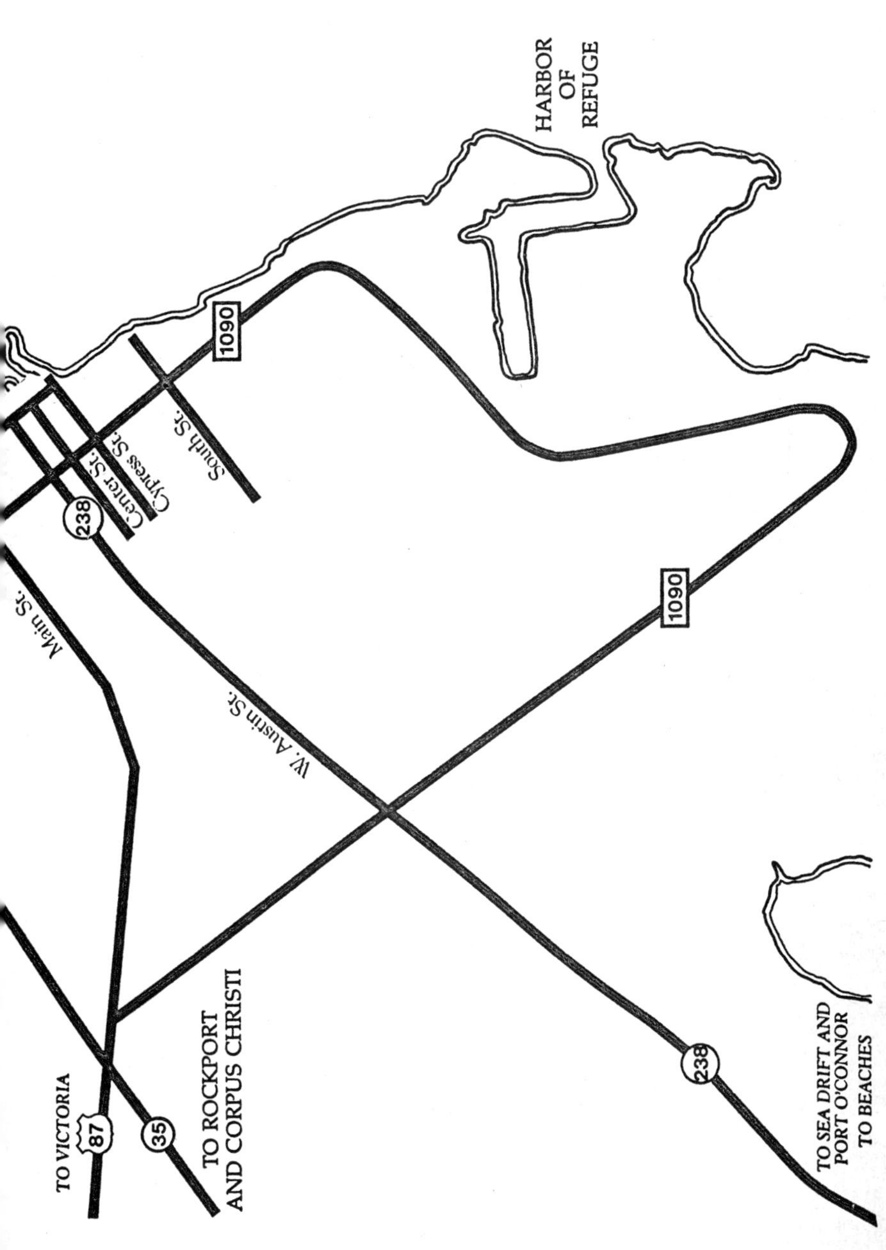
HARBOR OF REFUGE
1090
South St.
Cypress St.
Center St.
238
Main St.
W. Austin St.
1090
TO ROCKPORT AND CORPUS CHRISTI
TO VICTORIA
87
35
238
TO SEA DRIFT AND PORT O'CONNOR
TO BEACHES

devastating hurricanes in 1875 and 1886 virtually wiped Indianola from the map. Then the shipping business as well as the county seat was moved back to Port Lavaca where it remains to this day.

Today Port Lavaca is still a port, serving the major petrochemical and other industrial plants scattered up and down the nearby coast as well as commercial and sport fishermen. Its location on protected Lavaca Bay also attracts enthusiasts for boating and all types of water sports.

TOURIST SERVICES

PORT LAVACA-CALHOUN COUNTY CHAMBER OF COMMERCE
Bauer Community Center, 2300 Texas 35, just west of the Causeway
(P.O. Box 528, 77979)
552-2959
Monday–Friday 8:30–12, 1–5
W +

Information is available on both the city and the county. Be sure to get the free map with all the details of Port Lavaca on one side and Calhoun County on the other. Although not strictly a chart, this map provides information for anglers and boaters that includes the depths of local bays and waters out into the Gulf.

MUSEUMS

CALHOUN COUNTY MUSEUM
201 West Austin at Ann
552-2661
Tuesday–Friday 1:30–4:30, closed holidays
Free
W

One of the outstanding exhibits in this museum is scale model dioramas of four scenes of Indianola as it looked in 1875 before being destroyed by hurricanes. Also on display is the original Fresnel lens from the 1852 Matagorda Island Lighthouse, that except for a time during the Civil War, served as a guiding beacon for ships until 1977. Other displays include a textile collection and items relating to home and family life, local history, and natural history.

HISTORIC PLACES

HALFMOON REEF LIGHTHOUSE
2300 Texas 35, next to Bauer Community Center

Built in 1858 to warn mariners of the dangerous reef, this wooden building survived the Civil War, a number of hurricanes, and 90 years of service before being moved to this location where it is preserved as an important part of local history. Except for occasional special events, such as art shows, it is not open, so you can only view it from the outside.

LA SALLE'S CROSS
Grace Episcopal Church, 213 Austin
552-2805

The cross historians say was carried by the French explorer, La Salle, in 1685 when he landed at the place that would later become the port of Indianola is on view inside the church.

RANGER CEMETERY
Harbor St. off Broadway

There's a hundred years of local history in the gravestones here. The main problem is finding the cemetery because it's tucked in behind a fish cannery. Harbor is a short, commercial street with restricted parking. It may be best to park on Broadway and walk the block. The site was named for Margaret Peyton Lytle, the wife of the "poet" of the Texas Rangers, who was buried here in 1850. The oldest grave is that of Major James Watts, who was killed in a Comanche raid on the nearby community of Linnville in 1840. Watts and his recent bride had fled at the first sign of the Indians, but Mrs. Watts insisted on returning to their home for a gold watch they left behind. The Comanches were waiting and killed Watts and captured his wife. A posse later rescued Mrs. Watts, but not before an Indian shot an arrow at her that was deflected by the steel stays in her corset. Among the others buried here are ten Union soldiers who died in an epidemic during the Civil War.

OTHER POINTS OF INTEREST

PORT LAVACA STATE FISHING PIER AND PIER PARK
Texas 35 at the causeway over Lavaca Bay
552-4402
Fishing pier open seven days, summer 6 a.m. to midnight, winter 8 a.m. to midnight; park always open
Fishing $1 per device + tax
W Variable

This lighted fishing pier is built on the pilings of the old causeway from Port Lavaca to Point Comfort. It extends more than half a mile into the bay and local anglers claim it's a great place to catch speckled trout, flounder, and redfish. A fee is charged for fishing, but if you just want to stroll out and enjoy the view, that's free. The adjoining park has RV spaces (fee), a swimming pool (fee), a playground, restrooms and showers. Plans are in the works to put in a 1,000-foot beach for swimming starting at the Pier Park and extending to behind the Bauer Community Center. There will also be hike and bike trails.

SPORTS AND ACTIVITIES

Fishing

Landlubbers can fish off the lighted state pier (See State Fishing Pier) or from the many beaches. Or you can go out in a boat on the bay or the Gulf. Most of the guides and charter boats operate out of nearby Port O'Connor and are listed with the Port Lavaca-Calhoun County Chamber of Commerce (See Tourist Services).

Golf

HATCH BEND COUNTRY CLUB
Off Texas 35 west of the city
552-4730

Nine-hole course. Visitor's green fees: weekdays $7.50, weekends $10.

Hunting

Duck and other waterfowl hunting is a major wintertime sport in Calhoun County since there's lots of water around to lure the waterfowl migrating south for the winter. There's also deer hunting in season.

SIDE TRIPS

INDIANOLA
Take Texas 238 (Austin St.) southwest about two miles to where it meets Texas 316, then take 316 a little over eight miles to the Indianola site

What you can see here is a historical marker, a monument, and a beach park. What you can't see is the ghost of a town that once was one of the most bustling ports on the Gulf.

In the 1840s, huge concrete and stout wooden piers stretched out half a mile into the Gulf in what was then one of the finest ports on the Texas coast. In addition to the tons of cargo that went through the port, this was the main port of entry for new colonists coming to Texas, including the Germans who arrived with Prince Carl zu Solms-Braunfels to found the inland cities of New Braunfels and Fredericksburg. In the 1850s it was the main army supply depot for the western frontier, and it was here that Jefferson Davis, as U.S. secretary of war, shipped Arabian camels to start his experiment to replace army horses in the western desert. Indianola became so prosperous that the county seat was moved here from Port Lavaca.

The town survived Union shellings and capture and recapture by both sides during the Civil War, as well as yellow fever epidemics, and two hurricanes — in 1866 and 1875 — that partially destroyed it and killed more than 900 people. However, it was too prosperous to let die, so the residents rebuilt only to be struck by a third hurricane and tidal wave that leveled the town in 1886. This time there was no rebuilding. There wasn't even anything left to move when officials returned the county seat to Port Lavaca.

The 22-foot granite monument here is not to the people who withstood the three lashings from the elements before finally giving up, but to the French explorer, Rene Robert Cavelier Sieur de laSalle, who landed here in 1685.

There are covered picnic tables, barbecue pits, a boat ramp, and RV hook-ups at the little beach park and an assortment of rental cabins, bait shops and other small businesses along the beach. A little further north is Magnolia Beach (See following).

MAGNOLIA BEACH

Take Texas 238 (Austin St.) southwest about two miles to where it meets Texas 316, then take 316 to FM 2760 to the beach, approximately 14 miles from Port Lavaca

This shell beach offers facilities for boating, fishing, swimming, camping (fee) and other beach sports. Restrooms, cabanas with barbecue pits, and restaurants and other beach shops are available.

MATAGORDA ISLAND

See Port O'Connor

ANNUAL EVENTS

May

SUMMERFEST

Bayfront Peninsula, on the bay at the end of Main St. (US 87)
552-2959 (Chamber of Commerce)
Friday–Sunday of Memorial Day weekend
Free (admission to dances)
W Variable

An outdoor dance on Friday night kicks off this weekend festival that includes a variety of entertainment, an arts and crafts show, beauty pageant, carnival, and another dance on Saturday night.

June

CALHOUN COUNTY YOUTH RODEO

Calhoun County Fairgrounds Arena, County Rd. 101 off Texas 35
552-9747 (County Extension Service)
Usually weekend in middle of June
Adults $3, youth $1
W

To be a contestant in any event sponsored by the Texas Youth Rodeo Association you have to be able to sit on a horse — which in Texas could mean someone as young as 2 years old — and not be out of high school. You also have to be a good student. Most events are scaled down versions of adult rodeo events, like calf roping, pole bending, and cloverleaf barrel racing. But with the energy with which these kids compete, they don't look too scaled down.

October

CALHOUN COUNTY FAIR AND JUNIOR LIVESTOCK SHOW
Calhoun County Fairgrounds Arena, County Rd. 101 off Texas 35
552-9747 (County Extension Service)
Usually second week in October
Admission
W Variable

This fair starts with a parade and Go Texan Day activities on Saturday, then the main activities pick up again the following Wednesday through Saturday. All the typical county fair ingredients are here: livestock judging and auction, cookoffs, sports and contests (like hay-hauling), a variety of entertainment, and exhibits.

RESTAURANTS

($ = under $7, $$ = $7 to $17, $$$ = $17 to $25, $$$$ = over $25 for one person excluding drinks, tax, and tip.)

J & J RESTAURANT
503 W. Main
552-6235
Breakfast, lunch, and dinner Monday–Saturday, Closed Sunday
$
No Cr.
W

They've been serving up Tex-Mex dishes and seafood here for more than 15 years. If you want a sampling of the menu, try the Mexican Plate Deluxe that includes a *taco, chile con queso, a nacho, a chalupa, an enchilada,* rice and beans, all for under $5.

THE PANTRY
702 N. Virginia
552-1679
Lunch Monday–Friday, Closed Saturday–Sunday
$
Cr.
W

There are about a dozen tables in this cozy restaurant set up in the rear of the Greenhouse Flower Shop. The blackboard menu lists soups, sandwiches, salads, and the daily special which may be roast beef, or a seafood or chicken dish. There are also items like lasagna and banana split pie that are diet or low-fat even though they don't sound like it.

WAGON TRAIN
Texas 35, just east of Virginia (FM 1090)
552-3056
Breakfast, lunch, and dinner Monday–Saturday, Closed Sunday
$-$$
No Cr.
W
Children's plates

Barbecue is a major item here, but they also have steaks — from chicken-fried to T-bone — shrimp, catfish, oysters, and sandwiches. The building is set back off the highway a bit with parking in front, so look for the sign. Beer and wine.

ACCOMMODATIONS

($ = Under $45, $$ = $46-$60, $$$ = $61-$80, $$$$ = $81-$100, $$$$$ = Over $100)
Room Tax 13 percent

CHAPARRAL MOTEL
2086 Texas 35
552-7581
$
W + two rooms

There are 53 rooms in this two-story motel. Children under 12 stay free in room with parents. Senior discount. Cable TV with HBO. Room phones (local calls free). No pets. 24-hour restaurant adjoining. Outdoor pool. Free Continental breakfast. Same-day dry cleaning.

DAYS INN
2100 N. Texas 35
552-4511 or 800-325-2525
$
W + one room
No-smoking rooms

The 99 units in this Days Inn include one suite ($$$) and ten no-smoking rooms. Children under 18 stay free in room with parents. Senior discount. Cable TV with HBO. Room phones (local calls free) and coffeemakers in rooms. Pets OK. Restaurant, room service,and lounge open seven nights with occasional entertainment. Outdoor pool. Free coffee in restaurant. Self-service laundry and same-day dry cleaning. Small refrigerators in some rooms.

SHELLFISH INN
Texas 35 at the Causeway
552-3393
$
One no-smoking room

This one-story motel has 50 rooms. Children under 12 stay free in room with parents. Cable TV with HBO. Room phones (local calls free). Small pets OK. Outdoor pool and children's playground. Free coffee in lobby. Same-day dry cleaning. Small refrigerators in some rooms. On the bay.

VIKING INN
150 N. Texas 35
552-2981
$
W + two rooms
No-smoking rooms

This two-story motel has 70 rooms that include four no-smoking. Children under 12 stay free in room with parents. Senior discount. Cable TV with HBO and room phones (local calls free). Small pets OK. Restaurant and lounge open seven nights with occasional entertainment. Outdoor pool.

PORT MANSFIELD

WILLACY COUNTY	★	350	★	(512)

This is another one of those fishing holes that anglers don't even want to share with their friends. But the secret is out. Port Mansfield has been touted by several fishing magazines as one of the best fishing spots in the world.

It wasn't always so. Oh, the fish were there, it was just a long haul to reach them from way up or down the coast. Shrimpers and other commercial fishermen worked the area, but getting here was too much trouble for most sport anglers. Then, in the late 1940s, the officials of Willacy County worked out the financing, got 2,500 acres of the King Ranch that rested on the Laguna Madre, built a port and town from scratch, and dug a channel through Padre Island (now called the Mansfield Cut) to the Gulf opening up this great fishing area to the world.

TOURIST SERVICES

PORT MANSFIELD CHAMBER OF COMMERCE
P.O. Box O, Port Mansfield, 78598
944-2354

SPORTS AND ACTIVITIES

Fishing

The International Game Fishing Association has rated Port Mansfield one of the ten best fishing spots in the world. According to local experts, the currents are responsible. At one point, called Devil's Elbow, five different currents converge bringing big fish as close as eight to ten miles offshore.

If you don't want to go that far, there are lots of places close inshore where the fish bite. In addition to the deepsea fishing, you can boat fish the Gulf and Laguna Madre, try surf fishing on Padre Island, jetty fishing at the Mansfield Cut, and pier fishing in town. There is also barge fishing. The barges are really floating platforms with bunkhouses, some air conditioned, holding 6 to 12 fishermen. The barges are anchored where the fish are biting then the fishermen are ferried out to the barges at night. There they can fish and sleep and fish and sleep all night, depending on how the fish are biting and how long it takes to catch the limit. The cost varies, but averages $30 per person.

A guide for boat or wade fishing in Laguna Madre's Redfish Bay will run from $225 to $300 a day for two or three people. Offshore fishing in the Gulf runs from $400 to $600 a day depending on the size of the group and the boat and the kind of fish you want to go after.

Since fishing is the main business here, several excellent guides are available. For information on guides, barge fishing, and charter boats, contact the Chamber of Commerce or the Port Mansfield Guides Association at P.O. Box 148, 78598.

SIDE TRIPS

PADRE ISLAND NATIONAL SEASHORE

Several charter boats will take you to unspoiled Padre Island National Seashore near the Mansfield Cut for beachcombing, shell hunting, fishing, or camping. The trip usually costs between $75 and $150. For information contact the Chamber of Commerce or the Port Mansfield Guides Association at P.O. Box 148, 78598.

ANNUAL EVENTS

July

PORT MANSFIELD FISHING TOURNAMENT
944-2354 (Chamber of Commerce)
Usually Thursday–Sunday of third week in July

The Chamber of Commerce suggests this event for the whole family, and the tourney categories support that. The major divisions are Offshore and Bay/Surf, but for each there's an adult and junior division (through age 14). And for the little ones there's a Piggy Perch division, held at the pier, that is broken down for ages 1-4, 5-8, and 9-12. Trophies are awarded for just about every category of fish you could catch in Laguna Madre or the Gulf, from barracuda to blue marlin. Dinner and band nightly. Usually about 450 entrants take part in this tournament.

RESTAURANTS

($ = under $7, $$ = $7 to $17, $$$ = $17 to $25, $$$$ = over $25 for one person excluding drinks, tax, and tip.)

FISHERMAN'S INN RESTAURANT
Laguna and Legion
944-2882
Breakfast, lunch, and dinner seven days
$-$$

You can have your seafood, burgers, or steaks while you watch the boats moving in the harbor.

WINDJAMMER INN RESTAURANT AND LOUNGE
South Harbor Dr.
944-2272
Lunch and dinner seven days
$$
Cr.
W
Children's plates

Seated inside on the deck overlooking the harbor, you can dine on a variety of fresh seafood, charcoal broiled steaks, or entrée combinations of seafood and beef. Lounge. The "Inn" part of the name refers to four motel rooms with boat slips ($).

ACCOMMODATIONS

($ = Under $45, $$ = $46-$60, $$$ = $61-$80, $$$$ = $81-$100, $$$$$ = Over $100)
Room Tax 6 percent

CASA DE PESCADORES
201 S. Harbor Dr. (P.O. Box 81, 78598)
944-2333
$$$

The Pescadores has 11 two-story condominiums for rent, cable TV, no pets, boat slips, and lighted fishing pier.

FISHERMAN'S INN
Laguna and Legion (P.O. Box 135, 78598)
944-2882
$

The two-story inn has 14 units including seven motel rooms, three efficiencies and four apartments ($-$$), plus five condominium units with boat slips ($$$$-$$$$$). Cable TV with Showtime. No pets. Restaurant. Some covered parking.

HARBOR HOUSE INN
1132 South Port (P.O. Box 240, 78598)
944-2888
$

The two-story Harbor House has 26 motel rooms, six kitchenettes, and two suites ($$$). Cable TV. Pets Ok. Free freezer storage for your catch.

OTHER ACCOMMODATIONS

There are a few beach houses, apartments, and condominiums that can be rented by the day or longer. For a listing and prices contact the Chamber of Commerce or Bay House Rentals/Glaze Realty (944-2355), 701 Bayshore (P.O. Box 12) 78598; or Pier II Enterprises, (944-2519) 732 North Shore Dr. (P.O. Box 71) 78598.

PORT O'CONNOR

CALHOUN COUNTY ★ 900 ★ (512)

The town got its start late in the 1880s with a small settlement here called Alligator Head. By the turn of the century a railroad had reached Alligator Head and the American Townsite Company laid out and sold lots and renamed the town Port O'Connor after Thomas O'Connor, the man who owned the original land grant. The town's heyday ran from about 1909 to 1919 when it became a summer resort with excursion trains bringing in an estimated 10,000 tourists every summer. Business boomed and, at a time when few coastal communities even had seashell streets, the city even laid in cement sidewalks.

But the hurricane of 1919 brought all this to a halt. The town rebuilt, but after hurricanes hit again twice in the 1940s and again in the 1960s, it never regained its favor with long-term summer residents or tourists. Now Port O'Connor's fame and fortune rests almost squarely on its reputation as a great place for fishing.

Located at the southeastern tip of the peninsula that makes up most of Calhoun County, this village has Matagorda Bay on the east, the Barroom and Espiritu Santo Bays on the south and west, and Pass Cavallo leading to the Gulf between them. The Intracoastal Waterway also runs right by. All this adds up to make Port O'Connor one of the prime fishing spots on the coast — a spot that many fishermen tend to keep secret from all but their best fishing buddies — and often even from them. As one angler put it, "If the fish are biting anywhere along the coast, it'll probably be at Port O'Connor."

TOURIST SERVICES

PORT O'CONNOR CHAMBER OF COMMERCE
P.O. Box 701, 77982
983-2898

That phone number rings at a local store. The clerks there will take messages for the Chamber or give you other numbers to call if you need detailed information.

PORT LAVACA-CALHOUN COUNTY CHAMBER OF COMMERCE
Bauer Community Center, 2300 Texas 35, just west of the Causeway
(P.O. Box 528, 77979)
552-2959
Monday–Friday 8:30–12, 1–5
W +

SPORTS AND ACTIVITIES

Fishing

That's what it's all about here. There's a free fishing pier near Adams St. or you can go out in your own boat or one of several charter boats that operate out of the port. In addition to bay fishing, there's good fishing at the jetties by the Matagorda Ship Channel and in the surf off both Matagorda Peninsula and Matagorda Island. Billfishing is available just 60 miles offshore at the East Breaks. For information on guides and charter boats, contact the Chamber of Commerce here or at Port Lavaca (See Tourist Services).

One of the richest fishing tournaments on the Gulf is held in Port O'Connor each year, usually in mid-July. This is the Poco Bueno Invitational Offshore Fishing Tournament, a deep-sea contest in which prizes can reach over a quarter million dollars. Sorry, but it is invitational and to be one of the hundred or so who get invited you need a deep-sea fishing reputation plus a big boat and big bucks. The Chamber of Commerce also sponsors an annual fishing event that doesn't require an invitation nor a lot of cash (See Annual Events).

SIDE TRIPS

MATAGORDA ISLAND STATE PARK AND WILDLIFE MANAGEMENT AREA
983-2215 (Texas Parks and Wildlife office in Port O'Connor)

A barrier island, Matagorda stretches nearly 38 miles southwest from Pass Cavallo, near Port O'Connor, to the Aransas National Wildlife Refuge. By agreement with the U. S. Department of the Interior, which owns most of the island, Texas Parks and Wildlife Department (TPWD) manages the nearly 45,000 acres. About 36,000 of these acres are set aside as a wildlife management area to protect endangered species, but most of the rest is open to the public as a state park. However, this island is still in its near-natural state — no condos, no T-shirt vendors, in fact, no drinking water, no electricity, not much of anything except miles and miles of pristine beach where you can go swimming, fishing, picnicking (bring your own food and water), shell collecting, or bird watching.

The only way to get to the island and the park is by boat, your own or charter. If it's your own, check in first with the TPWD office at the docks in Port O'Connor for details on how to get there and the rules and regulations. Or, several charter skippers in the area will shuttle you to the park headquarters dock, which is about 22 miles from Port O'Connor, and bring you back for about $100 for a party of four. If prior arrangements are made, park personnel will drive you to where you want to go and arrange to pick you up, provided their work schedule permits. That's why it's best to call first. Charter boats will also take you to selected beach areas without going to the park headquarters. For a list of the skippers that provide this shuttle, contact the Chamber of Commerce.

ANNUAL EVENTS

May

CHAMBER OF COMMERCE FISHING TOURNAMENT
Local bays
Contact Chamber of Commerce (See Tourist Services)
Three days over Memorial Day weekend
Entrance fee $5

During this tourney you can win prizes in a variety of categories including biggest trout, redfish, flounder, and other catches from local waters. There's also a one-day children's tournament, usually off the piers, plus a fish-fry, street dance, and other activities.

ACCOMMODATIONS

There are several small motels in town that cater to fishermen, and local real estate agents occasionally have beach houses or condominium apartments available for short-term rental. For details contact the Chamber of Commerce at Port O'Connor or Port Lavaca (See Tourist Services).

RAYMONDVILLE

WILLACY COUNTY SEAT ★ 10,000 ★ (512)

Spanish explorers came through this area early, but the first real settlement was established when the King of Spain gave a land grant to Jose Narcisco Cavazos in 1790. Cavazos received 470,000 acres, the largest land grant in south Texas, for which he paid what would be the equivalent today of about $54.

Founded in 1904, the city is named after Edward Burleson Raymond, foreman of the El Suaz division of the King Ranch from the 1870s until his death in 1914. Raymond used his income to buy into what he knew best — land. At one time a barbed wire fence ran down the middle of what is now Hidalgo Ave. (Texas 186), the main east-west street in town, separating the vast expanse of the King Ranch on the north from the 24,000 acres of Raymond's ranch. Raymond used part of his land to experiment with types of vegetables that grew best in the area. One he discovered did particularly well was the Bermuda onion. As a result, in the 1920s, Raymondville became known as the "Onion Capital of the World" and the county was called the "Breath of the Nation."

Today, onions and other vegetables are major crops in Willacy County, but they also raise grain sorghum, cotton, and citrus fruit and ranching is still important.

For about two centuries salt was also a major product of the area. Two intermittent salt lakes: *La Sal Vieja* (Old Salt Lake) and *Sal Del Rey* (Salt of the King) are west of Raymondville. These were used as salt supply for all northern Mexico by the Spaniards as early as the mid-1700s, and there is evidence the Indians used these salt lakes thousands of years before them. The salt deposits were important to the Confederacy during the Civil War, and salt was shipped commercially from Raymondville until about 1920. Both lakes are abandoned now.

TOURIST SERVICES

RAYMONDVILLE CHAMBER OF COMMERCE
427 S. 7th (US 77 Bus)(P.O. Box 746, 78580)
689-3171
Monday–Friday 8–5
W

Located with Historical and Community Center.

MUSEUMS

HISTORICAL CENTER
427 S. 7th (US 77 Bus) at Harris
689-3171 (Chamber of Commerce)
Wednesday and Friday 2–5
Free
W

Some of the artifacts recovered from Spanish ships wrecked on nearby Padre Island in the mid-1500s are on display here. Most of the exhibits, however, relate to local history dating back to the original Spanish land grant and include memorabilia of the nearby King and Kenedy ranches. The Community Center and Chamber of Commerce office are located in this complex.

SPORTS AND ACTIVITIES

Golf

RAYMONDVILLE MUNICIPAL GOLF COURSE
US 77 Bus about one mile south of town
689-9904

Nine-hole course. Green fees: 9 holes about $3, 18 holes about $4.50.

SHOPPING

ARMANDO'S BOOTS
169 N. 7th
689-3521
W

Armando was trained at the Rios Boot Company which was the leading bootmaker in town for years. You can get custom-made boots, shoes, belts, and purses here. A pair of plain calfskin boots go for about $220 while boots made from alligator run about $1800. The waiting time for boots is about eight to ten weeks.

SIDE TRIPS

DELTA LAKE
Take Texas 186 west about 15 miles to FM 1015, then south to lake
Open at all times
W Variable

The county park on this small lake offers facilities for boating, fishing, water skiing, picnicking, and camping.

ANNUAL EVENTS

December

RANCH ROUNDUP
Rodeo Arena south on US 77 By-Pass between Raymondville and Lyford
689-3171 (Chamber of Commerce)
Weekend early in December
Admission
W Variable

This is not your ordinary rodeo. It's a competition among real cowboys in activities related (perhaps stretching the relationship a little) to what cowboys do on a ranch. Contestants must be regular employees of the ranch they represent. Events include Team Penning, in which a three-man team has four minutes to cut out three marked head of cattle from a herd and pen them; Wild Cow Milking, Team Branding, Head and Heel Roping, Steer Loading, and Wild Horse Riding.

RESTAURANTS

($ = under $7, $$ = $7 to $17, $$$ = $17 to $25, $$$$ = over $25 for one person excluding drinks, tax, and tip.)

BIG R BARBECUE
US 77 By-Pass approximately one mile north of town
689-5641
Lunch seven days, dinner Tuesday–Sunday
$
No Cr.
W
Children's plates

The barbecue choices include brisket, sausages, beef and pork ribs, and chicken, all cooked over mesquite. Mexican entrées are also on the menu. Smoked turkeys are available by special order. Beer and wine.

CASA BLANCA RESTAURANT
US 77 Bus south at FM 3168
689-3230
Breakfast, lunch, and dinner Tuesday–Sunday. Closed Monday
$-$$
No Cr.
W

In spite of the Mexican name and a few Mexican dishes on the menu, most of the entrée choices are American dishes including steaks and seafood. Their popular Sunday buffet usually features turkey, beef, ham, and chicken. Beer and wine.

ACCOMMODATIONS

($ = Under $45, $$ = $46-$60, $$$ = $61-$80, $$$$ = $81-$100, $$$$$ = Over $100)
Room Tax 11 percent

ANTLERS INN
US 77 By-Pass south at FM 3168 (P.O Box 160, 78580)
689-5531
$
No-smoking rooms

The two-story Antlers has 32 rooms that include four 4 no-smoking. Children under 15 stay free in room with parents. Senior discounts. Satellite TV. Room phones (local calls free). Pets OK (also kennel within walking distance). Lounge open seven nights (beer and wine only). Guest memberships available for health club and golf course. Free coffee. Same-day dry cleaning.

OTHER ACCOMMODATIONS

THE INN AT EL CANELO
Ten miles north off US 77 at El Canelo Ranch (P.O. Box 487, 78580)
689-5042
$$$$$

Two large bedrooms in the hacienda-style main house and two more in the guest house are available at this 3,200-acre ranch's main compound located five miles west of the highway. *All* meals are included in the room rate. Children and pets permitted only by special arrangement. Senior discount. Tennis court, nature trails, and family museum in historic ranch school house. Weekend cooking classes by hostess trained at several American and French cooking schools can be arranged for groups of four to eight.

ROCKPORT & FULTON

ROCKPORT: ARANSAS COUNTY SEAT ★ 6,500 ★ (512)

FULTON: ARANSAS COUNTY ★ 1,002 ★ (512)

Rockport was built in 1868 by the Morgan Steamship Company of New York upon the guarantee of the King-Kenedy and Coleman-Fulton cattle companies that they would ship at least $1,000 worth of hides, tallow, bones, and horns every ten days. With the development of the Texas cattle industry after the Civil War, huge herds were shipped here for slaughter and Rockport became a leading seaport in the state. The demand in the East was for hides for leather goods, tallow for candles and soap, bones for fertilizer, and horns for buttons and combs. The meat was considered a side-product. Some of the meat was salted, pickled, or dried and shipped out or sold to the army, but most of it was considered waste and thrown in the bay.

Fortunately for the environment, as the great cattle drives to the mid-Western railheads became commonplace, the packing industry in the area declined and finally died an early death. The town almost died, too, but the people soon turned their eyes to the bounty of the waters.

Aransas County is one of the smallest counties in Texas and most of it is covered with water. It was inevitable for fishing to become the major industry. Tourism wasn't far behind. At one time, in the "gay 90s," four passenger trains arrived and departed Rockport each day.

Today, these neighboring towns of Rockport and Fulton have grown together until most visitors now think of them as one. Located on a peninsula that rivals anything on the coast for natural beauty and protected by the barrier of San José Island, both are still important commercial and sport fishing centers and popular resort communities. Perhaps drawn by the rugged beauty of the area, a large number of artists have settled in both cities.

Also considered part of this resort area is the small town of Lamar that sits just across the LBJ Causeway (Texas 35) on the east side of Copano Bay. Established in 1838, shortly after the Texas Revolution, Lamar was one of the first towns settled in this area. It was during that Revolution that an unusual incident occurred near here in which a land force captured several enemy ships. It started when a company of mounted Rangers surprised and captured a merchant ship that was carrying supplies for the Mexican Army. They then used this ship as decoy to lure in and capture two other Mexican supply ships. For this exploit, this company of Rangers became known locally as the Horse Marines.

TOURIST SERVICES

ROCKPORT-FULTON AREA CHAMBER OF COMMERCE
404 Broadway (Texas 35) (P.O. Box 1055, 78382)
729-9952 or 800-242-0071, or 800-826-6441
Monday–Friday 9–5, Saturday 9–1
W

Among the many brochures and other publications available here are instructions for a self-guided driving tour of Rockport, Fulton, and Lamar.

BOAT TOURS

The five boats listed below offer tours to Aransas National Wildlife Refuge, usually from November 1st through early March, when the Whooping Cranes are there. The trips last about four hours. Fares run about $20 for adults and $12 for children 12 and under. Most offer senior citizen discounts. Although most skippers will take walk-ons, in the height of the whooping crane season *all* the boats fill up fast, so reservations are strongly recommended.

Capt. Ted's Whooping Crane Tour ***(Skimmer)***, Sandollar Pavilion, Fulton Beach Rd., 729-9589 or in Texas 800-338-4551. Daily whooping crane tours at 7:45 a.m. and 12:45 p.m. From April through July 4th, Capt. Ted operates Rookery Tours to see birds nesting on 12 different rookery islands. Reservations required.

Lucky Day, Rockport Harbor, 729-8571 or in Texas 800-782-BIRD. Daily whooping crane tours at 8 a.m. and 1 p.m.

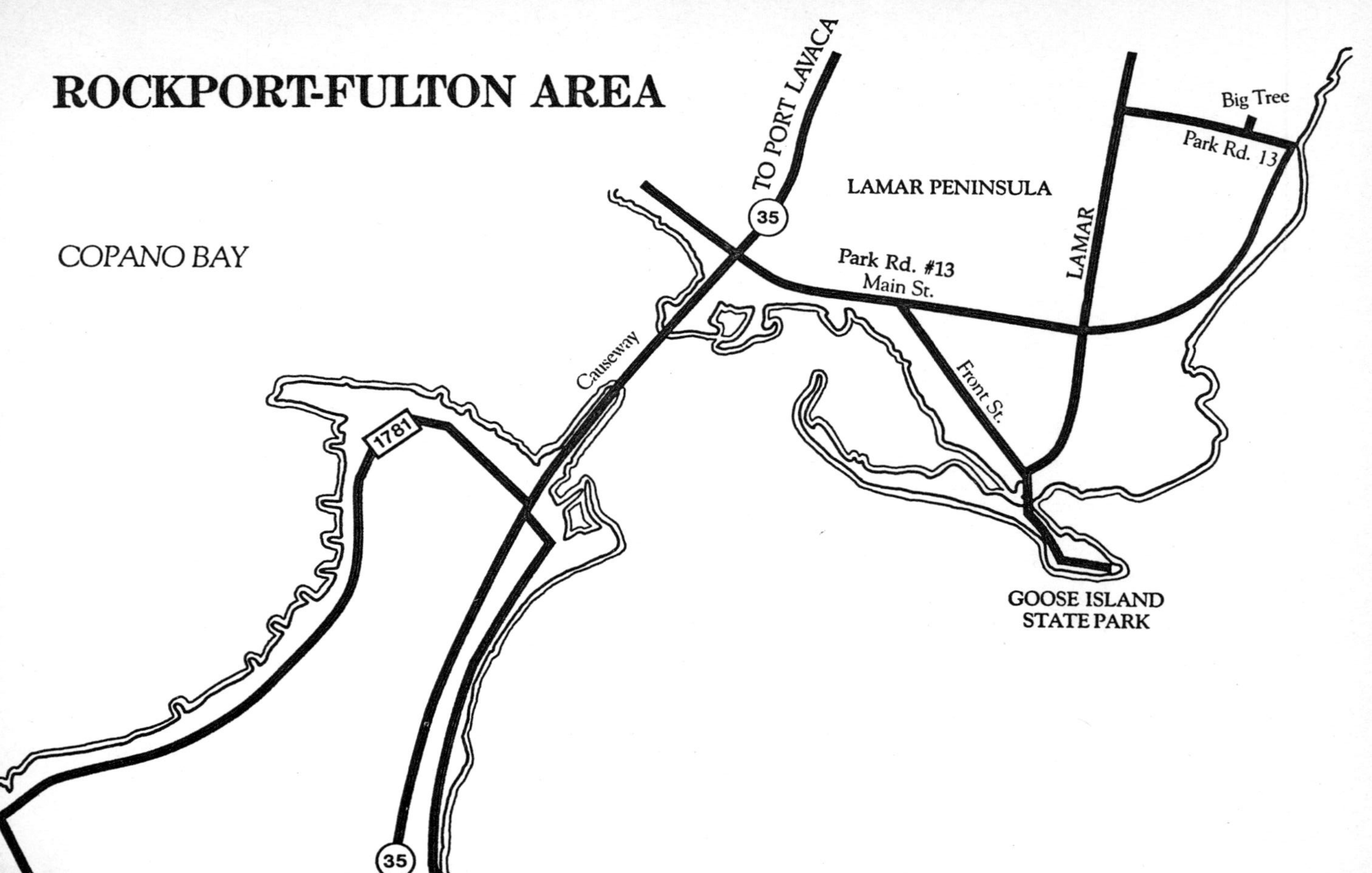
ROCKPORT-FULTON AREA
COPANO BAY
TO PORT LAVACA
35
LAMAR PENINSULA
LAMAR
Big Tree
Park Rd. 13
Park Rd. #13
Main St.
Front St.
Causeway
1781
GOOSE ISLAND
STATE PARK
35

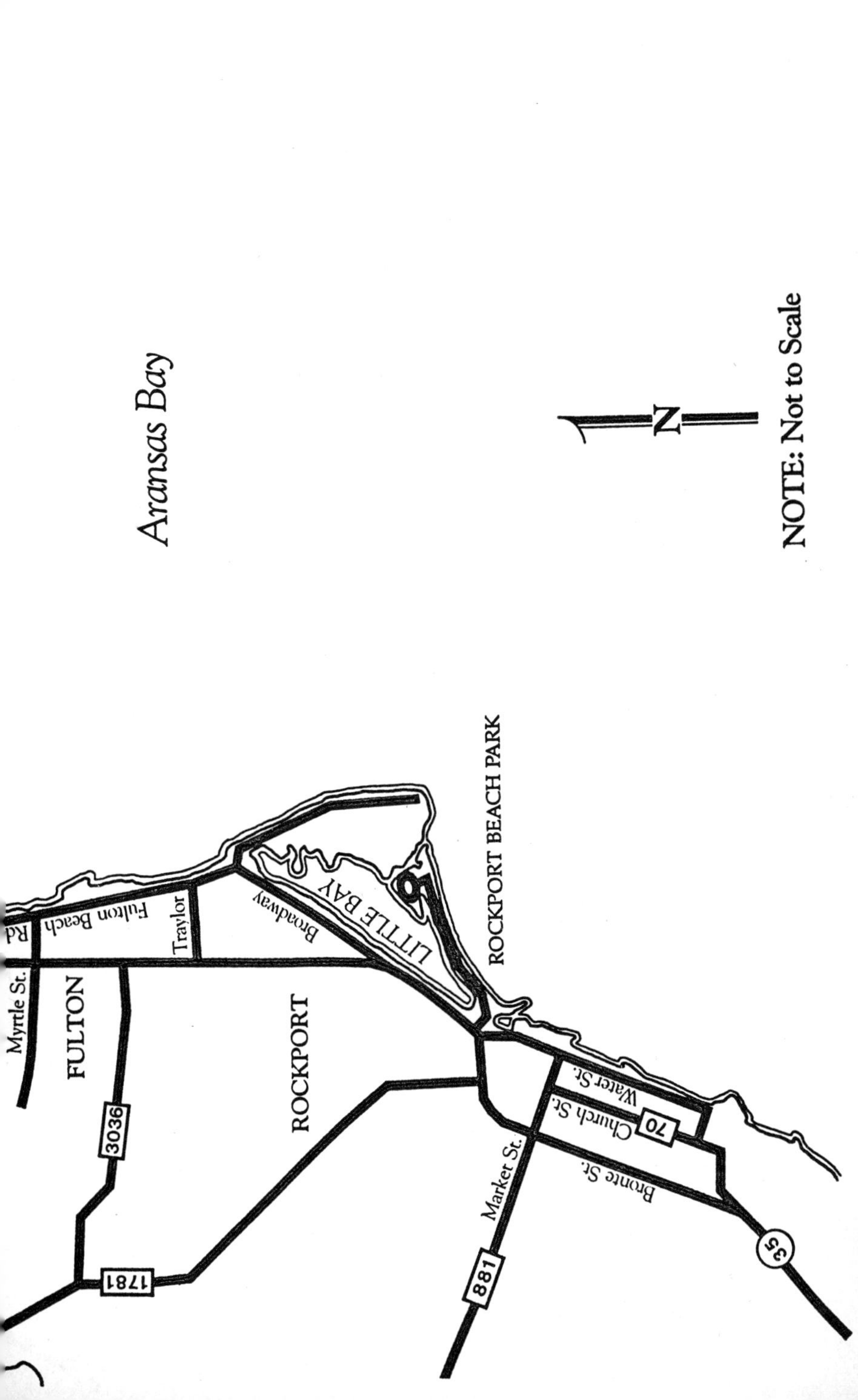

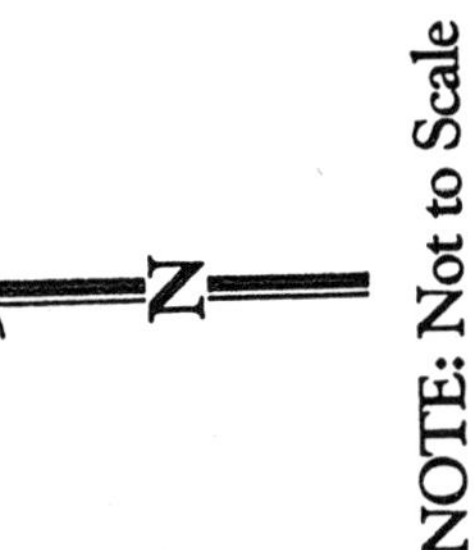
Aransas Bay
N
NOTE: Not to Scale
ROCKPORT BEACH PARK
LITTLE BAY
Broadway
Fulton Beach Rd
Traylor
Myrtle St.
FULTON
ROCKPORT
3036
1781
Water St.
Church St.
70
Market St.
Bronte St.
881
35

New Pelican, Rockport Excursions, Rockport Harbor, 729-8448. Daily whooping crane tours at 8 a.m. and 1 p.m.
Pisces, Rockport Harbor, 729-7525 or 729-4661. Daily whooping crane tours at 8 a.m. and 1 p.m.
Wharf Cat, Sea Gun Resort Hotel, Texas 35 North, 729-2341 or 749-5760. Whooping crane tours Wednesday, Thursday, Friday, and Sunday at 10 a.m. and 2 p.m.

GET-ACQUAINTED DRIVING TOUR

Start at the **Chamber of Commerce,** between the Harbor and Little Bay on Texas 35. The Cape Cod-style house across from it was built in 1868. From the rear of the Chamber building you can see the **Texas Maritime Museum** (See Museums), **Rockport Harbor,** and **Rockport Beach Park,** and the **Rockport Art Center** (See Other Points of Interest).

Leaving the Chamber, *turn right (north) on Broadway (Texas 35)* and drive along with Little Bay on your right. Don't be surprised if you see a large number of birds along here, perhaps even the endangered brown pelican, because this area is part of the Connie Hagar Bird Sanctuary, named after a well-known Rockport birdwatcher.

At the fork, *stay to the right,* on Broadway. From here on you'll be seeing more and more of the wind-sculptured, **leaning live oaks** that huddle together in twisted groups lining the road (See Other Points of Interest). Also note that almost every house and motel along here has a private fishing pier, each sticking out into the bay like a long, thin finger.

After about a mile, you'll *cross a small bridge and come to another fork.* To the left is Fulton Beach Rd., but for now, *continue straight* over the next little bridge to Key Allegro. The expensive homes on this small peninsula offer examples of just about every beach house style from Thailand to Disneyland. Make a loop through the area and, when you've satisfied your architectural curiosity, *go back over the last bridge and turn right on Fulton Beach Rd.*

On your left, about a half mile down, is **Fulton Mansion** (See Historic Places). Further on, on your right, is **Fulton Harbor** (See Other Points of Interest) with its commercial shrimp boats and pleasure craft sharing the anchorage. Next to the fishing pier, at the north end of the harbor, is the Paws and Taws building that is principally a recreation center for Winter Texans.

Fulton Beach Rd. goes along the water for about three more miles before it butts back into Texas 35. *Turn right on Texas 35* and go over the causeway. Locally this is called the Bay Causeway, but officially, it's the Lyndon B. Johnson Causeway. The remains of the old causeway can be seen next to the new one. Split in the middle, both ends are now lighted **fishing piers.** (See Sports and Activities-Fishing). A little way off the causeway, make a *right (east) on Park Rd. 13* that goes to the community of Lamar.

As you drive through the grove of trees that line this road, look for Front St. going off to your right at a fork. If you want to see the

Schoenstatt Shrine (See Historic Places) this is the road to take. It is about a quarter mile down. Otherwise, continue on Park Rd. 13. A little further down, on the left, is Driftwood St. which leads into Lamar. If you want to visit the **Stella Del Mar Chapel** (See Historic Places), you'd turn here and follow the Lamar Cemetery signs. But, once again, we'll continue on Park Rd. 13, to the crossroads where you see signs pointing to **Goose Island State Recreation Area** to your right and the **Big Tree** to your left (See Other Points of Interest). The park entrance is just a short distance away, but since there is an entrance fee and this is just a Get-Acquainted Tour, unless you really want to visit the park right now, *turn left*.

Drive carefully here. The road is narrow and deer occasionally pop out of the bushes. Look for and follow the signs to Big Tree — they're small, but they're there — leading to the 1,000 year old tree.

Once you've seen this impressive tree, *retrace your route back to Park Rd. 13, then turn right back to Texas 35 where a left (south)* will take you back over the causeway. Along Texas 35 you'll pass the airport, some small strip shopping centers, RV parks, small businesses, motels, and fast food places and eventually wind up back passing the fork where you originally took Broadway to go to Key Allegro and Fulton.

Continue on past the Chamber of Commerce (now on your left) and Rockport Harbor. *Stay to your left* and you'll soon be on Austin St. in the downtown area. Along this street are several popular restaurants (See Restaurants), art galleries (See Shopping) and gift shops. *Turn right on Market St.* (FM 881), then, in three blocks, *left on Church*. Going south on Church, you'll pass several of the historic homes in town. At 621 is the Mathis Home built in 1869-1870 by one of the founders of Rockport. Further along, the gray house at 712 was built in the early 1890s and the blue house across the street, at 717, was built a few years earlier. A block west of this house is a city park where General Zachary Taylor's army camped in 1845 while enroute to the Valley and what became the war with Mexico. The Chamber of Commerce can provide information on other historic homes in this section of town as well as the rest of the Rockport/Fulton area.

Turn right on King. The sprawling white block building with the pond behind at 501 King is the **Simon Michael School of Art and Gallery** (See Shopping). Where King ends *at Bronte St, turn right*. This will put you back on Texas 35 again and you can follow it back to your starting point at the Chamber of Commerce, winding up this get-acquainted tour.

MUSEUMS

TEXAS MARITIME MUSEUM
1202 Navigation Circle — Texas 35 at Rockport Harbor (P.O. Box 1836, 78382)
729-1271
Wednesday–Saturday 1–5, Sunday 12:30–5, Closed Monday, Tuesday, and some major holidays

Adults $2.50, children 4 to 12 $1, under 4 free
W + main floor only

Perhaps because of its size, few people realize that Texas is a maritime state with several hundred miles of coastline, 12 deep-water ports, and a history that goes from Spanish treasure ships to the Texas Navy to the modern treasures of black gold brought up by offshore oil rigs. This museum is dedicated to overcoming that lack of understanding by preserving our maritime heritage and explaining its impact on our lives. Exhibits include artifacts from shipwrecks of Spanish ships dating back to 1554 and paintings of all the sailing ships in the Texas Navy. There is also detailed coverage of a variety of topics including the importance of the steamboat river trade, boat and ship building, and the development of the commercial fishing industry. Upstairs is a hands-on mock-up of an old time freighter's flying bridge with wheel, compass, and engine order telegraph. Gift shop.

HISTORIC PLACES

FULTON MANSION STATE HISTORIC STRUCTURE

Fulton Beach Rd. at Henderson, Fulton, about three miles north of Rockport
729-0386
Wednesday–Sunday 9–noon and 1–4; last morning tour at 11:30, last afternoon tour at 3:30
Adults $2, children (6-12) $1, under 6 free
W first floor and basement only, lift in rear

When cattle baron George Fulton, founder of the town that bears his name, built this 30-room mansion in the mid-1870s, he used his engineering background to make it what we would now call "state-of-the-art." The exterior style is French Second Empire with its characteristic mansard roof, but inside the house had a central heat and ventilation system, hot and cold running water, flush toilets, gas lights fueled by a gas plant in the rear of the house, and crushed seashell insulation. In the larder, water was circulated through concrete troughs to cool perishable food. The mansion has been restored to its original splendor by the Texas Parks and Wildlife Department. Visitors are requested to wear flat, soft-soled shoes to prevent damage to floors and carpets. Because this is a major tourist attraction in the area, in summer you might want to call first to find out the waiting time. Groups of ten or more are requested to make reservations at least a month in advance. For information write: Park Superintendent, P.O. Box 1859, Fulton 78358.

HISTORIC HOMES

A listing of historic homes with a sketch map is included in the free Chamber of Commerce publication on Area Points of Interest. Among the oldest in the area are the *Baylor House*, 617 S. Water, built in 1868; the *Mathis Home*, 621 S. Church, built in 1870; and the *Wood Home*, 203 N. Magnolia, built in 1868.

SCHOENSTATT SHRINE
Front St., Lamar. Take Texas 35 north across the LBJ Causeway to Park Rd. 13, then right (east) to Front St.
729-2019
Call for open hours
W

This is an exact replica of the shrine in Schoenstatt, Germany, the center and mother house of the Schoenstatt Sisters of Mary.

STELLA DEL MAR CHAPEL
Lamar. Take Texas 35 across LBJ Causeway to Park Rd. 13, then right (east) to Driftwood, then follow Lamar Cemetery signs to Hagy St. and Chapel near the Cemetery
729-2880 or 729-3387 (Knights of Columbus)
Usually open Sunday 1–4 or by appointment
W

This chapel is the first recorded church in Aransas County and is reported to be the oldest surviving building in the county. Built in 1858, the chapel was originally located on property overlooking Aransas Bay. It was shelled twice by Union vessels during the Civil War, but was not severely damaged. It was moved to this site in 1986. Among the graves in the nearby Lamar Cemetery is that of Patrick O'Connor, who died in 1854, and was a direct descendent of Roderick O'Connor, the last King of Ireland.

OTHER POINTS OF INTEREST

THE BIG TREE OF LAMAR
Take Texas 35 north across the LBJ Causeway to Park Rd. 13, then right (east) to sign, then left to tree
Open at all times
W

This Texas Champion Coastal Live Oak has branches as big around as many other large tree trunks. Sometimes called the Lamar Oak, Bishop's Oak, or Goose Island Oak, it is best known as simply The Big Tree. While not the biggest tree in the state — that title goes to a bald cypress in East Texas — it is still impressive with a trunk that is more than 35 feet in circumference, a height of 44 feet above the ground and a crown spread of 89 feet. It is said that this was a council tree for the Karankawa Indians and it was also a hanging tree when the white settlers later dispensed frontier justice. The Big Tree is estimated to be well over 1,000 years old.

FULTON BEACH AND PIER
At Fulton Harbor
Beach open at all times
W Variable

In addition to a small swimming beach there is a 1,000-foot lighted public fishing pier. Use of the beach is free, but there is a small charge to use the pier.

GOOSE ISLAND STATE RECREATION AREA
Lamar. Take Texas 35 north across the LBJ Causeway to Park Rd. 13, then right (east) and follow signs to entrance
729-2858
Open seven days 8–8 for day use, at all times for camping
$2 per vehicle per day
W + But not all areas

This 314-acre park starts on the mainland and extends out onto a peninsula and several islands located in the conjunction of Aransas, Copano, and St. Charles Bays. Facilities are available for boating, fishing (there's a 1,620-foot long lighted fishing pier) swimming, water skiing, picnicking, and camping (fee). It is also an excellent location for birdwatching and other nature studies. For information write: Park Superintendent, Star Route 1, Box 105, Rockport 78382.

ROCKPORT ART CENTER
901 Broadway at Rockport Harbor
729-5519
Tuesday–Saturday 10–5, Sunday 2–5. Closed Monday
Free
W ramp in rear

This attractive 1890s Bruhl/O'Connor House set against the backdrop of the colorful harbor could itself be a subject for the artist's brush. Instead it is the home of the Rockport Art Association that has redesigned the structure to house four gallery display areas and three studio classrooms. Exhibits emphasize regional art and change every three to six weeks. The Rockport Art Association, which operates this center, also sponsors the annual Art Festival each July (See annual Events).

ROCKPORT BEACH PARK
Rockport Harbor off Texas 35
Open 5 a.m.–11 p.m.
729-6445 (Chamber of Commerce) or 729-2213 (City of Rockport)
Parking $2
W Variable

The heart of this park is the one and a quarter mile sandy beach on the shallow waters of Aransas Bay. Facilities include picnic cabanas, a fitness trail, saltwater swimming pool, playgrounds, lighted fishing pier, water ski area, pavilions with showers, restrooms, and concessions that rent water sports equipment including paddleboats and jet skis. For birders, there's an observation platform overlooking the Connie Hagar Wildlife Sanctuary that is home to thousands of shore and game birds during the winter. If you drive in expect a parking fee, but you can walk in free.

THE WINDSWEPT LEANING TREES
Mostly along Fulton Beach Rd., Fulton

The live oaks here appear to be hanging on in a fight with the elements for survival. Sculpted into bent and twisted shapes by the constant winds off the Gulf, at times they look like creatures bowing gracefully toward the earth; and, at other times, like a Disney version of a witch's forest.

SPORTS AND ACTIVITIES

Birdwatching

Close to 500 different species of birds have been spotted in the Rockport Area. For $1 ($1.50 by mail) you can get the 16-page "Birder's Guide to Rockport/Fulton" from the Chamber of Commerce (See Tourist Services). This colorfully illustrated and comprehensive guide includes a loop driving tour that takes in most of the birding spots in the area, a seasonal checklist of birds of the Coastal Bend, and other recommended birding sites ranging from Sinton to Corpus Christi. It also lists local birding organizations and birding hotlines (e.g., Coastal Bend Bird Hotline 512/364-3634). The Chamber of Commerce also sponsors an annual Hummer/Bird Celebration in September. For birding boat tours see Tourist Services.

Boating

Boating is excellent in all the area bays and the Gulf is just a short trip away through Aransas Pass. Sunfish sailboat races are scheduled every Tuesday evening from May though August in Little Bay. There are also several sailboat regattas held during the summer and the race/cruise to Port Isabel is held annually over Labor Day weekend.

Fishing

Without leaving land, you can fish from the jetty at Rockport, the private fishing piers owned by many of the motels on the shoreline, the Fulton public pier, or the Copano Bay Fishing Pier (See following). Two party boats operate out of Rockport harbor for bay fishing. They are the *Lucky Day* (729-9442 or 800-782-BIRD) and the *Pisces* (729-7525 or 729-4661). Fares run from about $16-$20. For information on these and on charter boats and guides for both bay and offshore fishing, contact the Chamber of Commerce (See Tourist Services).

COPANO BAY STATE PARK FISHING PIER
Texas 35 N at the LBJ Causeway, approximately five miles north of Rockport
Memorial Day through Labor Day open at all times, rest of year open seven days dawn until early afternoon
Adults $1 per fishing apparatus, children 50¢
W

Waste not, want not. That seems to be the excellent policy followed by the Texas Parks and Wildlife Department when it came to salvaging the old bridge to Lamar after the new causeway was built. The bridge has been converted into lighted piers extending from both north and south side (taking out the old drawbridge in the middle) for over a mile and a half. According to local historians, the day they announced that the old causeway would be used as a fishing pier, it was so crowded with fishermen that none of the men or equipment sent to remove the drawbridge could get near it. Snack bar, bait and tackle shop, and restrooms on both sides; public boat ramp on the south side.

PERFORMING ARTS

ROCKPORT COMMUNITY THEATRE
Charlotte Plumber's Party House, Fulton
729-8216
Tickets about $12
Reservations recommended
W

The season goes from February through November with a production every other month running for about five performances. Most of the plays are comedies. This is dinner theater with the buffet dinner provided by Charlotte Plumber's Restaurant.

SHOPPING

AUSTIN STREET GALLERY
501 S. Austin
729-5010
W

The works of a large number of regional and national artists are available here in a variety of media including paintings, pottery, sculptures, and woodcarvings.

AUSTIN STREET STATION
415 S. Austin
W

This corner mini-mall includes specialty shops offering ladies clothing, books, jewelry, arts and crafts, Texas gifts, and desserts and gifts. There are also a beauty shop and a restaurant (See Restaurants).

ESTELLE STAIR GALLERY
406 S. Austin
729-2478
W

Housed in a spacious building, built in 1892, this is a working gallery with no glitter or fancy lighting and almost half of the building is devoted to classes and space for artists to come in and paint. But the other half contains a large selection of original paintings by local and regional artists and limited edition prints for sale. Estelle Stair was one of the founders of the Rockport Art Association as well as one of the magnets that drew so many artists to settle here.

SIMON MICHAEL SCHOOL OF ART AND GALLERY
510 E. King
729-6233

Simon Michael gave his first one-man exhibition at the St. Louis Museum of Fine Arts in 1923 when he was 18, and he is still painting and teaching. As a result, most of the works on display and for sale are his; however, there are also a number of paintings and pieces of sculpture by other American and European artists for sale.

THE STEINER STUDIO
111 N. Austin
729-9561
W

Bradley Steiner does sculpture in crystal. How well he does it is evidenced by the fact that an original dragon he created in glass is in the permanent collection of the Corning Museum in Corning, New York. In his shop you'll find some small pieces for as low as $20 and items like a crystal rattlesnake that go for several thousand. Steiner uses a rare and dangerous technique of working with glass called lamp-working in which he subjects special glass rods to such intense heat and pulling and twisting that only about 2 percent of his work survives without shattering.

SWISS CHOCOLATE VILLA
Texas 35 north of fork with Broadway (H.C.R. Box 358K, 78382)
729-8009
W

This heaven on earth for chocoholics is owned by a couple who came from Switzerland by way of East Africa and Kenya. Marie-Claire Herzog's candy-making background includes a grandfather who was one of the founders of a Swiss chocolate factory. Her husband, Peter, ran a safari business in the Serengeti National Park and learned the chocolate cooking secrets from her. Now they both turn out European-style candies here. They offer a mail order catalog that includes both rich chocolate delights and sugar- and salt-free chocolates.

SIDE TRIPS

ARANSAS NATIONAL WILDLIFE REFUGE
Take Texas 35 north to FM 774 then northeast (right) to Austwell, then south (right) about seven miles on FM 2040 to Refuge; approximately 38 miles from Rockport
(512)286-3559

Open seven days sunrise to sunset. Wildlife Interpretive Center open seven days 7:30–5
$2 per vehicle
W Variable

With almost 55,000 acres, this is the largest national wildlife refuge in Texas. It is also the winter home of the whooping crane. These birds, which stand over five feet tall, migrate in October or November each year from their summer home in Canada. Only 21 whoopers were known to exist in the world in the early 40s when the United States and Canada started a joint program to save the bird from extinction. Slowly the efforts are paying off. Though still an endangered species, more than 100 whoopers usually winter in this colony alone. Their habitat is in the marshland along the shore so they can not be seen from the refuge roads. The best way to see them is from the refuge observation tower or on one of the boat tours (See Tourist Services). But there's a lot more to see than just the whoopers. On the 15-mile loop drive yo" may see many other species of birds, plus deer, coyotes, javelina, wild turkeys, armadillo, and even alligators. There are also over seven miles of walking trails and picnic areas. You must register and pick up a guide map at the Interpretive Center before touring. According to the park rangers, the most rewarding time to visit is November through March when both the migratory waterfowl and the whoopers are there. For information write: P.O. Box 100, Austwell, 77950.

ANNUAL EVENTS

March

FULTON OYSTERFEST
Fulton Park at Fulton Harbor on Fulton Beach Rd.
729-7529
First weekend in March
Free
W Variable

A gumbo cook-off and oyster-shucking and oyster-eating contest are just a few of the activities in this two-day festival. It also includes a parade, an arts and crafts show, entertainment, dances, and, of course, lots of food booths including some selling — guess what? It's sponsored by the Fulton Volunteer Fire Department.

July

ROCKPORT ART FESTIVAL
Near the Rockport Art Center at the harbor, just off Texas 35
729-5519
Usually weekend nearest July 4th

$1
W Variable

There are usually well over 100 booths set up in a colorful tent village at which artists and craftsmen from all over the Southwest, including Rockport's own artist community, display and sell their works in a variety of media. But it's not all art. There's plenty of music, and food booths are open during this two-day event sponsored by the Rockport Art Association.

September

ROCKPORT FIESTA EN LA PLAYA
Festival Grounds, Rockport Harbor
729-6418
Saturday and Sunday of Labor Day weekend
Free
W Variable

This is a fiesta with a Hispanic flavor. It features Mexican music and folkloric dancers, a piñata-breaking contest, the "most macho legs" contest, an arts and crafts show, a carnival, and plenty of Mexican food.

HUMMER/BIRD CELEBRATION
Various locations
729-6445 (Chamber of Commerce)
Thursday evening, Friday and Saturday of first weekend after Labor Day
Lectures and workshops free, fee for bus and boat field trips
W Variable

Close to 500 species of birds have been recorded in this area and one of them is the hummingbird that migrates here each fall in great numbers. Although the hummingbird is the focus of this weekend's activities, there are speakers, programs, and workshops on many other birds including, of course, the whopping crane. Bus and boat tours are available to see the hummers and other birds.

October

ROCKPORT SEAFAIR
Downtown and Rockport Harbor
729-3312 or 729-6445 (Chamber of Commerce)
Usually weekend preceding Columbus Day
Free
W Variable

A land parade, boat regattas, water shows, arts and crafts booths, crab races, a beauty pageant, a gumbo cook-off, live entertainment, a carnival, and a variety of contests (including the "Anything That Floats But a Boat Race") keep things moving at this two-day event. But the biggest draw remains the fresh shrimp, oysters, and other seafood cooked up and sold at the food booths operated by local civic groups.

OFFBEAT

BIG FISHERMAN RESTAURANT
FM 1069. Take Texas 35 about six miles south then right (west) on FM 1069 about a half mile
729-1997
Lunch and dinner seven days
$-$$
MC, V
W

The expression "that place is a zoo" fits this restaurant. They probably have as many birds and animals in the glassed-in aviaries and cages scattered throughout the several dining rooms as they have plates stacked up in the kitchen. Almost every room in this rambling building contains a collection of such birds as toucans, macaws, and peacocks. And for a change of pace, there are also a couple of young mountain lions. Take a tour of all the rooms to see the whole show, then go out back to see the menagerie there. Seafood, steaks, and chicken are on the menu. None are extraordinary, but it's good and reasonably priced; and eating is something to keep you occupied while you watch the bird and animal antics. Bar.

RESTAURANTS

($ = under $7, $$ = $7 to $17, $$$ = $17 to $25, $$$$ = over $25 for one person excluding drinks, tax, and tip.)

AUSTIN ST. PUB AND EATERY
415 S. Austin
729-4050
Lunch and dinner seven days in summer, Closed Sunday in winter
$-$$
MC, V
W rear entrance

Shrimp, beef, or chicken *fajitas* are the specialties here. Other entrées include seafood such as fried or grilled flounder, grilled chicken, U-peel-m shrimp, and a daily special. Also soups, salads, and sandwiches. Entertainment weekend evenings. Bar.

THE BOILING POT
Fulton Beach Rd., just north of the Fulton Mansion
729-6972
Lunch and dinner Friday–Sunday, dinner only Monday–Thursday
$-$$
MC, V, DIS
W

You are furnished a bib and a small mallet (for the crabs) and then the boiled Cajun-style crabs, shrimp, and crawfish, mixed with chunks of spicy sausage and potatoes or corn on the cob, are dumped on butcher paper on the table in front of you and you go at it. Beer, wine, and champagne.

CHARLOTTE PLUMMER'S SEAFARE
Fulton Beach Rd. and Cactus at Fulton Harbor
729-1185
Breakfast, lunch, and dinner seven days
$$
AE, MC, V
W +

The specialty is broiled and baked seafood with frying pretty much confined to the seafood platters. If you have three or more in your party you might want to try Charlotte's Seafare Special that includes shrimp steamed in beer, fish, oysters, and crab cakes — all served family style. Because they don't take reservations, the waiting can back up at times. They also supply the buffet for the Rockport Community Theatre's dinner theatre productions held at Charlotte's Party House across the street (See Performing Arts). Beer and wine.

CORKY'S
503 S. Austin
729-5161
Breakfast, lunch, and dinner seven days. Closed Tuesday in winter
$-$$
MC, V
W

This no-frills downtown restaurant has been going strong since 1947. The menu includes a little bit of all the standards from steaks to chicken, but the favorite seems to be the fresh seafood, especially the all-meat crab cakes. Beer and wine.

DUCK INN
701 Broadway (Texas 35), just north of the harbor
729-6663
Lunch and dinner Tuesday–Sunday, Closed Monday
$$
MC, V
W

Some of the recipes here go back to the original founder who opened it up right after World War II. The menu emphasizes seafood, but there are also steaks and chicken entrées. And the old recipes seem to have held up well. Lounge.

KLINE'S CAFE
106 Austin
729-8538
Breakfast, lunch, and dinner Friday–Wednesday, Closed Thursday

$-$$
No Cr.
W

Steaks and chops, fried chicken, hamburgers, seafood, and Mexican dishes are all on the menu, and they all come with homemade bread or corn bread. Wednesday night features all-you-can-eat fried fish. On display is the family collection of old clocks. Beer.

ACCOMMODATIONS

($ = Under $45, $$ = $46-$60, $$$ = $61-$80, $$$$ = $81-$100, $$$$$ = Over $100)

Hotels and Motels

(Rates are for double room in high season. Off-season rates are usually lower, sometimes considerably so.)
Room Tax 12 percent

BEST WESTERN ROCKPORT REBEL
800 Block of Texas 35 N, Fulton (P.O. Box 310, Fulton 78358)
729-8351 or 800-528-1234
$
W + One room
No-Smoking Rooms

This two-story Best Western has 72 units that include 24 kitchen unit suites ($$$$) and 24 no-smoking units. Children under 12 stay free in room with parents. Senior discount. Satellite TV with HBO. Room phones (local calls free). Pets OK ($25 pet deposit). Restaurant and room service. Outdoor pool. Free coffee in lobby and free newspaper. Self-service laundry and same-day dry cleaning. Fish cleaning station.

DAYS INN
1212 Laurel at Broadway (Texas 35), just north of the harbor
729-6379 or 800-325-2525
$-$$
No-smoking rooms

This two- and three-story inn has 29 rooms including two no-smoking. Children under 12 stay free in room with parents. Senior discount. Cable TV and room phones (local calls free). Pets OK. Outdoor heated pool. Free continental breakfast.

KONTIKI BEACH MOTEL
North end of Fulton Beach Rd., Fulton
729-4975 or in Texas 800-242-3407
$$-$$$

This three-story motel has 40 kitchenettes. Price includes up to four people in a room. Cable TV and room phones (local calls free). Pets

OK. Outdoor pool, tennis court, lighted fishing pier, docks and boat launch. Condominium adjoining has about 40 units in rental pool ranging from one to three bedroom ($$$-$$$$$).

LAGUNA REEF HOTEL
1021 S. Water St., entrance on Austin
729-1742 or 800-248-1057
$-$$
W + One room
No-smoking rooms

The 21 hotel rooms in the four-story Laguna Reef include two no-smoking, Children under 18 stay free in room with parents. Senior discount. Cable TV and room phones (charge for local calls). Coffeemakers in rooms. Pets OK ($25 pet deposit). Outdoor pool, and guest memberships available in country club in Portland. Small beach and 1,000-foot lighted fishing pier. Free Continental breakfast. Self-service laundry. An additional 47 units in the building are one- and two-bedroom condominium apartments, most of which are in the rental pool ($$$-$$$$).

SANDOLLAR RESORT
Texas 35, approximately five miles north of Rockport (H. C. R. Box 30, Rockport 78382)
729-2381
$-$$$

There are 49 motel rooms in this one- and two-story resort that runs between Texas 35 and Fulton Beach Rd. Cable TV and room phones (local calls free). Pets OK. Restaurant and lounge open seven nights with entertainment occasionally. Two outdoor pools. Free coffee in office. Self-service laundry. Children's playground. Marina and 500-foot lighted fishing pier. Some kitchenettes. Also 76 RV hook-ups, almost all in the shade, costing about $10 a night.

OTHER ACCOMMODATIONS

There are a number of condominiums in the area with units available for daily rental. For a list contact the Chamber of Commerce (See Tourist Services).

SEADRIFT

CALHOUN COUNTY ★ 1,277 ★ (512)

Located on San Antonio Bay, on the other side of the peninsula from Port O'Conner, this is also a village where the people earn their living primarily from the sea. Their pride in their hometown can be seen in the many murals depicting both past and present events painted on several buildings. Seadrift is also known as the finish-line for the intrepid canoeists who take part in the Texas Water Safari (See Annual Events).

TOURIST SERVICES

SEADRIFT CHAMBER OF COMMERCE
P.O. Box 251 (77983)

ANNUAL EVENTS

June

TEXAS WATER SAFARI
Bayfront Park

Free
W Variable

Billed as the "World's Toughest Boat Race," this event challenges teams to paddle non-stop 260 miles from San Marcos to Seadrift against a 100-hour deadline. Any muscle-powered craft can be used — and everything from racing sculls to kayaks to pedal-powered boats have been — but most teams stick to standard aluminum canoes, often rigged with lights for night travel. Trophies are awarded in several categories, from being first to being first over-40, solo, or novice. Those who survive the grueling trip down the San Marcos and Guadalupe rivers to cross the finish line here at Seadrift also earn the much-coveted Water Safari patch.

July

SHRIMPFEST
Bayfront Park
Usually held July 4th weekend
Mostly free
W Variable

The Blessing of the Shrimp Fleet, a Miss Shrimpfest contest, and a shrimp-eating contest are just a few of the activities that draw visitors who more than triple the population of this town during this festival. In addition to the many food booths, the Chamber of Commerce sponsors fried and boiled shrimp dinners. Each of the two days of activities is climaxed by a dance at the pavilion overlooking San Antonio Bay.

RESTAURANTS

($ = under $7, $$ = $7 to $17, $$$ = $17 to $25, $$$$ = over $25 for one person excluding drinks, tax, and tip.)

BARKETT'S
Texas 185 at north end of town
785-2441
Lunch and dinner Tuesday–Sunday, Closed Monday
MC, V
$-$$
W

Barkett's is not what could be classed as a seafood lover's find, but the kitchen does well enough here to put its menu a notch above many of the seafood restaurants on the coast. For example, on the seafood platter — that staple of every seafood menu — the shrimp are jumbo, the taste of crab in the stuffing is actually detectable, and the fish isn't overcooked. Plus the portions give good value for your money. Beer and wine. Gift shop.

ACCOMMODATIONS

($ = Under $45, $$ = $46-$60, $$$ = $61-$80, $$$$ = $81-$100, $$$$$ = Over $110)
Room Tax 6 percent

Bed & Breakfast

HOTEL LAFITTE
302 Bay Ave. (P.O. Box 489, 77983)
785-2319
$$-$$$

This restored three-story historic hotel has ten units that include two suites ($$$$). Cable TV with Showtime in some rooms. No pets. Free full breakfast and complimentary wine and dessert in the evening. This Victorian-style hotel was built in 1909 and offers a view of San Antonio Bay. One suite has an oversized jacuzzi tub. Children over 10 welcome.

SOUTH PADRE & PORT ISABEL

SOUTH PADRE ISLAND: CAMERON COUNTY ★ 1,600 ★ (512)

PORT ISABEL: CAMERON COUNTY ★ 5,000 ★ (512)

As you leave the mainland city of Port Isabel on the Queen Isabella Causeway, Texas' longest bridge, South Padre rises in front of you like a glowing island in the sun, luxurious and dreamlike. Here is the sun-bleached essence of the modern resort: a long, white beach — rated by some travel writers as one of the ten best beaches in the world — towering resort hotels and condominiums that offer all the pleasures of resort living, and a wide variety of activities for those who want more than just lazying on the sand or watching the sunset. Tourism is king here, accounting for close to 100 percent of the island's business. There are well over a thousand hotel/motel rooms and close to three thousand condominiums for rent. Only about 1,600 people actually live year-round on the island, but each year more than 1,200,000 visitors come to play at the shore and enjoy the casual life known as "Island-style" that blends small town ambiance with sophisticated living and dining.

SOUTH PADRE ISLAND AND PORT ISABEL

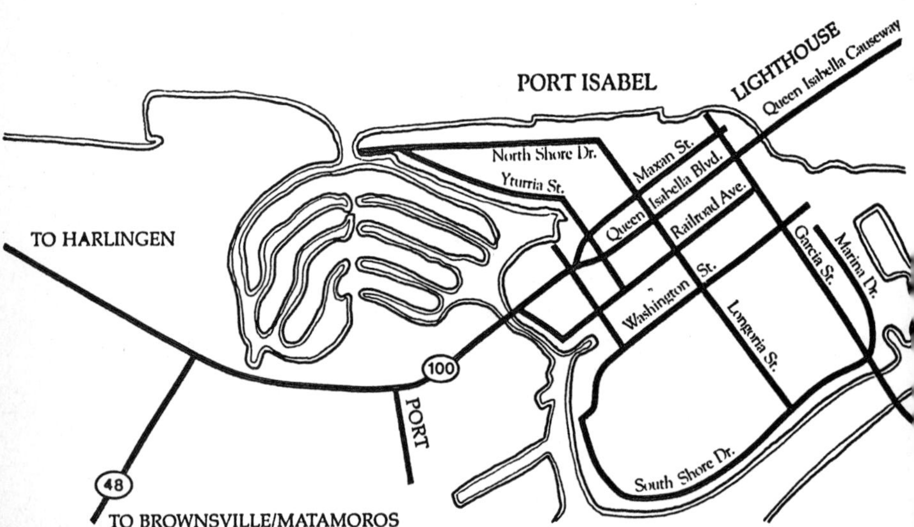

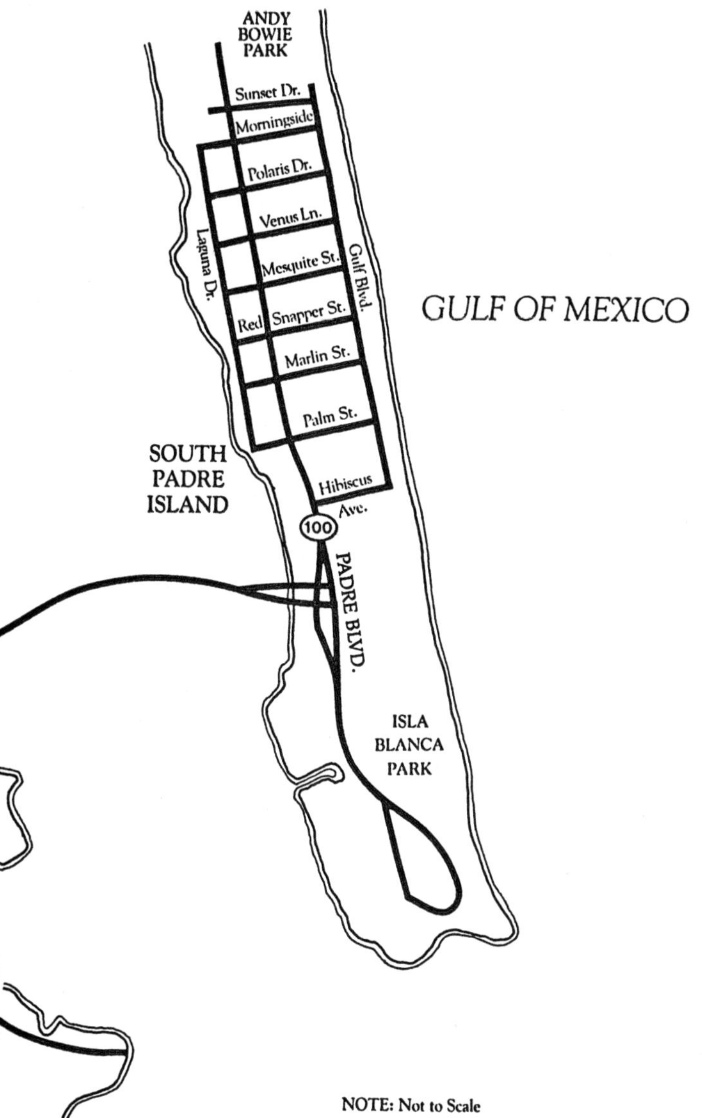

NOTE: Not to Scale

The town of South Padre is on the southern tip of Padre Island, a narrow strip of land — in reality a giant sandbar — running parallel to the coast for more than a hundred miles from Corpus Christi on the north to this beach resort town. It is one link in the chain of barrier islands that protects much of the Texas coast from the direct assault of the sometimes unfriendly sea.

The "South" in the name came to be when the Mansfield Cut, about 34 miles north, was completed in 1964 chopping Padre Island into two parts. Most of the land north of the cut is part of the Padre Island National Seashore (See Corpus Christi). South of the cut it's mostly private land, but only about five miles on the southernmost end have been developed into the town with the same name as the island. To the east is the Gulf of Mexico with its white-tipped waves. To the west are the calm waters of Laguna Madre. And only about 30 miles south is Mexico.

The width of this southern part averages about half a mile. Because it is long and narrow, the island town is easy to get around in. If you want, you can "catch the wave," bright blue trolleys that travel up and down the main street. (Fares are fifty cents a ride or one dollar a day.) The main street, running up the center of the island, is appropriately called Padre Blvd. (also Park Rd. 100). In much of the central part of town, two streets run parallel to Padre Blvd. The one between the Gulf and Padre Blvd. is called Gulf Blvd., and the one on the Laguna Madre side is — you guessed it — Laguna Dr. Padre Blvd. is the only paved road going north beyond the city limits, and then only for twelve miles. After that it's back to nature and 4-wheel drive country with beach, dunes, marshes, birds and other small creatures, tranquility, but no creature comforts. There are plans to develop to the north, including a possible huge, world-class resort, but so far they are still in the planning stages.

On the mainland, Port Isabel, originally established as a supply port in the 1840s for General Zachary Taylor's army in the Mexican War, grew up as a small fishing town. But the only way to reach the island from Port Isabel was by boat so, with the exception of a Coast Guard station, established in 1891, and a few fishing shacks and beach houses, for many decades the island remained much as it had been in 1804 when Padre Jose Nicolas Balli established the first settlement there on a land grant made by King Charles IV of Spain. Even the opening of the first causeway in 1954 didn't start a development rush. More beach houses and a few motels went up, but, in general, the island continued to be ignored for the next 20 years.

Then, in the early 1970s, two events changed the face of the island. The Texas Legislature passed laws forcing the insurance industry to provide hurricane coverage to coastal areas, and the new four-lane causeway was opened. The boom was on.

Overall, South Padre is a getaway island with all the conveniences. And Port Isabel, once known only for its fishing and as the gateway to South Padre, is coming into its own as the home port for day cruises and a tourist spot with several fine restaurants.

TOURIST SERVICES

SOUTH PADRE ISLAND CONVENTION AND VISITOR BUREAU
600 Padre Blvd., just north of the Causeway (P.O. Box 3500, 78597)
761-6433 or 800-343-2368 (U.S. and Canada), in Mexico 1-95-800-343-2368.
Monday–Friday 9–6, Saturday and Sunday 10–5
Free
W

In addition to a wealth of brochures on South Padre, Port Isabel, and the Lower Rio Grande Valley, you'll also find newspapers covering island activities, and helpful counselors who can answer your questions. If you want a preview of the island, send $8 to the Bureau for a video tour.

PORT ISABEL CHAMBER OF COMMERCE
213 Yturria, Port Isabel
943-2262 or in Texas 800-527-6102
Monday–Friday 8–5
W

You can get your questions about Port Isabel answered at this small office in the Community Center.

GRAY LINE TOURS
2505 Padre Blvd.
761-4343 or 800-321-8720
Open seven days 8–5
Tours $12–$99

The 3½-hour tour of South Padre Island and Port Isabel costs about $12 including admissions. They also run daily sightseeing and shopping tours to nearby Matamoros, Mexico ($15) and weekend tours to Monterrey, Mexico (3-days, 2-nights, $99). Tours can be booked through most hotels/motels.

VALLEY ADVENTURE TOURS
708-B Padre Blvd., in Shand's Travel Agency
761-1641 or 800-338-0560
Tours $13-$20

They offer a variety of tours including a daily tour to Matamoros, Mexico ($13), and tours to the zoo and Confederate Air Force Museum in Harlingen (about $15).

BIRD'S-EYE VIEW

PORT ISABEL LIGHTHOUSE
Port Isabel, Texas 100 and Tarvana at the Causeway
943-1172
Open seven days 10–11:30, 1–5
Adults $1, children 50¢ (under 6 and over 65 free)

Sitting in the middle of one of the state's smallest parks is the only lighthouse on the Texas coast that's open to the public. Completed in 1853, this guardian of the coast cast its light up to 16 miles out into the Gulf for more than half a century, until it closed in 1905. During that time it survived occupation by both sides in the Civil War, several hurricanes, and a six-year shutdown while a legal battle took place over the ownership of the lighthouse. It seems the government had neglected a minor point when it built the lighthouse — acquiring the land it was built on. From the top, on a clear day you can see almost forever. At least you'll get an unobstructed view of Port Isabel, the Causeway, South Padre Island, and well out into the Gulf. But this bird's-eye view doesn't come easy. To reach the top you have to climb more than 70 winding steps including three short ladders. A small park is being established on the grounds.

POINTS OF INTEREST

ISLA BLANCA PARK (CAMERON COUNTY PARK)
South of Causeway at southern end of the island (P.O. Box 2106, 78597)
761-5493
Open at all times, office open seven days 8 a.m.–10 p.m.
$1 per vehicle per day
W Variable

In addition to containing the only RV camping area on South Padre, this park also has over a mile of beach and a separate children's beach, marina, boat ramps, a fishing jetty, picnic areas, cabins and day-use cabanas, marine science exhibits, a bike trail, the Chapel by the Sea, a Civic Center, a Coast Guard station, and restaurants. Plans are in the works for a 68-suite motel near the Sea Ranch Marina.

THE *LADY BEA*
Port Isabel, Beulah Lee Park, Texas 100 near the Causeway (Laguna Madre Museum Foundation, P.O. Box 1916, Port Isabel, 78578)
Free

The shrimp boat the *Lady Bea* is a monument to the local shrimping industry and the first installment of what the Laguna Madre Museum Foundation hopes will eventually be a combined maritime and local history museum. Through windows cut into the hull you can see the interior of the 45-foot vessel including the captain's cabin and the engine room. There's a ramp up to the deck where you can peer into the wheelhouse and crew quarters. Standing guard nearby is a statue of the pirate Jean Lafitte who historians say often visited this area.

QUEEN ISABELLA CAUSEWAY
Between Port Isabel and South Padre Island
Open at all times

Measuring 2.6 miles, this causeway across Laguna Madre Bay is in the record books as Texas' longest bridge. Dedicated in 1974, it replaced the original two-lane causeway. At the center, the span is 73 feet above mean high tide permitting seagoing ships to pass underneath. It was built to withstand threefold hurricane force winds. About 5.5 million vehicles cross it each year.

PADRE BALLI STATUE
At South Padre Island end of Queen Isabella Causeway

Padre Jose Nicolas Balli was the first American-born Spaniard ordained by the Catholic Church in this continent. In 1765 his mother gave him the land grant she had received from the king of Spain, which included the island that now bears his name. He actually settled the island in 1804. His statue stands in the center of the highway at the entrance to the island, arms wide as if welcoming people to his home.

SHRIMP FLEET
Port Isabel Docks

When combined with the large numbers of shrimp boats berthed in nearby Port Brownsville, this is one of the largest fishing fleets on the coast. The boats can be seen at the docks all along the waters around Port Isabel and from the jetty as they go out into the Gulf. You can't buy shrimp from the boats, but their fresh catch is available in area shops.

UNIVERSITY OF TEXAS/PAN AMERICAN UNIVERSITY COASTAL STUDIES LAB
Isla Blanca County Park (P.O. Box 2591, South Padre Island 78597)
761-2644
Sunday–Thursday 1:30–4:30. Closed Friday and Saturday
Free ($1 per vehicle for entrance to park)
W +

Research at this lab focuses on the coastal ecosystems of southern Texas and northern Mexico with emphasis on Laguna Madre and Padre Island. Many species of marine life found in local waters, including Kemp's ridley sea turtles, stingray, redfish, grouper, snapper, and bighead sea robins are on display in aquariums. You can also see a small octopus or watch a hermit crab feed. If you find shells on the beach, you can compare them to ones in the lab's extensive collection. If you find one you can't match, the lab's experts will identify it for you.

SPORTS AND ACTIVITIES

Birdwatching

If you want to see something besides the laughing gulls that are omnipresent on the beach, try the tidal flats near the Causeway. With a 4-wheel drive vehicle you can visit the beaches and bayside marsh habitats north of the town up to the Mansfield Cut. And the Laguna Atoscosa Wildlife Refuge is on the mainland just about 20 miles northwest of town.

Boating

Small craft can use the waters of the Laguna Madre while larger craft are just minutes away from the waters of the Gulf. Sailboats can be rented by the hour or the day. Rental places include Bay Sailing and Water Sports, 200 W. Ling (761-5344) and Island Sailboat Rentals, 212 W. Dolphin (761-5061). They also offer lessons. Charter boats for short term — like a sunset cruise — or long term are also available. Most charter boats operate out of Port Isabel. For listings check the phone book or contact the South Padre Island Convention and Visitor Bureau (761-6433).

Fishing

South Padre offers anglers a full range of opportunities. You can pay big bucks to go out in the Gulf after trophy game fish on a high-powered charter boat, pay a lot less for a half-day on a party boat in the Gulf or the bay, wade fish on the flats of Laguna Madre or in the surf or throw a line off a jetty. For charter boats and guides, check the phone book or contact the South Padre Island Convention and Visitor Bureau (761-6433) or the Port Isabel Chamber of Commerce (943-2262). Party boats operating out of Jim's Pier, 209 W. Whiting, 761-2865 (P.O. Box 2249, South Padre Island, 78597), include the 48-foot *Danny B* for bay fishing and the 48-foot *Risa Ann* for Gulf fishing. Operating out of the Sea Ranch Marina are the 65-foot *Laguna Queen* for bay fishing (Colley's Fishing Service, P.O. Box 944, Port Isabel, 78578; 761-2623) and the 85-foot *Thunderbird III* for Gulf fishing (P.O. Box 444, Port Isabel 78578; 761-2764).

Horseback Riding

ISLAND EQUESTRIAN CENTER
Andy Bowie Park, Park Rd. 100 about four miles north of causeway
761-1809

You can ride the beach from here. Also instruction and pony rides available.

Scuba Diving

The Rio Grande Artificial Reef is building up in 80-foot of water in the Gulf about seven miles southeast of the jetties. Items such as sunken boats, trucks, and steel structures are used to attract fish, plants, and other marine creatures to set up their homes there. Local dive shops can arrange trips to the reef.

Windsurfing

Good winds and warm waters have combined to lure windsurfers, or boardsailers, to the island and make this a growing sport here. Sitting between the flat waters of the Laguna Madre and the Gulf surf, the 34-mile island offers a variety of sailing conditions that make it attractive for novices and experts alike. *Wind Surf* magazine has rated South Padre as one of the ten great windsurfing destinations. Several windsurfing competitions are held here each year (See Annual Events) and the Convention and Visitor Bureau has published a brochure on the sport and the island that includes information on these events plus details on five major windsurfing areas and a listing of sailing shops.

SHOPPING

ART GALLERIES
6300 Padre Blvd. at Bahia Mar Resort
761-2282

This small gallery and gift shop is located in a separate building at the north end of the resort. Most of the paintings on sale are sea scenes by local artists.

IVY'S ART GALLERY
5504 Padre Blvd.
761-9522
W entrance in rear

Original art in all media and crafts are featured here. Most of the works are by local artists.

THE MALL AT SUNCHASE
1004 Padre Blvd.
761-7711
W +

The lower two floors of this compact, four-story mall provide covered parking for customers going to the dozen or so specialty shops on the upper two floors. The anchor store is Jones & Jones Department Store.

RARE ART ESTATES SALES
708 Padre Blvd. in Franke Center
761-5510

It looks like a combination museum, art gallery, and antique shop with oriental and Persian rugs, bronzes, paintings, sculpture, period furniture, crystal and old glass, and estate jewelry. In addition to regular sales, there are periodic auctions.

SISTERS TRADING COMPANY
410 Padre Blvd., opposite the Causeway
761-2896
W

Featured here are original designer gifts and jewelry, fine linens, and both American and European antiques.

TEXAS SHELL FACTORY
Laguna Heights, Texas 100 approximately three miles west of Port Isabel
943-1709
W

"She sells sea shells by the seashore" has a real meaning here. This is just one of the many shell shops in the area. It is the retail outlet of a wholesale dealer, so if what you're looking for is made out of seashells you'll probably find it here. The emphasis is on novelty items that make forgettable souvenirs, but if you want untarnished samples of nature's art, there are shelves and open boxes filled with all kinds of shells and preserved marine life.

KIDS' STUFF

GLADYS PORTER ZOO
(See Harlingen.)

JEREMIAH'S LANDING
Padre Blvd. at Gulfpoint, just south of the Causeway
761-2131
Open seven days 12–9 (until 2 a.m. weekends in high season). Usually closed November–February

Packed into this small park is a 240-foot, three-flume water slide; an 18-hole mini-golf course (with three holes in the middle of the water slide hill), a video game room, souvenir shop, snack bar and open-air bar (beer and wine). From June through September, Jeremiah's usually has live entertainment nightly.

SIDE TRIPS

BROWNSVILLE/MATAMOROS
Take Texas 100 to Port Isabel then southwest (left) on Texas 48 approximately 20 miles to Brownsville and continue on to the International Bridge to Matamoros
(See Brownsville.)

HARLINGEN
Take Texas 100 to US 77/83, then northwest to city
(See Harlingen.)

LAGUNA ATASCOSA NATIONAL WILDLIFE REFUGE
Go west on Texas 100 past Laguna Heights and turn onto FM 510. Continue west to Bayview, then turn north (right) and go about four miles until the road intersects with FM 106. Turn east (right) until FM

106 dead-ends, then north (left) about two miles to park headquarters
748-3607
Open seven days dawn to dusk
Free
W Variable

This 45,000-acre coastline sanctuary lies on the Laguna Madre behind Padre Island. It is the southernmost refuge in the United States on what's called the Great Central Flyway along which waterfowl and other birds migrate annually between Canada and the Gulf. It is also the largest parcel of land in the Rio Grande Valley preserved for native plants and animals. Its name in Spanish means "muddy lagoon." More than 300 species of birds have been recorded here. The refuge visitor center, located near the entrance, is open daily from 10-4 from October through April; on weekends only from September through May. It is closed June through August. Bayside and lakeside tour roads provide ample opportunities for wildlife observation and photography. These are open daily from 7 to 7 year round. There are also walking trails. For information contact: P.O. Box 450, Rio Hondo 78583.

LE MISTRAL
1250 Port Rd., Port Isabel
943-1324 or 800-292-7022
Cruises start at $35
No children under 7 allowed
Call for cruise schedule
Parking at Port Isabel dock $3

How about an abbreviated version of life on a cruise ship? That's what this 600-passenger seagoing vessel offers as it travels south off the coast of Mexico. Entertainment, games and contests, sunbathing, dancing, all-you-can-eat buffet, and — once out in international waters — Las Vegas-style gambling. Cruises last about six hours. Day cruises Wednesday, Saturday and Sunday. Evening cruises Thursday, Friday and Saturday.

ANNUAL EVENTS

March

SPRING BREAK
Various locations on the island
761-6433 (Convention and Visitor Bureau)
Time depends on various schools' spring break schedules
Most events free
W Variable

When you get right down to it, this is a big, boisterous beach bash for tens and tens of thousands of college students from all over the U.S. and Canada who convene here when their schools close for spring break. Organized activities include concerts, sports events, contests of all kind, and many other events aimed at keeping the young crowd happy and their boundless energy in check (so they will leave the town in one piece when they depart).

May

SOUTH PADRE ISLAND WINTER PARK BLOW-OUT
Various locations
761-6433 (Convention and Visitor Bureau)
First weekend in May
Free to spectators
W Variable

One of the largest amateur windsurfing events in the United States, this tournament draws boardsailing enthusiasts from all over the country. Contestants vie for trophies in slalom, triangle, and long-distance races.

August

TEXAS INTERNATIONAL FISHING TOURNAMENT
Headquarters at South Point Marina, Port Isabel
943-TIFT (943-8438)
Usually first week of August
Free to spectators
W Variable

With its 50th anniversary well behind it, this is the second oldest fishing competition on the coast, bowing only to the Deep Sea Roundup at Port Aransas. Trophies and awards are given for both bay and offshore fishing. Entry fees range from about $15 for children under ten — every child who catches a fish and weighs it in gets a trophy — to about $75 for adults. The entry fee includes social events most nights during the tourney.

December

CHRISTMAS BY THE SEA AND ISLAND OF LIGHTS
Various locations on the island
761-6433 (Visitor and Convention Bureau)
Weekend early in month
W Variable

They don't have snow for a White Christmas at South Padre, so instead they have a Sandman-Building Contest, a land parade and a lighted boat parade that's slow moving but worth waiting for. Other activities include a tree-lighting ceremony, concerts, Christmas caroling, and a community Christmas party. The town is also lit-up with more than 300,000 lights.

OFFBEAT

ILA LOETSCHER, THE TURTLE LADY
5805 Gulf Blvd. near Parade Dr.
761-2544
Programs for visitors: Tuesday and Saturday; May–August at 9 a.m., October–April at 10 a.m. Group tours at other times by reservation only
$1 donation (for Sea Turtle, Inc.)
W

Turtles dressed in costumes for a show may look silly, but if being silly or putting on a corny show will raise money and educate the public to save sea turtles from extinction, that's what octogenarian Ila Loetscher and her volunteer helpers will do. Their lofty purpose is to save the Kemp's ridley sea turtle and seven other endangered species of marine turtles from extinction. In her show, the Turtle Lady uses a cast of turtles — both her pets and injured turtles being nursed back to health at her refuge — to acquaint visitors with their lives and the programs to save them from extinction. In her earlier years, Ila Loetscher was one of the first woman pilots in the United States.

THE SONS OF THE BEACH
P.O. Box 2694, 78597
761-5943

During Spring Break in 1987, more than 5,000 volunteers constructed what was then the world's longest sand castle on South Padre Island, a structure that measured more than two miles in length and earned a place in the Guiness Book of World Records. The project was organized and guided by sand castle building wizards "Amazin' Walter" McDonald and Lucinda "Sandy Feet" Wierenga, founders of The Sons of the Beach (S.O.B.s). On most summer Saturdays, the S.O.B.s can be found building their intricate sand castles with towers, spiraling staircases, and gravity-defying arches on the beach in front of the Holiday Inn Beach Resort.

RESTAURANTS

($ = under $7, $$ = $7 to $17, $$$ = $17 to $25, $$$$ = over $25 for one person excluding drinks, tax, and tip.)

Dinner For Two

GRILL ROOM AT THE PANTRY
708 Padre Blvd. in Franke Center
761-9331
Dinner only Wednesday–Sunday (Days vary by season, call to confirm)
Reservations suggested
$$-$$$
Cr.
W +

Among the seafood entrées are Red Snapper *Provence*, lump crab St. Charles, and a variety of shrimp dishes including Cajun baked, grilled, and Newburg. The menu also offers steaks, lamb chops, and grilled quail. All served in a cozy and comfortable dining room. The Pantry, attached, is a deli open for breakfast and lunch and offering sandwiches and light lunch items ($) as well as gourmet foods. Bar.

THE YACHT CLUB
Port Isabel, 700 Yturria, about two blocks north of Texas 100
943-1301
Dinner only Thursday–Tuesday. Closed Wednesday
Reservations suggested
$$$
Cr.
W
Children's plates

It hasn't been a yacht club since the Depression, but it still retains the air of substance — nothing cheap and nothing ostentatious — that one associates with old money. The cuisine carries out this promise at a more moderate cost than expected, featuring fresh seafood with just a dash of beef entrees. A house specialty, when available, is red snapper throats, a dish that will please the seafood-lover despite its unpleasant name. The full snapper fillet is available broiled, blackened, *Meuniere* (dipped in egg wash and sauteed in wine, butter, and parsley sauce), and Amsterdam Style (sauteed and topped with shrimp, *beurre blanc* and caviar). The wine list offers over 150 selections. No-smoking area. Bar.

Breakfast and Lunch

MANUEL'S RESTAURANT
100 E. Swordfish at Padre Blvd. in Miramar Hotel
761-9563
Breakfast and lunch seven days
$
No Cr.

You can get an American-style breakfast or lunch here, but why when you can fill-up on their inexpensive and hearty Mexican dishes like breakfast tortillas (touted as the biggest tortillas on the Island) with *chorizo* and egg and the lunch *fajita* plate. Beer and wine.

ROVANS RESTAURANT AND BAKERY
5304 Padre Blvd.
761-6972
Open 6–6 Wednesday–Monday. Closed Tuesday
$
MC, V
W
Children's plates

A variety of bountiful breakfasts are served here all day. They also offer reasonably priced plate lunch specials, sandwiches, steaks, chops, salads, and fresh-from-the-oven bakery goodies. It's popular and doesn't take reservations, so expect to wait in high season.

TED'S
5717 Padre Blvd.
761-5327
Breakfast and lunch seven days
$
No Cr.

One of the most popular dishes here is simply called "Our Specialty." The specialty is Ted's award winning *fajitas* served with two eggs, and hash browns or refried beans, available for breakfast or lunch. *Fajitas* share the lunch menu with salads, burgers, and sandwiches, including the poorboy "Philly," sliced roast beef grilled with sauteed onions and melted cheese. Beer and wine.

Italian

MARCELLO'S ITALIAN RISTORANTE
110 N. Tarnava at Texas 100, about two blocks from the Causeway, Port Isabel
943-7611
Lunch and dinner Monday–Saturday, dinner only Sunday
Reservations suggested
$-$$
Cr.
W
Children's plates

All the familiar Italian standbys are on the menu here. There's a variety of pasta dishes including spaghetti with pesto sauce, *lasagna, linguini* with white or red clam sauce, *cannelloni, fettucini Alfredo,* and several veal and chicken entrées, plus *Sicilia-* and *Napolitana-*style pizza. And they also take advantage of their location on the Gulf to offer fresh seafood choices like *scampi linguini* and flounder filet *parmigiana*. Bar.

SERGIO'S BY THE BAY
205 W. Palm, inside Bermuda's Night Club
761-4308
Dinner Monday–Saturday, Closed Sunday
Reservations suggested
$$-$$$
AE, MC, V

The menu is billed as Mediterranean fare that means the seafood, pasta, and chicken dishes range from Italian to Greek. Among the entrées are shrimp in a wine sauce and seafood *crespelle* (a pasta filled with crab, oysters, and shrimp in a a white sauce). If you pick your time carefully, your dinner will be enhanced by the view of the sun setting over the bay — and they offer sunset specials, too. Bar.

Seafood

BLACKBEARD'S
103 E. Saturn, off Padre Blvd. two miles north of the Causeway
761-2962
Lunch and dinner seven days
No reservations
$-$$
Cr.
W (ramp)

Although well-known by the beach crowd for its burgers, sandwiches, and steaks, the main order of business is seafood. The top of the line is the Seafood Platter Supreme that includes shrimp, stuffed crab, stuffed shrimp, fish, and scallops for about $14. Bar.

CAPUCINNO'S
317 E. Railroad, one block south of Texas 100, Port Isabel
943-4201
Dinner only Monday–Saturday. Closed Sunday
Reservations suggested
$$-$$$
Cr.
W Call ahead
Children's plates

Long known for its Italian food, Capucinno's is putting more and more emphasis on seafood. You can still indulge your tastes for pasta and Italian-style veal and chicken entrees, but now there is also a variety of fish, shrimp, and seafood combinations on the menu. It is housed in the oldest building in Port Isabel, built in 1899. No smoking area. Lounge upstairs.

CRABBY HARRY'S
1200 W. Hwy 100
943-1977
Breakfast, lunch, and dinner seven days
$-$$
Cr.
W

Seafood dishes include shrimp *veracruzana* and stuffed flounder. And there's a moderately priced all-you-can-eat Friday night fish fry. Steaks, chicken, soups, salads, and sandwiches are also available. Bar.

SEA RANCH RESTAURANT
1 Padre Blvd., at entrance to Isla Blanca Park
761-1314
Breakfast, lunch, and dinner seven days

Reservations suggested weekends
$$-$$$
AE, MC, V
W +
Children's plates

Located next to the Sea Ranch Marina, this waterside restaurant specializes in fresh seafood ranging from *ceviche* to red snapper (and snapper throats) to lobster tails. But it also offers steaks, chicken, burgers, deli sandwiches, and Mexican dishes including *fajitas*. Outdoor deck with live entertainment in season. No smoking area. Bar.

SCAMPI'S
206 W. Aries at Laguna
761-1755
Dinner only Wednesday–Monday. Closed Tuesday
Reservations suggested
$$-$$$
AE, MC, V
W downstairs only

How about an appetizer of "Alligator Bits?" Of course, if you're more conventional they also have appetizers like Oyster Rockefeller, Scallop *Ceviche*, or Peel-Your-Own Shrimp. Since *scampi* in Italian means shrimp, there are a a variety of shrimp dishes on the menu including shrimp & *fettucini* and Cajun-style B B Q Shrimp. Entrées also include choices like Swordfish Citron, swordfish steak with a lemon *blurre blanc*. For variety there are some steak and chicken dishes. No smoking area. Patio dining in good weather. Lounge upstairs.

ACCOMMODATIONS

($ = Under $45, $$ = $46-$60, $$$ = $61-$80, $$$$ = $81-$100, $$$$$ = Over $100)
Rate symbols are for high season (Spring Break and summer). Off-season rates are substantially lower.
Room Tax 13 percent

BAHIA MAR RESORT AND CONFERENCE CENTER
6300 Padre Blvd. (P.O. Box 2280, 78597)
761-1343 or in Texas 800-292-7502, outside Texas 800-531-7404
$$$-$$$$

This 12-story resort has 200 hotel rooms and 137 two-and three-bedroom condominium units ($$$$$). Children under 12 stay free in room with parents. Package plans available. Cable TV with HBO. Room phones (charge for local calls). No pets. Restaurant. Two outdoor pools, outdoor whirlpool, two lighted tennis courts, putting green, guest memberships available in country club and health club. Self-service laundry and same-day dry cleaning. Gift shop. On the beach.

BEST WESTERN FIESTA ISLE
5701 Padre Blvd.
761-4913 or 800-528-1234
$$$$$
W + two rooms
No-smoking rooms

The two-story Best Western has 58 rooms including eight no-smoking. Children under 16 stay free in parent's room. Senior discount. Cable TV and VCR rentals. Room phones (charge for local calls). Pets OK ($25 pet deposit). Outdoor pool, outdoor whirlpool, and guest memberships in health club. Free continental breakfast and free newspaper. Self-service laundry and same-day dry cleaning. Most rooms have kitchenettes.

DAYS INN
3913 Padre Blvd.
761-7831 or 800-325-2525
$$$
W + four rooms
No-smoking rooms

The 57 rooms in this two-story Days Inn include 10 no-smoking rooms. Package plans available and senior discount. Cable TV and VCR rentals. Room phones (charge for local calls). No pets. Outdoor pool, outdoor whirlpool, and guest memberships in country club. Free coffee in lobby and free continental breakfast. Self-service laundry. All rooms have kitchenettes (but no plates or utensils).

HOLIDAY INN BEACH RESORT
100 Padre Blvd., just south of Causeway near Jeremiah's Landing
761-5401 or in Texas 800-292-7506, outside Texas 800-531-7405
$$$$-$$$$$
W + five rooms
No-smoking rooms

The four- and six-story Holiday Inn offers 227 units that include eight suites ($$$$$) and 17 no-smoking rooms. Children under 12 stay free in room with parents. Package plans available and senior discount. Cable TV with HBO and Showtime. VCR rentals. Room phones (charge for local calls). No pets. Restaurant, club open seven nights with entertainment every night. Two outdoor pools (one heated), wading pool, outdoor whirlpool, two tennis courts, and rental bicycles. Self-service laundry and same-day dry cleaning. On the beach.

SHERATON SOUTH PADRE ISLAND BEACH RESORT
310 Padre Blvd., south of Causeway
761-6551 or in Texas 800-672-4747, outside Texas 800-222-4010
$$$$$
W + four rooms
No-smoking rooms

The 12-story Sheraton offers 250 units including 50 suites ($$$$$) and 24 no-smoking rooms. Children up to 17 stay free in room with parents. Package plans available and senior discount. Cable TV with HBO and VCR rentals. Room phones (charge for local calls). Fire sprinklers in rooms. No pets. Two restaurants, room service, and two clubs open Monday-Saturday with live entertainment every night. Indoor/outdoor heated pool with pool bar in season, children's pool, outdoor whirlpool, four lighted tennis courts, and guest memberships available in country club. Free newspaper. Self-service laundry and same-day dry cleaning. Gift shop. On the beach.

RADISSON RESORT ON SOUTH PADRE ISLAND
500 Padre Blvd. (P.O. Box 2081, 78597), just north of Causeway
761-6511 or 800-333-3333
$$$$$
No-smoking rooms

The 12- and 14-story Radisson Resort offers 145 hotel rooms, including five no-smoking, and 80 one- and two-bedroom condominium units ($$$$$). Children under 18 stay free in room with parents. Package plans available and senior discount. Cable TV with HBO and pay channel. Room phones (charge for local calls). No pets. Restaurant, room service, and club open seven nights with live entertainment every night but Sunday. Five outdoor pools, seven outdoor whirlpools, eight tennis courts (two lighted), and guest memberships available in country club and health club. Self-service laundry in condominiums. Same-day dry cleaning. Gift shop. Limited covered parking. On the beach.

THE TIKI CONDOMINIUM APARTMENT HOTEL
6608 Padre Blvd.
761-2694 or in Texas 800-292-1382, outside Texas 800-325-3140
$$$-$$$$$

The two-story Tiki has 144 one-, two- and three-bedroom apartments. Children under 6 stay free in room with parents. Cable TV. Room phones (charge for local calls). Small pets OK ($10 pet charge). Restaurant open for lunch and dinner, room service, and bar. Two outdoor heated pools, indoor whirlpool, sauna, guest memberships available in health club. On the beach.

THE YACHT CLUB HOTEL
700 Yturria, about two blocks north of Texas 100, Port Isabel
943-1301
$-$$
(Room tax 10 percent)

This two-story hotel has 24 units including four suites ($$). Cable TV. No pets. Restaurant (See Restaurants, above), bar. Outdoor heated pool. Free continental breakfast. A classic, it was built in the 1920s and restored to near original condition.

OTHER ACCOMMODATIONS

There are twice as many condominium units on South Padre Island as there are hotel and motels rooms. Of course, not all of the condos are available for rent, but thousands are, giving the renter more choices than anywhere else on the Texas coast. High season rates for a two-bedroom condo start at about $90 a day and go up to $200 or more with the location and number of amenities matching the price. Weekly rates are usually available.

Fortunately, finding a condo rental on South Padre is not difficult because almost all the rental units are listed with rental agencies. For a current listing and brochures of condominiums with rental units and rental agencies, contact the South Padre Island Convention and Visitor Bureau (See Tourist Services, above).

BIENVENIDOS TO THE RIO GRANDE VALLEY

To be technical, the Rio Grande Valley really isn't a valley at all. It's a wide delta. But that's the name it has been known by for years and years so let's live with it. The Rio Grande Valley covered in this guidebook has two parts, the lower valley and the upper valley. These distinctions are largely disregarded in the listings that follow, but it might help you enjoy your visit if you understand the differences between them.

The Lower Valley

The lower valley — which is what Texans mean when they refer to "The Valley" — is a strip about 100 miles long and 20 miles wide along the Rio Grande River from Brownsville west to Falcon Lake, just past the historic town of Roma. The climate here is often referred to as semi-tropical which means it has short, mild winters with only slight chance of a freeze and snow, and palm trees and other lush, colorful tropical-type vegetation. The climate is so hospitable, in fact, that the growing season here lasts about 320 days a year giving area farmers at least two yields a year of more than 40 different commercial crops that range from vegetables and citrus fruits — almost all the citrus grown in Texas is grown here — to sugar cane and cotton. But what really makes the lower valley thrive is water. It would be arid brushland except for irrigation canals that bring water to more than 800,000 acres of fertile soil.

LOWER RIO GRANDE VALLEY

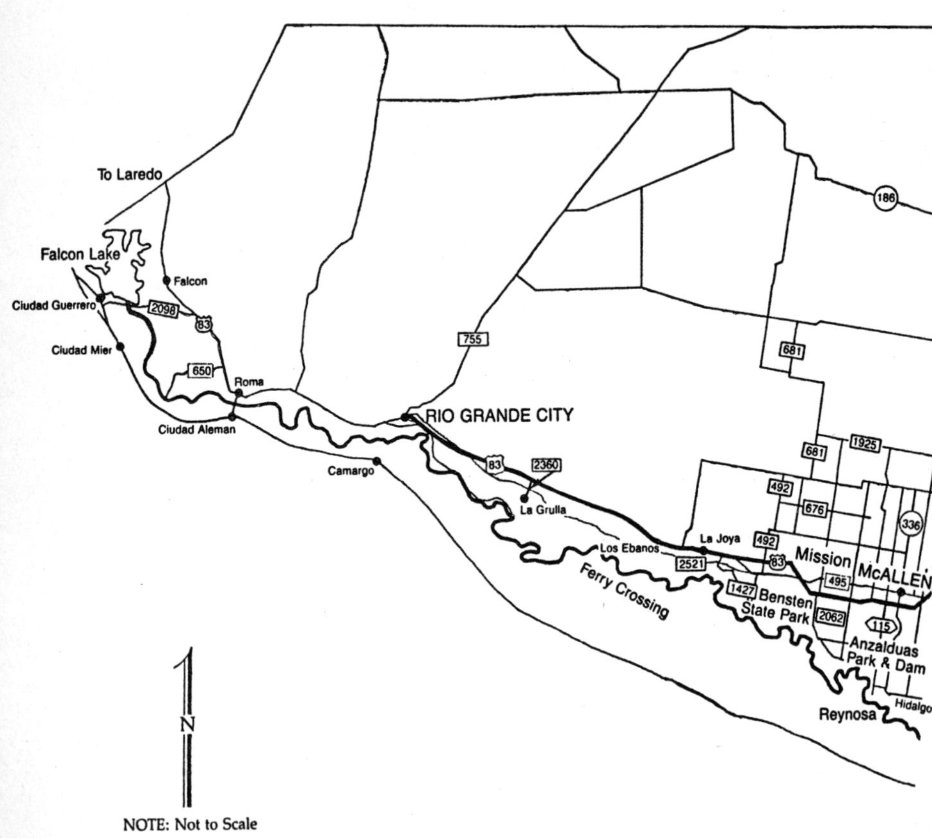

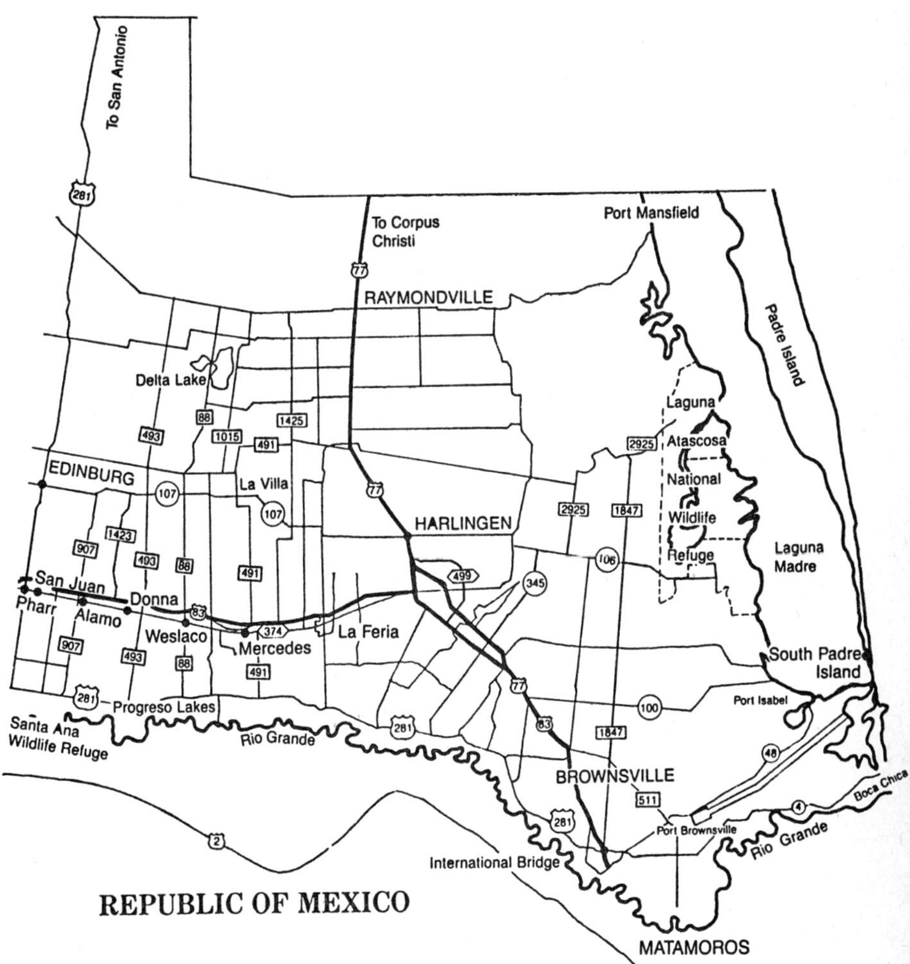
To San Antonio
281
To Corpus Christi
77
Port Mansfield
RAYMONDVILLE
Padre Island
Delta Lake
88
1425
493
1015
491
Laguna
2925
Atascosa
National
Wildlife
Refuge
EDINBURG
107
La Villa
107
77
HARLINGEN
2925
1847
1423
907
493
88
491
499
106
345
Laguna
Madre
San Juan
Pharr
Alamo
Donna
83
Weslaco
374
Mercedes
La Feria
907
493
88
491
South Padre
Island
77
281
Progreso Lakes
100
Port Isabel
Santa Ana
Wildlife Refuge
Rio Grande
281
83
1847
48
BROWNSVILLE
511
Boca Chica
4
281
Port Brownsville
Rio Grande
2
International Bridge
REPUBLIC OF MEXICO
MATAMOROS

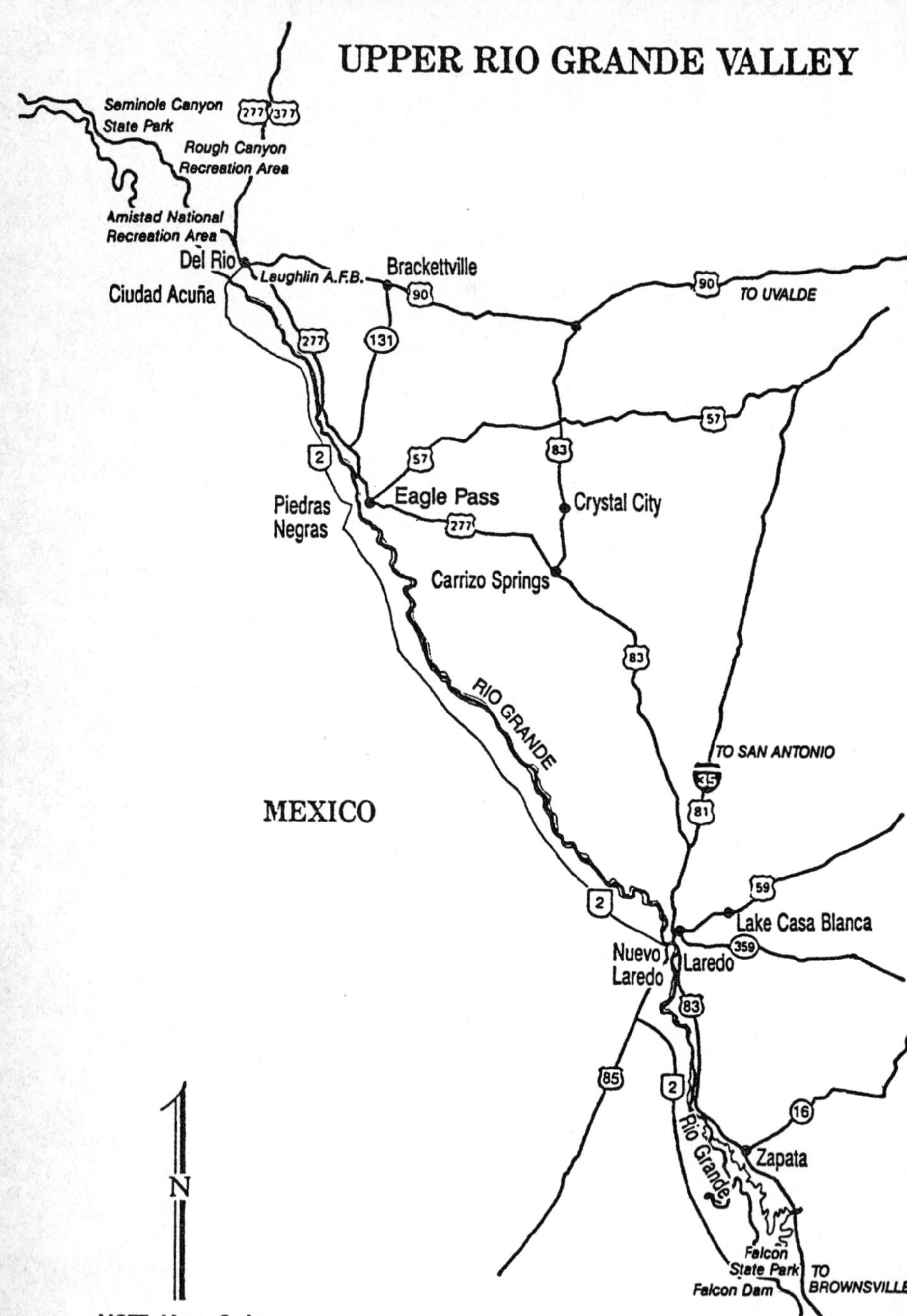

NOTE: Not to Scale

About 35 communities line up almost shoulder-to-shoulder in the lower valley with some 675,000 permanent residents. (More than twice that number of people live in the border cities across the river in Mexico.) Another 125,000 or more (estimates go as high as 200,000) semi-permanent visitors come to the area in the winter. Greeted with open arms by the residents, these "Winter Texans" come to avoid the cold weather in the northern states and Canada and spend from three to six months here. Most of them stay in the more than 400 RV/Mobile Home parks in the area, many returning to the same park year after year. To keep these repeat visitors coming back, the Valley offers even more activities for visitors during the winter than it does during the rest of the year.

The Upper Valley

The upper valley continues west up the Rio Grande from Falcon Lake to just past Lake Amistad and just short of the Big Bend region. This is a semi-arid area, also with mild winters — though there's a slightly higher chance of a freeze and even some snow — and desert-type vegetation. This area includes the widely-dispersed cities of Laredo, Eagle Pass, and Del Rio.

Enjoying the Whole Valley

Two highways will take you almost the entire length of the valley. U.S. 83 goes from Brownsville to Carrizo Springs, near Eagle Pass where you pick up U.S. 277 to go the rest of the way up to Del Rio.

There's plenty to do in both parts of the Rio Grande Valley — from visiting Brownsville's world-famous Gladys Porter Zoo to wine tasting at the oldest winery in Texas in Del Rio. But one of the major attractions is that Mexico waits just across the river. No trip to any of the Texas border cities would be complete without experiencing a visit to our neighbor to the south. Whether it's to Matamoros, a city of more than half million people across from Brownsville, or to tiny Camargo across from Rio Grande City, it's an opportunity you shouldn't pass up. And all it takes is a simple, no-hassle trip across one of the many international bridges (See Crossing into Mexico in the Introduction).

There you can eat, drink, and be merry and not spend a small fortune doing it. You can also shop. The Mexican border towns are a bargain hunter's heaven. And if you like to haggle, it's a double delight because, with a few exceptions in the exclusive or fixed price shops, haggling is a way of life for the Mexican shopper. Just remember the Mexican shopkeepers are THE experts at haggling. If you work at it, you can talk them down a little — perhaps a lot — but you can be sure they'll still make a profit on the sale. Haggling is a fun game because everybody wins a little.

With the large Hispanic population on the U.S. side of the border, the Mexican influence is felt in another way that is also a big attraction for visitors to the Rio Grande Valley. Even though there's lots to do, there's a gentle pace to daily life — not quite the full spirit of *mañana*, but almost.

ALAMO

HIDALGO COUNTY ★ 6,000 ★ (512)

Originally named Ebenezer after a nearby clubhouse where land-buying prospects were entertained, in 1919 the town was re-named for the Alamo Land and Sugar Company. It is a center for gift fruit shippers.

ALAMO CHAMBER OF COMMERCE
802 Austin (78516)
787-2117

SANTA ANA NATIONAL WILDLIFE REFUGE
Take FM 907 south approximately seven miles to US 281, then east (left) about ¼ mile to entrance
787-7861
Trails open sunrise to sunset, Visitors Center: weekdays 8–4:30, weekends 9–4:30
Free
W + Visitors Center and a trail for the handicapped

Most of the 2,080 acres are in subtropical native growth demonstrating how the area looked before the development of agriculture in the early 1900s. Because the lower Rio Grande Valley is on the convergence of two major flyways, Central and Mississippi, the refuge provides habitat for an amazing diversity of bird species, many of which can not be found elsewhere in the United States. A birdwatcher's checklist of well over 370 species is available at the Visitors Center. Also at the Center are maps and brochures, slide programs, films, and exhibits on the refuge and area wildlife. Three nature trails, including one that is paved, leave from the Visitors Center. During the winter tourist season the Frontera Audubon Society operates a tram tour Thursday through Monday. The tour lasts about 1½ hours and costs $2 for adults and $1 for children. (The Society also operates a hot line for recent sightings of rare species throughout the Valley — 565-6773). For information write: Refuge Manager, Route 1, Box 202A, Alamo 78516.

BRACKETTVILLE

KINNEY COUNTY SEAT ★ 1,860 ★ (512)

Like many towns in sparsely settled regions, Brackettville grew up as a supply village for nearby Fort Clark that was founded in 1852. The town was named after O. B. Brackett who built and operated the first store. While most such forts were deactivated when the frontier was settled, turning the dependent villages into ghost towns, Fort Clark remained an active U.S. Army cavalry post until 1946. This gave the town time to develop as a trade center for the county's ranchers and farmers.

With the exception of Spofford, a small Southern Pacific Railroad center, about ten miles away, Brackettville is the only town in Kinney County, a county 22 square miles larger than the state of Rhode Island.

Still living in the town are descendants of the Black Seminole Indian scouts who served at Fort Clark during the Indian campaigns. The Seminole Indian Scout Cemetery is located south of town (See Historic Places).

TOURIST SERVICES

KINNEY COUNTY CHAMBER OF COMMERCE
P.O. Box 386, 78832
563-2466

HISTORIC PLACES

FORT CLARK
US 90, east edge of town
563-2493
W Variable

The Fort was founded in 1852 to guard the San Antonio-El Paso road and to stop Indian raids in the area. It was from here, in May 1873, that Colonel Ranald S. Mackenzie, operating on secret orders to cross the Rio Grande if necessary, lead the 4th U.S. Cavalry, accompanied by the Black Seminole Indian Scouts (See following), 80 miles into Mexico to strike at the Lipan and Kickapoo Indians who had been raiding in Texas. Many infantry units, including the 9th and 10th Infantry's Black "Buffalo Soldiers," and virtually all the army's cavalry units were stationed at this post during its more than 90 years of service. Among the officers who served here and later became famous in World War II are Generals George C. Marshall, George S. Patton, and Jonathan M. Wainwright. Today, many of the historic fort buildings remain and there is a small museum in the Old Guardhouse that is open Saturday and Sunday afternoons. The fort is on the property of the Fort Clark Springs Association which, fortunately, is interested in preserving the historic buildings on the post and has restored several of them. You can get a pass at the security gate to visit the fort area. The Association also operates a motel and restaurant on the grounds (See Accommodations).

ST. MARY MAGDELENE CATHOLIC CHURCH
El Paso and Sweeney

Built in 1878, it was used as a church until 1964. Now it is a religious education building and not open to the public. It is registered with the Texas Historical Commission.

SEMINOLE INDIAN SCOUT CEMETERY
About three miles south on FM 3348

The Seminoles were descendants of slaves who escaped from their white masters in Georgia and took refuge among the Indians in Florida. They intermarried and took up Indian customs and identity. Supposedly, they became known as "Seminoles" after the Spanish word for "runaway." After the Seminole War in Florida, the Black Seminoles were relocated to Oklahoma, but many of them then migrated into Texas and Mexico. The army hired about 150 as scouts assigned to Fort Clark. The Seminole Indian Scouts proved themselves brave and loyal during the many battles with the Indians to settle the frontier. A number of them are buried in this cemetery, including four who earned the nation's highest military honor, the Congressional Medal of Honor.

OTHER POINTS OF INTEREST

ALAMO VILLAGE MOVIELAND
Shahan Ranches (P.O. Box 528, 78832). Take RR 674 north about seven miles to entrance
563-2580
Open seven days 9–5 except closed Christmas Week (December 21–26)
Adults $5, children over six $2.50
W Variable

The largest reproduction of The Alamo ever built was constructed here in the late 1950s for the John Wayne epic *The Alamo*. The replica still stands, with its battered walls and buildings in ruins, just as it was at the end of the filming after the battle was over. Nearby, and more entertaining, is an Old West town complete with a jail, general store, stagecoach barn, a blacksmith's shop, a bank, and more than a dozen other buildings that make up a set right out of a western movie. Many of the buildings are furnished and open to visitors. During June, July, and August there's live entertainment — four shows a day consisting of music, singing, and western comedy melodrama, plus staged gunfights in the streets. You can also see a herd of owner J. T. "Happy" Shahan's Texas Longhorn cattle. Food available in the Cantina runs from Mexican specialties to hamburgers. Movie-making is still big at Alamo Village. More than three dozen feature films and TV movies have been shot here, plus over a hundred TV shows and commercials. If one is shooting when you visit, you're welcome to watch. An end-of-summer highlight is the annual Cowboy Horse Races held on Labor Day. Anyone who rides western style on a fast horse is invited to enter the races that are held on the main street in the afternoon after a barbecue lunch. Other activities that day include live entertainment by celebrity C&W stars, staged gunfights, and trick gun acts.

SPORTS AND ACTIVITIES

Golf

FORT CLARK SPRINGS GOLF COURSE
Fort Clark Springs, US 90 at east edge of town
563-9204

Eighteen-hole course. Green fees; weekdays $10.60, weekends and holidays $12.72. Closed Monday.

ACCOMMODATIONS

Room Tax 6 percent

FORT CLARK SPRINGS MOTEL
Fort Clark Springs, US 90, east edge of town
563-2493
$
W + two rooms

There are 38 rooms in two buildings in this two-story motel. Golf package plans available. TV. Pets OK. Restaurant, lounge open seven nights. Outdoor spring-fed pool. Par-3 and 18-hole golf course. The motel is located in the restored limestone barracks on the grounds of the resort community.

BROWNSVILLE

CAMERON COUNTY SEAT ★ 115,000 ★ (512)

Brownsville might also be called Bargainsville because it offers the opportunity for low cost vacationing and shopping in both the largest American city and the largest Mexican city in the Rio Grande Valley. It is also just a short drive from the sparkling beach on South Padre Island.

Although separated by a national boundary, Brownsville and Matamoros (population 450,000) share a common Spanish culture. Matamoros was a full-blown city long before Brownsville existed and its customs and heritage lapped over to its younger sister. So strong is this feeling of a common bond that many of the residents on both sides of the Rio Grande think of the two cities as one. Each year more than 30 million border crossings are recorded at the two bridges connecting them, and the vast majority of these crossings are by locals going to shop, visit, or work on the other side. More evidence of this cultural relationship can be seen in Brownsville's downtown shopping district where, perhaps more than anywhere else in the city, Spanish is the predominant language heard on the streets and seen in the signs in most shops.

Brownsville originated as a fort in 1846, a fort that played a part in setting off the Mexican War. A major cause of that war was a dispute over whether the Nueces River or the Rio Grande was the border between Texas and Mexico. The Mexicans contended the Nueces was the border while the government of the new Republic of Texas claimed the Rio Grande. The festering dispute became a major issue between the United States and Mexico when Texas joined the Union. In 1846, to reinforce the American claim, General Zachary Taylor deliberately built a fort on the Rio Grande across from Matamoros. The Mexicans considered this an invasion and attacked the fort — and the war was on. Among the first casualties was Major Jacob Brown. The fort, and then the city, was named after him.

In 1848, after the war ended, Charles Stillman, one of the many New England merchants who had previously set up shop in Matamoros before the war, bought the land around Fort Brown and laid out a townsite.

The sister cities survived revolutions, border skirmishes, the Civil War, hurricanes, and bandits who raided on both sides of the river. In 1851, the citizens of Matamoros repulsed an attack by revolutionaries earning the official designation of "Heroic Matamoros" — one of only three cities in Mexico to hold that title. Today many signs and all official documents continue this tribute to valor with the letter "H" for *heroica,* before the city's name.

During the Civil War, for a time, Brownsville was the only unblockaded port of the Confederacy, shipping cotton and tobacco and other products from the southern states and bringing in armaments and supplies. The vast cotton yards, where Amigoland Mall now stands, are said to have held about 10,000 bales at any one time. But this ended when Union troops recaptured the city in late 1863. However, the Confederates never stopped trying to regain control and they engaged the Union forces at Palmito Hill, about 14 miles east of Brownsville in what has been called "The Last Battle of the Civil War." Because of the poor communications at that time, the battle took place six weeks after Lee had surrendered at Appomattox.

Today life is much quieter along the border. Texas' southernmost city, Brownsville is located at the same latitude as Miami, Florida. The subtropical climate, tempered by cool, and surprisingly dry, Gulf breezes, encourages a leisurely lifestyle. It also encourages year-round gardens of bougainvillea, hibiscus, oleander, and roses (to name just a few), all set against a background of stately palms, banana and citrus trees, bamboo, and the ubiquitous oak and mesquite. And scattered around the town are the resacas, the lagoons left behind as, over the centuries, the then untamed Rio Grande jumped from one course to another.

The leisurely pace does not mean Brownsville is a backwater. In addition to being a trade center for agricultural products of the valley, the city is an industrial center and an international seaport, connected to the Gulf by a 17-mile ship channel, and is the Texas terminus of the Intracoastal Waterway. It is also the home of one of the largest shrimp fleets on the Texas coast.

BROWNSVILLE

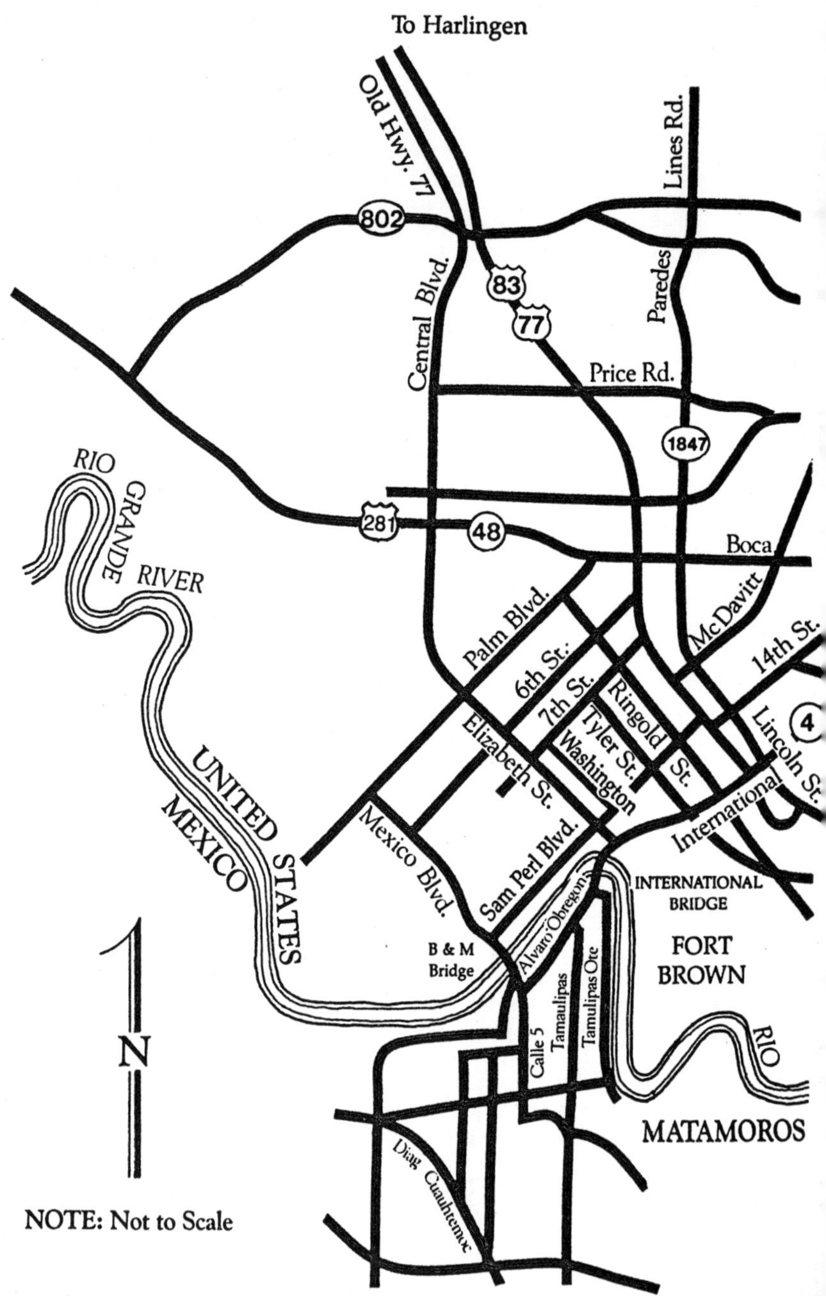

TO PORT ISABEL
802
Coffee Port Rd.
Old Port Isabel Rd.
48
Central Ave.
Vermillion Ave.
Chica Blvd.
4
To Boca Chica Beach
Billy Mitchell Blvd.
BROWNSVILLE INTERNATIONAL AIRPORT
Blvd.
30th St.
Southmost Rd.
East. Ave.
Calle Milpa Verde
GRANDE RIVER

TOURIST SERVICES

BROWNSVILLE CONVENTION AND VISITORS BUREAU
US 77/83 at FM 802 (P.O. Box 4697, 78523)
546-3721 or 800-626-2639
Monday–Friday 8:30–5
Free
W +

The pyramid-style building is stacked with free brochures and the helpful staff is loaded with information on just about anything you'd like to know about shopping, accommodations, restaurants, local sights, and sightseeing tours. A satellite office is located in the Chamber of Commerce building at 1600 E. Elizabeth, just north of the Gateway International Bridge. It is also open Monday-Friday 8:30-5.

BRO-MAT TOURS
544-6292

This small tour company conducts personalized sightseeing and shopping tours of Matamoros for groups of two to six people that last about 3 – 3½ hours. Prices are $35 for two or $15 each for three or more. The tour van frequently parks at the Convention and Visitors Bureau, but pick-ups will be made anywhere in the city.

GRAY LINE TOURS
761-4343

Regularly scheduled tours of Matamoros are offered both mornings and afternoons Monday through Saturday. You can book at most hotels/motels and travel agencies. The tours last about 3½ hours and cost $12.50 per person.

TOUR GUIDES IN MATAMOROS

Licensed, English-speaking tour guides can be hired at the Tourist Information booth on the right just across the Gateway International Bridge. They charge about $25 for a carful and they provide the car. The regular sightseeing and shopping tour lasts about 2½ hours, but you can personalize it almost any way you want for close to that price. To be sure your guide is licensed, ask to see the wallet-sized permit from the Mexican Tourism Department that guides are required to carry.

TEXAS TRAVEL INFORMATION CENTER
(See Harlingen)

VALLEY ADVENTURE TOURS
123 E. Price
761-1641 or 800-338-0560
Tours $13–$20

They offer a variety of tours including a daily sightseeing and shopping tour to Matamoros ($13), and tours to the zoo.

A GET-ACQUAINTED DRIVING TOUR

The logical place to start is the Brownsville Convention and Visitors Bureau at US 77/83 and FM 802. Here you can pick up a map and brochures on the places you'll see on this tour.

Go *south* on US 77/83 to *Boca Chica Blvd. exit.* Turn *right (west)* on Boca Chica, then almost immediately, *left (southwest) on Palm Blvd.* Take Palm about ½ mile to the traffic light on *Ringgold,* then turn *left (southeast).* On your left, a short distance down Ringgold, you'll see the **Camille Lightner Playhouse,** the home of the local community theater group (See Performing Arts). The playhouse is in **Dean Park,** a 12-acre park that includes a playground, swimming pool, and picnic areas. A little further on, on your right, is the **Gladys Porter Zoo**. This is a jewel among zoological parks — frequently listed among the ten best in the country — so if you don't stop to visit now, make sure you do before you leave Brownsville.

Swing through the zoo's free parking lot on your left and *retrace your route back to Palm,* then turn *left (southwest).* Continue down Palm to **Amigoland Mall** (on your left), one of the two major malls in the city. Turn *left (southeast) on Mexico St.* Follow Mexico to Sam Perl Dr. (E. 12th St.) just past the railroad overpass. If you continue on Mexico St., you'll wind up crossing the **B&M International Bridge** to Mexico. This is a railroad bridge that is also open to vehicle traffic. But this tour is just of Brownsville, so Matamoros will have to wait as you turn *left (northeast) on Perl/E. 12th* and drive parallel to the Rio Grande (behind the levee) for a few blocks. When Perl becomes one-way against you, you're *shunted over to E. 13th St.* (the main bridge to Matamoros, the Gateway International, will be on your right). In a little over a block, E.13th intersects with Elizabeth St. *Turn right (southeast) on Elizabeth.* This street was named in the late 1840s by Charles Stillman, founder of the city, for his bride-to-be, Elizabeth Goodrich. *Stay on Elizabeth,* past the bridge on your right, and cross International Blvd. Be especially watchful when passing the bridge. The traffic here, both the cars and the pedestrians, always seem to be in a rush.

After crossing International Blvd., the next cross street is Taylor. On your left is the Chamber of Commerce Building, where the Convention and Visitors Bureau has a small information office, and on your right the city's **International Friendship Pavilion**. This circular building is often used for cultural exhibits and art and fashion shows featuring other countries in our hemisphere.

Continue down palm-shaded Elizabeth, past the **Fort Brown Hotel and Resort** (See Accommodations) to the end of the street. *Turn right (southwest)* to loop back around the *resaca. Taking the left at the fork* will take you past the **Brownsville Art League Gallery and Museum** (See Museums). The league's headquarters is in the old house on your left and the museum in the larger building just past that.

Continuing on past the museum, the loop will quickly bring you to Taylor. *Go straight on Taylor,* past the **Fort Brown Memorial Civic Center** on your left, a complex that provides facilities for conventions, concerts, and other large recreational and social activities. The street ends at the parking lot of **Texas Southmost College** (See Colleges and Universities). Behind this, sharing the same campus, is the **University of Texas/Pan American University at Brownsville** (See Colleges and Universities). Several of the old buildings you see in this area are part of old **Fort Brown** (See Historic Places) and are now used by the college.

Turn left (northwest) and go one block to *International Blvd. and take another left (southwest).* Get over in the right lane as soon as you can safely, because the next turn is just two short blocks away. *Turn right (northwest) on Washington St.* This will put you on a typical, narrow downtown shopping street.

Stay to the right. On the corner of Washington and E.13th is the **Stillman House**, built in 1850 by the founder of Brownsville, now a museum (See Museums). *Turn right (northeast) on 13th,* go two blocks and *turn left (northwest) on Jefferson.* On your left is the **Immaculate Conception Cathedral**, built in 1859. At 12th and Jefferson, diagonally across from the cathedral, is the **old courthouse**, now a Masonic Lodge. Continue on Jefferson to *10th,* then *turn left (southeast).* The imposing building on the corner of 10th and Elizabeth is the **U.S. Courthouse**.

Turn right (northwest) in one block on *Levee* and take it all the way to Palm Blvd. A *right on Palm and then an immediate left (northwest)* puts you on Elizabeth again, which is now two-way and is also US 77/83 Bus. Follow this business route signs when the road *veers right (north)* off Elizabeth and becomes *Central Blvd.* Central will take you through an area of small businesses, restaurants, and Mom and Pop motels about two miles back to your starting point at the Convention and Visitors Bureau, completing a circle of downtown Brownsville and ending this get-acquainted tour.

MUSEUMS

BROWNSVILLE ART LEAGUE GALLERY AND MUSEUM

230 Neale Dr. (P.O. Box 3404, 78520)
542-0941
Monday–Friday 9:30–3, or by appointment
Free (donations accepted)
W

One gallery houses the Brownsville Art League's eclectic permanent collection that ranges from the works of well-known artists of the Southwest to Hogarth prints. The other gallery is used for traveling exhibitions, lectures, art films, and classes. If the museum isn't open during the hours posted, try next door at the League's headquarters in the Neale House, the oldest frame building in the city, where someone will probably be available to give you a tour. The League usually sponsors major art shows in March and November. The old Fort Brown bandstand is also on the property.

CASA MATA MUSEUM
Matamoros, Santos Degollado between Guatemala and Panama
Usually open Tuesday–Sunday 9:30–5:30, Closed Monday
Admission

This small, thick-walled fort, built in the early 1800s, now serves as a city museum. Unless you read Spanish, the labels and descriptions on the exhibits may be hard to decipher. However, many of the items on display tell a story that often needs no further explanation. With a little diligence, you can pick out a few words of international understanding that indicate the significance of many of the documents and artifacts, such as a *charro* suit that once belonged to Pancho Villa and the names on the photographs of patriots of the Mexican Revolution.

CORN MUSEUM (MUSEO DEL MAIZ)
Matamoros, Avenida Constitucion and 5th
6-3763
Tuesday–Sunday 9:30–5
Free
W

The domestication of corn was an important factor in the growth of civilization in Mexico and Central America. Using more than a dozen large tableaus and displays, this museum traces the history of corn and its utilization and importance in Mexico. Guided tours are available.

HISTORIC BROWNSVILLE MUSEUM
E. Madison and 6th
548-1313
Tuesday–Saturday 10–4:30
Adults $2, children 50¢
W

This is a private museum owned and operated by a historic association dedicated to telling the history of Brownsville and the surrounding area. Housed in a 1928 Southern Pacific Railroad depot, the museum staff is slowly building its permanent collection of historical documents, photos and prints, furniture, and clothing. Outside are a small engine used by the Rio Grande Railroad connecting Brownsville and Port Isabel in the 1870s and two cabooses from more recent times. The museum sponsors about five traveling exhibits each year. Gift shop.

STILLMAN HOUSE AND MUSEUM
1305 E. Washington
542-3929
Monday–Friday 10–12 and 2–5, Closed Saturday–Sunday
Adults $1, children 15¢
W

This restored one-story, pink-brick house is one of the oldest buildings in the city. It was built in 1850 by Charles Stillman, a merchant from Connecticut who originally set up a business in Matamoros and then, after the Mexican War, was the founder of Brownsville. Many of the furnishings and memorabilia inside were donated by the Stillman family in New York and date to the mid-1800s. The oldest item is a 1790 grandfather clock in the central hallway. The house is listed in the National Register of Historic Places. Street parking is a problem in this downtown area. There is a small lot next door, but if it is filled, parking is usually available at Adams and 14th.

HISTORIC PLACES

FORT BROWN
600 International, just east of Gateway International Bridge
W

Now it is part of the campus of Texas Southmost College, but during the 102 years from its founding in 1846 until it was closed in 1948, this border post saw a lot of action. Its very construction in an area of dispute between Mexico and the United States was one of the immediate causes of the Mexican War. General Zachary Taylor first called it Fort Texas Across from Matamoros, but renamed it in honor of Major Jacob Brown who died defending the fort against a Mexican attack. It was fought over and occupied by both sides in the Civil War and, as a border post, used to defend the area against bandits well into the 1900s. The post hospital, now the college administration building, was where Dr. W. C. Gorgas started his research into tropical diseases, reportedly against the orders of the Fort's commander, that eventually led to his important contribution in the control of yellow fever. Other fort buildings still standing include the post headquarters, guard house, the medical laboratory, and the morgue.

IMMACULATE CONCEPTION CATHEDRAL
Jefferson and 12th
546-3178
W

Completed in 1859, this church was a haven for Catholic priests fleeing the anticlerical revolutions in Mexico. The first bishop of the area and a number of former parish priests are buried in the small graveyard by the entrance. The church is listed in the National Register of Historic Places.

MEXICAN WAR BATTLEFIELDS
Marker commemorating the battles of Palo Alto and Resaca de la Palma at intersection of FM 1847 and FM 511

When Texas entered the Union, it brought with it a long-standing border dispute with Mexico. The Texans — and the United States — claimed the border was the Rio Grande, while the Mexicans contended it was the Nueces River because it had been the southern boundary of the old province of Texas. The dispute led to a breaking off of relations between the two countries. President Polk sent General Zachary Taylor with an army of about 4,000 troops to Corpus Christi and deployed the navy along the coast of Mexico. When the dispute couldn't be resolved, Polk ordered Taylor into the disputed territory.

When Mexican troops wiped out an American cavalry patrol and then laid siege to Fort Texas which Taylor had established across from Matamoros, Taylor moved to reinforce the fort. On May 7, 1846, he left his supply base at Point Isabel (now Port Isabel) with about 2,300 troops. The next morning, at Palo Alto, some ten miles from the fort, the Americans clashed with a Mexican force of about 6,000. Taylor's light horse artillery was a major factor in the battle. Dashing from position to position, the "Flying Artillery," under the command of Major Samuel Ringgold, laid down deadly fire that overcame the almost 3-to-1 odds and forced the Mexicans to withdraw. One of the nine Americans killed in the battle was Major Ringgold. More than 300 Mexicans were killed.

When Taylor pressed on the next morning, the Mexican Army was waiting, dug into a strong position in a dry streambed called Resaca de la Palma. In this second battle, the Americans once again drove off the Mexicans. This time about 120 Americans were killed or wounded and the Mexican Army lost over a thousand. Among the American infantry company commanders in this second battle was Second Lieutenant Ulysses S. Grant who later noted that the Mexican soldiers were brave, but poorly led.

While this battle was taking place, word finally reached President Polk that the cavalry patrol had been wiped out. On May 13, 1846, war was declared against Mexico.

PALMITO HILL BATTLEFIELD

Marker on Texas 4, approximately 14 miles east of downtown

While Mexican War battles around Fort Brown were fought before the war was officially declared, the Civil War battle of Palmito Hill was fought about six weeks after that war was officially over. But the word of Lee's surrender had not reached the 300 Confederate soldiers from Fort Brown when they went out to successfully drive off about 1,600 Union troops trying to capture the cotton stored in the warehouses at Brownsville. Coincidentally, this Civil War battle took place on May 12 and 13, 1865, and the 13th was the same day that war had been declared against Mexico just 19 years before.

OTHER HISTORIC BUILDINGS

There are a number of other Brownsville buildings still surviving that were built in the mid and late 1800s. Among the oldest are the old *City Hall* (1852) at 1100 E. Adams, the *San Roman* Building (1850) at 1231 E. Elizabeth, and the *Yturria Bank* Building (1853). The *Browne-Wagner House* at 812 E. St. Charles was built in 1894 and is listed in the National Register of Historic Places. There are also a number of early 1800s buildings scattered around Matamoros. One of the oldest is the Cathedral of Our Lady of Refuge on the Main Plaza at 5th and Morelos which was completed in 1831.

OTHER POINTS OF INTEREST

GLADYS PORTER ZOO
Ringgold and 6th
546-2177 (activities recording) or 546-7187
Gates open seven days 9–5 with extended hours on weekends and in the summer (once inside, visitors may remain until dark)
Adults $4, children (under 14) $2
W +
Guarded parking lot at entrance $1. Free lot across street

This zoo is consistently ranked by zoo professionals as one of the ten best in the country and is proof that good things do come in small packages. Although the ingenious design and landscaping give the appearance of open spaces, the more than 1,800 mammals, birds, and reptiles from five continents are actually squeezed into only 31 acres. Viewing the zoo will take you through four major areas of the world: Africa, Asia, Australia and Indonesia, and tropical America. In each, the animals live in miniaturized naturalistic habitats on islands or in large open areas separated from visitors by moats or waterways — no bars or cages. The Children's Zoo includes both an animal nursery for viewing newborns and a petting zoo stocked with barnyard animals. Other facilities include the Herpetarium that houses reptiles, amphibians, spiders, and insects; the Aquatic wing specializing in local marine and freshwater fishes and invertebrates; and the free-flight Aviary and the Bear Grottos. The zoo has also earned a reputation as a haven and breeding facility for endangered species such as the Jentink's Duiker, considered the rarest antelope in the world. Strollers and wheelchairs available for rent. Tour train makes a half-hour narrated tour Sunday afternoons between 1:30 and 3:30 (Adults $1, children 50¢). Concession stands, gift shop. A visual delight, this is what a zoo should be — and a must see.

MATAMOROS
To call Matamoros direct from Brownsville, dial 011-52-891 and then the 5-digit local number

First settled in the late 1700s, it was organized as a village in 1821 and named for Farther Maiano Matamoros, a hero killed in the 1810 revolution. The town became prominent in the 1860s when the Confederates used it as a shipping point for getting around the Union blockade. At the same time, the French helped conservative Mexicans put Maximilian on the Mexican throne and many Europeans began moving to the area. Money poured in; great mansions and buildings like the recently restored *Theatro Reforma* were built.

Today, with a population of close to half a million, Matamoros is one of Mexico's 15 major cities and the largest city on both sides of the border in the Rio Grande Valley. In addition to continuing its role as a major port of entry, it is both an industrial and a commercial city, and tourism is a major factor in the local economy.

You can get to Matamoros over either of two bridges. The main one is the Gateway International Bridge at the end of International Blvd. Further south, at Perl Blvd./E. 12th is the privately-owned old railroad bridge that is open to vehicle and pedestrian traffic. There's a toll to cross the bridges. Buses and taxis also run across the bridges. Both bridges come out on Avenida Alvaro Obregon, a major street with many shops and restaurants listed in this guide, so it is easy to just walk across. Obregon starts at the Gateway Bridge and the railroad bridge intersects it a few blocks south.

A small Mexican Tourism office is located inside the building on the Matamoros side of the Gateway bridge just past the Mexican customs office (phone 2-3630). It is sometimes staffed with English-speaking personnel. You can get a Matamoros map here. A little further on, on the right hand side of the street is a booth housing licensed guides (See Tourist Services). There are also taxi stands in this area. Before you hire a guide or a taxi, make sure you settle on a fair price. Most of the drivers and guides are honest and genuinely friendly, but there are always some out to stick it to the *turista*.

An inexpensive way to get around Matamoros is by maxi-cab. You'll usually find a herd of them gathered on the first street to the left after you cross the Gateway Bridge. These are small passenger vans that follow definite routes within the city, but will stop almost anywhere to pick-up or let off a passenger. They cost pennies to ride and go to the markets and other places of tourist interest. The destination of each maxi-cab is marked on the front, and with a map and an understanding of a few, simple Spanish words you should be able to get around. For example, if you want to go to the Juarez Market (See Shopping) look for a cab marked *Mercado*. To get back to the bridge from almost anywhere in the city, look for one marked *Puente* (bridge). A maxi-cab marked *Sexta* travels up and down Calle Sexta or 6th St., a major north-south street in the city. Simple — and fun!

PORT OF BROWNSVILLE
Intersection of Texas 48 and FM 511, about ten miles northeast of downtown
831-4592 (Brownsville Navigation District)
W Variable

A 17-mile ship channel, opening into the Gulf of Mexico at South Padre Island, makes this a deep-sea port. It is also the end of the line for the Intracoastal Waterway. The 44,000-acre port services both the Rio Grande Valley and northeastern Mexico, handling more than 5 million tons of cargo every year. The Shrimp Basin in the port area services one of the largest shrimp fleets in the world.

SABAL PALM GROVE SANCTUARY
8834 Ernest Ortiz Rd. off FM 1419 (Southmost Rd.)
541-8034
November–April: Thursday–Monday 8–5, May–October Saturday–

Sunday 8–5
Adults $2, children $1

The sabal palm (*Sabal texana*), the only palm native to extreme south Texas, is now considered endangered in Texas. This Audubon Society sanctuary preserves 32 acres of these scarce palms and the native plant and animal life associated with them. Visitors are welcome for wildlife and plant observation and photography. There is an interpretive trail through the palm jungle, a visitor's center, and an observation blind. Because the sanctuary is small, there are no roads open to the public. For information write: Refuge Manager, National Audubon Society, P.O. Box 5052, Brownsville, 78520.

SPORTS AND ACTIVITIES

Birdwatching

More than 370 bird species share the refuges and wild places in and around Brownsville, including many tropical bird species seen nowhere else in the United States. A free, colorful "Birder's Guide" is available from the Brownsville Convention and Visitors Bureau (See Tourist Services). This compact, but comprehensive fold-out brochure lists recommended birding sites in Brownsville and the Valley, maps, information on birding activities, a checklist of birds seen in the area, and colored illustrations of 17 of these birds.

Fishing

Freshwater and channel fishing is recommended in the old beds of the Rio Grande, in canals, and from the banks of the Brownsville Ship Channel. A colorful fold-out "Fishing Guide" available free from the Brownsville Convention and Visitors Bureau also includes information on bay fishing in the Laguna Madre off South Padre Island and deep-sea fishing in the Gulf.

Golf

BROWNSVILLE COUNTRY CLUB
1800 W. San Marcelo
541-2582

Eighteen-hole course. Green fees: weekdays $10, weekends $15.

FORT BROWN GOLF COURSE
300 River Levee, south of Fort Brown
542-9861

Eighteen-hole course. Green fees: about $5.

RANCHO VIEJO COUNTRY CLUB
US 77/83 at Rancho Viejo Dr., approximately nine miles north of downtown
350-4000

Two 18-holes courses. Non-members' green fees: $25.

RIVER BEND RESORT
US 281 about three miles west
548-0191

Nine-hole course. Green fees: 9 holes $6, 18 holes $10.

VALLEY INN AND COUNTRY CLUB
Central Blvd. and FM 802
546-5331

Eighteen-hole course and 9-hole Executive Course. Non-members must acquire guest card at registration desk. Call for non-member green fees.

Horse Racing

TURF CLUB
Matamoros, 5th and Hidalgo
2-5187

You can place bets here on horse races at all the major U.S. tracks. Open daily starting at 11 a.m.

COLLEGES AND UNIVERSITIES

TEXAS SOUTHMOST COLLEGE
1614 Ridgley Rd.
544-8200
W + But not all areas

The 50-acre campus is on what was once the center of Fort Brown, the U.S. Army post established by General Zachary Taylor in 1846. The college administrative offices are housed in the old hospital. A two-year community college, it offers academic and vocational/technical courses to its more than 6,000 students. Visitors are welcome to plays and musical performances, some of which are performed at the Marion Hedrick Smith Memorial Amphitheater that fronts the Fort Brown *resaca* (lagoon).

UNIVERSITY OF TEXAS/PAN AMERICAN UNIVERSITY AT BROWNSVILLE
1614 Ridgley Rd., on the campus of Texas Southmost College
542-6882
W + But not all areas

This upper-level university offers about 20 programs leading to bachelor's and master's degrees. For the long-term visitor, the school also offers a wide variety of non-credit seminars, presentations, and workshops.

PERFORMING ARTS

CAMILLE LIGHTNER PLAYHOUSE
Dean Porter Park, across from Gladys Porter Zoo
542-8900
W

This community theater features five or six plays and musicals by the local theater group during the September though May season. General admission runs about $6. There is also a summer children's theater production. The theater is also used for concerts and other activities.

SHOPPING

To call Matamoros direct from Brownsville, dial 011-52-891 and then the 5-digit local number

AMIGOLAND MALL
301 Mexico at Palm
546-3788
W

Dillard's, Penney's, and Ward's anchor the more than 60 other stores, fast food stalls, movie theater, and cafeteria. This is the closest mall to the bridges to Matamoros, so it is especially popular with Mexican shoppers.

BARBARA DE MATAMOROS
Matamoros, 37 Avenida Alvaro Obregon, about four blocks south of Gateway International Bridge
2-5058

Looking for a life-sized brass monkey? Or how about a colorful larger-than-life *papier-mache* macaw on a perch? These are just a few of the Sergio Bustamente originals elegantly displayed, and elegantly priced, in this shop. There are also ceramics, jewelry, and other selected items from the interior of Mexico. Upstairs is a fashionable boutique featuring clothing of Barbara's own design.

DON BREEDEN ART GALLERY
2200 Boca Chica
542-5481

Wildlife paintings and drawings in various media are the specialty of artist-owner Don Breeden.

MARY'S
Matamoros, 26 Avenida Alvaro Obregon, about four blocks south of the Gateway International Bridge
6-2431

St. Francis must be this shop's patron saint because carved wooden statues of him are scattered thoroughout both its display floors. In a lighter vein, there are gobs of *papier-mache* animals, clowns, and other funny-looking creatures to brighten a child's room. Other offerings include furniture, clothing, chess sets, silver, gifts and other fine curios. If you want a cooling respite from shopping, there's a cocktail lounge in the middle of it all.

MERCADO JUAREZ
Matamoros, Matamoros at Calle Nueve (9th St.)
W Variable

There are two markets here. The old on one side of the street and the new market on the other. Each is made up of many small shops under a low roof. You'll find both the gaudy and the good here. The key is to know what you want, how much it costs elsewhere, and how much you're willing to pay. Then bargain. Just remember, the shopkeepers here are both hard-sell salesmen and bargaining experts. Even if they knock the price down, they always make a profit. However, you can at least have fun at the game and lower the price a bit—perhaps a lot.

SUNRISE MALL
2370 N. Expressway 77/83 and FM 802
541-5302
W

Beall's, K-Mart, and Sears anchor about 50 other shops and food booths.

SIDE TRIPS

BRAZOS ISLAND STATE PARK
Take Texas 4 approximately 22 miles east

There are no facilities at this undeveloped park, but you can camp, fish, swim, surf, or just soak up the sunshine on the wide and isolated beach. A 4-wheel drive vehicle is strongly recommended if you drive on the beach.

ANNUAL EVENTS

February

CHARRO DAYS
Various locations in Brownsville and Matamoros
546-3721 (Convention and Visitors Bureau)
Thursday through Sunday in middle or end of February
Admission to some activities
W Variable

A *grito*, the Mexican cowboy's yell of exuberance, shouted at the Gateway International Bridge usually opens this two-country fiesta. *Charro* refers to landowning Mexican horsemen whose formal attire was the traditional black or striped pants covered with fancy chaps, a bolero jacket with ornamental embroidery, and a sombrero covered with silver or gold filigree. The *charro* traditions and costume have been adopted by a number of *charro* associations on both sides of the border, and it is the spirit of the *charro* coupled with that of the hell-bent for pleasure Mexican cowboy who rides to town to spend his hard-earned wages that set the theme for this celebration. Festivities include parades, fiestas, dances, floor shows, sports events including a *charreada* (Mexican rodeo). Many participants and spectators wear traditional Mexican dress.

September

FIESTA INTERNATIONAL
Various locations in Matamoros and Brownsville
546-3721 (Convention and Visitors Bureau)
Three-day weekend near September 16, Mexican Independence Day
Admission to some activities
W Variable

This is a two-nation celebration of Mexican Independence Day. The main events are in Matamoros where there are parades, receptions, and fireworks. But there are other activities on both sides of the border as the citizens of the sister cities entertain each other.

RESTAURANTS

($ = under $7, $$ = $7 to $17, $$$ = $17 to $25, $$$$ = over $25 for one person excluding drinks, tax, and tip.)
To call Matamoros direct from Brownsville, dial 011-52-891 and then the 5-digit local number

THE DRIVE-IN
Matamoros, Sexta (6th) and Hidalgo, approximately one mile southwest of Gateway International Bridge
2-0022
Lunch and dinner seven days
$-$$$
Cr.
W

Don't let the name fool you — you can't drive in. In fact, the parking is across the street, and inside the crystal chandeliers, red plush seats, an aviary with tropical birds, and the extensive continental menu will quickly dispel any lingering thoughts of fast food. The menu offers mostly Continental cuisine with choices that include *chateaubriand*, lobster, frogs legs, shrimp, steaks and, of course, Mexican dishes. But be aware that the kitchen's efforts can be erratic. Bar.

THE FISH HOUSE
5424 E. 14th, north of Boca Chica Blvd.
831-8226
Lunch and dinner Tuesday–Sunday, Closed Monday
$$
AE, MC, V
W

If you are not familiar with the many ways seafood can be prepared, the menu explains each. Then it offers some fine examples such as trout *amandine* and redfish *parmesan*. There are also blackboard specials and a small selection of beef, chicken, and pasta dishes. Bar.

GARCIA'S
Matamoros, Obregon and Anapolas
3-1209
Lunch and dinner seven days
$-$$
Mc, V

Like Phoenix rising from the ashes of the fire that destroyed the popular restaurant near the bridge, Garcia's is back — but at a new location about six blocks south, near the family-owned Hotel Del Prado (See Accommodations). Many among its long-term devotees say both the food and the service are even better than before. The extensive menu includes steaks, turkey, lobster, crab, quail, and Mexican dishes. Still the most popular are the game dinners and the combos in which you pick two entrées. Bar with musicians.

LOS PORTALES
Matamoros, Sexta (6th) and J.J. de la Garza
2-3338
Lunch and dinner seven days
$-$$
AE, MC, V
W

The parking lot is decorated with old wagon wheels and this rustic decor is carried over inside the restaurant. Specialties are almost all meats including large portions of *cabrito*, steaks, *shish kabobs*, and ribs. They also have the more popular Mexican dishes. Bar.

PALM COURT RESTAURANT
2235 Boca Chica, about one block east of Expressway 77/83
542-3575
Lunch only Monday–Saturday
$-$$
AE, MC, V
W

As its name implies, the interior of this restaurant is designed to give the feeling of eating in an elegant open court — provided you can find a courtyard with a crystal chandelier. The menu offers salads from fresh fruit to shrimp, soups including *gaspacho* and *tortilla,* sandwiches from chicken or tuna salad to a super sub, and entrées that include *lasagne, quiche,* and chicken *crepes,* plus luscious desserts like coco mocho pie and Manhattan cheesecake. No smoking area. Beer and wine.

PANCHO VILLA'S
Matamoros, 55 Avenida de la Rosa
6-4840
Lunch and dinner seven days
$$
MC, V

The specialty of the house is called *Basto Corte de Fajita Sin Filetar,* which the menu very loosely translates as "A big chunk of meat taken the way the man of the revolution cooked it." Charbroiled meats (*carnes asadas*) that include steaks, and ribs, and chicken, dominate the rest of the menu, but it also offers some seafood such as red snapper and shrimp. Old photos of Pancho Villa and other revolutionaries look down at you from the walls as you eat. Limited parking in front. Bar.

ACCOMMODATIONS

($ = Under $45, $$ = $46-$60, $$$ = $61-$80, $$$$ = $81-$100, $$$$$ = Over $100)
To call Matamoros direct from Brownsville, dial 011-52-891 and then the 5-digit local number
Room Tax 13 percent

FORT BROWN HOTEL
1900 E. Elizabeth
546-2201 or 800-582-3333
$-$$$
No-smoking rooms

This two- and three-story hotel has 278 units that include four penthouse suites ($$$$$) and 12 no-smoking rooms. Children under 12 stay free in room with parents. Package plans available and senior discount. Cable TV with HBO. Room phones (local calls free). Coffeemakers in rooms. Fire intercom system. No pets. Two restaurants, room service, and club open seven nights with entertainment nightly. Two outdoor pools, outdoor whirlpool, two lighted tennis courts, guest memberships available in health club and for golf. Playground. Free airport transportation to Brownsville and Harlingen. Free coffee in lobby in morning, free cocktail at check-in. Same-day dry cleaning. Located on 17 acres in walking distance of Gateway International Bridge.

HOTEL DEL PRADO
Matamoros, 249 Avenida Obregon
3-9440
$$

This two-story hotel has 124 units that include two suites ($$$). Children under 14 stay free in room with parents. Cable TV with HBO, Cinemax, and Showtime. Room phones (local calls free). Pets OK. Restaurant, room service, and lounge open seven nights with entertainment nightly. Outdoor heated pool and outdoor whirlpool. Free Mexican-style breakfast. Colorful garden. Secured outside parking. Close to bridges.

HOLIDAY INN
1945 N. Expressway (US 77/83), just south of FM 802
546-4591 or 800-HOLIDAY
$$-$$$
W + one room
No-smoking rooms
This two-story Holiday Inn has 159 rooms that include 16 no-smoking rooms. Children under 12 stay free in room with parents. Senior discount. Satellite TV with Showtime and pay channel. Room phones (local calls free). Pets OK. Restaurant, room service, lounge open seven nights with entertainment Monday-Saturday. Outdoor heated pool, exercise room, outdoor whirlpool, and guest memberships available in health club. Free airport transportation to Brownsville and Harlingen. Free newspaper. Self-service laundry, and same-day dry cleaning.

LA QUINTA
55 Sam Perl (southern extension of 12th St.)
546-0381 or 800-531-5900
$
W + two rooms
No-smoking rooms
The two-story La Quinta offers 143 rooms that include 20 no-smoking. Children under 12 free in room with parents. Senior discount. Satellite TV with Showtime. Room phones (local calls free). Small pets OK. Restaurant next door. Outdoor pool. Free coffee in lobby. Same-day dry cleaning. Located between the two bridges to Matamoros.

RANCHO VIEJO RESORT
US 77/83 at Rancho Viejo Dr., approximately nine miles north of downtown
350-4000 or in Texas 800-292-7263, outside Texas 800-531-7400
$$$$$ (+6 percent room tax)
This resort offers about 100 hotel rooms plus a number of two- and three-bedroom villas that are in the rental pool. Children under 14 stay free in room with parents. Package plans available. Cable TV with HBO. Room phones (local calls free). No pets. Two restaurants, two lounges with entertainment in one most nights. Outdoor pool with swim-up bar (in season), children's pool, two lighted tennis courts, and two 18-hole golf courses. Same-day dry cleaning. Rental bicycles. Boutique shop and men's shop. Beauty salon and barbershop. The resort is spread over 1,400 acres.

SHERATON PLAZA ROYALE
3777 N. Expressway (US 77/83)
350-9191 or 800-325-3535
$$$
W + four rooms
No-smoking rooms

The two-story Sheraton has 142 units that include two suites ($$$$$) and 20 no-smoking rooms. Children under 17 stay free in room with parents. Cable TV with HBO and pay channel. Room phones (charge for local calls). Fire sprinklers in rooms and fire intercom system. Small pets OK. Restaurant, room service, and lounge open seven nights with entertainment nightly. Two pools (one outdoor with swim-up bar (in season), one indoor-outdoor heated pool), outdoor whirlpool. Guest memberships available for Country Club. Free airport transportation to Brownsville and Harlingen. Free coffee Monday-Friday and free newspaper. Same-day dry cleaning.

DEL RIO

VAL VERDE COUNTY ★ 35,000 ★ (512)

Del Rio, the largest city between San Antonio and El Paso, was originally named San Felipe del Rio (St. Phillip of the River). Some say it was named by Spanish explorers after their monarch, King Phillip, and others say it was named by Spanish missionaries who arrived here on St. Phillip's Day in the early 1600s. Either way, the name survived more than two centuries, until the 1880s when the Post Office suggested shortening it to Del Rio to avoid confusion with another Texas town named San Felipe de Austin.

There are some 400 archaeological sites in Val Verde County, many giving evidence to the presence of Indians in this area thousands of years ago. For example, pictographs painted on the walls of area caves have been dated back some 8,000 years.

Like most towns in semi-arid regions, Del Rio came into being because it was an oasis. The San Felipe Springs, just off US 90 East, gush forth from a subterranean river at a rate of more than 90 million gallons a day. In the early days the springs were an important watering stop on the historic Chihuahua Rd. that connected Mexico's Chihuahua City with the bustling Texas port of Indianola. Later they also served as a watering stop for stagecoaches on the San Antonio to San Diego trail.

DEL RIO

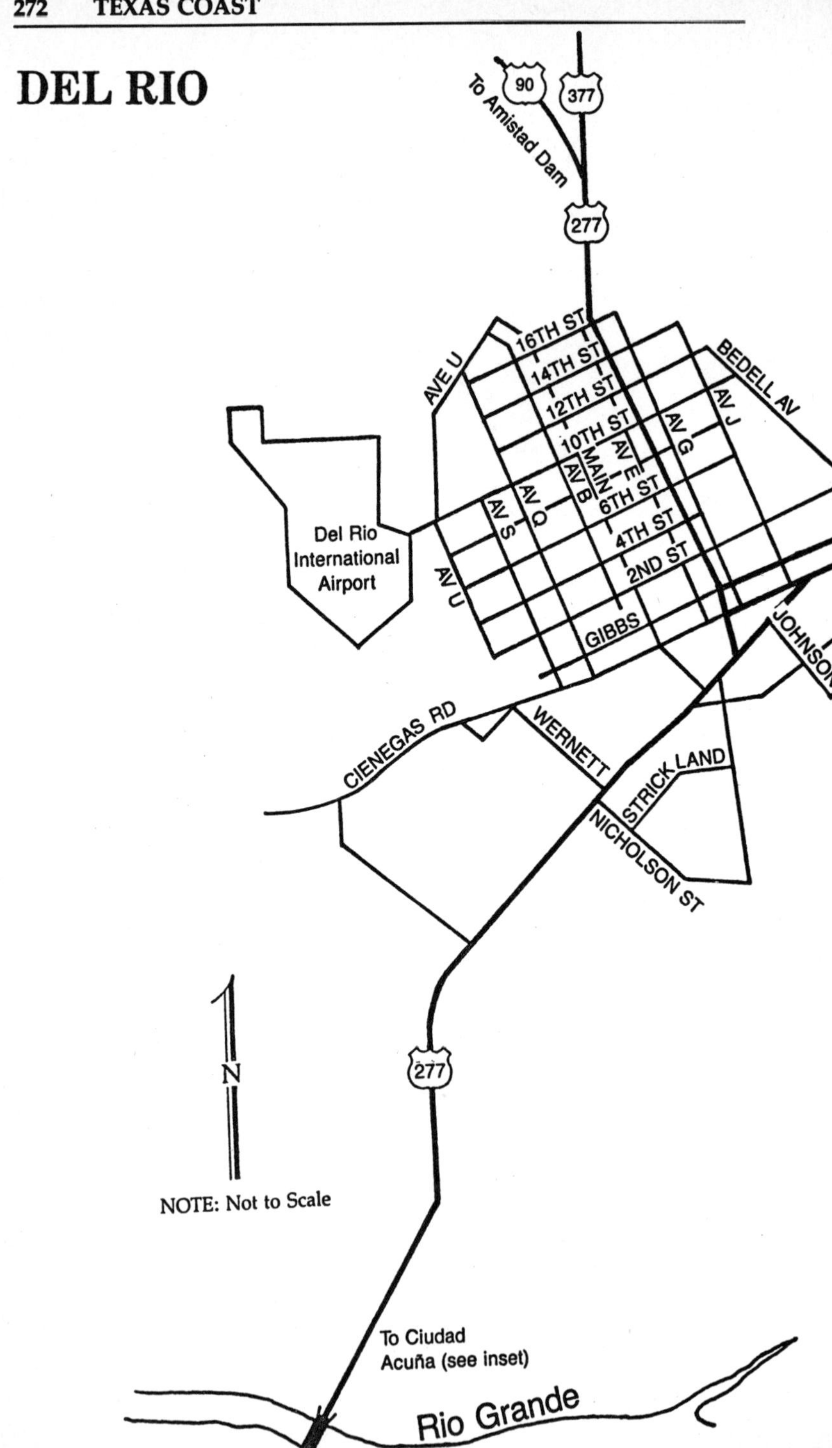
90
377
To Amistad Dam
277
16TH ST
14TH ST
12TH ST
10TH ST
AVE U
BEDELL AV
AV J
AV G
AV E
MAIN
AV B
AV Q
AV S
6TH ST
4TH ST
2ND ST
Del Rio International Airport
AV U
GIBBS
JOHNSON
CIENEGAS RD
WERNETT
STRICKLAND
NICHOLSON ST
N
NOTE: Not to Scale
277
To Ciudad Acuña (see inset)
Rio Grande

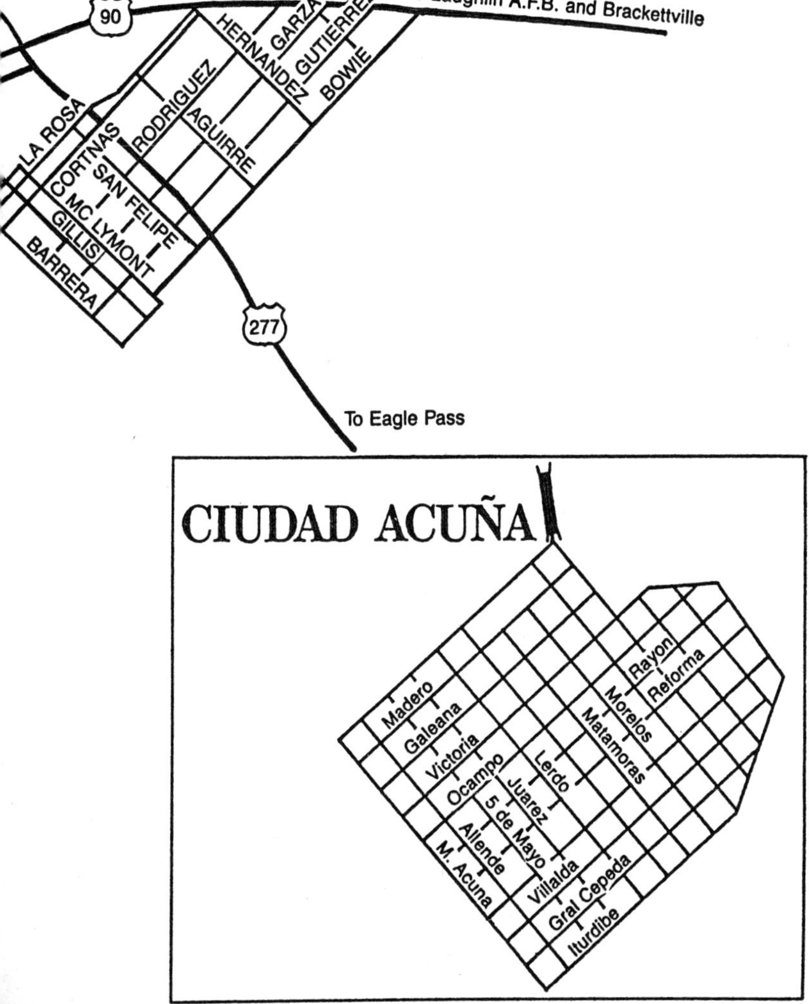

90
To Laughlin A.F.B. and Brackettville
GARZA
HERNANDEZ
GUTIERREZ
BOWIE
RODRIGUEZ
AGUIRRE
LA ROSA
CORTNAS
SAN FELIPE
MC LYMONT
GILLIS
BARRERA
277
To Eagle Pass
CIUDAD ACUÑA
Rayon
Reforma
Morelos
Matamoras
Madero
Galeana
Victoria
Ocampo
Lerdo
Juarez
5 de Mayo
Allende
M. Acuna
Villalda
Gral Cepeda
Iturdibe

But the first real settlement grew up here after the Civil War when a group of ranchers moved in and dug an irrigation system based on the springs.

Irrigated farming is still important, however farmers soon discovered that sheep and goats could thrive on the sparse vegetation in the surrounding hills. Today Del Rio claims to be the wool and mohair capital of the world. Other Texas cities, like San Angelo, contest that claim, but there's no doubt that Val Verde County is among the top producers in the state of sheep, lamb, wool, and mohair.

An outstanding feature of downtown Del Rio is the number of native limestone buildings. These were constructed by Italian stonemasons who came to build the infant city after finishing the construction of Fort Clark at Brackettville and the stone embankments for the Galveston, Harrisburg and San Antonio Railroad that reached Del Rio in 1882. Some of the Italians also planted vineyards and built a winery that is now called the Val Verde Winery, the oldest winery in Texas.

To the northwest is Amistad Lake, an international reservoir that is located partially in Texas and partially in Mexico. About three miles south, across the Rio Grande, is the Mexican city of Acuña with a population of roughly 120,000.

TOURIST SERVICES

DEL RIO CHAMBER OF COMMERCE
1915 Ave. F (78840), in rear of Civic Center
775-3551
W

Among the things you can get here are a free city map, a walking tour brochure, and information on going to Mexico.

AMISTAD TOURS
US 90W (HCR#3, Box 44, 78840)
775-6484 or 800-LAKEFUN (800-525-3386)
Tours seven days
$15–$35
W Call ahead

They provide boat tours of Amistad Lake and the Pecos and Rio Grande Rivers on launches. Sights include the Indian pictographs on the canyon walls, the dam, and the high bridges. Most tours last about four hours. They also offer land tours of Del Rio and Ciudad Acuna and to interior Mexico.

HIGH BRIDGE ADVENTURES
Box 816, Comstock, 78837
(915)292-4462
Tours $20–$25

Tours are on a pontoon boat holding six passengers that cruises the Pecos and Rio Grande Rivers to see the Indian pictographs and the highest bridge in Texas. Tours last three to four hours.

MUSEUMS

FIREHOUSE ART GALLERY
120 E. Garfield
775-0888
Monday–Friday 8:30–5:30, and November–December on Saturday 10–4
Free
W (side door)
Parking on east side of building in gun shop lot

Traveling art exhibitions in a variety of media are usually rotated through here about once a month. In May there's the annual juried "Western Art Show and Sale." The building is a 1932 structure that served as Del Rio's City Hall and Fire Station. The Gallery is in the old City Hall area with the rest of the building occupied by Gallery's parent organization, the Del Rio Council for the Arts. In November and December the Gallery becomes a Christmas shop with art and hand-crafted items for sale.

WHITEHEAD MEMORIAL MUSEUM
1308 S. Main at Wallen
774-7568 Ext 244
Tuesday–Saturday 9–11:30, 1–4:30. Closed Sunday, Monday, and major holidays
Adults $1, children 50¢
W Variable

In 1962, the old Perry Mercantile Building, dating from the 1870s and once the largest store between San Antonio and El Paso, was given to the city for a museum by the Whiteheads, a local ranching family. Since that time, the museum has grown to include seven buildings on several landscaped acres. The entrance to the grounds is through the Hacienda. In addition to the small visitors center and gift shop, this building houses The Chapel, which is dedicated to the memory of the Spaniards who brought Christianity to the region. The Perry Store is now an exhibition area for pioneer history. The Hal Patton Office, built in 1905, features both Black history and the story of the Seminole Scouts (See Brackettville). A replica of the Jersey Lilly, the saloon/court operated by the famous Judge Roy Bean is also on the grounds and behind it are the graves of the Judge and his son, Sam. The original Jersey Lilly saloon is located in Langtry, about 60 miles west of Del Rio. Judge Bean named it after English actress Lillie Langtry who he thought was the most wonderful woman in the world. It was in this saloon that he dispensed his own brand of justice that made him a legend as "The Law West of the Pecos." Other buildings on the grounds include The Log Cabin, which was built by local Boy Scouts in 1924 and now contains exhibits about the early settlers; and The Barn, which houses exhibits about prehistoric man and the Indians who lived in the area. Guided tours are available.

HISTORIC PLACES

A brochure guide to Historic Del Rio is available from the Chamber of Commerce. This includes a walking tour of the downtown Courthouse Square area as well as a map locating the historic buildings in the rest of the city.

COURTHOUSE SQUARE AREA

The oldest building here is the Old Jail, on the northeast corner of the Square, which was built in 1885. Nearby, at 400 Pecan, is the Courthouse, built in 1887, which is listed in the National Register of Historic Places. The old Sacred Heart Church (1892) is at 310 Mills. The original French stained glass windows from this church are now in the new church immediately north.

OTHER AREAS OF THE CITY

There are a number of other historic buildings scattered throughout the city. The ones listed here were all built in the late nineteenth century; *Tardy-Borroum Home*, (1883), 703 Losoya; *Brodbent-Hamilton Home*, (1895), 404 Spring; *Chris Qualia Home*, (1898), 901 S. Main; *Tagliabue Home*, (1881), 609 Pecan; *Taylor-Rivers House* (1870), 100 Hudson, built by one of the founders of Del Rio and now the oldest existing house in town; *Mason-Foster House*, (1887), 123 Hudson; and the *Val Verde Winery*, (1883), 139 Hudson (See Other Points of Interest).

OTHER POINTS OF INTEREST

AMISTAD LAKE AND AMISTAD NATIONAL RECREATION AREA

Take US 90 northwest about ten miles
775-7491 (National Park Service Office, 4121 US 90 West — open 8-5 seven days.) or 775-6722 (Ranger Station)
Open at all times
Free
W Variable

The eagle is a symbol of both the United States and Mexico, so it's appropriate that seven-foot high bronze U.S. and Mexican eagles stand at the border between the two countries in the center of the joint U.S.-Mexican Amistad Dam across the Rio Grande. It was at this site that the presidents of the two countries, Richard Nixon and Gustavo Diaz Ordaz, dedicated the dam on September 8, 1969. You can drive into Mexico across the toll-free road atop the six-mile long dam from 10 a.m. to 4 p.m. daily. A Visitors Center, near the customs station on the dam, is operated daily from 10-6 during the summer by the National Park Service.

The dam impounds an international lake that reaches 74 miles up the Rio Grande, 25 miles up the Devil's River, and 14 miles up the Pecos River with more than 67,000 water surface acres (44,000 acres are in Texas) and 850 miles of shoreline (540 in Texas).

More than a million visitors come to the U.S recreation area every year. There are facilities for boating and houseboating (rentals available), swimming, water skiing and other water sports, fishing, limited hunting, nature study, primitive camping, and picnicking. Park facilities are mostly on the east end of the lake; however, the Pecos River Area (44 miles west of Del Rio) has a boat ramp and picnic tables.

You can fish on both sides of the international boundary that runs through the lake, and there is no closed season, but a Texas fishing license is required in U.S. waters and a Mexican license in Mexican waters. Check with the Park Headquarters or the Chamber of Commerce for places where you can get both these licenses on the American side. The Chamber can also provide a list of fishing guides. The phenomenal visibility of the water in fall, winter, and spring, makes this lake a choice place for scuba shops across the state to bring their students for check-out dives. There are also several commercial campgrounds along the shoreline.

On the Mexican side are a swimming beach, picnic facilities, and a marina with launching ramp. However, the President of Mexico has announced "top priority" plans to build a $50 million resort on the lake including a "five-star" resort hotel and a golf course.

In addition to a map/brochure of the area, the National Park Service offers a brochure outlining a self-guided tour of the major attractions in the Pecos River District including the Indian pictographs at the Panther and Parida Caves. For information contact Superintendent, Amistad National Recreation Area, P.O. Box 420367, Del Rio 78842-0367.

BRINKLEY MANSION
512 Qualia Dr.
Not open to the public

In the 1930s, during the Depression, Dr. John R. Brinkley built this mansion with the profits from his controversial goat gland implants for men that was supposed to restore their youthful vigor. To sell his services he built radio station XER across the border in Acuña. At that time, this station had 500,000 watts of output — which could reach radio sets as far away as Canada — making it one of the most powerful radio stations in the world. The station is still on the air today. It still has a strong signal, but not as powerful as when Dr. Brinkley owned it, since it has been reduced to an output of 200,000 watts.

CIUDAD ACUÑA
Take Garfield Ave. (Spur 239) west approximately three miles to International Toll Bridge
To call directly from Del Rio to Acuña, dial 011-52-877 and then the number.

This city of about 120,000 is named for Manuel Acuña, a romantic poet of the Mexican Revolution. The central plaza, called *Plaza Benjamin Canales*, after another revolutionary hero, is worth a visit. On this tree-lined plaza is the *Palacio Municipal* (City Hall). In 1960 Presidents

Eisenhower and Lopez Mateo addressed the people from its balcony when they met to conclude the agreement to build Amistad Dam. Most tourist shopping is near the bridge, especially along Avenida Hidalgo. The shops here offer a variety of Mexican handicrafts, gifts, souvenirs, and curios. Most shopkeepers speak English and deal in American dollars. As in most tourist shops, there's a lot of junk for sale, but there are also genuine bargains if you know what you're looking for and what it would cost in the States. There are also several restaurants and nightclubs in Acuña that are popular with American visitors. You can drive your car over, but if you do it's suggested you pick up Mexican auto insurance at one of the insurance agencies in Del Rio. (See Crossing Into Mexico in the Introduction.) If you don't wish to drive, you can park near the bridge and walk across (it's about ¾ mile to the shopping area) or take a taxi or bus. You can also pick up the bus to Acuña in downtown Del Rio. Del Rio and Ciudad Acuña jointly celebrate Fiesta Amistad in October each year (See Annual Events).

LAUGHLIN AIR FORCE BASE
US 90 approximately six miles east
298-5201 (Public Affairs Office)

This is an Air Force jet pilot training base. Tours are available for groups only. However, you can call and if there is a tour group scheduled and there's space, you may be able to join it.

VAL VERDE WINERY
139 Qualia Dr.
775-9714
Monday–Saturday 9–5
Free Tour

This is the oldest winery in Texas. Started in 1883 by Frank Qualia, an immigrant from Milan, Italy, it is still operated by the Qualia family more than 100 years later. For years it was the only licensed winery in the state. The tour takes about 20 minutes and covers all the steps in wine-making from growing the grapes to bottling. You will see the vineyard (look for the geese that are used for weeding), storage vats, aging room, and other facilities. Eight different wines are produced here, including the *Lenoir* that was the first wine produced by the winery in the 1880s, and all are usually available for tasting (and sale) during the tour. Diagonally across Hudson at N. 100, is the Taylor-Rivers Home, built in 1870 and now the oldest existing house in Del Rio, and further down Hudson, at 512, is the Brinkley Mansion (See above).

SPORTS AND ACTIVITIES

Golf

SAN FELIPE COUNTRY CLUB GOLF COURSE
US 90 E at San Felipe Springs Rd.
775-3953

Nine-hole course open to the public. Visitor green fees: weekdays $10, weekends $15.

Fishing

See Other Points of Interest-Amistad Lake. List of fishing guides available from the Chamber of Commerce.

House Boating

LAKE AMISTAD RESORT & MARINA
US 90W at Diablo East Recreation Area (P.O. Box 420635, 78842)
774-4157

Fifty-foot and 36-foot houseboats are available for rent at this Amistad National Recreation Area concession. Each one accommodates up to ten people and is equipped with bunk beds, stove, oven, refrigerator and ice chest, barbecue grill, cooking and eating utensils, and a shower. You must provide your own bedding, linens, towels, and food. No special boat license is required, but you must take instruction on the safe operation of the boat and its equipment from the concessionaire before setting out. From June 8 to September 2, rates run from about $220 for one night to $1,095 for seven nights. From September 3 through June 7 rates run from about $135 for one night to $665 for seven nights. There is also a damage deposit required, and you pay for your own gas.

Hunting

Limited free hunting is available at the Amistad National Recreation Area (See Other Points of Interest). A listing of member ranches offering hunting is available from the Chamber of Commerce. The following is an example of one of these.

DOLAN CREEK HUNTING
P.O. Box 420069 (78842)
775-3129 or 775-6163

Hunters are picked up at local motels and guided on a hunt on about 50,000 acres for white-tailed deer and wild turkey. A three-day hunting package runs about $1,400. This includes some meals and a good chance of coming out with a buck, two does, and a turkey.

PERFORMING ARTS

PAUL POAG THEATRE
746 S. Main
774-3277
Admission varies by event
W Call ahead

A 1940s era movie theater has been renovated by the Del Rio Council for the Arts and turned into a 726-seat performing arts theater with a proscenium stage. The calendar includes popular musicals, mysteries, and comedies performed by the community theater group, and the community concert and entertainment series that bring in outside talent.

SHOPPING

(To call directly from Del Rio to Acuna, dial 011-52-877 and then the number.)

LANDO CURIOS
Ciudad Acuña, 290 Hidalgo
2-1269

Mexican crafts, liquor, jewelry, and brass items are just a few of the things you'll find here. Free parking with purchase.

LA RUEDA (THE WHEEL)
Ciudad Acuña, 215 Hidalgo East
2-1260

The wagon wheel that hangs over the shop entrance is old, but inside much of the stock is modern Mexican designer clothes for women, priced from about $50 to $200, and designer jewelry.

PANCHO'S MARKET
Ciudad Acuña, 299 Hidalgo East
2-0466

If you get weary shopping this store for leather goods, liquor, jewelry, clothes, etc., etc., you can take a break in Pancho's Lounge in the rear. They also advertise prompt curb service.

PLAZA DEL SOL MALL
2205 Ave. F (US 90) near Garner
774-3634
W

Beall's, K-Mart, and Penney's anchor this small mall that includes a 3-screen cinema, a cafeteria, and a couple of dozen stores and fast food shops.

SIDE TRIPS

ALAMO VILLAGE MOVIELAND
Take US 90 east 29 miles to Brackettville, then RR 674 seven miles north
1-563-2580

See Brackettville.

SEMINOLE CANYON STATE HISTORICAL PARK
Take US 90 west about 45 miles to Park Rd. 67, just east of the Pecos River Bridge
(915) 292-4464
Open seven days 8–10 for day use, at all times for camping
$2 per vehicle per day
W + But not all areas

In the canyon of this 2,173-acre park is Fate Bell Shelter that contains some of North America's oldest pictographs — some believed to be painted 8,000 years ago. These paintings are considered by many experts to be among the most important rock art finds in the New World. Guided tours of this ancient rock art are conducted Wednesday through Sunday at 10 and 3, weather permitting. Because some moderately strenuous hiking is involved, persons planning to go on the tour should be in good physical condition. The park's Visitors Center contains exhibits depicting the life-style of early man based on the rock art and artifacts found in the area. There are picnic areas, RV and tent campsites (fee), and a six-mile (round- trip) hiking trail that leads to a scenic overlook 200 feet above the Rio Grande. For information contact: Park Superintendent, P.O. Box 820, Comstock, TX 78837. Just west of the park, on US 90, is the Pecos River Bridge. At 273 feet above the river's normal waterline, this is the highest highway bridge in Texas.

ANNUAL EVENTS

May

GEORGE PAUL MEMORIAL BULL RIDING COMPETITION
Del Rio Race Track, 2001 N. Main
775-3551 (Chamber of Commerce)
Competition usually first Sunday in May with other events in week preceding
$8–$15
W

Top-ranked bull riders are matched against top-ranked bulls in this competition that offers one of the biggest bull-riding purses in the world.

October

FIESTA DE AMISTAD
Most events in downtown Del Rio
775-3551 (Chamber of Commerce)
Usually week nearest October 24th
Most events free
W Variable

This bi-national fiesta commemorates the visit of Presidents Eisenhower and Lopez Mateo to Del Rio and Ciudad Acuña on October 24, 1960. A highlight of the fiesta is the International Parade from Del Rio to Ciudad Acuña, reportedly the only parade in the world that starts in one country and ends in another. Other activities during the week include a Battle of the Bands, the *Senorita Amistad* and Miss Del Rio pageants to choose the U.S. and Mexican ladies who will reign over the Fiesta, the *Abrazo* (friendship embrace) Ceremony, an open house and air show at Laughlin Air Force Base, an arts and crafts show, a bicycle race and a 10 K International Run.

RESTAURANTS

($ = under $7, $$ = $7 to $17, $$$ = $17 to $25, $$$$ = over $25 for one person excluding drinks, tax, and tip.)
(To call directly from Del Rio to Acuña, dial 011-52-877 and then the number.)

ASADERO LA POSTA
Ciudad Acuña, 348 Allende
2-2327
Breakfast, lunch, and dinner seven days
$-$$
MC, V
Parking lot across street

Roasted and grilled steaks, beef ribs, and other meats are the house specialty in this cozy, brick-walled restaurant. A special *fajita* plate with onions, *quesadilla*, and *guacamole* goes for about $5. Organ music on Friday and Saturday nights. Bar.

CRIPPLE CREEK SALOON
US 90 W about one mile north of the "Y" with US 277/377
775-0153
Dinner only Monday–Saturday, closed Sunday
$$
MC, V
W
Children's plates

Outside the log cabin style building there's a small animal farm to entertain the kids. Inside, while owner, George Aubry, plays barrel house piano and occasionally leads sing-alongs, the kitchen dishes up entrées that include a variety of mesquite-grilled steaks, swordfish steaks, and chicken, plus prime rib, lobster, shrimp, king crab, catfish, frog legs, and quail. Bar.

CROSBY'S
Ciudad Acuña, 195 Hidalgo
2-2020

Breakfast, lunch, and dinner seven days
$-$$
MC, V
W

It started back in the 1930s and, even though the owners have changed, its still going strong and holding onto its reputation of being one of the best places to eat in Acuña. Inside the etched glass entrance, old photos from the Mexican Revolution and masks from Oaxaca decorate the walls. The menu includes both continental and Mexican entrées ranging from *cabrito* and *fajitas* to seafood, quail and a house specialty: Portuguese Chicken. Bar and piano bar.

LANDO'S RESTAURANT AND BAR
Ciudad Acuña, 270 Hidalgo
2-1205
Lunch and dinner seven days
Reservations recommended on weekends
$$
MC, V
W
Secure parking in rear

The walls are covered with elegant wallpaper, the ceiling is mirrored, and there's a chandelier to round out the plush atmosphere. The menu features both Mexican and Continental entrées. Disco Thursday through Saturday nights. Bar.

LA PALAPA DE LANDO'S
Ciudad Acuña, 1190 S. Guerrero Blvd.
2-3982
Lunch and dinner seven days
$
MC, V
W
Children's plates
Secure parking

While the downtown Lando's is elegant and cozy, this walled restaurant is bright and wide-open and dining on the patio is a big attraction. The menu offers a variety of Mexican dishes, including *Tampiquena* for about $4, and broiled steaks. A little out of the way, it's still not hard to get to. Two blocks past the bridge, turn left on Iturbide, go nine blocks to Guerrero and turn left again — or take a taxi. Bar.

MEMO'S
804 E. Losoya
775-8104
Lunch and dinner Monday–Saturday, Dinner only Sunday
Reservations suggested for Tuesday night jam sessions
$-$$
W

One of the people in the many celebrity photos that line the walls of this Mexican restaurant is always Moises (Blondie) Calderon. Blondie, (whose hair is now black but was blonde when he was young) runs the family's restaurant when he's in town, but he is also the band leader and piano player for C & W singer Ray Price, which makes him a celebrity in his own right. When he's not on the road, Blondie and his local band play and have a jam session on Tuesday nights. The food? Well, the family has been serving up Tex-Mex and American dishes here since 1936, so it must be pleasing the customers. The menu runs from *chalupas, tacos, enchiladas,* and *fajitas* to T-bone and chicken-fried steaks. The dining room overlooks the San Felipe Creek. Bar.

MEXICAN KITCHEN
807 E. Losoya
774-2280
Lunch and dinner Monday through Saturday, closed Sunday
$-$$
MC, V
W
Children's plates

One of the specialties here is *Encebollada* — small, tender beef filets and onions grilled in butter and garnished with avocado, tomatoes, and jalepeno slices. They also offer a wide variety of other Tex-Mex dishes including *fajitas, flautas* and *Chimichanga* — tender beef inside a flour tortilla. Beer and wine.

ACCOMMODATIONS

($ = Under $45, $$ = $46-$60, $$$ = $61-$80, $$$$ = $81-$100, $$$$$ = Over $100)
Room Tax 13 percent in city, 6 percent outside

AMISTAD LODGE
US 90 W near Amistad Lake, ½ mile east of Diablo East Marina (HCR 3, Box 29, 78840)
775-8591
$
W

Some of the 40 rooms include kitchenettes. Children under 12 stay free in room with parents. Cable TV. Room phones (local calls free). Pets OK. Restaurant, room service, lounge open seven nights. Outdoor pool. Free airport transportation. Boat parking. Fish cleaning house. Texas and Mexican fishing licenses for sale. Overlooks the lake.

BEST WESTERN INN OF DEL RIO
810 Avenue F (US 90 W)
775-7511 or 800-528-1234
$-$$
No-smoking rooms

This two-story Best Western has 62 rooms including six no-smoking. Senior discount. Cable TV with HBO. Room phones (local calls free). Pets OK (pet charge $3/day). Outdoor pool and whirlpool. Free airport transportation. Free coffee in lobby, free cocktail hour, and free full breakfast. Self-service laundry and same-day dry cleaning. Boat parking.

HOLIDAY INN
2005 Ave. F (US 90 W)
775-7591 or 800-HOLIDAY
$-$$
W + one room
No-smoking rooms

The two-story inn has 101 units that include one suite ($$$$) and 11 no-smoking rooms. Children under 18 stay free in room with parents. Senior discount. Cable TV with The Movie Channel. Room phones (local calls free). No pets. Restaurant, room service, lounge open Monday-Saturday. Outdoor pool. Free airport transportation. Free coffee in lobby in morning. Self-service laundry and same-day dry cleaning. Boat parking.

LAGUNA DIABLO RESORT
Sanders Point Rd. on Devil's River Arm of Lake Amistad (P.O. Box 420608, 78842)
774-2422
$$-$$$

The ten units in this resort consist of six 2-bedroom and four 1-bedroom apartments with full kitchen, bath, and living and dining area. No pets. Two night minimum for reservations. Call or write for directions to this hideaway on the lake.

RAMADA INN
2101 Ave. F. (US 90 W)
775-1511 or 800-2-RAMADA
$$
No-smoking rooms

A two-story Ramada with 95 units including one suite with jacuzzi ($$$$$) and 27 no-smoking rooms. Children under 18 stay free in room with parents. Package plans available, senior discount, and weekend rates. Cable TV with HBO and VCR rentals. Room phones (local calls free). Pets OK (pet deposit required). Restaurant, room service, lounge open seven nights with occasional entertainment on weekends. Outdoor heated pool and whirlpool, exercise room. Free transportation to airport and bridge. Self-service laundry and same-day dry cleaning. Boat parking, beauty shop.

EAGLE PASS

MAVERICK COUNTY SEAT ★ 25,000 ★ (512)

The city takes its name from a ford across the Rio Grande that the Spanish named *Paso del Aguila* (Pass of the Eagles) for the eagles that nested nearby. In 1848, the commander of a company of the Texas Volunteer Militia, who set up a camp here to guard the border, translated that into the Camp at Eagle Pass in his reports. A year later, the U.S. Army took over the border duty and built Fort Duncan. And in 1850, John Twohig, a San Antonio banker who owned much of the land along the river, laid out a townsite near the fort and officially named it Eagle Pass. The same year, a Mexican garrison was established on the opposite side of the river and the village of Piedras Negras grew up around it.

The county was established in 1856 and named for Samuel Maverick, one of the signers of the Texas Declaration of Independence. Maverick's name became part of our language because he refused to brand all his cattle. As a result, any unbranded animal found on the range was considered one of his — a maverick. The term is still in use with cattle, but has also come to mean an independent thinker who doesn't follow the herd.

During the Civil War, the Confederates controlled Fort Duncan and it was near here, on July 4th, 1865, that General Joseph O. Shelby crossed the Rio Grande with his brigade of Missouri Cavalry who had refused to accept Lee's surrender. Shelby ordered the last Confederate flag to fly over his men buried in the river. According to a poem written about the event, Shelby, Southern gentleman to the last, then took the plume from his hat and threw it in the river after the flag.

During the 1870s, the Seminole Indian Scouts were assigned here and fought with the army to put down the hostile Indians. But the Indians weren't the only trouble. Outlaws from both sides of the border gave the place the reputation of being lawless. Conditions were so bad at times that the county judge, fearing for his life, dared not sleep in his own home. Eventually, the Texas Rangers moved in and restored a semblance of order.

But trouble erupted again when the Mexican Revolution started in 1910. By 1916 the whole border was aflame. Fort Duncan, which had faded in importance since the Indian fighting days, suddenly became the garrison for 16,000 troops. The troops stayed until after World War I.

Today, Eagle Pass is a quiet border town that is the trading center for the surrounding irrigated agricultural area as well as a base for some light industry and oil and gas production. It is also a gateway to Mexico with US 57 continuing in Piedras Negras as Mexico Hwy 57 that leads to Saltillo, San Luis Potosi, and Mexico City.

TOURIST SERVICES

EAGLE PASS CHAMBER OF COMMERCE
400 Garrison (P.O. Box 1188, 78852)
773-3224
W +

Maps of Eagle Pass and Piedras Negras and brochures in both English and Spanish are available for visitors in this office located just a couple of blocks east of the bridge.

MUSEUMS

FORT DUNCAN MUSEUM
Fort Duncan Park, Bliss between Monroe and Adams
773-2748
Monday–Friday 1–5
Free
W

This small museum is located in the old headquarters building of the fort. The exhibits feature both the archaeological story of the area and local history including exhibits on the Kickapoo Indians who live near here. The headquarters is just one of the eleven surviving old post buildings that date back through the Indian fighting days almost to the Mexican War. Established in 1849, the fort was occupied by the Confederates during the Civil War. Union forces regarrisoned it in 1868 and it remained active until about 1900. It was reactivated in 1916 to protect

PIEDRAS NEGRAS

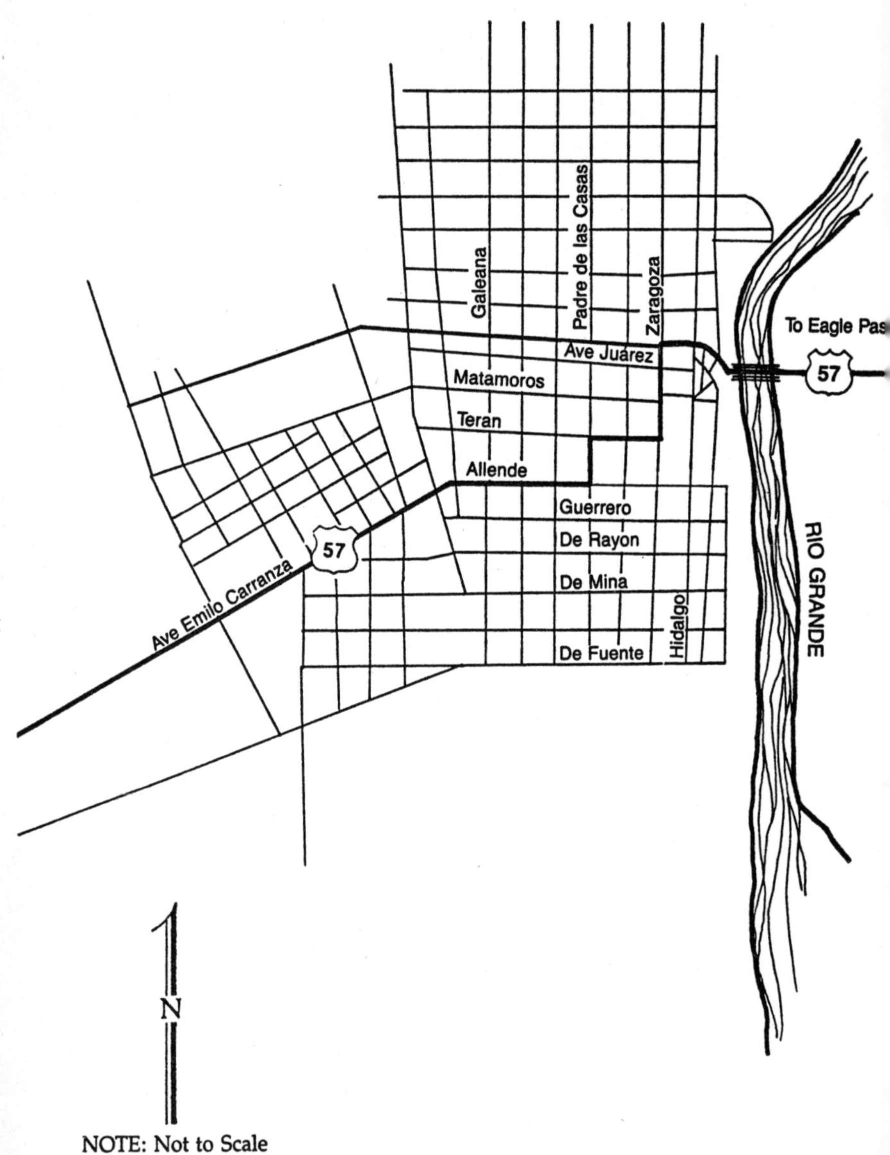

NOTE: Not to Scale

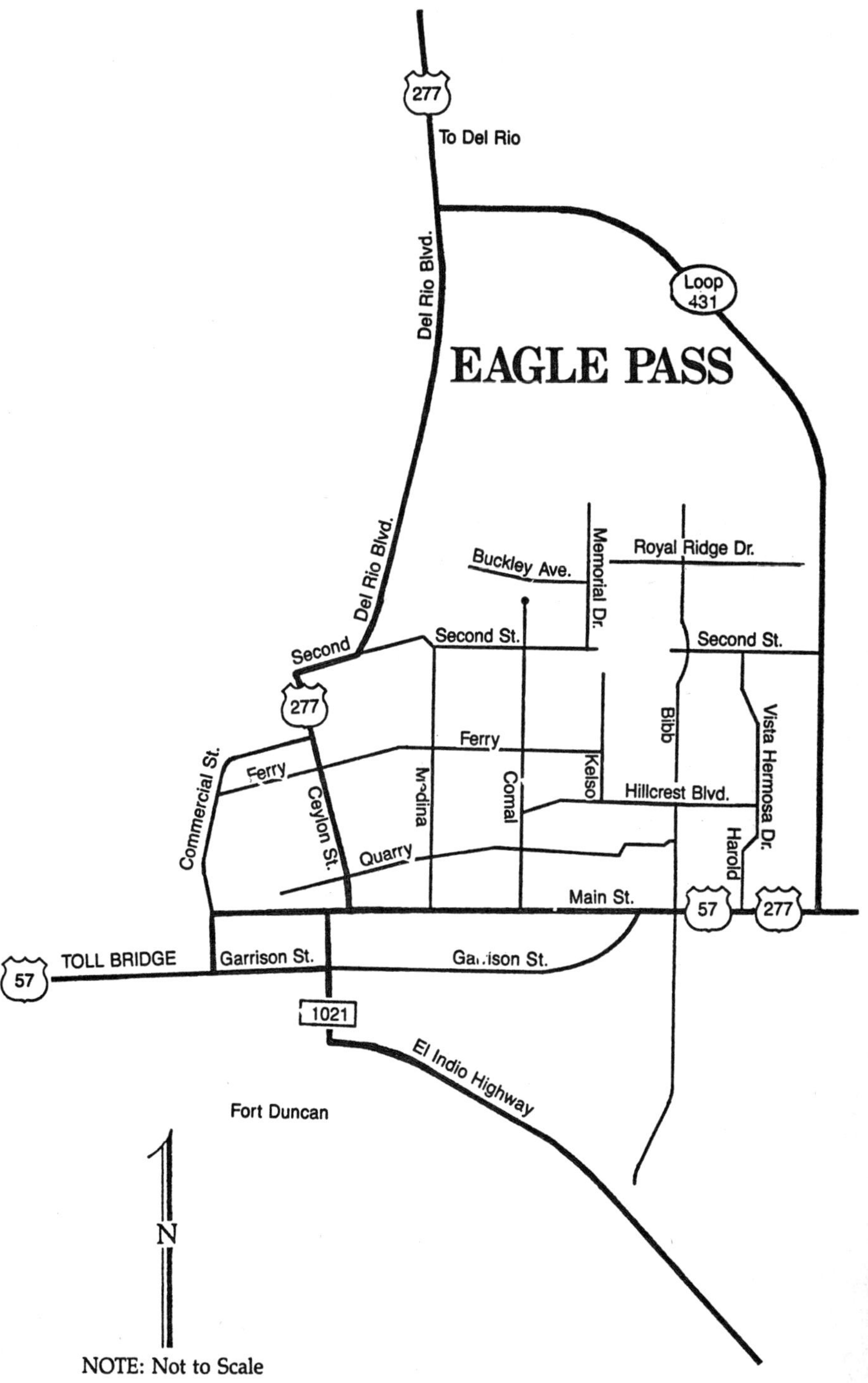

NOTE: Not to Scale

the border during the Mexican Revolution and served as a training base during World War I. After that war it fell into a caretaker status and in 1938 was acquired by the city and turned into a city park. Throughout its history, many colorful officers either commanded or were stationed here. These included Phil Sheridan, William R. Shafter, John L. Bullis, Zenas R. Bliss, Terry Allen, James Doolittle, Matthew Ridgeway, and James Van Fleet.

HISTORIC PLACES

There are a number of turn-of-the-century homes on Ceylon St. (US 277 Bus), especially in the 400 to 600 blocks.

MAVERICK COUNTY COURTHOUSE
500 Main
Built in 1885, the crenellation suggests a fortress.

OTHER POINTS OF INTEREST

PIEDRAS NEGRAS
Take Garrison St. (US 57) across the International Bridge
To call Piedras Negras from Eagle Pass, dial 011-52878 and then the five-digit local number.
The "black rocks" (*piedras negras*) for which the city is named were coal deposits. For a time, during the late 1880s and early 1900s, coal was mined on both sides of the border. Today, the city has a population of around 200,000, about eight times that of Eagle Pass. The main shopping area and the most popular restaurants are within an easy walk of the bridge. Just as you cross the bridge, at Hidalgo and Abasolo, is the *Estrella del ProNaf* (See Shopping), a small national shop that sells folk art and handicraft items guaranteed authentic by the government. The central market is on Zaragoza St., one block further west. There are also many reputable shops that cater to tourists along this street. If you want to walk across, you can park your car free at the Chamber of Commerce at 400 Garrison, near the bridge. You can drive your car across, but if you do you should pick up Mexican auto insurance at one of the insurance agencies in Eagle Pass. (See Crossing into Mexico in the Introduction.)

SPORTS AND ACTIVITIES

Bullfighting

PLAZA DE TOROS, MONUMENTAL ARIZPE
Piedras Negras, Avenida Lopez Mateos
773-3224 (Eagle Pass Chamber of Commerce)
Admission: Sunny side about $5, Shady side about $12

The bullfights in this small ring are put on mostly by the lesser known matadors on a circuit. Schedules are erratic, but there are usually bullfights here one Sunday a month from Memorial Day to Labor Day.

Golf

MAVERICK COUNTY GOLF COURSE
Fort Duncan Park
773-9761

Nine-hole course. Green fees for all day: weekdays $7.50, weekends and holidays $10.75.

Horse Racing

MODERNO DERBY CLUB
Piedras Negras, Zaragoza at Allende
2-0684

This is a combination restaurant/nightclub/off-track betting parlor. You can place bets on races at most U.S. tracks. (See Restaurants, following.)

Hunting

A list of guides and leases for hunting on both sides of the border is available from the Eagle Pass Chamber of Commerce (See Tourist Services).

SHOPPING

ESTRELLA DEL PRONAF
Piedras Negras, Hidalgo and Abasolo, at the bridge
2-1087
Monday–Saturday 9–7, Sunday 9–noon

You won't find a "Made in Taiwan" stamp on the bottom of any of the items for sale here. This is a Mexican government shop so everything is guaranteed to be made in Mexico. The emphasis is on authentic and original folk art from all over the country and in many forms including pottery and jewelry. There's no bargaining here; prices are fixed and range from about 100 pesos up to a million (at the rate of exchange when this guidebook went to press, that's from about a nickel up to around $400).

MALL DE LAS AQUILAS
445 South Bibb
773-9033
W

The main shopping mall in Eagle Pass, it is anchored by Beall's, Penney's, and Wal-Mart.

ZAPATERIA "ESTRELLA"
Piedras Negras, Padre de las Casas and Teran
2-2164

They hand make cowboy boots, jackets, belts, and bags in this little shop about five blocks west of the bridge. Calfskin boots run about $100, while ostrich cost about $450. It usually takes about two weeks for handmade boots, but they can do a pair in two days if necessary. For information you can write the shop at its Eagle Pass mailing address: P.O. Box 2074, 78852.

SIDE TRIPS

ALAMO VILLAGE MOVIELAND
Take US 277 northwest to Texas 131, then right (north) to Bracketville, then RR 674 north seven miles. Approximately 50 miles.

(See Bracketville)

GUERRERO, MEXICO
Take Mexico Hwy 57 southwest about three miles to Mexico Hwy 2, then left (southeast) to Guerrero. Approximately 35 miles from Piedras Negras

This is the site of the Spanish missions that was the jumping off place for the establishment of the Texas missions. Some historians consider it one of the most historically significant sites along the entire U.S.-Mexico border. The town plaza is surrounded by colonial buildings. Just north of town are the ruins of the San Bernardo mission founded in 1702. Part of Santa Anna's army stopped in Guerrero on its way to the Alamo in 1836. This is beyond Mexico's 12 mile federal border zone, so you will need a Mexican tourist card. (See Crossing into Mexico in the Introduction.)

ANNUAL EVENTS

March

INTERNATIONAL FRIENDSHIP FIESTA
Downtown and Fort Duncan Park area
773-3224 (Chamber of Commerce)
Usually last week in March
Free
W Variable

Although the main events are on the weekend, a carnival and food and game booths open at Fort Duncan Park several days before. Festivities include a parade, a dance, a chili cookoff, and sporting events.

RESTAURANTS

($ = under $7, $$ = $7 to $17, $$$ = $17 to $25, $$$$ = over $25 for one person excluding drinks, tax, and tip.)
To call Piedras Negras from Eagle Pass, dial 011-52878 and then the five-digit local number.

CLUB MODERNO

Piedras Negras, Zaragoza and Allende
2-0098
Lunch and dinner seven days
$-$$
Cr.
Parking in lot behind

The menu includes both continental and Mexican cuisine with large portions at moderate prices. At the Moderno Derby Club, in the building, they offer off-track betting and live music for dancing.

DON CRUZ RESTAURANT

Piedras Negras, Morelos between Teran and Allende
2-1092
Lunch and dinner seven days
$-$$
Cr.
Garage parking

A varied menu, but the best entrées are the Mexican dishes like *huachinango veracruzano*, red snapper Vera Cruz style.

ACCOMMODATIONS

($ = Under $45, $$ = $46-$60, $$$ = $61-$80, $$$$ = $81-$100, $$$$$ = Over $100)
To call Piedras Negras from Eagle Pass, dial 011-52878 and then the five-digit local number.
Room Tax 13 percent (in Eagle Pass only)

HOLLY INN

2421 Main (US 57)
773-9261
$

Built on one level, this motel offers 86 rooms including two suites ($$). Children under 18 stay free in room with parents. Cable TV with HBO. Room phones (local calls free). Pets OK. Restaurant, room service, lounge open seven nights with DJ Wednesday-Saturday. Outdoor heated pool, outdoor whirlpool, exercise room. One free cocktail in lounge. Free newspaper. Same-day dry cleaning.

LA QUINTA INN
2525 Main (US 57)
773-7000 or 800-531-5900
$$
W + six rooms
No-smoking rooms

The two-story La Quinta on the American side offers 130 rooms that include 39 no-smoking. Children under 18 stay free in room with parents. Senior discount. Cable and satellite TV with HBO, Showtime and pay channel. Room phones (local calls free). Pets OK. Restaurant adjoining. Outdoor pool. Free coffee in lobby and free news magazine in room. Same-day dry cleaning.

LA QUINTA MOTOR HOTEL
Piedras Negras, 1205 Avenida E. Carranza
2-2154
$

This motel offers 38 rooms and two suites ($$). Cable TV with HBO. Room phones (free local calls). Pets OK (*but check on animal controls on returning to U.S. before taking them across border*). Restaurant, room service, lounge with entertainment open seven nights. Outdoor pool. There's no connection between this motel and the American one of the same name. Check-out time is 24 hours after you check in.

POSADA ROSA
Piedras Negras, Avenida Sinaloa and San Luis. From bridge take Abasolo five stop lights to San Luis, then left to hotel
2-5011
$$-$$$
No smoking rooms

This two-story hotel has 91 units including nine suites ($$$) and some no-smoking rooms. Cable TV. Room phones (local calls free). No pets. Restaurant and cafeteria, room service, lounge with entertainment open seven nights. Outdoor pool, exercise room, tennis courts. Gift shop and beauty salon. Secured parking, some covered.

EDINBURG

HIDALGO COUNTY ★ 30,000 ★ (512)

The city was originally founded on the Rio Grande (near the present location of Hidalgo) in the early 1850s when John Young secured a license to operate a ferry on the river. He called the town that grew up around his ferry and general store Edinburgh, after his home in Scotland. It was named the county seat of the new Hidalgo County that was named after Miguel Hidalgo, the famous liberator of Mexico. In addition to its importance as a ferry site, Edinburg soon became a steamboat town.

Despite the efforts of the Texas Rangers and other lawmen, the years from the 1850s until the early 1880s were times of trouble for the settlers in this area. Rustlers and other bandits raided almost constantly and sheriffs didn't last long, either suddenly deciding to resign or dying "with their boots on." Then, in 1882, John Closner became a local peace officer. It took him until 1896, but Sheriff Closner finally cleaned up Hidalgo County — without killing a single man.

Then Closner developed a steam-driven irrigation pump that drastically increased the quality of the sugar cane produced on his plantation and won him the 1904 St. Louis World's Fair Gold Medal for the finest sugar cane in the world. That distinction created interest in the Valley and started a land boom.

The Rio Grande flooded frequently in those days. In 1886, Edinburgh was washed away by a flood and the county seat was moved to nearby Hidalgo. When the floods of 1907 threatened the courthouse at Hidalgo, officals decided to move the county seat to safer ground. Closner offered some land in the brush about 16 miles northeast. A referendum was held and the new site approved. But, as often happened in those days, the opposition wouldn't give up the county records. So, under cover of darkness, Closner and a group of heavily armed men removed the records from Hidalgo and took them to the new county seat in the brush. Once they had the records, they built the town starting with a barn-like temporary courthouse. When the new town was founded in 1908 it was called Chapin, but in 1911 its name was changed to Edinburg (without the "h").

Today, Edinburg is the western gateway to the Lower Rio Grande Valley for those traveling down US 281. In addition to agriculture, one of the mainstays of the local economy is the annual influx of winter Texans.

TOURIST SERVICES

EDINBURG CHAMBER OF COMMERCE
521 S. 12th at Champion (P.O. Box 85, 78540)
383-4974
Monday–Friday 8:30–5
W

MUSEUMS

HIDALGO COUNTY HISTORICAL MUSEUM
121 E. McIntyre, on north side of the Square
383-6911
Tuesday–Friday 9–5, Sunday 1–5
Adults $1 children under 12 25¢
W East door

The building was originally the county jail. If you look up when you first walk in, you can see the steel trap door of the hanging room in the tower over the entrance. According to the records, the only hanging here took place in 1913. The major part of this small, but well organized museum is upstairs. The exhibits depict the rich cultural heritage of the Rio Grande Valley from the pre-historic times, when the Coahuiltecan Indians lived here, to life on the ranches in the 1900s. One exhibit of special interest is on river steamboats that includes a model of a "mud skimmer," a type of Rio Grande paddlewheel steamboat that earned its name because it only drew two feet of water. Gift shop.

SPORTS AND ACTIVITIES

Golf

EDINBURG MUNICIPAL GOLF COURSE
300 Palm Dr.
383-1244

Nine-hole course. Green fees: $4 for 9 holes, $5.25 for 18.

MONTE CRISTO GOLF COURSE
Take US 281 north about two miles, then east on FM 1925
383-0964

Eighteen-hole course. Green fee: $5 for 9 holes, $6.50 for 18 holes

COLLEGES AND UNIVERSITIES

UNIVERSITY OF TEXAS-PAN AMERICAN UNIVERSITY
1201 W. University Dr.
381-2011
W + But not all areas
Visitor parking on both ends of campus

Originally founded in 1927 as a junior college, it is now the Valley's largest institution of higher learning with the more than 12,000 students on this 200-acre campus taking courses leading to a bachelor's degree in about 40 fields and a master's degree in about 20 fields in liberal arts and sciences, business, and education. The university is also a sports and cultural center for both the residents of the area and visitors. The school participates in most major intercollegiate sports except football. (Sports information and tickets: 381-2221). Faculty, student, and traveling art exhibits are held at the Gallery in the Communication Arts and Sciences Building (381-3480). Four to six theater productions are put on each academic year in the University Theater Auditorium (381-3581). An additional three productions, including a musical, are usually produced during the summer. The school's Jazz Dancers and Folkloric Dancers also give public performances (381-3501). The South Texas Chamber Orchestra and the Valley Symphony, two organizations that combine outside professional musicians with faculty and students from the Music Department, give frequent concerts in the Fine Arts Auditorium (381-8682) and in various other cities in the Valley. And if you get hungry while on campus, the cafeteria in the University Center is open to the public.

ANNUAL EVENTS

February

FIESTA HIDALGO
Various locations

383-4974 (Chamber of Commerce)
Usually about three weeks in February
Free. Admission to some events
W Variable

When Edinburg (then Chapin) became the county seat, in 1908, some people opposed moving the city north to its present location. So, under the cover of darkness, a group of men moved the courthouse records by mule cart to the new site. This fiesta celebrates that event. Activities, spread over much of the month, include a parade, dance, square dance jamboree, carnival, a rodeo, an arts and crafts show, a youth livestock show, entertainment, and several sports tournaments.

RESTAURANTS

($ = under $7, $$ = $7 to $17, $$$ = $17 to $25, $$$$ = over $25 for one person excluding drinks, tax, and tip.)

SHEA-MARTIN CAFE
217 S. Closner
380-0401
Breakfast and lunch only Monday–Friday
$
AE, MC, V
W

Lunches like shrimp and crab Louis, and roast beef with mushroom wine sauce are popular with both the courthouse and the university crowds that congregate here. Other items on the menu are some Tex-Mex dishes, sandwiches, and salads. Usually also open on weekends when the university has theater performances.

ACCOMMODATIONS

($ = Under $45, $$ = $46-$60, $$$ = $61-$80, $$$$ = $81-$100, $$$$$ = Over $100)
Room Tax 13 percent

ECHO MOTOR LODGE
1903 S. Closner at E. Palm
383-3823 or 800-422-0336
$-$$

This two-story motel has 128 rooms. Children under 12 stay free in room with parents. Senior discount. Satellite TV. Room phones (charge for local calls). Coffeemakers in rooms. No pets. Restaurant, room service, lounge open Monday-Saturday. Outdoor pool, children's pool. Guest memberships available in health club. Free airport transportation. The lodge is located on 16 acres.

HARLINGEN

CAMERON COUNTY ★ 55,000 ★ (512)

This town, named for a city in the Netherlands, was founded by Lon C. Hill in 1903, decades after the settlement of the wild West, but Harlingen's early days were reminiscent of those shoot'em-up times. At first it was peaceful. The railroad came to this town, in 1904, and by 1907, miles of canals had been dug to irrigate thousands of acres of farmland. But a few years later the chaos of the Mexican Revolution spilled over and bandit raids became commonplace. A company of Texas Rangers was stationed in the town plus members of the U.S. Customs mounted patrol. With all those guns around, the railroad people started to call the town "Sixshooter Junction." Rumor has it that there were more sidearms than citizens. The law was generally regarded as the thing you carried in your holster. Eventually, the bandit situation became so terrifying that the National Guard was called in to join forces with the Rangers and order was finally restored.

Today Harlingen is at the crossroads of U.S. Highways 77 and 83, four lane thoroughfares linking the rest of Texas to the Valley. It is a processing, distribution, and marketing center for the major citrus orchards and vegetable farms of the fertile Rio Grande Valley.

In the works are plans for the Arroyo Colorado State Recreation Area to be developed in an area about 15 miles northeast of the city.

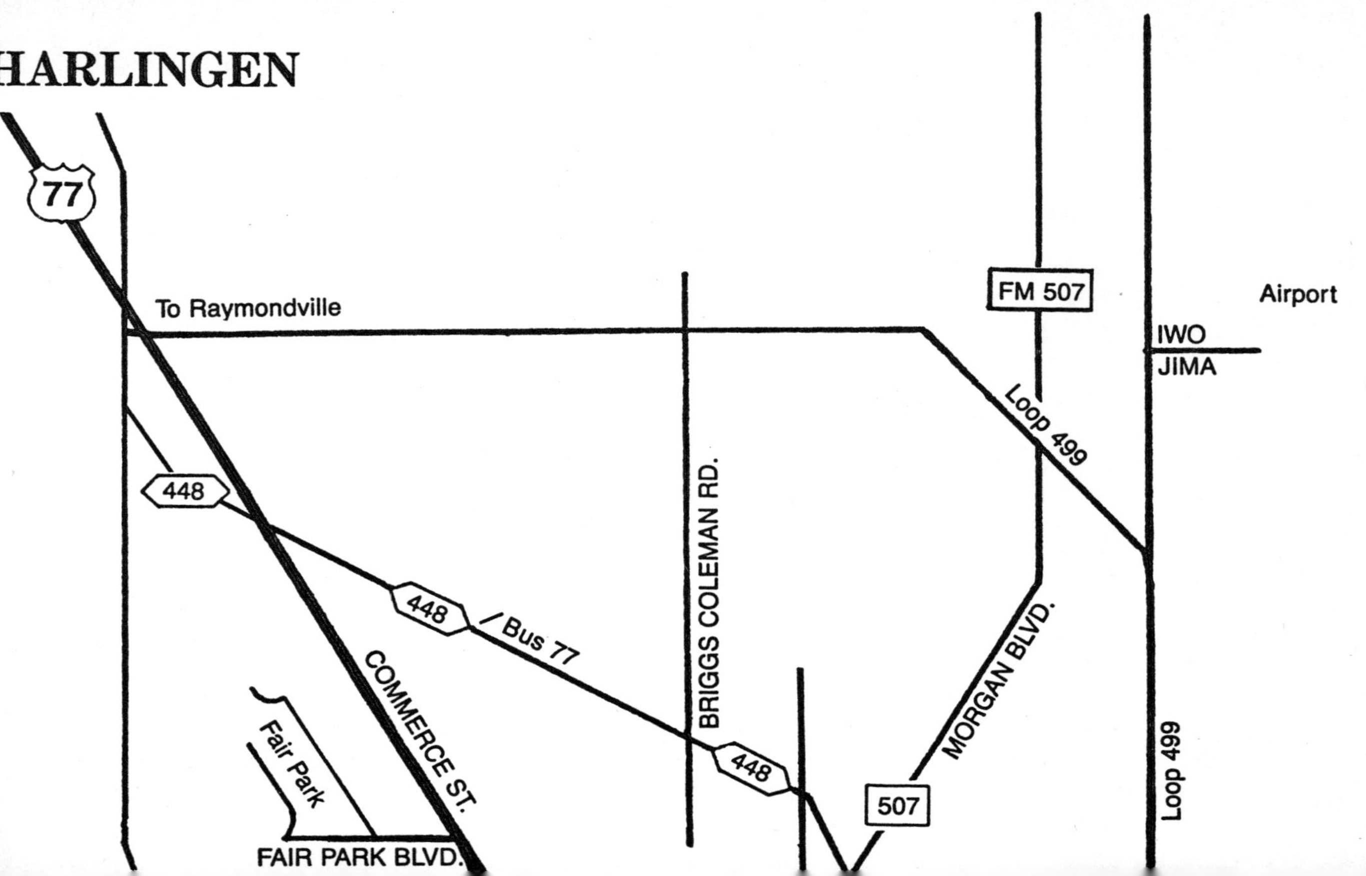
HARLINGEN
77
To Raymondville
448
448
Bus 77
COMMERCE ST.
Fair Park
FAIR PARK BLVD.
BRIGGS COLEMAN RD.
448
507
MORGAN BLVD.
FM 507
Loop 499
IWO JIMA
Airport
Loop 499

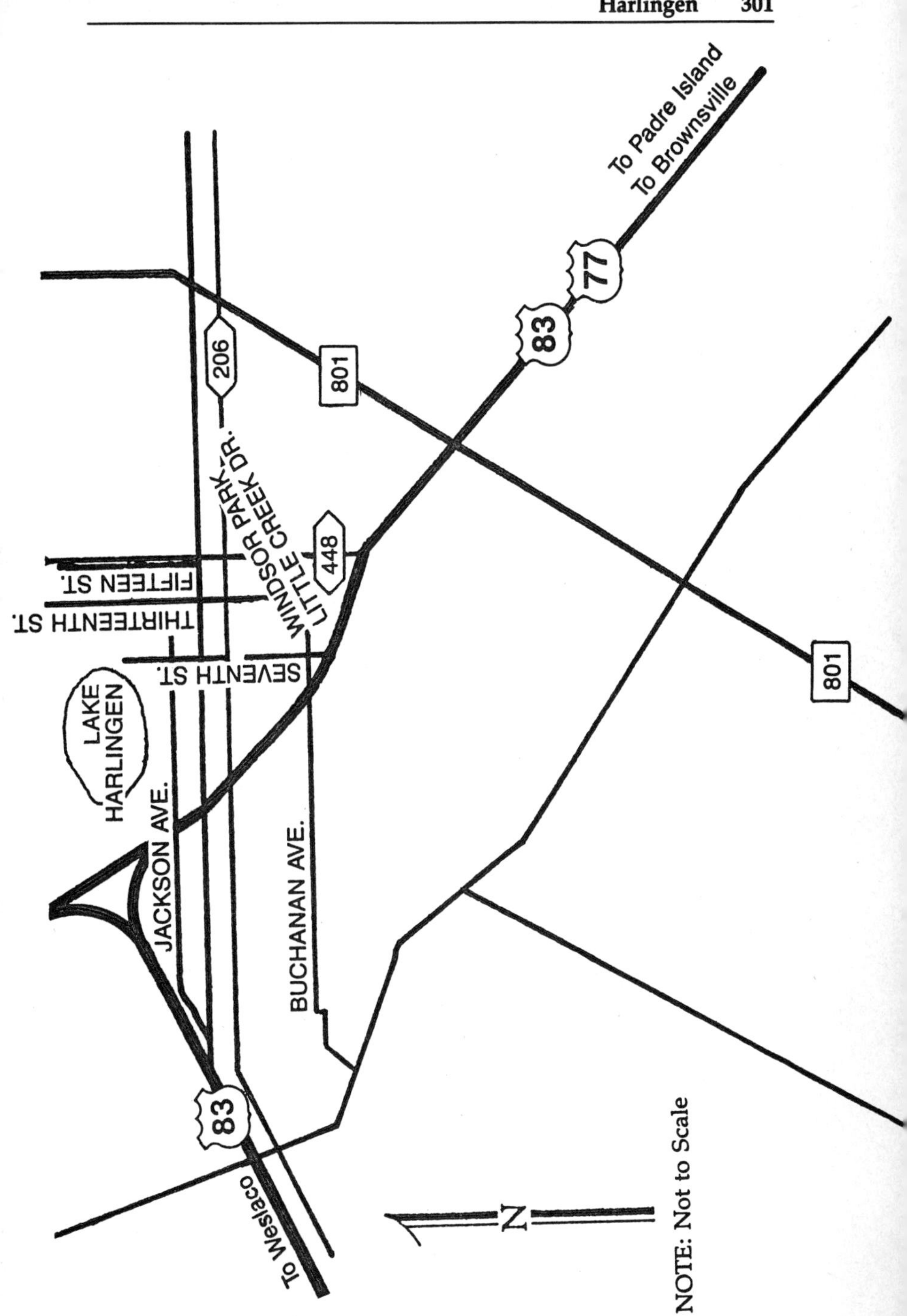
To Padre Island
To Brownsville
77
83
801
206
WINDSOR PARK
LITTLE CREEK DR.
448
FIFTEEN ST.
THIRTEENTH ST.
SEVENTH ST.
LAKE HARLINGEN
JACKSON AVE.
BUCHANAN AVE.
83
To Weslaco
N
NOTE: Not to Scale

TOURIST SERVICES

HARLINGEN CHAMBER OF COMMERCE
311 E. Tyler at 3rd St. (P.O. Box 189, 78551)
423-5440
Monday–Friday 8:30–5
W

In addition to providing maps, brochures, and other information on the city and the Valley, this office is the outlet for tickets for just about anything going on in Harlingen.

HARLINGEN TOURIST CENTER
201 E. Madison
423-9932
Open 10 a.m. to late in evening
W +

Although primarily a center for activities for the thousands of Winter Texans, it is open year round and brochures and other information on Harlingen are available.

TEXAS TRAVEL INFORMATION CENTER
2021 W. Harrison (Junction US 77 and US 83)
428-4477
Open seven days 8–5
Free
W +

One of 12 roadside information centers operated by the Texas Department of Highways and Public Transportation on key highways entering the state. Bilingual travel counselors can provide a wealth of free information, official highway maps, and tons of other travel literature on the Rio Grande Valley and the rest of Texas. Even if you're not interested in all the goodies available, this is an excellent rest stop. The building is cool and quiet, the restrooms are clean, and there is a small reflecting pool in a courtyard outside that is relaxing just to sit by.

VALLEY ADVENTURE TOURS
421-2262 or 800-338-0560
Tours $13–$20

In the Harlingen area, they offer tours that include the Gladys Porter Zoo and the Confederate Air Force Museum. Tours are also available to Matamoros.

MUSEUMS

CONFEDERATE AIR FORCE FLYING MUSEUM
Harlingen Industrial Air Park (Rebel Field), Valley International Airport
425-1057

Monday–Saturday 9–5, Sunday and holidays 1–6, except closed Christmas Day
Adults $3, children (6 to 12) $1.50
W

You didn't know the Confederates had an Air Force? Well the headquarters is sitting right here. The Confederate Air Force (CAF) "Ghost Squadron" includes an almost complete collection of American World War II combat aircraft plus a number of rare and classic aircraft of the Royal Air Force, German Luftwaffe, and the Imperial Japanese Navy. All are flyable or in the process of restoration. Usually about a third of the aircraft are at this museum. The others are either on tour at air shows, working in movies, or scattered throughout the more than 70 squadron chapters world-wide.

The museum building offers displays of uniforms, weapons, and other memorabilia from both sides in World War II. But the main attractions are in the display hangers and on the airport aprons — the restored planes themselves. Here side by side you may find a Japanese Zero, a German Messerschmitt, a U.S. B-29 Superfortress, and a P-39 Aircobra. All clearly marked with plenty of information. For the airplane buff, the World War II historian, and children (young and old), this is a don't-miss museum. For information write P.O. Box CAF, Harlingen 78551. *(Unfortunately, the museum has outgrown the quarters it has ocupied for more than 20 years and, because there's no room at the Harlingen Airport for it to expand, the CAF is moving to Midland — a move that may occur at any time so call before visiting.)*

RIO GRANDE VALLEY HISTORICAL MUSEUM COMPLEX
Boxwood and Raintree off Loop 499, Harlingen Industrial Air Park, near Valley International Airport
423-3979
Tuesday–Friday 9–noon and 2–5, Sunday 2–5. Closed Saturday, Monday, and major holidays
Free (donations accepted)
W Variable

This is really four museums in one. The **Historical Museum** building features the cultural and natural history of the Lower Rio Grande Valley. One of the outbuildings is the restored nineteenth-century **Paso Real Stagecoach Inn** that charged thirty-five cents a night for meals and a bed. It was used until 1904 when the railroad came to the Valley. Another building is Harlingen's first hospital, built in 1923, and now restored as a **medical museum**. The fourth building is the **Lon C. Hill Home.** Built in 1905 by the city's founder, this home was the headquarters of the Hill Plantation. Hill believed that irrigation would bring prosperity to the region. By 1907 he had 26 miles of canals in operation and 5,000 acres under irrigation. This house was visited by such notables as William Jennings Bryan. Hill's wife and the youngest of their nine children died in a typhoid fever epidemic just before the house was completed.

OTHER POINTS OF INTEREST

ALOE VERA INFORMATION CENTER
US 83 W and Altas Palmas Rd.
425-2585
June–September: Monday–Friday 10–4; October–May: Monday–Saturday 10–6
Free
W

You'll have to put up with some soft selling here because the center is run by Forever Living Products that sells Aloe Vera in many forms. But if you're interested in learning about this fascinating plant the soft sell is worth it. There's a twenty minute film on the history of aloe vera and the company, a brief tour of the fields, and a free test of the various health, cosmetic, and nutritional products. They also give each visitor a free baby aloe plant.

MARINE MILITARY ACADEMY AND TEXAS IWO JIMA WAR MEMORIAL
320 Iwo Jima Blvd., across from Valley International Airport
423-6006
Open seven days except for school holidays
W Variable

If you've ever wanted to see a Marine Corps precision drill or parade, but couldn't get to the real thing, this academy offers a good substitute. Students at this private military prep school wear uniforms similar to the U.S. Marines and follow the customs and traditions of the Corps as well. Check the Public Affairs Office for parade and activities to which visitors are welcome. The Iwo Jima War Memorial on the campus is always open to visitors. This is the original working model used to cast the famous bronze memorial that stands in Arlington National Cemetery. The 32-foot high figures are shown erecting a 78-foot steel flagpole from which a cloth flag flies 24 hours a day. (The Marine placing the flag pole in the ground was Corporal Harlon H. Block, from Weslaco in the Valley, who was later killed in battle). Across from the monument is a small museum with WWII memorabilia and a gift shop.

SPORTS AND ACTIVITIES

Golf

FAIRWAY GOLF COURSE
2524 W. Spur 54 off US 77 N
423-9098

Nine-hole course. Green fees: 9 holes $3, 18 holes $4.25

TONY BUTLER MUNICIPAL GOLF COURSE
Approximately half mile south on M St. off US 77/83
423-9913

Twenty-seven hole course. Green fees: weekdays $6, weekends $5.50.

Greyhound Racing

VALLEY GREYHOUND PARK
Ed Carey Dr., about 1.5 miles southwest of US 77/83
428-0161
Admission , Parking fee
W Variable

They have races about 300 nights a year here and matinees on Wednesday and Saturday. No racing on Tuesday. Seating for about 2,500 in a covered grandstand ($2). Eighteen kennels can house more than 1,000 dogs. Two restaurants and lounge.

Tennis

HEB TENNIS CENTER
Pendleton Park, Morgan Blvd at Grimes
423-4230

Twelve lighted courts. $1 hour. Also public pool and playground.

VICTOR PARK
M St. and US 77/83
423-4230

Eight lighted courts. Free. Also public pool and playground.

PERFORMING ARTS

BROADWAY THEATER LEAGUE
Performances at Harlingen Municipal Auditorium, Fairpark Blvd. (also called Valley Fair Blvd.) and Wichita
423-5440 (Chamber of Commerce)
Admission varies by performance
W +

This organization usually sponsors three touring Broadway-type musicals between October and April. Tickets run from about $8 to $40 depending on the show and seat location.

THE COUNTRY PLAYHOUSE
423-2111 or 423-5440 (Chamber of Commerce)
Admission
W Variable

This community theater group puts on about three productions a year in its November to April season. Shows are held either at the Municipal Auditorium or Memorial Junior High School. Tickets, which usually run $5-$7, are available at the Chamber of Commerce.

HARLINGEN MUNICIPAL AUDITORIUM
Fairpark Blvd. (also called Valley Fair Blvd.) and Wichita
423-5440 (Chamber of Commerce)
Admission varies by event
W +

This 1,860 seat auditorium plays host to a variety of performing arts events including the touring shows brought in by the Broadway Theater League, Country Playhouse productions, concerts of all types, and the Harlingen Concert Ballet.

SHOPPING

HAND OF MAN STAINED GLASS
1201 W. Jackson at South K St. (entrance on South K)
428-4562
W

This is both a custom shop and a stained glass hobbyist's supply store. Stained glass for sale frequently includes salvaged windows from old houses.

SUGAR TREE FARMS
Bass Blvd. off US 83 W
423-5530
Usually open November–April, depending on harvest season
W

This shop is a typical example of many in the area that sell local and imported citrus and fruits. You can buy by the pound, the sack, or the gift pack. They also sell fresh squeezed orange juice, nuts, dried fruits, imported glazed fruits, honey, jellies, and aloe vera products.

VALLE VISTA MALL
2020 S. Expressway 83, intersection of US 77 and 83
425-8374
W

Anchored by Beall's, Dillard's, Penney's, and Sears, this one-story mall contains about 70 other shops, fast food restaurants, a cafeteria, and a 3-screen cinema.

SIDE TRIPS

LAGUNA ATASCOSA NATIONAL WILDLIFE REFUGE
Take FM 106 east approximately 25 miles until it dead-ends, then north (left) about two miles to park headquarters
748-3607
Open seven days dawn to dusk
Free
W Variable

This 45,000-acre coastline sanctuary lies on the Laguna Madre behind Padre Island. It is the southernmost refuge in the United States on what's called the Great Central Flyway along which waterfowl and other birds migrate annually between Canada and the Gulf. It is also the largest parcel of land in the Rio Grande Valley preserved for native plants and animals. Its name in Spanish means "muddy lagoon." More than 300 species of birds have been recorded here. The refuge visitor center, located near the entrance, is open daily from 10-4 from October through April; on weekends only September and May. It is closed June through August. Bayside and lakeside tour roads provide ample opportunities for wildlife observation and photography. These are open daily from 7 to 7 year round. There are also walking trails. For information contact: Refuge Manager, P.O. Box 450, Rio Hondo 78583.

ANNUAL EVENTS

April

RIOFEST
Fair Park, Valley Fair Blvd.
425-2705
Three day weekend in mid-April
$2 admission
W Variable

This is a cultural arts festival featuring artists and artisans and almost continuous musical entertainment set up in a tent city. In the "Art in Action" area you can witness the evolution of art from mind to creation. A celebrity guest star performs during at least one evening's entertainment.

November

HARLINGEN GO-KART GRAND PRIX
Fair Park, off Valley Park Blvd. and Wichita
423-5440 (Chamber of Commerce)
Usually second Saturday and Sunday in November
Free
W Variable

If you think of go-kart racing as a little kids' sport played with toys consider that the carts in this competition reach speeds of over 100 mph. How'd you like to drive at that speed while sitting in a seat that clears the ground by less than an inch? All the speed and fun — and some of the danger — of big time racing is here, just scaled down to an easy size to watch.

RESTAURANTS

($ = under $7, $$ = $7 to $17, $$$ = $17 to $25, $$$$ = over $25 for one person excluding drinks, tax, and tip.)

LONE STAR
Palm Blvd, one mile east of US 83
423-8002
Lunch and dinner seven days
$-$$
AE, MC, V
W

Barbecue is the name of the game here and the mesquite-smoked offerings include ribs, brisket, and chicken. And if someone in your party doesn't like barbecue, the menu also has a few seafood and Tex-Mex items. Bar.

MAMACITA'S
521 S. Sunshine Strip (US 77 Bus)
421-2561
Lunch and dinner seven days
$-$$
Cr.
W
Children's plates

The house specialties include Mexican style ribs grilled over mesquite, *tortilla* soup, salads served in edible *tortilla* shells, and sizzling *fajitas*. The menu also features special variety dishes for parties of two, three, or four. Bar.

MESQUITE TREE
803 S. Sunshine Strip (US 77 Bus)
425-3542
Lunch seven days, dinner Monday–Saturday
$-$$
Cr.
W

They seem to have a little-bit-of-everything on the menu — ribs, brisket, chicken, *fajitas* — most cooked over mesquite. They also have what looks like a mile-long soup and salad bar. Lounge.

VANNIE TILDEN BAKERY
203 E. Harrison at S. 2nd (Downtown)
423-4602
Breakfast and lunch only Monday–Saturday, Closed Sunday
$
No Cr.
W

As soon as you walk in you're face-to-face with temptation in the form of pastry delights on display in an old wooden case. You can give into temptation and fill up on pastries and coffee or have a regular full breakfast or breakfast tacos. For lunch there are soups, salads, sandwiches, chili, chicken 'n' dumpling, plus daily specials. They've been in business since 1930.

ACCOMMODATIONS

($ = Under $45, $$ = $46-$60, $$$ = $61-$80, $$$$ = $81-$100, $$$$$ = Over $100)
Room Tax 13 percent

BEST WESTERN HARLINGEN INN
W. Expresssway 83 at Stuart Place Rd.
425-7070 or 800-528-1234
$-$$
W + one room
No-smoking rooms

This two-story Best Western has 102 units that include one suite ($$$$) and 20 no-smoking rooms. Children under 12 stay free in room with parents. Weekend rates. Cable TV and VCR rentals. Room phones (local calls free). No pets. Restaurant, room service, lounge open Monday-Saturday with entertainment Wednesday-Saturday. Outdoor heated pool. Free airport transportation. Same-day dry cleaning.

HOLIDAY INN
1901 W. Tyler at junction of US 77 and 83
425-1810 or 800-HOLIDAY (800-465-4329)
$$-$$$
W + one room
No-smoking rooms

The two-story Holiday Inn has 148 units that include six suites ($$$) and 15 no-smoking rooms. Children under 18 stay free in room with parents. Package plans available, senior discount, and weekend rates. Satellite TV with Showtime and pay channel, VCR rentals. Room phones (local calls free). Pets OK. Restaurant, room service, lounge open seven nights with entertainment Monday-Saturday. Outdoor heated pool. Guest memberships available in health club. Free airport transportation. Self-service laundry and same-day dry cleaning.

LA QUINTA MOTOR INN
1002 S. Expressway 83 at M St. exit
428-6888 or 800-531-5900
$
W + four rooms
No-smoking rooms

The two-story La Quinta has 130 rooms that include 39 no-smoking. Children under 18 stay free in room with parents. Senior discount. Cable TV with Showtime and pay channel. Room phones (local calls free). Small pets OK. Restaurant adjacent. Outdoor pool, guest memberships available in health club. Free airport transportation. Free coffee in lobby. Self-service laundry and same-day dry cleaning.

LAREDO

WEBB COUNTY SEAT ★ 128,000 ★ (512)

Laredo was one of the first settlements in Texas not established as a mission or a *presidio* (fort). It was settled in 1755 by three families lead by Don Tomas Sanchez de la Barrera y Gallardo, an officer in the Royal Army of Spain. He named it for the city of the same name in Spain. The original site was on the river near what is now St. Augustin Plaza.

By 1836, after the successful revolutions in Mexico and Texas, a census showed there were 2,000 citizens in Laredo and ranching and farming were thriving. During the next ten years Laredo was virtually the capital of a no-man's land. Mexico contended that the boundary with the new Republic of Texas was the Nueces River while the Texans claimed it was the Rio Grande. In 1840, some of the Mexican citizens in the disputed area, charging that the government in Mexico City neglected them, formed a coalition of three northern Mexican states and southwest Texas and set up an independent Republic of the Rio Grande with Laredo as the capital. This rebellion lasted 283 tumultuous days before it was crushed by the Mexican Army. During that time the flag of the short-lived republic flew over Laredo, giving it the distinction of having seven flags fly over it while the rest of Texas had only six.

The boundary dispute was settled by the Mexican War that set the Rio Grande as the border between the United States and Mexico. After that war many Laredoans moved to the section of the city south of the river to preserve their Mexican citizenship and renamed it Nuevo Laredo. This is now the larger of the sister cities with a population of well over a quarter of a million.

Not one, but two railroads came to Laredo in the early 1880s. One, the Texas Mexican from Corpus Christi, made it even though two of the railroad's prospective investors were robbed and tied to trees by highwaymen. The other, the International and Great Northern, one of Jay Gould's holdings, came down from San Antonio. These were linked to the National Lines from Mexico and the ensuing prosperity turned the sleepy town into the "Gateway to Mexico" and a center of international freight traffic.

One of the bloodiest political battles in the history of the West was fought in Laredo in 1886. After winning an election, one of the contending factions, called the *Botas* (boots), decided to stage a mock funeral of their opponents, the *Huaraches* (sandals). A shootout resulted, which included the firing of what was formerly a ceremonial cannon. Seventeen Laredoans were killed and troops from nearby Fort McIntosh had to be brought in to halt the carnage. As things worked out, the *Botas* and the *Huaraches* patched up their differences after this and formed the Independent Club that remained a dominant force in local politics until the 1970s.

Don Tomas, the city's founder, served as its leader almost continuously from its beginning in 1755 until he resigned as mayor in 1792, at the age of eighty-two. A son, Santiago Sanchez, served several terms, and through the years, more than half a dozen of Don Tomas' descendants held that post including Albert Martin, a direct sixth generation descendant who was elected mayor in 1926 and served in that post for fourteen years. Then in 1954, a nephew and a seventh generation descendant, J. C. Martin, Jr. was elected to that office.

The city's status as the "Gateway to Mexico" was reinforced in 1954 when the Pan American Highway was completed to Nuevo Laredo providing dependable access by road to the major cities of northern Mexico as well as Mexico City.

Today, the diversified economy of Laredo is based on import/export businesses, cattle raising, farming (Bermuda onions are a specialty crop), manufacturing, tourism, and oil and gas production. Nuevo Laredo's principal source of income is the import/export industry. It is the largest port of entry on the Mexico-United States border and tariff and customs collections are larger than any other customs office in the Republic of Mexico. This trade often causes traffic congestion on both sides of the river and the bridges. To alleviate this, a new bridge has been built at Columbia, Mexico, northwest of the city that should draw off some of the commercial traffic.

Most of the residents of the sister cities of Laredo and Nuevo Laredo maintain that they live in one city that just happens to exist on both sides of an international border, a city they often refer to as *Los Dos Laredos* (The Two Laredos).

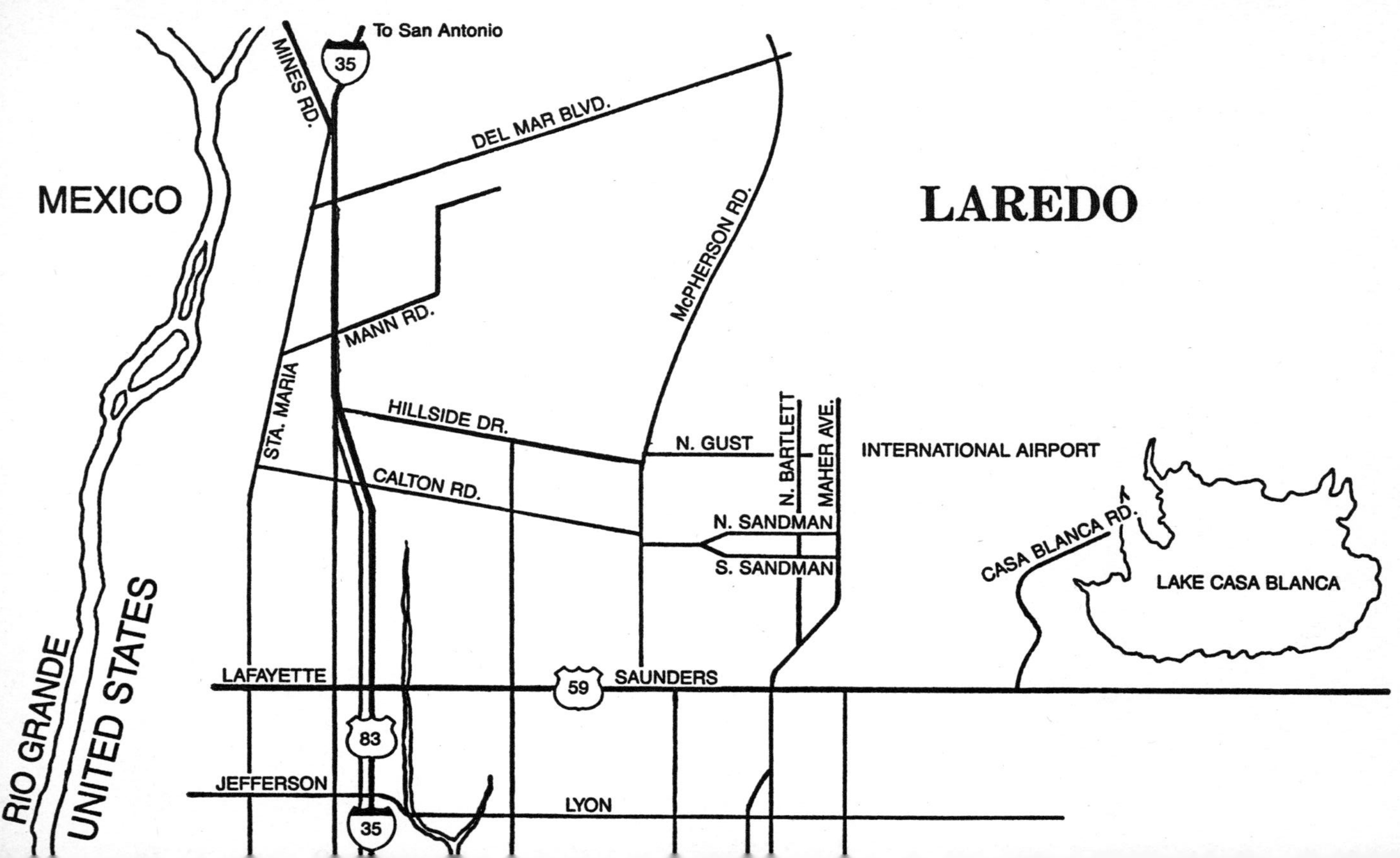
To San Antonio
35
MINES RD.
DEL MAR BLVD.
MEXICO
LAREDO
McPHERSON RD.
MANN RD.
STA. MARIA
HILLSIDE DR.
N. GUST
N. BARTLETT
MAHER AVE.
INTERNATIONAL AIRPORT
CALTON RD.
N. SANDMAN
S. SANDMAN
CASA BLANCA RD.
LAKE CASA BLANCA
RIO GRANDE
UNITED STATES
LAFAYETTE
59
SAUNDERS
83
JEFFERSON
LYON
35

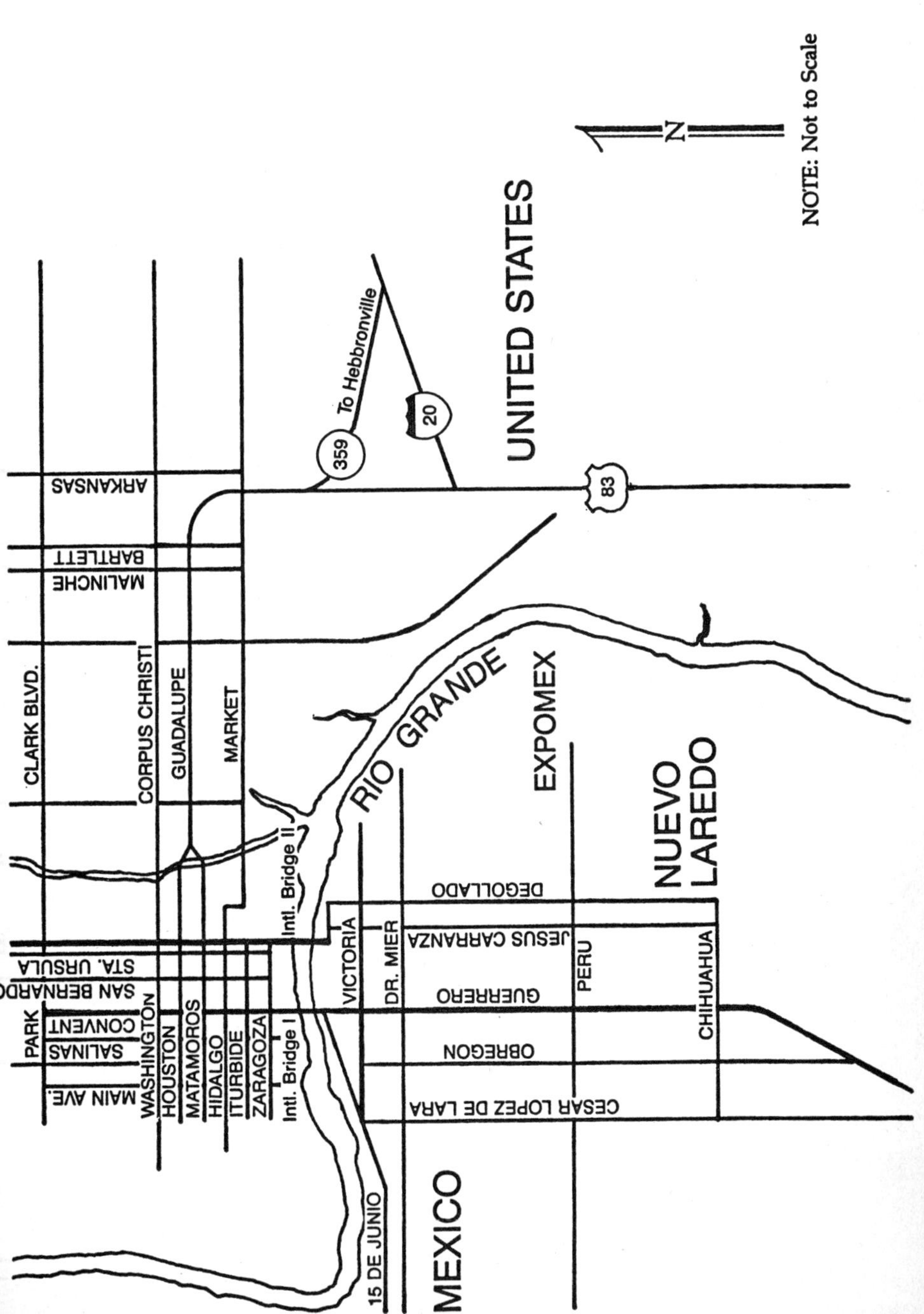
NOTE: Not to Scale
N
UNITED STATES
To Hebbronville
359
20
83
ARKANSAS
BARTLETT
MALINCHE
CLARK BLVD.
CORPUS CHRISTI
GUADALUPE
MARKET
RIO GRANDE
EXPOMEX
NUEVO LAREDO
Intl. Bridge II
Intl. Bridge I
DEGOLLADO
JESUS CARRANZA
GUERRERO
OBREGON
CESAR LOPEZ DE LARA
VICTORIA
DR. MIER
PERU
CHIHUAHUA
STA. URSULA
SAN BERNARDO
PARK
CONVENT
SALINAS
MAIN AVE.
WASHINGTON
HOUSTON
MATAMOROS
HIDALGO
ITURBIDE
ZARAGOZA
15 DE JUNIO
MEXICO

TOURIST SERVICES

LAREDO CONVENTION AND VISITORS BUREAU
2310 San Bernardo at Laredo Civic Center (P.O. Box 790, 78042)
722-9895 or 800-292-2122
W

In addition to general information on Laredo and Nuevo Laredo, you can also get border crossing tips and a brochure on a self-conducted walking tour of the historic district.

OLE' TOURS
Family Gardens Inn, 5830 San Bernardo (P.O. Box 43, 78042)
726-4290

Daily tours of Nuevo Laredo are run morning and afternoon Monday through Saturday and Sunday morning. The tour lasts about 4½ hours and costs about $11 (children half price). Also offered are bullfight and nightclub tours, day or overnight trips to Monterrey, Mexico, and train tours on Mexican National Railway to several Mexican cities.

TEXAS TRAVEL INFORMATION CENTER
I-35 about six miles north
722-8119
Open seven days 8–5
Free
W +

One of 12 roadside visitor centers operated by the Texas Department of Highways and Public Transportation on key highways entering the state. Bilingual travel counselors can provide a wealth of free information, official highway maps, and tons of other travel literature on the Laredo area and the rest of Texas. Located on the north-bound side of I-35. For southbound visitors, there is a parking lot off I-35 with a walkway over the highway to the center.

WEBB COUNTY HERITAGE FOUNDATION WALKING TOURS
727-0977 or 724-7346
$2
By appointment only

These are one-hour walking tours of Laredo's historic district. Tours can be tailored for groups.

GET-ACQUAINTED DRIVING TOUR

Start at the Laredo Convention and Visitors Bureau at the Civic Center, 2310 San Bernardo, where you can pick up a map of the city and plan your route. *Drive south on San Bernardo.* At about an eighth of a mile you'll pass Bruni Plaza and the city library. A block past this, *turn left on Victoria* then *right onto Santa Ursala,* the southbound I-35 access road. Stay to the right and follow Santa Ursala to the end and *turn right on Zaragoza*. This is the **San Augustin Historical District**. On your right will be the **San Augustin Church** built in 1872 and opposite it the **Ortiz House** (915 Zaragoza) that was built in stages between the late 1700s and 1870. This will bring you into San Augustin Plaza that was the center of the original Spanish town and was also the scene of a bloody shoot-out between the rival political groups, the *Botas* (Boots) and *Huaraches* (Sandals), in 1886 that left seventeen dead. (Be careful here, the traffic becomes two way around the plaza.) On your left, tucked in between the buildings of the **La Posada Hotel** (See Accommodations), is a small building built in 1830 that was once the **Capitol Building of the Republic of Rio Grande** and is now a museum dedicated to the history of that short-lived Republic (See Museums). Just past the La Posada Hotel, if you look to your left at Convent Street, is **International Bridge #1** that leads to Avenida Guerrero, a main shopping street in Nuevo Laredo.

Go four more blocks and *turn right on Davis*. Go three blocks to *Lincoln and turn right again*. This reverses your direction and you'll be going east again. There are lots of signs in Spanish along here because this is a prime shopping area for the Mexicans who come over from Nuevo Laredo. Go past the square containing the old city hall — now converted into a restaurant and shops and called the *Mercado* — and *turn left on San Augustin*. The grocery store on the corner of San Augustin and Hidalgo has been a grocery most of the time since the building was constructed in 1875.

Continue on to *Houston and turn left*. On your right is the **County Courthouse**, built in 1909 by noted Texas architect Alfred Giles, and on your left the **Courthouse Annex** that was built in 1916 as the exclusive Latin American Club where Laredo gentlemen met to bowl, shoot billiards, and play dominos and chess. Just past this, on your right is the new **City Hall**. At the corner of Houston and Salinas is the old **Hamilton Hotel**, the original wing of which was built in 1892 the remainder completed at turn of the century. Across from the hotel are the **Federal Building** and **Post Office. St. Peter's Church**, at Houston and Santa Maria, was built in 1896 as Laredo's second Catholic church and the first for English speakers. What was the **First Baptist Church** in the city, built in 1901, is at Houston and Main.

Go two more blocks on Houston and *turn right on Santa Rita*. The Classical Revival style house on the corner on your right is the **Russell House**, built in 1901 and on the corner on your left is the **Richter House** built in 1908.

Go two blocks to *Washington and turn left*. Follow this street over the bridge over the railroad tracks to the joint campus of **Laredo Junior College** and **Laredo State University** (See Colleges and Universities). Continue on the same street. Note the 15 mph speed limit on campus. Some of the old buildings along here were part of the old Fort McIntosh. Some were officers' quarters and others were warehouses. *At the "T" turn left* and go on to the **Nuevo Santander Museum Complex** (See Museums). The museum is open Monday-Friday 9-4 and Sunday 1-5 but visitors must go to the old Fort Chapel first. If you want to explore the college, drive around and work your way back to the Washington St. exit. Otherwise, just swing around in the museum parking lot and *go back the way you came.*

A little way down Washington, the two-way ends and you are *forced to make a right.* Go one block to *Victoria, then left. Continue on to I-35.* If you turned right you'd go over **International Bridge #2** to Nuevo Laredo. But we'll *turn left* and take the highway going north. After about a mile and a half you'll pass the exit to US 59. This is the turnoff if you wanted to go to **LIFE Downs** (See Sports and Activities) or **Lake Casa Blanca** (See Other Points of Interest). Another two miles along I-35 you'll see **Mall del Norte** (See Shopping) on your right. Just past this is the *Mann Rd. exit where you'll turn off.*

Follow Mann Rd. east. Continue on it when it turns left and becomes Spring Rd. About a block down on the right is the entrance to **Regency Park,** one of the highest-priced housing areas in Laredo. If you like to look at expensive homes, loop through the streets of this area and then *work your way back* to Spring Rd., Mann Rd. and I-35. *Go under I-35 and turn left* on the access road which is San Bernardo. After a short way this becomes motel row. If your motel is on this stretch, you might as well end your tour here, because there are no major sights between here and the Civic Center. Or, if you want to complete the loop back to your starting point, just continue down San Bernardo to the Convention and Visitors Bureau where this get-acquainted tour officially ends.

MUSEUMS

MUSEUM OF THE REPUBLIC OF THE RIO GRANDE
1003 Zaragoza, by the La Posada Hotel on San Augustin Plaza
727-3480
Tuesday–Sunday 10–5, closed Monday
Free
W
Limited free parking across street in San Augustin Church lot on weekends, pay on weekdays

By 1840, northern Mexico had become the center for opposition to the centralist government in Mexico City that paid little attention to this remote area and failed to protect the settlers from marauding Indians. In January 1840, the settlers in three northern states of Mexico banded together in Laredo and formed The Republic of the Rio Grande. Their capitol was this small rock building. About 300 Texans, from the newly established Republic of Texas, joined the revolutionary army of this new republic. The Mexican forces moved to crush the revolutionaries and several months of bitter battles followed in which first one side and then the other was victorious. It all ended on November 6, 1840 when the revolutionaries were granted amnesty and surrendered. The Republic of the Rio Grande had lasted 283 days and almost everything that is preserved from it is in this building. The original structure, consisting of three rooms decorated as a period house, was built in 1834. The large display room at the front of the building was added in 1860. Exhibits include furniture, weapons, and clothing as well as documents and artifacts relating to the Republic. The Republic also gave Laredo a seventh flag, over and above the six normally considered to have flown over the rest of Texas.

NUEVO SANTANDER MUSEUM
Laredo Junior College, west end of Washington St.
721-5321 Ext 321
Monday–Thursday 9–4, Friday 9–noon, Sunday 1–5, closed Saturday
Free
W

Situated in several restored buildings of old Fort McIntosh, this museum is named after the original Spanish province in which Laredo was established in 1755. The main museum in the old Fort Chapel contains exhibits on the cultural history of the region. The chapel is the only building regularly open. If you want to visit any other museum buildings you must go here to pick up a tour guide. The other buildings are The Guardhouse, which houses exhibits on military history with emphasis on Fort McIntosh, and The Commissary and Commissary Warehouse (both located several blocks away), which house a small art museum and a small science and technology collection.

HISTORIC PLACES

FORT McINTOSH
Laredo Junior College, west end of Washington St.
W Variable

Established in 1849, Fort McIntosh anchored the center of the chain of forts along the border that ran from Fort Brown at the mouth of the Rio Grande to Fort Bliss in El Paso. Phillip Sheridan, who later achieved fame in the Civil War, was stationed here in 1854, and Lieutenant Colonel Robert E. Lee visited the fort in 1860 while commanding the Department of Texas. During the Civil War, the post was occupied by Confederate troops who protected the cotton routes to Mexico after the Union forces took control of the south Texas coast from Corpus Christi to Brownsville. In 1910, one of the first airfields in the United States was established here. The fort was closed in 1947. Today most of the remaining old fort buildings, including former officers' quarters and the one remaining barracks building, are used by Laredo Junior College.

SAN AUGUSTIN CHURCH
East side of San Augustin Plaza
W

The oldest church in Laredo was built in 1872 on the site of two previous churches.

OTHER HISTORIC BUILDINGS

Most of the nineteenth-century buildings are clustered in the downtown area. These include the *Ortiz House*, 915 Zaragoza, various parts of the structure date from the late 1700s to the 1870s; the *Bruni-Cantu* Building, 1101 Zaragoza, built in 1884 (now The Tack Room of the La Posada Hotel); *Leyendecker House,* 204 Flores, built in 1870; *Southern Hotel,* 1216 Matamoros, built in 1890; *Orfila House,* 1701 Matamoros, built in 1895; and the *McKnight House,* 1503 Farragut, built in 1883.

OTHER POINTS OF INTEREST

CASA BLANCA PARK AND LAKE CASA BLANCA
Go east on US 59 to turn-off on left just past the airport
Open daylight hours for day use, at all times for campers
W + But not all areas

This park contains a 1600-acre lake and offers facilities for boating, boat rentals, fishing, picnicking, swimming, water skiing, and RV camping (no hook-ups). The park also includes a **Natural Science Center** and the **Casa Blanca Golf Course** (See Sports and Activities). Work has started on long-range plans to upgrade this to a state park.

NUEVO LAREDO
Take I-35 south across International Bridge #2 or Convent St. south across International Bridge #1
To call from Laredo, dial 011-52871 plus the five-digit local number

This bustling city of more than a quarter of a million offers bargain shopping, inexpensive dining, some interesting nightclubs, professional baseball and occasional bullfighting. Since the downtown areas of each city come right up to the bridges, the simplest way to go over is to walk. You can park your car in the free lots along the river below Riverdrive Mall (off Zaragoza St.) and walk across Bridge #1 at Convent St. that connects with Avenida Guerrero, a major shopping street in Nuevo Laredo. You can also drive over either bridge, but first be sure your insurance covers your car in Mexico (See Crossing into Mexico in the Introduction) and realize that parking is often difficult in downtown Nuevo Laredo. The **Nuevo Laredo Chamber of Commerce** at 810 Guerrero (2-0399 or 2-7707) usually has someone who speaks English on duty.

SPORTS AND ACTIVITIES

Baseball

MEXICAN LEAGUE
West Martin Field, 2200 Santa Maria in Laredo (722-8143) and Fairgrounds Stadium in Nuevo Laredo (2-1331)
Admission
W

The professional Mexican League team, *Tecolotes de los Dos Laredos,* plays on both sides of the border during the regular season.

Bullfighting

LA FIESTA BULLRING
Nuevo Laredo, on Monterrey Highway just past turn-off to airport
722-9895 (Laredo Chamber of Commerce)
Admission $4–$10 depending on sunny or shady side and fame of matadors
W Variable

There is no regular schedule here, but the season usually starts on Washington's birthday and lasts through September with bullfights most often held on major American holidays. There are also two mini-bullrings in Nuevo Laredo. One is at 125 Washington St. and the other at Bolivar and Juarez adjacent to the Don Lauro Restaurant. Both are used primarily for amateur bullfights.

Golf

CASA BLANCA GOLF COURSE
Casa Blanca Lake Rd., off US 59 just east of airport
727-9218
Open Tuesday–Sunday

Eighteen-hole course. Green fees: weekdays $6, weekends and holidays $8.

Horse Racing

LIFE DOWNS
Laredo, US 59 east of airport and Lake Casa Blanca
722-5662
Admission
W Variable

This small track, used mostly for quarter horse races, is on the Laredo International Fair and Exposition (L.I.F.E.) grounds.

NUEVO LAREDO TURF CLUB
Bravo and Ocampo, Plaza Juarez (turn left immediately after crossing Bridge #1 and go one block)
2-3802
Open seven days
W Variable
Customer parking in rear

It's not plush — the furnishings are mostly school-type tables for the no-nonsense players to work out bets — but they offer wagering on races at major U.S. and Mexican tracks. Bar.

COLLEGES AND UNIVERSITIES

LAREDO JUNIOR COLLEGE
West end of Washington St.

721-5140 (Public Information)
W Variable

This community college offers occupational/technical and academic programs to about 4,000 students on its 196-acre campus. A number of the older buildings on campus are the remains of **Fort McIntosh**. Visitors are welcome to sports events, opera workshops, and other music, dance, and theater productions. The **Nuevo Santander Museum Complex** is on campus (See Museums).

LAREDO STATE UNIVERSITY
West end of Washington St. (co-located with Laredo Junior College)
722-8001
W Variable

About half the 1,100 students enrolled in this upper-level university are in undergraduate programs and about half in graduate programs including one leading to a M.B.A. in International Trade. The school is now part of the Texas A&M System.

PERFORMING ARTS

CIVIC CENTER
2400 San Bernardo
722-8143
Admission depends on event
W +

Events here include concerts by C&W, Latin, and other groups; a music/dance series that brings in touring artists; and performances by the Laredo Philharmonic and the Laredo Junior College Civic Symphony.

LAREDO LITTLE THEATRE
602 Thomas
723-1342
Admission $5–$6
W

The theater group here puts on about four productions in its regular season that runs from fall through spring and a summer theater for children.

LAREDO PHILHARMONIC ORCHESTRA
727-8886

A professional orchestra that plays four or five concerts a year during the fall to spring season. Most performances are at the Civic Center. It also sponsors a chamber music series and a youth symphony.

SHOPPING

(To call Nuevo Laredo from Laredo, dial 011-52871 plus the five-digit local number.)

BLUE GATE ANTIQUES
719 Corpus Christi at Logan
727-4127
W

The stock here includes china, crystal, silver, oriental porcelains, jewelry, and some early American furniture.

DEUTSCH'S
Nuevo Laredo, 320 Guerrero
2-2066
W

This jewelry store is best known for its custom-made gold and silver jewelry. Unlike most Nuevo Laredo tourist area shops that seem to be always open, Deutsch's has limited hours just four or five days a week. So, if you're interested in buying, you may have to make an appointment.

FOSTER'S
1004 Hillside, behind Mall del Norte
723-3653
W

Prized locally for its quality merchandise and service, Foster's offers a variety that includes home furnishings and accessories, china, cookware, brass fittings, wallpaper, fabrics, and linens.

LA CASA DEL CAFE
Nuevo Laredo, Matamoros and Hidalgo
W

The thing to remember here is that a kilo is about 2.2 pounds. So when you buy a kilo of coffee beans or fresh ground coffee for about $5, you're getting a bargain. Even if you don't buy anything, a brief stop at this corner shop is worth it just for the aroma.

MALL DEL NORTE
5300 I-35 just north of Calton
724-8191
W

In addition to the anchor stores of Beall's, Dillard's, Sears, and Wards, this mall contains more than 125 other shops (including the well-known Joe Brand men's store), restaurants, and a 4-screen cinema. It is unique among malls in that it also houses a 5,000 sq. ft. Catholic church.

MARTI'S
Nuevo Laredo, 2933 Victoria at Guerrero
2-3137
W Variable

Probably the best-known shop in Nuevo Laredo, if not along the whole Mexican border, Marti's offers a wide assortment of hand-picked items that includes unique designer clothes, jewelry, perfumes, antique and custom furniture, crystal, pottery, tableware, woven rugs and blankets, and tapestries. There is also an art gallery that features Mexican fine art including the colorful *papier-mache* animal creations of Sergio Bustamante and the surrealistic sculptures of Pedro Friedeberg. Everything is of the highest quality — with prices to match.

NUEVO MERCADO DE LA REFORMA
Nuevo Laredo, Guerrero at Belden
W (ground floor only)

This is called the New Market because it replaced the old one that was burned down when someone accidently tossed a match into a fireworks shop. The one-block, two-story market is a collection of shops selling souvenirs and tourist doodads, clothing, jewelry, toys, leather goods, baskets, candy, and a wide variety of other items. Bargain hunting here can be fun — the merchants expect you to haggle on price — and the careful shopper will probably find some treasures hidden among the junk.

OSCAR'S ANTIQUES
1002 Guadalupe at Hendricks
723-0765
W

American, European, and Mexican furniture are featured here. There are also Pre-Columbian artifacts and Spanish Colonial architectural columns and doors.

RAFAEL DE MEXICO
Nuevo Laredo, 3902 Reforma (Mexico Hwy 85) near the El Rio Motor Hotel
4-2588
W

You'll find a wide variety of gifts, arts and crafts here, even Christmas tree ornaments in season, but Rafael's is best known as a builder of custom-made furniture. They make everything from custom-designed boxes to dining room sets to elaborate hand-carved mantels in the workshop in the building.

RIVERDRIVE MALL
1600 Water, just west of International Bridge #1
724-8241
W Variable

A small, two-level mall with more than 50 stores and fast food places anchored by Penney's and Weiners. Its free 1,600 space parking area is a good place to park if walking across the bridge. It also has a studio for a local TV news program that you can watch through a large picture window.

SIDE TRIPS

MEXICAN NATIONAL RAILWAYS EXPRESS TO MEXICO CITY

First-class train travel has been reborn in Mexico. A new train, called the *Regiomontano*, now offers daily runs between Nuevo Laredo and Mexico City with stops in Monterrey, Saltillo, and San Luis Potosi. The full-service train is equipped with first class coach, club, dining, and Pullman cars. All tickets include meals on the train, covered 24-hour secured parking in Laredo, transfers from Laredo to the Nuevo Laredo Train Depot, and tourist card processing. (To obtain a tourist card one of the following is required: valid passport, copy of birth certificate, or voter's registration card.) Fares range from about $45 roundtrip to Monterrey to about $140 roundtrip by Pullman to Mexico City. Reservations are suggested at least 72 hours in advance for first class coach seats and 15 days in advance for Pullman accommodations. Tickets and a brochure listing destinations, fares, schedules, and packages for this and other Mexican National Railway full-service trains are available from Mexico By Rail, 1016 Grant, across from the La Posada Hotel (P.O. Box 3508, 78044-3508) (727-3814 or 800-228-3225).

ANNUAL EVENTS

January

WINTER TEXAN FESTIVAL
Various locations in city
722-9895 or 800-292-2122 (Convention and Visitors Bureau)
Friday–Sunday late in January
Free
W Variable

This celebration is a thank you to the many visitors from the north who winter in warm Laredo, but everyone is welcome. Activities include a fishing derby, horseshoe tossing tournament, folk art displays, a radio controlled aircraft show at the airport with miniature planes flown by nationally known operators, an antique car exhibit, square dance, and a bullfight in Nuevo Laredo on Sunday.

February

GEORGE WASHINGTON'S BIRTHDAY CELEBRATION
Various locations in Laredo and Nuevo Laredo
722-9895 or 800-292-2122 (Convention and Visitors Bureau)
Ten days in mid-February
Admission to some events
W Variable

It's doubtful that our First President ever heard of Laredo, but that doesn't stop the people here from celebrating his birthday in a grand manner — something they've been doing since 1898. Among the many activities are parades, pageants, fireworks, concerts and dances, entertainment by Mexican celebrities, sports contests, and a carnival. One highlight is the Jalapeno Festival that includes a contest to see who can eat the most of what locals call "border grapes," and a "Some Like It Hot" recipe contest.

March

LAREDO INTERNATIONAL FAIR AND EXPOSITION
LIFE Fairgrounds, US 59 east of airport and Lake Casa Blanca
722-5662
Five days in second week in March
General Admission $1 per car, plus admission to special events
W Variable

Livestock exhibits and judging, arts and crafts show, food and other contests, chili cook-off, dance, rodeo, and quarter horse racing are all part of the festivities.

July

BORDERFEST
Laredo Civic Center, 2310 San Bernardo
722-9895 or 800-292-2122 (Convention and Visitors Bureau)
Three-day weekend around Fourth of July
Admission to some events
W with assistance

Patterned after the Texas Folklife Festival, this festival not only celebrates the Fourth of July, but also Laredo's heritage under seven flags and seven cultures. Starting with a parade on Friday, there is almost continuous entertainment, an arts and crafts show, food booths, mock shoot-outs, and folk singing and dancing.

September

TAMAULIPAS REGIONAL FAIR AND EXPOSITION
Nuevo Laredo, Viveros Park, take Guerrero south from International Bridge #1 to Calle Peru, then left (east) to park
4-1200 or 4-1253 or in Laredo 722-9895 or 800-292-2122 (Laredo Convention and Visitors Bureau)
Two weeks around Mexican Independence Day, September 16
Admission
Secured parking available

The popular name for this annual fair is EXPOMEX. Comparable to a Texas county fair, it features livestock shows, government and commercial exhibits, arts and crafts booths, a midway, and entertainment that ranges from cockfights to shows put on by Mexican entertainment celebrities. In recognition of its north-of-the-border friends, EXPOMEX offers a special Laredo Day, San Antonio Day, and Texas Day.

RESTAURANTS

($ = under $7, $$ = $7 to $17, $$$ = $17 to $25, $$$$ = over $25 for one person excluding drinks, tax, and tip.)
(To call Nuevo Laredo from Laredo, dial 011-52871 plus the five-digit local number.)

Dinner for Two

TACK ROOM
1000 Zaragoza (La Posada Hotel, San Augustin Plaza)
722-1701
Dinner only Monday–Saturday. Closed Sunday
$$$-$$$$
Cr.

This cozy, upstairs restaurant, with its racing stable motif, is housed in a charming restoration of a nineteenth-century house that once also served as Laredo's telephone exchange. The menu leans toward beef dishes, like Carpet-Bagger Steak (12 oz broiled sirloin stuffed with oysters and herbs) and Baby Canadian Spare Ribs, but there are also a few seafood selections. If you like *shish kabobs* you can choose from combinations of shrimp, oysters and scallops; chicken breast and *fajitas;* or beef tenderloin, shrimp and chicken breast. These are called the Royal Flaming Daggers and, as you might guess, are delivered to your table flaming on daggers. Piano bar downstairs.

Barbecue

COTULLA-STYLE PIT BAR-B-Q
4502 McPherson, south of Calton Rd.
724-5747
Breakfast and Lunch Tuesday–Sunday, closed Monday
$
MC, V
W
Children's plates

Elsewhere in Texas, *tortillas* filled with a variety of ingredients are known as breakfast tacos, but in Laredo they go by the name *mariaches.* This restaurant offers almost two dozen choices of fillings for this morning favorite and has made it into an all-day best seller. Not far behind in popularity is the pit barbecue, brisket cooked over mesquite coals for hours, and *fajitas.* The menu also offers a wide choice of Mexican entrées and some fried seafood dishes. No-smoking area. Beer.

Italian

FAVORATO'S
1916 San Bernardo
722-9515

Lunch and dinner Tuesday–Sunday. closed Monday
$$-$$$
Cr.
W

Although it has a reputation as one of the better Italian restaurants in Laredo, there is really only a small part of the menu listing Italian entrées such as *Scaloppine al burro* and *Fettucine Favorato*. The rest offers a wide variety of steaks, seafood, and continental cuisine. Bar.

Mexican

EL TIO HUT RESTAURANT
601 E. Calton Rd.
723-5430
Lunch and dinner Monday–Saturday, closed Sunday
$-$$
AE, MC, V
W
Children's plates

Just about all the most popular Tex-Mex dishes are on the menu from *chili con carne* to *mariaches* to *tostadas*. But they put an interesting twist on some of the favorites such as *Fajitas A' La Ray* that serves up the grilled beef skirt in hot tomato sauce, and *Enchiladas Suizo* that are cheese *enchiladas* smothered with a *salsa verde*. Also steaks and diet plates. Bar.

LA PALAPA
Nuevo Laredo, 3301 Reforma (Mexico Hwy 85)
2-9995
Laredo, 5300 San Dario, I-35 northbound access road by Mall Del Norte
727-7115
Lunch and dinner seven days
$-$$
Cr.
W

The name refers to the thatched roofs that top these two restaurants. The menu offers a variety of Mexican entrées, but the specialty is beef and chicken *fajitas* broiled over mesquite that can be bought by the plate or — for a group — by the kilo (2.2 pounds). Bar.

MEXICO TIPICO
Nuevo Laredo, 934 Guerrero
2-1525
Lunch and dinner seven days
$
No Cr.
W
Parking in rear

The charcoal broiler sits in a place of honor in the courtyard patio under a big sombrero, giving testimony that the specialties here are grilled meats, including *cabrito*. They are also known for their small sandwiches, called *tortas*, made from hard Mexican rolls filled with meat and *guacamole* and other fillings. *Mariachis* play nightly. Bar.

VICTORIA 3020
Nuevo Laredo, 3020 Victoria at Matamoros
3-3020
Lunch and dinner seven days
$$-$$$
Cr.
W With assistance

The cuisine in this former town mansion is interior Mexican, often a far-cry from border Tex-Mex. Examples are shrimp in a tequila base sauce and *pollo pibil yucateco*, a spiced chicken breast steamed in a banana leaf and served on rice with a special sauce. There are also a number of mesquite-grilled entrées on the menu including *cabrito* and *tacos al pastor*. Bar.

Oriental

CHINA BO
1015 Matamoros
725-8388
Lunch and dinner seven days
$-$$
AE, MC, V
W
Validated parking across street

If you have taste buds that only come to life in the presence of spicy hot dishes, but are tired of the jalapeno cuisine of Tex-Mex, this simple restaurant offers an intriguing alternative with its Szechuan-style entrées. Its *kung pao* chicken, for example, opens up a whole new world of peppers. For those with milder tastes, the menu offers a variety of less incendiary choices, including American dishes like the ubiquitous chicken-fried steak.

Variety

THE UNICORN RESTAURANT
500 San Augustin
726-9102
Lunch and dinner seven days
$$
Cr.
W

The old City Hall building, now called *The Mercado*, is the site of this bright and airy restaurant that has a menu offering a little bit of everything. There are *enchiladas* and *chalupas* and *Carne Asada,* Egg Plant *Parmagiana,* Chicken *Teriyaki,* Stuffed Flounder Filet and Red Snapper *Veracruzano,* mesquite-broiled steaks, burgers, and diet plates. Large patio. Bar with margaritas available by the pitcher. Other locations at 600 E. Calton (722-7978) and, with a different menu, at 3810 San Bernardo (727-4663).

CLUBS AND BARS

CADILLAC BAR
Nuevo Laredo, Belden and Ocampo
2-0015
Open seven days
No cover
Cr.
W

"Meet you at the Cadillac." This is the restaurant/bar where tourists have met for decades. And they'll probably continue to meet here until it falls down even though the food is not up to that served in many of the restaurants in the area. It's one of those places that every tourist should stop and sip at least one beer — or the Cadillac's famous Ramos gin fizz — just to be able to say "I've been there."

WINERY PUB AND GRILL
Nuevo Laredo, 308 Matamoros
2-0895
Open seven days
No cover
Cr.
W ground floor only

A good place to stop for a cooling margarita in the comfortably dark lounge after a sunny day wandering around the dusty streets of downtown Nuevo Laredo. The upstairs restaurant offers good, if unremarkable, fare.

ACCOMMODATIONS

($ = Under $45, $$ = $46-$60, $$$ = $61-$80, $$$$ = $81-$100, $$$$$ = Over $100)
(To call Nuevo Laredo from Laredo, dial 011-52871 plus the five-digit local number.)
Laredo Room Tax 14 percent

EXECUTIVE HOUSE HOTEL
7060 N. San Bernardo (Del Mar exit off I-35)
724-8221
$
W + three rooms
No-smoking rooms

The two-story Executive House has 137 units including two suites ($$-$$$) and ten no-smoking rooms. Children under 18 stay free in room with parents. Senior discount. Coffeemakers in rooms. Cable TV with HBO. Room phones (local calls free). No pets. Restaurant, room service, lounge open Monday-Saturday with entertainment Tuesday-Saturday. Outdoor pool. Free transportation to airport and bridge. Same-day dry cleaning.

FAMILY GARDENS INN
5830 San Bernardo (Mann Rd. exit off I-35)
723-5300 or 800-292-4053
$-$$
W + one room
No-smoking rooms

This two-story inn has 170 units in two buildings that include 18 suites ($$$$) and 38 no-smoking rooms. Children under 18 stay free in room with parents. Senior discount. Cable and satellite TV with HBO. Room phones (local calls free). Pets OK (kennel-$1 deposit). Restaurant open for lunch and dinner, room service, lounge open Monday-Saturday. Outdoor pool, three outdoor whirlpools, playground. Convenience store. Package store. Free airport transportation. Free coffee, free newspaper, and free breakfast. Self-service laundry and same-day dry cleaning. Microwaves and refrigerators in some rooms. Upstairs rooms in main building have large porches. Seventy rooms in Garden Square building built around indoor garden with waterfall.

HACIENDA MOTOR HOTEL
Nuevo Laredo, 5530 Reforma (Mexico Hwy 85) about eight miles south of Bridge #1
4-4666
$

The Hacienda is a two-story motel with 72 units including two suites ($$$). Children under 10 stay free in room with parents. Cable TV with Showtime. Room phones (local calls free). Fire sprinklers in rooms. No pets. Restaurant, room service, lounge open seven nights. Outdoor pool, lighted tennis court. Same-day dry cleaning.

HOLIDAY INN-CIVIC CENTER
800 Garden St. (US 59 exit off I-35 southbound. Entrance on Santa Ursala, southbound I-35 access road)
727-5800 or 800-HOLIDAY
$$$
W + two rooms
No-smoking rooms

This 14-story Holiday Inn has 200 units that include six suites ($$$$-$$$$$) and 26 no-smoking rooms. Children under 17 stay free in parent's room. Senior discount. Satellite TV with HBO. Room phones (local calls free). Fire sprinklers in rooms. No pets. Restaurant, room service, lounge open seven days with live entertainment Monday-Saturday.

Outdoor pool, outdoor whirlpool, exercise room. Free transportation to airport and bridge. Free coffee in lobby in morning. Self-service laundry and same-day dry cleaning. Gift shop. Free parking in four-story garage. Good view of downtown from upper floors on south side.

LA POSADA HOTEL
1000 Zaragoza at San Augustin Plaza
722-1701 or in Texas 800-292-5659 or outside Texsa 800-531-7156
$$$-$$$$

The two- and four-story La Posada has 227 units that include a 55 suites ($$$$$). Children under 8 stay free in room with parents. Senior discount and package plans available. Cable and satellite TV with HBO and pay channel. Room phones (charge for local calls). No pets. Three restaurants (two dinner only), room service, four bars and lounges with live entertainment in one lounge Tuesday-Saturday. Two outdoor pools, one with swim-up bar. Free transportation to airport, train station, and country club. Guest memberships available in country club. Same-day dry cleaning. Free parking in underground garage. Concierge floor ($$$$$). Part of hotel complex in converted 1916 high school. Next to International Bridge #1.

LA QUINTA MOTOR INN
3600 Santa Ursala (southbound I-35 access road)
722-0511 or 800-531-5900
$$
W + four rooms
No-smoking rooms

The two-story La Quinta has 152 units that include one suite ($$$) and 36 no-smoking rooms. Children under 12 stay free in room with parents. Senior discount. Satellite TV with Showtime. Room phones (local calls free). Pets OK. Restaurant next door. Outdoor swimming pool. Free coffee in lobby and free national news magazine in rooms. Same-day dry cleaning. Electronic card keys.

TRES CAMINOS MOTOR HOTEL
Nuevo Laredo, 2450 Chihuahua
4-9300
$

This two-story motel has 38 units that include two suites ($$). Children under 12 stay free in room with parents. TV, room phones (local calls free). Fire sprinklers in rooms, fire intercom. Pets OK ($20 pet deposit). Restaurant, room service, lounge open seven nights with occasional entertainment. Two outdoor pools. Free newspaper. Self-service laundry and same-day dry-cleaning. Valet parking.

EL RIO MOTEL
Nuevo Laredo, 4402 Avenida Reforma (Mexico Hwy 85), approximately 3.25 miles south of Convent Street International Bridge #1 (P.O. Box

746, Laredo 78041)
4-3666
$-$$

The two-story El Rio has 152 units including two suites ($$$). Children under 12 stay free in room with parents. Package plans available and senior discounts. Cable TV. Room phones (local calls free). Fire intercom system. No pets. Restaurant, room service, lounge open seven nights with occasional entertainment. Two outdoor heated pools. Free coffee in lobby and free cocktails. Self-service laundry and same-day dry cleaning. Valet parking. Day care available.

McALLEN

HIDALGO COUNTY ★ 95,000 ★ (512)

The city is named for an early settler, John McAllen, who came to the area from Scotland in the 1850s when Hidalgo County was just being formed. He and a friend, John Young, settled south of present day McAllen in what is now the town of Hidalgo. Young soon married into a wealthy local family, and when he died, McAllen married his widow in 1862. The county was plagued by bandits and cattle rustlers until the 1890s when Sheriff John Closner established law and order, reportedly without the use of guns. Meanwhile, John McAllen had continued to increase his land holdings and by 1904 owned 80,000 acres. At that time he founded a town he called West McAllen, although no one was really sure what it was west of. In 1907, James Briggs, another land developer, bought 8,000 acres from Sheriff Closner (at $3 an acre) and founded East McAllen. There was not much going on in either town, both were struggling to survive, but still a rivalry grew. East won out when the enterprising members of the newly formed McAllen Businessman's Club installed a horse trough in that town to attract cowboys and ranchers to stop to water their horses and buy supplies. As a result, West McAllen literally dried up and died.

With the rivalry settled, and partly spurred by the arrival of the railroad in 1905, McAllen began growing. By 1911 it had grown large enough to hold an election to decide if it should be incorporated. Just about every male in the proposed town boundaries who was over 21 was allowed to vote — and 45 of them did with a majority for incorporation.

Water again proved a major factor in the city's fortunes when the Rio Bravo Irrigation Company dug canals and soon more than 27,000 acres of land were ready for irrigation. With fertile soil, irrigation, and a mild climate allowing the cultivation of two and sometimes three crops a year, agriculture boomed becoming the number one industry in the area.

But 1916 saw trouble come again. This time it was the spill-over of a series of revolutions and counter-revolutions in Mexico. World War I was underway in Europe and there were rumors that German agents were stirring up the trouble. Soon 12,000 soldiers of the 69th New York Infantry were sent to protect the nearly 1,000 residents of McAllen. Naturally, business boomed with this huge jump in population and the impact of the soldiers' $30-a-month salary on the local economy. (Some wealthy New Yorkers in the 69th, like Cornelius Vanderbilt paid gouging rents of up to $250 a month on the larger houses.) When the border was quiet again, the soldiers left. But by that time the city was set for further growth.

In 1936, McAllen became the first city in the world to try to deliver mail across an international border by rocket. Five mail carrying rockets were launched from each bank of the Rio Grande River. The first rocket from the U.S. side blew up scattering rocket pieces and mail all over the river. The second — designed to fly a mere 1,000 feet — just kept going and going and wound up hitting a street in Reynosa. The other three made it successfully. Three of the five rockets launched from the Mexican side also made it, but the other two blew up. Of the 1,500 pieces of mail launched, 922 made it across the river intact. After that, the project rocketed into oblivion.

Today, in addition to agriculture, which is still number one, McAllen's economy is boosted by the expanding industrial base in the McAllen Foreign Trade Zone and "twin-plant" operations. Another boost comes from the thousands of "Winter Texans" who come down from the mid-West and Canada to avoid the cold winters in "The City of Palms," as it is now called. Among these Winter Texans are a number of nationally recognized square dance callers and round dance cuers who have set up a schedule that offers the chance to dance almost every hour of the day and well into the night, any day of the week (See Sports and Activities), leading McAllen to also lay claim to a new title as "The Square Dance Capital of the World."

About ten miles south of the city is the Mexican border city of Reynosa that is a major industrial and oil refining center with a population estimated to be more than half a million (See Other Points of Interest).

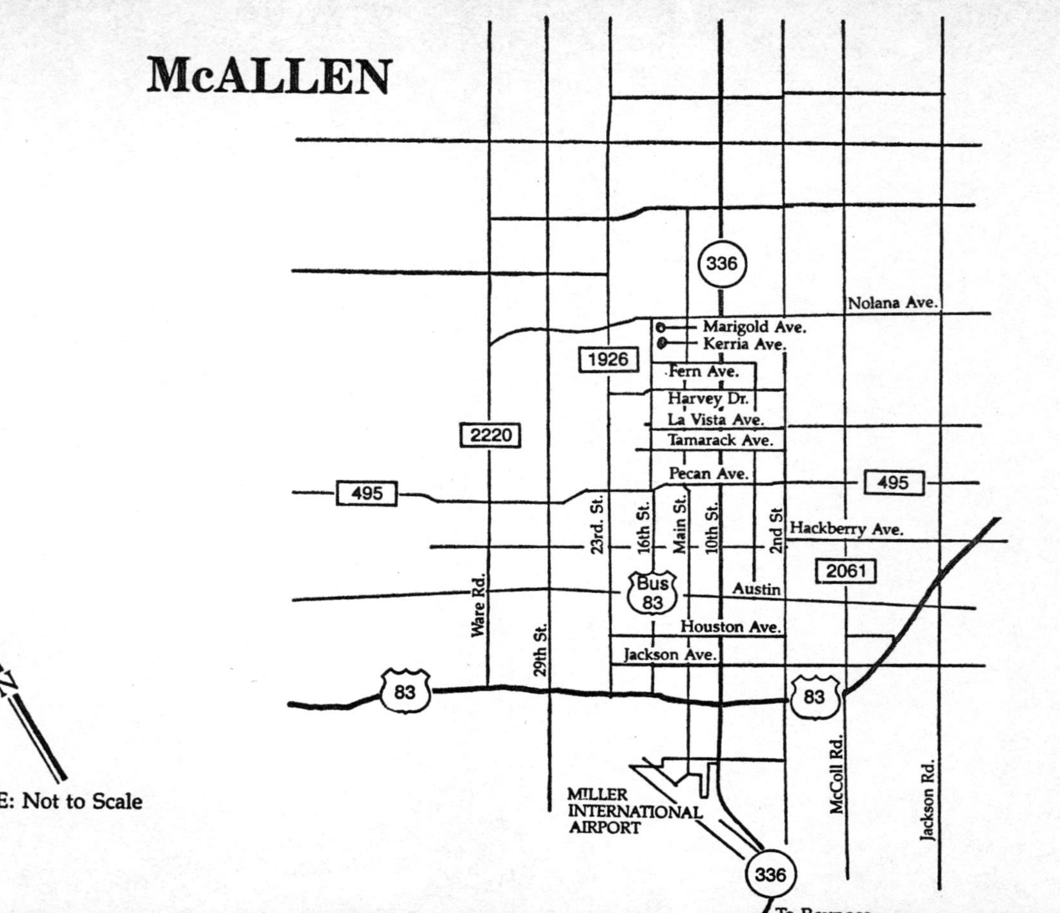
McALLEN
336
Nolana Ave.
Marigold Ave.
Kerria Ave.
1926
Fern Ave.
Harvey Dr.
La Vista Ave.
2220
Tamarack Ave.
Pecan Ave.
495
495
23rd. St.
16th St.
Main St.
10th St.
2nd St
Hackberry Ave.
2061
Bus 83
Austin
Ware Rd.
29th St.
Houston Ave.
Jackson Ave.
83
83
MILLER INTERNATIONAL AIRPORT
McColl Rd.
Jackson Rd.
336
To Reynosa
N
NOTE: Not to Scale

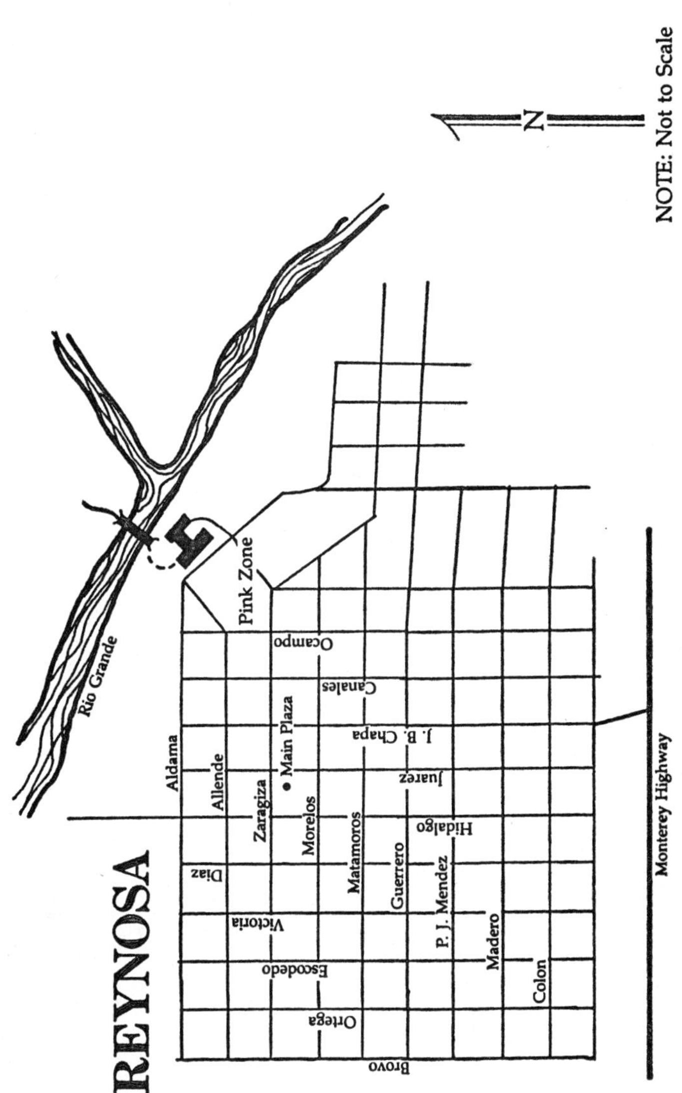
REYNOSA
Rio Grande
Pink Zone
Main Plaza
Aldama
Allende
Zaragiza
Morelos
Matamoros
Guerrero
P. J. Mendez
Madero
Colon
Ocampo
Canales
J. B. Chapa
Juarez
Hidalgo
Diaz
Victoria
Escodedo
Ortega
Brovo
Monterey Highway
N
NOTE: Not to Scale

TOURIST SERVICES

McALLEN CONVENTION AND VISITORS BUREAU
Chamber of Commerce Building, 10 N. Broadway, just north of US 83 Bus (P.O. Box 790, 78502)
682-2871
Monday–Friday 8:30–5
W +

Operates an information center where you can get a free copy of "McAllen Visitors Guide," a brochure providing detailed information on McAllen and nearby cities in the Rio Grande Valley.

MUSEUMS

McALLEN INTERNATIONAL MUSEUM
1900 Nolana at north end of Bicentennial
682-1564
Tuesday–Saturday 9–5, Sunday 1–5. Closed Monday
Free (donations accepted)
W +

The permanent collection, used in rotating exhibits, includes Mexican folk art, masks and textiles, contemporary American and regional prints, and the Caton collection of sixteenth- to nineteenth-century European paintings. There are also exhibits on the natural sciences in the earth science gallery that includes an exhibition of dinosaur tracks. The museum hosts some twenty traveling exhibitions annually and in December holds its annual Christmas Tree Forest exhibit featuring about three dozen decorated trees. Gift shop.

HISTORIC PLACES

OLD HIDALGO COUNTY COURTHOUSE AND JAIL
Bridge St. and Flora, Hidalgo. Take Texas 336 (10th St.) or Loop 115 (23rd St.) approximately ten miles south to Hidalgo

The Courthouse complex was built in 1886 and is listed in the National Register of Historic Places. It served the county until 1908 when the county seat was moved to Edinburg. The jail was the home of the city's first newspaper from 1904 to 1908. Both have been restored as offices by the current owner, a local bank.

OTHER POINTS OF INTEREST

McALLEN BOTANICAL GARDENS AND NATURE CENTER
Approximately 2.5 miles west on US 83 Bus just past Ware Rd.
682-1517 (Parks and Recreation)
Open seven days until dark
Free
W Variable

This twenty-acre park includes a sunken garden graced by waterfalls and ducks, a cactus garden, a main garden featuring many of the trees indigenous to Texas, and nature trails. Register at the main house by the parking lot before touring.

REYNOSA
Take Texas 336 (10th St.) or Loop 115 (23rd St.) south about ten miles to the International Bridge
To call dial 011-52892 plus the five-digit local number.

Founded in 1749, Reynosa is now a city of more than half a million people that offers visitors bargain shopping, inexpensive dining, some interesting nightlife, sightseeing, and, occasionally, the opportunity to attend a bullfight. You can drive over, but first be sure you have insurance covering your car in Mexico (See Crossing into Mexico in the Introduction) and also realize that parking can be difficult in the downtown area. Or you can park your car in inexpensive pay lots on the American side and walk over. You can also take a bus from the Valley Transit Bus Station at 120 S. 16th in downtown McAllen to the bridge or the Reynosa bus station. Buses depart every 20 or 30 minutes. The last bus departs Reynosa for McAllen at 11 p.m. For information call 686-5479.

There is a tourist information booth (phone 2-1308) at the end of the bridge just past the Mexican customs office. English speaking counselors are available and you can get a map of Reynosa and a variety of brochures on the city. There are usually licensed guides near the bridge. Before you hire one, ask to see their wallet-sized license from the Mexican Tourism Department and make sure you settle on the details of the tour and the fee before starting out.

Many of the shops and restaurants in Reynosa are in the *Zona Rosa* (Pink Zone) within an easy walk from the bridge. If you need assistance, an English-speaking policeman is always on duty at the Tourist Branch Police Precinct in the *Zona Rosa* — call 2-9988. If you want to go to the Main Plaza or the Zaragoza Market (See Shopping), it might be best to take a taxi, making sure you first fix the fare with the driver. One of the sights at the Main Plaza is The Cathedral of Our Lady of Guadalupe of Reynosa. The church itself is fairly new, but the bell tower dates from the original mission church built in 1789.

SPORTS AND ACTIVITIES

To call Reynosa dial 011-52892 plus the five-digit local number.

Baseball

The *Parque Beis-Bol* on the Monterrey Highway in Reynosa is the home of the Reynosa Broncos of the Mexican League. In addition to the regular season games, the team often plays exhibition games in the winter. For information about the schedule call the Reynosa Chamber of Commerce at 2-3734.

Bullfighting

There are two bullrings in Reynosa, however the bullfighting schedule is erratic and so is information about it which is usually only released just before the event. For information try the McAllen Convention and Visitors Bureau (682-2871) or the Reynosa Chamber of Commerce (2-3734).

Darts

McAllen is working toward becoming the dart center of the Valley. As it is played here, the sport is quite different from the game you played as a kid, tossing plastic darts at a cheap target board. It's now a big boys' game with precision equipment, leagues, rules, and regional and national tournaments. A recent three-day tournament in McAllen offered $10,000 in prize money. For information contact the Tropical Dart Association at 631-6397 or the Convention and Visitors Bureau (682-2871).

Fishing And Hunting

A list of guides for fishing and hunting in Texas and Mexico is in the McAllen Visitors Guide available from the Convention and Visitors Bureau.

Golf

PALM VIEW GOLF COURSE
1.5 miles south on Ware Rd.
687-9591

Twenty-seven-hole course. Green fees: $4.75 for 9 holes, $6 for 18.

Horse Racing

REYNOSA TURF CLUB
Reynosa, 915 Aldama
2-8318
Open seven days
W Variable

You can bet here on the races at many of the major horse tracks in the U.S. and Mexico. Open daily from about 9:30 a.m. until after the last race. Bar.

Square Dancing

Various locations
682-2871 (Convention and Visitors Bureau)

For the past few years the McAllen area has claimed the title of "Square Dance Capital of the World" because of the number of dancers and dances, and the number of callers and round dance cuers who either live in the Valley or winter here and set the pace for this popular pastime. Each year, the McAllen Chamber of Commerce sponsors what it modestly calls "The World's Largest Beginners Square Dance Class," a ten-week schedule of free Monday morning square dance classes held each January through March that has attracted as many as 500 new dancers at one time to learn how to do-si-do. With all this square dance activity, it is possible to dance just about every hour of the day and well into the night, any day of the week, in McAllen and nearby towns. The "Magic Valley Square and Round Dance Directory," published by the association of the same name, lists pages of scheduled dances, workshops, and classes all across the Valley. This directory is available at the McAllen Convention and Visitors Bureau (See Tourist Services).

Stock Car Racing

RIO GRANDE VALLEY SPEEDWAY
S.10th St. about four miles south of US 83 Expressway
843-2787
Admission
W Variable

Races on clay oval track most Saturday nights from March through December. Racing divisions include mini, hobby, late model, super stock, and bombers.

Tennis

There are 16 lighted courts open to the public every evening at McAllen High School, 23rd and La Vista, and four courts open evenings at Travis Junior High, 600 Houston. There is a small fee for public use.

PERFORMING ARTS

McALLEN INTERNATIONAL CIVIC CENTER
1300 S. 10th at US 83 Expressway (North access road)
686-3382 (Tickets: 686-4221)
Admission depends on event
W

The Civic Center complex — Municipal Auditorium, Convention Center, Tourist Center — has concerts, musical events, trade and home shows, and other events scheduled throughout the year. The McAllen Performing Arts sponsors touring shows and the Rio Grande Valley Ballet also performs here.

McALLEN PERFORMING ARTS
Civic Center Auditorium, 1300 S. 10th
631-2545 (Ticket ofice at Chamber of Commerce)
Admission depends on event
W

This is a non-profit corporation that brings in professional touring theater productions and entertainment not available through other local agencies. It usually sponsors four to six productions in its October through April season. Attractions range from musicals and music greats to drama and children's theater. Individual tickets depend on the production and go from about $5 to $40.

RIO GRANDE VALLEY BALLET
205 Pecan
682-2721

This semi-professional local company and touring companies put on several ballets a year. Performances are usually at the McAllen International Civic Center and tickets range from $4 to $6.

THEATRE McALLEN
9717 N. 10th
380-0413
Admission
W

About one weekend a month during its fall-to-spring season, this group puts on productions that range from drama to comedy to melodrama. Tickets run about $15.

SHOPPING

To call Reynosa dial 011-52892 plus the five-digit local number.

EGGERS ACRES
Shary Rd. (FM494), west of McAllen and 2.5 miles north of US 83 Bus
581-7783
Monday–Saturday 10–6, Sunday 12–5, Closed Tuesday in summer
W

If you want to, you can pick your own fruit from the trees in the orchard (in season) at this family citrus market run by Mardi Eggers, the granddaughter of Dr. J. B. Webb, the discoverer of the famed Ruby Red grapefruit. Gift fruit packs are available from about $17 to $30. The citrus fruits season runs from November though March. The adjoining garden center, which is open all year, is so filled with lush tropical and other exotic and landscape plants (for sale) that a walk through it is almost like going through a botanical garden.

GABII'S
Reynosa, 1097 Avenida Los Virreyes
2-3433

Mexican designer dresses are among the fine items in this woman's clothing store. Also folk art and crafts and gifts from Mexico and Central and South America.

KLEMENT'S GROVE
Fm 1924 (3 mile line) and Taylor Rd., west of McAllen. Take Taylor Rd. north off US 83 Bus
682-2980
Open Monday–Saturday in citrus season (October–April), Closed Sunday
W

You can get your fresh fruit from baskets in the store or pull a little kid's wagon out into the grove and pick your own citrus right from the trees (in season). Gift fruit packs available from about $12 to $40. They also have mesquite and wildflower honey, pecans and pecan brittle, fruitcakes, and fresh baked pies.

LA PLAZA MALL
2200 S. 10th, just south of US 83 Expressway
687-5251
W

Beall's, Dillard's, Penney's, and Sears are the anchor stores. Here you'll also find a number of national chains and local stores, including Jones and Jones, considered by some to be the Neiman Marcus of South Texas; a food court and a cafeteria.

LUPE'S
820 N. 10th at Ivy
686-1264

This is not your run-of-the-mill giftshop. Lupe Weir has converted an older house into a shop in which she stocks fine gift items like hand-made *Buccellati* sterling from Italy and everything in the Royal Doulton line for children. In addition to silverware, china, crystal, and a smattering of antiques, she also offers several unusual items such as Reuge music boxes from Switzerland that play three or four different songs, Russian lacquer boxes and painted plates, and rare books with even more rare "fore-edge" painting on them.

SAHADI IMPORTED FOOD
709 N. 10th between Gumwood and Hackberry
682-3419
W

This looks like a deli, but it's more than that. In addition to the typical deli fare of coldcuts and cheeses — which you can eat in the small restaurant section of the store — it also stocks food from all over the world. Side by side, you'll find biscuits from England, barrels of olives from Greece, fine wines from Europe, Swiss chocolates, and Oriental and European beers.

ZARAGOZA MARKET
Reynosa, Hidalgo and Matamoros, just south of the Main Plaza
W Variable

This is a typical tourist-oriented border market with dozens of small shops where bargaining over price is a way of life. For the smart shopper, there are some bargain treasures among the tourist souvenirs. It closes at sundown. Hidalgo St. is a pedestrian mall between the market and the Main Plaza.

ANNUAL EVENTS

January–February

RIO GRANDE VALLEY INTERNATIONAL MUSIC FESTIVAL
Various locations in the Valley
686-1456
Admission varies with event
W Variable

A week of musical events that features orchestras like the Fort Worth Symphony and well-known guest performers. For information write: P.O. Box 2315, McAllen, 78501.

March

SPRINGFEST
Various locations around city
682-6221
Nine days early in March
Free. Admission to some events
W Variable

The wide range of activities during this fiesta includes a parade, beauty pageant, antique car show, a variety of bands and other entertainment, a dance, German Night, sports tournaments, and Fiesta in the Park with arts and crafts and food booths. For information contact McAllen International Spring Fiesta, P.O. Box 720264, 78504.

December

CANDLELIGHT POSADA
Main activities in Archer Park at Ash between Broadway and Main
682-2871 (Convention and Visitors Bureau)
First Friday and Saturday in December
Free
W variable

These festivities open the Christmas season. *La Posada,* in Spanish, means inn or lodging and *Las Posadas* is a traditional Mexican re-enactment of Mary and Joseph's search for a place to spend the night. This ancient drama and procession, held on Saturday evening, is the highlight of the two-day festival that also includes a live nativity scene; caroling; entertainment by choirs, bands, and folk dancers; *luminarias;* twinkling lights; food booths; and the arrival of Santa Claus.

RESTAURANTS

($ = under $7, $$ = $7 to $17, $$$ = $17 to $25, $$$$ = over $25 for one person excluding drinks, tax, and tip.)
To call Reynosa dial 011-52892 plus the five-digit local number.

American

THE PATIO AT JONES AND JONES
La Plaza Mall, 2100 S. 10th
687-1171
Lunch Sunday–Tuesday, lunch and dinner, Wednesday–Saturday
Reservations requested
$$-$$$$
Cr.
W

Mall restaurants are for convenience, not fine dining, right? Well, there are exceptions, and this is one. Just as Jones and Jones is the Valley's most up-scale department store, The Patio makes its mark as an up-scale restaurant. The dinner menu features choices like prime rib, broiled trout, and lobster. Bar.

PEPPER'S BURGERS AND STEAKS
4800 N. 10th
631-2082
Lunch and dinner Monday–Saturday
$-$$
Cr.
W

They offer 12 different style burgers from avocado to the pizzaburger. Actually there's a 13th burger on the menu called the "Famous Rolex Burger," a regular burger wrapped with a solid gold Rolex watch. It goes for only $10,000, but so far they haven't had any orders for it. Other offerings include a *fajita* platter, a variety of chicken and steak dishes, fried vegetables, and catfish and shrimp. Bar.

TOM AND JERRY'S
401 N. 10th
687-3001 at Date Palm
Lunch and dinner Monday–Saturday
$
Cr.
W

The setting is simple — an old brick house on the corner with a porch, a patio, and bench seats. And the menu is simple, too. There are only a little over a dozen items on it including several types of burgers, beef or chicken *fajitas,* the ever-present chicken-fried steak, chili, hot dogs, and only one dessert — french cream cheese cake. Also in Mission at 2415 Griffin Parkway (581-2375). Beer and wine.

Continental

LA CUCARACHA
Reynosa, Aldama and Ocampo, about three blocks southwest of bridge
2-0174
Lunch and dinner seven days
$$-$$$
Cr.
W

The menu at this plush restaurant includes *Chateaubriand* and lobster thermidor, but the most popular items are the inexpensive two-meat special dinners that can be topped off with a flaming dessert. Entertainment. Dancing nightly except Monday. Secured valet parking. Bar.

LA MANSION DEL PRADO
Reynosa, Emilio Portes Gil at Mendez, about five blocks southeast of the bridge
2-9914
Lunch and dinner seven days
$-$$
MC, V
W

The menu includes *alambres (shish kebab),* beef *medallions* with sherry sauce, chicken *chichingaro* and other traditional Mexican dishes, large steaks, and a variety of seafood. Note the intricate tile work throughout the restaurant. Private parking. Bar.

Italian

IANNELLI RISTORANTE ITALIANO
N. 10th and La Vista
631-0666
Lunch and dinner seven days
$-$$
Cr.
W

All the traditional southern Italian dishes are on the menu here including seven different spaghetti dishes and a variety of other home-made pastas. Or you can try a deep dish vegetarian pizza. Other choices on the menu include a wide range of chicken, veal, and seafood entrées. Beer and wine.

Mexican

JOHNNY'S MEXICAN FOOD
1012 Houston
686-9061
Lunch and dinner seven days
$

MC, V
W

This no-frills Mexican restaurant north of the border offers most of the typical Mexican and Tex-Mex choices from breakfast *tacos* and *migas* to *cabrito* and *chili rellenos*. Also steaks and vegetarian dishes. Order at the counter and they call when it's ready. Bar.

SAM'S
Reynosa, Allende at Ocampo, one block west of the bridge
2-0034
Lunch and dinner seven days
$-$$
Cr.
W

The two-meat dinner here, with all the trimmings, runs around $7. You can do better on price in this border city, but they've been serving it up to diners since 1932 so they must be doing it better than the competition in some way. The menu features several Northern Mexican dishes and you can expect to be serenaded by *mariachis*. Parking lot on corner. Bar.

Oriental

LOTUS INN
1120 N. 10th at Kendlewood
631-2693
Lunch and dinner seven days
$-$$
AE, MC, V
W

The menu is small compared to some Chinese restaurants, but the selection of Hunan and Mandarin specialties is more than adequate and includes choices like hot and sour soup, citrus chicken, Mandarin lamb, and Imperial shrimp with water chestnuts. And behind this white, Chinese-style building is a large patio for pleasant outdoor dining. Bar.

Seafood

RICO'S
Reynosa, 585 P. Diaz at Mendez, about two blocks southwest of the Main Plaza
2-2315
Breakfast, lunch, and dinner seven days
$-$$
DC, MC, V
W

There is a variety of seafood selections on the menu, but shrimp seems to be the name of the game in this no-frills restaurant. They make it in a half dozen different ways, all good. A good place to hit when visiting the Zaragoza Market or the Main Plaza. Bar.

CLUBS AND BARS

AUSTIN STREET INN
1110 Austin
687-7703
Closed Sunday
No Cover
Cr.
W downstairs

An old-fashioned saloon with tin ceiling, wooden floor, and a large bar. Specialty is drinks in hurricane glasses. Parking in bank lot across street.

23rd ST. SPORTSPUB
821 N. 23rd, north of Hackberry
687-9399
Open seven days
No cover
CR.
W

You can play'em or watch'em here while you drink. There are pool tables, professional darts, shuffleboard, foosball, and video games, plus big screen TVs and a dozen TV monitors scattered around that are fed by two satellite dishes that can broadcast ten different sporting events simultaneously.

TREVINO'S
Reynosa, 30 Virreyes, near the bridge
2-1444
Open seven days
No cover
Cr.
W

In the front it's a gift shop selling expensive jewelry, perfume, and crystal. But behind this is a large lounge and piano bar that is popular with both visitors and locals as a great stopping-off place coming from or going to the bridge.

ACCOMMODATIONS

($ = Under $45, $$ = $46-$60, $$$ = $61-$80, $$$$ = $81-$100, $$$$$ = Over $100)
Room tax 13 percent

COMPRI HOTEL CASA DE PALMAS
100 N. Main, just north of US 83 Bus
631-1101 or 800-274-1102 or 800-4-COMPRI
$$$

W + sixteen rooms
No-smoking rooms

This three-story hotel has 161 units that include several suites ($$$$$) and 52 no-smoking rooms. Children under 18 stay free in room with parents. Package plans available and senior discount. Satellite TV with HBO and The Movie Channel. Room phones (charge for local calls). Fire sprinklers in rooms. No pets. Restaurant, room service, and bar. Outdoor heated pool, exercise room, and guest memberships available in country club. Free airport transportation. Free coffee, free newspaper, two free drinks per guest, free full breakfast, and late night snacks available in lounge. This is a charmingly restored, Spanish-style hotel originally built in 1918.

EMBASSY SUITES
1800 S. 2nd off Texas 83 Expressway (take 2nd St. exit westbound, 10th St. exit eastbound)
686-3000 or 800-EMBASSY
$$$$
W + ten suites
No-smoking suites

This nine-story Embassy offers 168 two-room suites including 60 no-smoking. Children under 17 stay free in room with parents. Package plans available, senior discount, and weekend rates Friday-Saturday. Satellite TV with HBO and pay channel. Room phones (charge for local calls). Coffeemakers in rooms. Fire sprinklers in rooms. No pets. Restaurant, room service, and lounge open seven nights with entertainment Monday-Saturday. Heated indoor pool, children's pool, whirlpool, exercise room, steam bath, sauna, and guest memberships available in country club. Free transportation to airport and mall. Complimentary two-hour cocktail party and full breakfast. Free newspaper. Self-service laundry and same-day dry cleaning. Gift shop. Suites have microwaves and small refrigerators. Top three floors are private condominiums.

FAIRWAY RESORT
2105 S. 10th, across from La Plaza Mall
682-2445 or 800-432-4792
$$-$$$
No-smoking rooms

This resort is composed of 26 separate one- and two-story buildings offering 245 units that include 10 suites ($$$-$$$$$) and 26 no-smoking rooms. Package plans available and senior discount. Satellite TV with HBO. Room phones (charge for local calls). Pets OK. Restaurant, room service, lounge open seven days with entertainment Monday-Saturday. Three outdoor pools (one heated), two lighted tennis courts, shuffleboard courts, jogging trails with exercise stations, and guest memberships available for country club. Free transportation for airport and shopping. Free coffee in lobby in morning. Self-service laundry and same-day dry cleaning. Most units are drive-up and have small patio. Set on 17.5 acres of landscaped gardens.

HOLIDAY INN-CIVIC CENTER
2nd St. at US 83 Expressway (take 2nd St. exit westbound, 10th St. exit eastbound)
686-2471 or 800-HOLIDAY
$$$
W + one room
No-smoking rooms

This two-story Holiday Inn has 173 units that include two suites ($$$$$) and 35 no-smoking rooms. Children under 19 stay free in room with parents. Package plans available and senior discount. Cable TV with HBO. Room phones (local calls free). Pets OK. Restaurant, room service, lounge open seven nights with DJ nightly. Game room, putting green, whirlpool, bar, and indoor pool, outdoor pool, two lighted tennis courts, sauna, and guest memberships available in country club. Free coffee Monday-Friday morning. Free transportation to airport and medical centers. Free champagne reception weeknights. Self-service laundry and same- day dry cleaning.

McALLEN AIRPORT HILTON INN
721 S. 10th, across from the airport
687-1161 or 800-HILTONS (800-445-8667)
$$-$$$
W + three rooms
No-smoking rooms

The five-story Hilton has 149 units that include one suite ($$$$$) and 32 no-smoking rooms. Children under 18 stay free in parents room. Senior discounts. Satellite TV with pay channel. Room phones (charge for local calls). Fire sprinklers in rooms. Small pets OK (pet deposit $50). Restaurant, room service, lounge open seven nights. Outdoor heated pool, outdoor whirlpool, tennis court. Free transportation to airport and mall. Free coffee in morning. Same-day dry cleaning.

MISSION

HIDALGO COUNTY ★ 32,500 ★ (512)

The city is named after the tiny chapel of the nearby La Lomita Mission (See Historic Places). As the story goes, it was here that the Oblate Fathers planted oranges and grapefruit and discovered that the area was ideal for growing citrus crops. John Shary, a land developer who moved here from Nebraska in the early 1900s, recognized the commercial aspects of growing citrus. During the period from 1906 to 1910, Shary and a partner developed approximately 250,000 acres of land in south Texas. In 1915 he planted the first large commercial citrus orchard in the Valley. He also built the first modern commercial packing plant in Mission. Because of this first large scale venture and his continuing activities in the development of every phase of the citrus industry, Shary has become known as "the father of the Texas citrus industry, " and Mission is called "The Home of the Grapefruit."

Shary's original home in Mission is located about 3.75 miles north of US 83 Bus on Sharyland Rd. The estate includes a memorial chapel. The mansion is privately owned and not open to the public, but it can be viewed from the road.

Downtown, at W. 8th and S. Conway, is the Plaza de la Lomita, a combination plaza and a 1,000-seat sunken amphitheater decorated with fountains. The garden here contains more than 175 native plants and trees that have low water-demands reflecting the natural concept of landscape water conservation. Plays, musicals, and other events are performed in the amphitheater, many of them free.

TOURIST SERVICES

MISSION CHAMBER OF COMMERCE
220 E. 9th at Miller (US 83 Bus) across from City Hall (P.O. Box 431, 78572)
585-2727
Monday–Friday 8–5
W

In addition to free brochures and a city map, you can also buy tickets to area events here.

HISTORIC PLACES

LA LOMITA MISSION CHAPEL
FM 1016 about three miles south of US 83
581-2725
Open seven days 8:30–4:30
Free
W

Originally built in 1865 by the circuit-riding Oblate Fathers who served Catholics on the ranches between Brownsville and Roma, *La Lomita,* which means "little hill" in Spanish, was a rendezvous campsite for these priests who were known as the "Padres' Mounted Posse." The chapel has been rebuilt several times — the present chapel being built in 1889 — and relocated to its present site in 1899. The tiny (approximately 16 by 30 feet) building with hand-hewn mesquite wood window and doorsills, is still used for weddings and such. It is set in a seven-acre park with picnic facilities.

GREGG WOOD HOME
1215 Doherty
585-5768
Open by appointment only
Free

This simple, bungalow-style house was built in 1917 by the mayor of Mission for his family. The second story was added in 1920.

WILLIAM JENNINGS BRYAN HOME
Byran Road north of FM 495 at 3-Mile Line

William Jennings Bryan and his family spent two winters in this house, which was built in 1910, before he was called back to serve as secretary of state under President Woodrow Wilson. You may have to search a little for the marker, which is difficult to see. The home is not open to the public.

OTHER POINTS OF INTEREST

ANZALDUAS DAM AND PARK
From US 83, take FM 1016 about three miles south to FM 494, then one mile west. South of La Lomita Mission on Rio Grande River
Park open seven days 7–10
$2 per vehicle
W Variable

The international boundary runs through the center of this dam which is used to divert water from the Rio Grande to a large irrigation canal in Mexico. The 96-acre Hidalgo County Park offers facilities for boating, waterskiing, RV camping, fishing, and picnicking.

BENTSEN-RIO GRANDE VALLEY STATE PARK
From US 83 west of Mission, take FM 2062 (Bentsen Palm Dr.) about three miles to Park Rd. 43 then three miles to park
585-1107
Open seven days 8–10 for day use, at all times for camping
$2 per vehicle per day (Over 65 free)
W + But not all areas

Located on the banks of the Rio Grande River, this 587-acre park has been set aside to preserve the native flora and fauna of the lower Rio Grande Valley. Facilities are available for boating, camping (fee), picnicking, and nature studies. A checklist of 221 species of birds that have been sighted here over the years may be picked up at the park office on entry. Detailed lists and booklets on the mammals, herbs, plants, and butterflies seen in the park are also available as well as a booklet that guides you along "The Singing Chaparral Trail," so named because the birds usually provide background singing for the tour through the park's woodlands and brushlands.

SPORTS AND ACTIVITIES

Golf

MARTIN VALLEY RANCH GOLF COURSE
US 83 about 4.5 miles west
585-6330

Eighteen-hole course. Call for green fees.

MEADOW CREEK COUNTRY CLUB
1 mile south on inspiration
581-6262

Eighteen hole course. Call for green fees.

SHARY MUNICIPAL GOLF COURSE
2201 Mayberry at Lions Park
580-8770

Eighteen-hole course. Call for green fees.

SHOPPING

EGGERS ACRES
Shary Rd. (FM 494), east of Mission and 2.5 miles north of US 83 Bus
581-7783
Monday–Saturday 10–6, Sunday 12–5, Closed Tuesday in summer
W

If you want to you can pick your own fruit from the trees in the orchard (in season) or take it from baskets in the store at this family citrus market run by Mardi Eggers, the granddaughter of Dr. J. B. Webb, the discoverer of the famed Ruby Red grapefruit. Gift fruit packs are available from about $17 to $30. The citrus fruits season runs from November though March. The adjoining garden center, which is open all year, is so filled with lush tropical and other exotic and landscape plants (for sale) that a walk through it is almost like going through a botanical garden.

KLEMENT'S GROVE
Fm 1924 (3-Mile Line) and Taylor Rd., east of Mission. Take Taylor Rd. north off US 83 Bus
682-2980
Open Monday–Saturday in citrus season (October–April), Closed Sunday
W

You can get your fresh fruit from baskets in the store or pull a little kid's wagon out into the grove and pick your own citrus right from the trees (in season). Gift fruit packs available from about $12 to $40. They also have mesquite and wildflower honey, pecans and pecan brittle, fruitcakes and fresh baked pies.

SIDE TRIPS

LOS EBANOS FERRY
Take US 83 west about 14 miles to FM 886, then south to ferry
Operates seven days 9–5
$1 per vehicle, 25¢ per person

The wooden two-car ferry is hand-pulled back and forth across the Rio Grande by the Mexican crew, linking the dirt roads on the Texas and Mexican sides. It is the only government-licensed hand-pulled ferry on any U.S. border. You can have your car ferried across or you can ride over as a pedestrian, but there's not much to see on the other side even if you drive the two miles to Diaz Ordaz, the nearest Mexican town. A historical marker at the site explains the history of the ferry.

ANNUAL EVENTS

January

TEXAS CITRUS FIESTA
Various locations
585-9724 or 585-2727 (Chamber of Commerce)
One week near end of January
Admission to some events
W Variable

Since its beginnings in 1932, the Fiesta has evolved into a prolonged celebration to honor the bountiful harvest of the citrus crops. It features a wide variety of events including The Parade of Oranges with fruit covered floats, The Coronation of Queen Citrianna and King Citrus, an arts and crafts show, barbecue, golf tournaments, carnival, dances, and prize citrus judging. A unique event is the Product Costume Style Show. Rules dictate that all visible parts of the costumes must be covered by some type of Valley-grown product, including, of course, citrus. In the early days the costumes were just covered with vegetables or citrus or other products. But today, science has stepped in and, although the costumes are often spectacular, the products are just as often dehydrated, pulverized, tinted with natural dyes, blended, and microwaved to the point that they are barely recognizable in their finished state.

December

TOURIST FEST
Primarily at Lomita Plaza, W. 8th and S. Conway
585-2727 (Chamber of Commerce)
Three days in middle of December
Free
W Variable

Music and dancing are a big part of these festivities. There are square and round dance exhibitions with professional callers, clogging, and Mexican dancers. Musical entertainment includes blue grass, C & W, jazz, mariachis, and choral. Other activities include an arts and crafts exhibition and the Garden Club's American Poinsettia Show. A wide variety of this colorful Christmas flower can be seen at this nationally judged show that is held in the Chamber of Commerce building (220 E. 9th).

RESTAURANTS

($ = under $7, $$ = $7 to $17, $$$ = $17 to $25, $$$$ = over $25 for one person excluding drinks, tax, and tip.)

LA PARILLA
1800 E. US 83 Bus, in Palm Village
580-1498
Lunch and dinner seven days
$-$$
AE, MC, V
W

As you could expect from the name, the menu offers a variety of familiar Tex-Mex staples like *enchiladas* and *fajitas*, but they also offer enticing non-Mexican entrees like fried butterfly shrimp. Bar.

TACO OLE
2316 N. Conway
581-7431
Breakfast, lunch and dinner
Wednesday-Monday. Closed Tuesday
$-$$
No Cr.

Tex-Mex and American dishes including hamburgers and some seafood.

PHARR

HIDALGO COUNTY ★ 35,000 ★ (512)

In 1909, the Valley's first sugarcane craze attracted Louisiana sugarcane plantation owner Henry N. Pharr, who with a partner, John C. Kelly from Waco, bought 20,000 acres (at $17.50 an acre). The partners laid out a town and decided to name it after one of them. So it might have been called Kelly, but for reasons unknown now, Pharr's name won out.

Today, sugarcane has just about faded from the scene, but agriculture — winter vegetables, citrus, and cotton — is still Pharr's major industry. Coming in second are tourist-related industries. As a home for many Winter Texans who come to stay in their RV's, the city has been called the "RV Park Capital of Texas."

TOURIST SERVICES

PHARR CHAMBER OF COMMERCE
308 W. Park (P.O. Box 1341, 78577)
787-1481
Monday–Friday 8–5
W

In addition to providing detailed information on Pharr and the surrounding area, the Chamber also arranges trips to Mexico that last from three-days to a week.

MUSEUMS

OLD CLOCK MUSEUM
929 E. Preston (one block S of US 83 Bus, behind the Leather Factory)
787-1923
Usually open 10–12 and 2–6
Free (Donations accepted and given to charity)
W

James Shawn started collecting clocks in the mid-1960s. It wasn't long before his collection, which now numbers close to 2,000 timepieces, antique phonographs, and clock accessories, outgrew his home and he opened this museum next door, one of only five such museums in the nation. Among the prizes in the collection are more than 200 clocks in numbered cases casted by famed foundryman Nicolas Muller from the 1870s on. The collection of cuckoo clocks is especially popular with children. If the museum is closed, try knocking at the Shawn house next door for a tour.

SHOPPING

THE LEATHER FACTORY
904 E. US 83 Bus at Huisache
781-8997
Store open regular business hours
Free factory tours October–April, Monday–Saturday 10 a.m. and 2 p.m. Tours by appointment only May–September
W

This factory outlet store sells coats, jackets, boots, purses, belts, and other leather items at discount prices. Most of the items come from their own factory, but they also carry other name brand leather products. They'll also do custom fitting. The tour includes explanations of the types of leather used, tanning processes, cutting and trimming and each stage of garment construction.

ANNUAL EVENTS

December

ALL VALLEY WINTER VEGETABLE SHOW
Pharr Civic Center, 1011 W. Kelly
787-1481 (Chamber of Commerce)
Friday–Saturday early in December

Free
W Variable

The variety and richness of the Valley's vegetable industry are on display here. More than 60 different classes of vegetables are exhibited. Activities include a Vegetable Show Queen contest, exhibits of vegetables by local 4-H and FFA chapter members, a parade, awards, auctions, and the famous "Sack Sale," more commonly known as the "Vegetable Dash." In this event, held after the awards ceremony, the public can purchase brown grocery bags at a set price and at the whistle race to fill up the sacks with vegetables.

RESTAURANTS

($ = under $7, $$ = $7 to $17, $$$ = $17 to $25, $$$$ = over $25 for one person excluding drinks, tax, and tip.)

TEXAS "T" SMOKEHOUSE
120 E. Park, Bldg. C
781-5845
Lunch and dinner seven days
$
AE, MC, V
W

Some barbecue places specialize in just one or two kinds of meat; this one has them all — beef, chicken, sausage, *fajitas,* ham, beef ribs, and pork ribs. And, in keeping with its location near the border, the menu also offers everything but the ribs served in flour *tortillas.*

RIO GRANDE CITY

STARR COUNTY SEAT ★ 12,500 ★ (512)

In the mid-1700s, Jose de Escandon, Count of Sierra Gorda in Spain, opened the Rio Grande Valley to colonization by establishing about twenty towns near the river including Reynosa, present day Laredo, and the town of Camargo. In 1753, an area across the river from Camargo was given to the de la Garza family who made it a ranching community they called Carnestolendas, meaning "carnival." In 1846, after a lengthy Spanish-style courtship, an American named Henry Clay Davis married a daughter of the de la Garza family and they were given Carnestolendas as their home.

Just a few months after the wedding, the Mexican War broke out. Carnestolendas was the head of navigation for the steamboats carrying supplies for the American Army. Since Davis owned the land, the Americans started calling it Davis Landing. As part of the treaty ending that war, the American government was obligated to protect the people of northern Mexico — and of course, the Texans — from attacks by marauding Indians and outlaws. To do this, Fort Ringgold (See Historic Places) was built here in 1848 as part of a line of forts spaced approximately 100 miles apart along the border. At about the same time, Starr

County was formed and Davis and his associates founded Rio Grande City.

In 1852, the 500 or so residents of the city had a grandstand view of an attack by a filibustering army formed in Rio Grande City that crossed the river to conquer the neighboring border town of Camargo. The army, composed of both Mexicans and American soldiers-of-fortune including some American soldiers from Fort Ringgold who deserted to join the expedition, was attempting to set up "The Republic of Sierra Madre" in northern Mexico. But the Mexican militia, well aware of the invasion plans, met the invaders near the river, routed most of the force and surrounded the rest. Since most of those surrounded were American, Henry Clay Davis, who had remained aloof from the expedition, decided he had to do something to rescue them. He enlisted a band of Carrizo Indians and lead them as they carried out the rescue operation, making this a unique instance in the history of the West in which the Indians rather than the cavalry came to the rescue.

By 1859 the head of navigation had moved up river another 14 or so miles to Roma, but by then Rio Grande City had been established as a commercial center. It remained so until about 1890 when the railroads arrived in the Valley. At that time the river steamboats, which often had trouble navigating the unpredictable Rio Grande, were replaced by the more efficient railroads and, because the railroad stopped short of Rio Grande City, that city died as a center of commerce.

Today, farming and ranching are the mainstays of the local economy.

Camargo (See Other Points of Interest), a Mexican town of about 10,000 population, is about two miles south of the International Bridge. Founded in 1749, it is one of the oldest Spanish colonies in the Valley. It used to sit right on the river, but frequent flooding forced its relocation to higher ground. Up the river about 14 miles, on the American side, is the historic city of Roma (See Side Trips). Opposite it is Miguel Aleman, a Mexican city of about 30,000 established in the 1920s. It offers a little more in the way of border shopping than Camargo. A little further on is the historic city of Mier (See Side Trips).

TOURIST SERVICES

RIO GRANDE CITY AND ROMA CHAMBER OF COMMERCE
207 E. 2nd at East
(P.O. Box 2, 78582)
487-3024
Monday–Friday 8–5

Information is available on both cities plus the rest of Starr County and the nearby Mexican cities of Camargo, Miguel Aleman, and Mier. For the history buff, they have an Historical Trail map/brochure that cites all the important historical buildings in both Starr County and the northwest part of the Mexican state of Tamaulipas, which includes all the mentioned towns.

HISTORIC PLACES

FORT RINGGOLD
US 83 at east end of town
W Variable

Built in the late 1840s, after the Mexican War, Fort Ringgold was one of a line of forts established every 100 miles along the Mexican border. Its mission was to secure the border and stop Indian and bandit raids. The fort was established by General Zachary Taylor and named after Major Samuel Ringgold. Major Ringgold was killed while commanding Taylor's "Flying Artillery" which played a major role in winning the battle of Palo Alto, the first battle of the Mexican War. Among the surviving buildings are the old barracks, officers' quarters, stables, bakery, and storerooms. Perhaps the most historically significant building is the Lee House. This simple frame building was occupied by Colonel Robert E. Lee for a short time in April 1860 during his investigation of a bandit raid on Rio Grande City that resulted in a battle between the bandits and the U.S. Cavalry and the Texas Rangers. The bandits came out second best.

The Confederates occupied the fort during the Civil War. One of the things the Confederate commander did was order anti-secessionist, John Peter Kelsey, a local store-keeper and rancher, to not only get out of town, but out of the country. Kelsey lived out the war in Camargo. After Lee's surrender at Appomattox, Kelsey was commissioned to raise "a battalion of men" to go to Rio Grande City and take the fort and city back. He could only find three men willing to go with him. And when he raised the Union flag over his old store, it was suddenly pierced by a rifle shot. That unfriendly welcome made him decide to return to Camargo for another 12 years.

The fort is now the home of the city's school system and as such entrance is restricted during school hours on school days. It is open to the public evenings, weekends, and during the summer and other school vacation periods.

OTHER HISTORIC BUILDINGS

Among other historic buildings in the city are the *Henry Clay Davis House*, southeast corner of Britton and Mirosoles, built in 1848; *Samuel Stewart Home*, San Antonio and Water, built in early 1850s; *John Peter Kelsey Building*, Main and Washington, built in 1877 and now the home of El Pato Del Rio Mall (See Shopping); and the *Silverio de la Pena Building*, northwest corner of Main and Lopez, built in 1886 by well-known border architect and builder Heinrich Portscheller and now listed in the National Register of Historic Places. Another building listed in the National Register is the *LaBorde House*, 601 E. Main at Garza, completed in about 1899 as the home and border store of Francoise LaBorde and now a well-known historic inn. (See Accommodations).

OTHER POINTS OF INTEREST

CAMARGO, MEXICO

Take Diaz St. south to the International Bridge, then continue south about two miles to city

Founded by Jose de Escandon in 1749, this is one of the oldest towns in the Valley. Soon after the start of the Mexican War, in 1846, General Zachary Taylor's army occupied Camargo. Steamboats brought troops and supplies up the Rio Grande to Camargo where they were unloaded and moved overland into Mexico. The outcome of the Mexican War, which made the Rio Grande the border, made Camargo a border town.

Over the years the inhabitants had to contend with bandits and revolutionaries. In June 1866, a battle was fought at Santa Gertrudis, about three miles east of the city, between the forces of the Emperor Maximilian and those opposed to his foreign regime. Maximilian's soldiers were defeated and after that the French pulled out of northern Mexico. A year later, the Mexicans, lead by Juarez, were victorious and Maximilian was executed.

Today, Camargo is a town of about 10,000 people. Among the many historic buildings here is the Catholic church on Libertad St. which was built in 1750. Although tourism is not a major factor in the economy here, with a little hunting you'll find shops that offer bargains in everything from liquor to leather goods.

OUR LADY OF LOURDES GROTTO

Immaculate Conception Church, Britton Ave. across from the Starr County Courthouse

Open at all times

This is a replica of the famous Shrine of Our Lady of Lourdes in France. It was constructed almost entirely of rocks and petrified wood in 1927 by the Oblate Fathers. The statues of the Virgin and the peasant girl Bernadette Soubirous were made in Paris.

SANTA CRUZ RANCH CROSS

US 83 about four miles east of city

A small ebony cross was first placed on this hill in 1880 by the Pena family to signify that this was the Santa Cruz ranch. Over the years the family has replaced the cross several times, each time with a larger one. The family holds a religious service at the cross each year during the first week in May to which the public is invited.

SPORTS AND ACTIVITIES

Golf

FORT RINGGOLD GOLF COURSE
4350 E. US 83
487-5666

Nine-hole course. Green fees: about $5.

SHOPPING

EL PATO DEL RIO MALL
Main and Washington
487-3386
W

John Peter Kelsey, the anti-secessionist merchant who had to flee the city during the Civil War, would probably be pleased that this building he built in 1877, after his return from exile in Mexico, is now once again occupied by merchants. The two stories built around a courtyard house a mini-mall that includes specialty shops for jewelry, women's clothing, antiques, and gifts, plus a restaurant.

SIDE TRIPS

FALCON STATE RECREATION AREA
Take US 83 through Roma and continue north about 10 miles to FM 2098, then left to Park Rd. 46 to the Recreation Area; about 30 miles from Rio Grande City
848-5327
Day use hours vary by season, open for camping all year
$2 per vehicle per day
W Variable

The 572-acre recreation area is located on the eastern shore of 87,000-acre Falcon Reservoir that is jointly owned by the U.S. and Mexico. Facilities are provided for boating, fishing, swimming, water skiing, hiking, picnicking, and tent and RV camping (fee). The rugged south Texas brush country in the park also makes it an excellent spot for birdwatching of both resident birds of the American Southwest and some tropical species. The international crossing over the nearby Falcon Dam into Mexico is free. The dam itself is five miles long (two miles on the U.S. side and three on the Mexican).

ROMA
Take US 83 west about 14 miles

In the late 1800s, when Roma was in its heyday as a riverport and a major ford across the Rio Grande for trade from Mexico, a number of local landowners employed Heinrich Portscheller, a German stonemason, to build their homes and business buildings. Many of Portscheller's buildings — characterized by double doors, high windows, hand-carved brick borders, and New Orleans ironwork — have survived and his work dominates the historic district around a wide street known as the Plaza. Most of the center of the town is included in a National Historic District.

Possibly the biggest event in Roma's recent history was its use as a set for a Mexican town in the 1950s filming of the movie *Viva Zapata* with Marlon Brando and Anthony Quinn. At the present time, Roma has a population of about 5,000. Across the International Bridge is the Mexican city of Miguel Aleman. The bridge, which dates from 1927, is the only suspension bridge left on the Rio Grande.

Roma Historical Museum
Lincoln and Estrella
849-1411 (City Hall)
Monday–Friday 8–5 or by appointment
Free
W

Located in a building built in the 1840s, this small museum features displays depicting various aspects of Roma's history from education and religion to farming and ranching.

Other Historic Buildings

Many of the historic buildings are on Estrella St., which runs parallel to US 83, or on Convent St., which runs from Estrella to the river. At Estrella and Convent, on the Plaza, is *Our Lady of Refuge Catholic Church.* The church was built in 1966, but the bell tower was built in 1854 by Father Pierre Keralum, a priest responsible for the construction of a number of churches in the Valley. Across from the church is the *Old Convent,* built by Portscheller in the 1880s and now used as the parish hall. Down the Plaza, just north of Water St., is the *Cox House,* which was one of the first two-story houses in Roma when built in 1853. Another Portscheller building is the *Manuel Guerra Store,* at Convent and Portscheller, constructed in 1884. From the park at the end of Convent St. you can see the suspension bridge over the river and the Mexican city of Miguel Aleman.

Miguel Aleman, Mexico
Across the International Bridge from Roma

You can walk across the bridge here and be right in the shopping section of Miguel Aleman. This is a relatively new city, built in the 1920s, so there's not much of historical interest; however, there are several curio and other shops that cater to visitors and several restaurants.

MIER, MEXICO

From Roma, go over the International Bridge to Miguel Aleman, then take Mexico Hwy 2 west (right) about eight miles to Mier

This is another town colonized in the 1750s by Jose de Escandon. Its narrow streets, plazas, and historic buildings are typical of towns founded in that time. The Catholic Church here was completed in 1798, making it one of the oldest churches in the Valley. The clock tower, added in 1872, was built by Heinrich Portscheller.

Mier is famous, or infamous, in Texas history for giving its name to the Mier Expedition of 1842 that lead to the "Black Bean Incident." The Expedition, of about 750 men, was sent by Sam Houston, President of the Republic of Texas, as a demonstration in force to persuade the Mexicans to stop causing border incidents. Unfortunately, after taking Laredo, dissention broke out in the Army's ranks and the commanding general and more than half the force went back to Texas while the remainder, about 300 men, went on to attack Mier. The attack was unsuccessful. A larger Mexican force captured the Texans and marched them as prisoners into the interior of Mexico. Soon after, the Texans staged a mass escape, but most were recaptured by the Mexicans. Mexican dictator Santa Anna, ordered that one in ten be put to death. Those to be executed were chosen by picking beans from a pitcher. The 17 who picked the black beans were executed.

At present, there are no Mexican checkpoints between Miguel Aleman and Mier, so a tourist card is not required to make the trip.

RESTAURANTS

($ = under $7, $$ = $7 to $17, $$$ = $17 to $25, $$$$ = over $25 for one person excluding drinks, tax, and tip.)

CARO'S RESTAURANT
205 N. Garcia just north of US 83 on west side of town
487-2255
Lunch and dinner seven days
$
No Cr.
W
Children's plates

This may be a small restaurant with a short menu, but its Tex-Mex cooking is well-known in the upper Valley (as well as at its other restaurants in Fort Worth and Arlington.) A specialty of the house is puffed *tostadas*. Beer.

ACCOMMODATIONS

($ = Under $45, $$ = $46-$60, $$$ = $61-$80, $$$$ = $81-$100, $$$$$ = Over $100)
Room Tax 6 percent

FORT RINGGOLD MOTOR INN
4350 E. US 83
487-5666
$-$$
W + One room

The 64 units in this motel include one suite ($$$). Children under 12 stay free in room with parents. Cable TV with HBO. Room phones (charge for local calls). No pets. Restaurant, room service, club open Tuesday-Sunday with entertainment nightly. Outdoor pool. Self-service laundry. Public golf course adjoining.

LaBORDE HOUSE
601 E. Main at Garza
487-5101
$-$$

This two-story historic inn has 21 units that include eight historical rooms ($$) and nine efficiency apartments in rear ($). Children under 12 stay free in room with parents. Senior discount. Cable TV. Room phones (local calls free). No pets. Parking in lot across Garza St. Restaurant (lunch seven days, dinner Friday-Sunday). Lounge open seven night. Guest memberships available in country club. Free coffee and Mexican *pan dolce* in morning. Self-service laundry. Gift shop. The authentic restoration was made in coordination with both Texas Historical Commission and U. S. Department of the Interior. Historical rooms are furnished with Victorian antiques. Listed in the National Register of Historic Places.

SAN JUAN

HIDALGO COUNTY ★ 10,000 ★ (512)

Oddly, in a section of the Valley where most of the population is of Hispanic origin, this is the only city between Mercedes and Mission with a Hispanic name. San Juan is derived from the Spanish name given to John Closner by his employees. Closner was the owner of San Juan Plantation and in 1910 founded the town from a section of his plantation. He came to the area from Wisconsin and started out in Rio Grande City as a mail stage driver. In 1882 he became Deputy Sheriff of the newly created Hidalgo County, a position he held until 1912. In the early 1900s he bought the plantation and in 1904 his sugar cane won a medal at the St. Louis World's Fair.

TOURIST SERVICES

SAN JUAN CHAMBER OF COMMERCE
(P.O. Box 1192, 78589)
787-2725
W

POINTS OF INTEREST

SHRINE OF LA VIRGEN DE SAN JUAN DEL VALLE
400 W. Nebraska Ave. just south of US 83 Expressway (San Juan exit)
787-0033
Open seven days 6 a.m.–8 p.m.
Free
W

Knowing that his Hispanic parishioners had a special devotion to the Virgin of San Juan de los Lagos, in 1949, Oblate Father Jose Azpiazu placed a replica of the statue of the Virgin in his parish church. It soon became known as the Virgin of San Juan of the Valley and attracted so many pilgrims from Texas and Mexico that in 1954 a shrine to the Virgin was dedicated in a ceremony attended by more than 60,000 pilgrims. However, in 1970, while a Mass was going on, a pilot flew his small plane into the church — some say deliberately. Miraculously no one at the Mass was hurt. But, the resulting fire destroyed all but the tower and the statue of the Virgin which was rescued from the flames. For ten years pilgrims continued to visit the statue temporarily located in a cafeteria on the grounds. Then in 1980, the present shrine was completed, at a cost of $5 million, paid mostly from small contributions. Even if you are not a Catholic, the shrine is impressive with its spacious interior seating 1,800, gigantic ceramic altar, the statue of the Virgin enshrined in a niche in the center of a 50-by-100 foot wall, and colorful stained glass windows. About 20,000 visitors come to the shrine each weekend.

RESTAURANTS

DON PANCHO'S
107 N. Nebraska, just south of US 83 Expressway, across from the Shrine
781-3601
Lunch and dinner Tuesday–Sunday. Closed Monday
$-$$
No Cr.
W

Well known in the Valley for its Tex-Mex specialties like *chile relleno, enchiladas,* and *mammoth panchos,* this restaurant also serves some American dishes. *Mariachis* usually entertain on weekends. Beer and wine.

ACCOMMODATIONS

($ = Under $45, $$ = $46-$60, $$$ = $61-$80, $$$$ = $81-$100, $$$$$ = Over $100)
Room Tax 7 percent

SAN JUAN HOTEL
125 W. US 83 Bus at Lincoln
781-5339
$

This historic two-story hotel offers 22 rooms. Children under 16 stay free in room with parents. Package plans available and senior discount. TV. Room phones (local calls free). Pets OK. Restaurant (closed Sunday and Monday dinner). Outdoor pool. Parking in lot in rear. Three enclosed patios. This is a historic Spanish colonial style hotel built in 1919. Some rooms are furnished with antiques. Owners will be delighted to show you a four-minute segment on the hotel from the "Eyes of Texas" TV show.

WESLACO

HIDALGO COUNTY ★ 25,000 ★ (512)

The name is composed from the initials of the **W. E. S**tewart **La**nd **Co**mpany which in 1919 sold a parcel of land to the town's developers. For a time, in the early 1940s, Weslaco was known as the "City with the Neon Skyline." The neon lights of downtown were darkened during World War II. During that war, one of the casualties from the city was Corporal Harlon Block, a Marine who was killed shortly after he was pictured in a photo that made history — the planting of the flag on Iwo Jima (See Harlingen — Marine Military Academy).

Because it is located in the heart of the vast Rio Grande Valley agricultural belt, the citrus, sugar, vegetable, and cotton industries all have major facilities in the area for processing, packaging, and shipping their products. It is also the home of agricultural research facilities operated by the United States Department of Agriculture, Texas A & M University, and Texas A & I University (See Other Points of Interest).

TOURIST SERVICES

RIO GRANDE VALLEY CHAMBER OF COMMERCE
US 83 Expressway and FM 1015 east of city
(P.O. Box 1499, 78596)
968-3141
Monday–Friday 8:30–5
W

This is the information center for all the cities and towns in the lower and central Valley. They publish an inexpensive (about 50¢) — but invaluable — guidemap to the Valley that gives the big picture from South Padre on the east to Falcon Lake on the west and includes smaller street maps of all the towns with lists of points of interest. They also publish the Rio Grande Valley Vacation Guide that you can pick up free at the Chamber or have them mail it to you for $1.

WESLACO AREA CHAMBER OF COMMERCE
1710 E. Pike, north access road of US 83 Expressway, exit Pike/Airport
(P.O. Box 8488, 78596)
968-2102
Monday–Friday 8–5
W

Provides detailed information on Weslaco, the Valley, and nearby Mexican border cities.

MUSEUMS

WESLACO BI-CULTURAL MUSEUM
521 S. Kansas, next to library
968-9142
Wednesday–Thursday 1–3, Friday 10–12, 1–3
Free
W

The exhibits portray the daily life of early Spanish and Anglo settlers and the dual culture of the area. Displays range from an ox cart to a silver glove stretcher used to stretch the fingers in kid gloves. The museum features changing exhibits. Because it is staffed by volunteers the hours sometimes vary from those posted.

OTHER POINTS OF INTEREST

TEXAS A & I UNIVERSITY CITRUS CENTER
312 N. International Blvd. (FM 1015), just north of US 83 Expressway
968-2132
Tours by appointment
Free

The major work of this research center is developing new citrus varieties, finding new methods to control pests and plant diseases, and improving citrus production and marketing techniques. You must call in advance for the tour that consists of a 30-minute slide show and an hour-long guided walking tour of the orchards. Texas A & I University is now part of the Texas A & M University System (See following), so some consolidation and changes to tour arrangements may occur in the future.

TEXAS AGRICULTURAL EXPERIMENT STATION
International Blvd (FM 1015) and US 83 Bus

As a part of the Texas A & M University System, the station conducts research to improve Valley crops. Among its accomplishments is the development of the Ruby Red grapefruit and the 1015 onion. No tours, but you can drive through part of the grounds.

VALLEY NATURE CENTER
301 S. Border, in Gibson Park just south of US 83 Bus
969-2475
Monday–Saturday 9–1. Closed Sunday and holidays
Free
W

In the building are exhibits on native birds and other nature items from this area ranging from insects to rocks. Outside is a four-acre park filled with native flora — including cactus — all nicely labeled. Guided tours are available if you call in advance. Gift shop.

WESLACO CITY HALL
Kansas and 5th

Among the features of this attractive Spanish Renaissance style building, built in 1928, are ornate cast stone sculpture — considered a lost art — adorning the entrance and cupola. The sculpture molds were destroyed to prevent duplication.

SPORTS AND ACTIVITIES

Golf

VILLAGE EXECUTIVE COURSE
FM 1015 about two miles south of US 83 Bus
969-3445

Nine-hole course. Green fees: $4 for 9 holes, $5 for 18.

PERFORMING ARTS

WESLACO TOWER THEATER
120 S. Kansas
968-3257
Admission
W

When the city built a large water tank tower in 1938, the huge concrete ground level water storage tank, constructed ten years earlier, became a white elephant because its massive walls made it too costly to tear down. For years it was used as a storage building for city supplies. Then, in the 1960s, the city manager, who had done some theater work in college, started a long term project to turn it into a theater. Now, instead of holding 150,000 gallons of water, the old reservoir holds 130 seats and a stage and is the home of the Mid Valley Civic Theater. If no answer at the number listed, call the Chamber of Commerce (968-2102) for performance information.

SIDE TRIPS

DELTA LAKE
Take FM 88 north to Elsa then continue on approximately eight miles north to the lake
Open at all times
W Variable

The county park on the east side of FM 88 provides facilities for bank fishing and picnicking. Fishing permits ($1 per day) are sold at lake concession on FM 88.

DONNA AMERICAN LEGION POST NO. 107
Donna. Take US 83 Bus west to Donna, turn south (left) on S. Main and go three blocks to Silver
Hours vary

When it opened in 1920, this was the first post-owned Legion Hall in the country. It now houses the **Donna Hooks Fletcher Museum** — a tribute to the woman after whom the new town was named in 1904. The museum features early photographs of the Valley. For information contact the Donna Chamber of Commerce, 464-3272 (129 S. 8th, 78537).

NUEVO PROGRESO, MEXICO
Take FM 1015 south about seven miles to International Bridge

Benito Juarez Avenida, the main shopping street of this border town, starts right at the bridge. The majority of the stores and restaurants are in the first few blocks, so you can park on the Texas side (about $1) and walk across. (See Crossing into Mexico in the Introduction.) The shopping choices aren't as varied as in many other border towns, but careful shoppers will still find bargains. Two stores that carry a little bit of everything from liquor to clothing to souvenirs are **El Disco** (on your right in the first block), which, as its name suggests, also sells records, tapes, and cassettes; and **Canada** (about three blocks down on the right) which specializes in shoes made in Mexico. Also just a block from the bridge, on your left, is **Arturo's** (See Restaurants) and a little further on, upstairs, is the **Garcia Gomez Restaurant**. Both are consistently popular with border-crossers from Weslaco.

ANNUAL EVENTS

March

RIO GRANDE VALLEY LIVESTOCK SHOW
Take US 83 Expressway east to Mercedes, then north on N. Texas Ave. to Showgrounds
565-2456
Wednesday–Sunday mid–March
Admission
W Variable

In addition to five days of livestock activities and competitions, there's a downtown parade, almost continuous family entertainment during the day and in the evening, a rodeo, a carnival, and nightly C&W dances.

RESTAURANTS

($ = under $7, $$ = $7 to $17, $$$ = $17 to $25, $$$$ = over $25 for one person excluding drinks, tax, and tip.)

ARTURO'S
Nuevo Progreso, about one block south of the International Bridge
Lunch and dinner seven days
$-$$
MC, V
Secured parking

From the outside it looks like a converted nightclub. Inside it is probably the plushest-looking restaurant in the Weslaco area with red jacketed waiters, tablecloths, cloth napkins, and even that rarity among silver settings in most Texas restaurants — salad forks. The menu offers both Mexican and American entrees with so many choices that it could be broken up and the pieces used as full menus in several different restaurants. The game dinner is especially popular. Don't expect a gourmet meal — the kitchen isn't up to it — but you'll certainly get your money's worth, and then some. Bar.

CIRO'S
502 W. Pike at Republica
969-2236
Lunch and dinner seven days
$-$$
MC, V

There are almost a dozen shrimp entrées on the menu (most giving you a dozen shrimp) that go from the simple *Camaron a la Pancha* (broiled in butter) to *Camaron Veracruzano* (with tomato sauce, tomato, onions, pimentos, olives, capers, jalapenos, parsley, garlic, wine and other spices). They also have red snapper and other fish, meats including steaks, *fajitas*, and even Kosher Ribs, and a variety of Mexican plates.

HAROLD'S COUNTRY KITCHEN
Donna
2111 E. US 83, on the east side of Donna
464-2185
Lunch and dinner seven days
$
No Cr.
W

Harold's has an all-you-can-eat buffet (they call it a Buffeteria) with several meats and seafood, salads, fresh vegetables from the Valley, coffee or tea and dessert for about $6 weekdays and $7 for the "Deluxe" one on Sunday. The turn-over is fast so the food in the steam tables stays hot without drying up. Overall, it's like home cooking at down-home prices. And to add to the homey atmosphere, it's in a converted home — a rambling house with a spacious lawn and banana trees.

MILANO'S ITALIAN RESTAURANT
2900 W. Pike Blvd., just west of Milano's Rd.
968-3677
Dinner only Tuesday–Sunday, Closed Monday
$$
Cr.
W

They've been pleasing customers with Neapolitan style Italian cuisine here since 1955. If you want a taste of why, try the pasta combination platter that includes *lasagna, ravioli, manicotti*, and *spaghetti*. In addition to a selection of pasta entrées, there is also a good selection of veal, chicken, and seafood dishes, all served with spaghetti, and a variety of pizzas. No smoking area. Bar.

OYSTER BAR VI
1501 W. US 83 Bus
968-9002
Lunch and dinner Tuesday–Sunday, closed Monday
$$
Cr.
W

The "VI" refers to the fact that this is #6 in a growing chain of seafood restaurants that stretch along the Valley from Brownsville to Laredo. The simple menu includes flounder, snapper, and other fish available fried or broiled; shrimp boiled, fried, or stuffed; oysters, deviled crabs, and sea scallops. For the light-eater, or those who prefer to sample several dishes, half orders are available on most entrées. Bar.

ACCOMMODATIONS

($ = Under $45, $$ = $46-$60, $$$ = $61-$80, $$$$ = $81-$100, $$$$$ = Over $100)
Room Tax 13 percent

BEST WESTERN PALM AIRE MOTOR INN
415 S. International, US 83 Expressway and FM 1015
969-2411 or in Texas 800-248-6511 or outside Texas 800-528-1234
$$-$$$
No-smoking rooms

The 121 units in this two-story Best Western include two suites and 20 no-smoking rooms. Children under 12 stay free in room with parents. Satellite TV with HBO. Room phones (local calls free). Fire intercom system. No pets. Restaurant, room service, lounge open Monday-Saturday with entertainment Wednesday-Saturday. Three outdoor pools, outdoor whirlpool, exercise room, lighted tennis court, weight room, racquetball courts, sauna, steam room. Free breakfast. Self-service laundry and same-day dry cleaning. Shops.

VALI-HO MOTEL
2100 E. US 83 Bus
968-2173 or 800-445-1993
$
No-smoking rooms

The 37 rooms in this 1-story motel include six no-smoking. Cable TV. Room phones (local calls free). Coffeemakers in rooms. No pets. Outdoor heated pool. Free airport transportation. Same-day dry cleaning. All rooms have apartment refrigerators.

INDEX

B

I

J

K

L

P

Q-R

S